LACLAU AND MOUFFE

Laclau and Mouffe: The Radical Democratic Imaginary is one of the first book-length studies of two of the most significant political theorists writing today. Anna Marie Smith provides both a clear and accessible overview of the work of Ernesto Laclau and Chantal Mouffe and a thoughtful and challenging consideration of some of the weaknesses in their work. Throughout, she links their work and criticism of it with some of the key themes in contemporary social and political theory.

Anna Marie Smith shows first how the work of Laclau and Mouffe seeks to retrieve the strongest elements of both the liberal democratic and socialist traditions, emphasizing its valuable contribution to radical democratic pluralism. She goes on to show how they have combined the insights of three important currents: Gramsci's political theory, anti-foundational themes found in post-structuralist theory, and aspects of psychoanalytic theory and how these have been brought to bear on traditional political theory. She demonstrates how Laclau and Mouffe have combined these perspectives to develop a compelling theory of social identity and power relations in contemporary political societies.

Laclau and Mouffe: The Radical Democratic Imaginary also considers some of the weaknesses in Laclau and Mouffe's work. Anna Marie Smith examines their problematic approach to historically structured conditions of political practice and demonstrates that certain themes in their work have been anticipated by critiques in feminist and race theory, lesbian and gay studies and multiculturalism. Underpinning these discussions is careful consideration of the implications these dimensions have for the notions of hegemony, essentialism and power that are central to any understanding of Laclau and Mouffe's work.

Laclau and Mouffe: The Radical Democratic Imaginary provides fresh insights into the work of two key contemporary political theorists; these insights are linked to central concerns in contemporary thought and illustrated by lively discussions of British and American politics. It will be of interest to all those engaged in the study of political and social theory, philosophy, cultural studies and gender studies.

Anna Marie Smith is Assistant Professor of Government at Cornell University. She is the author of *New Right Discourse on Race and Sexuality: Britain 1968–1990*.

LACLAU AND MOUFFE

The radical democratic imaginary

Anna Marie Smith

London and New York

First published 1998
by Routledge
11 New Fetter Lane, London EC4P 4EE

Simultaneously published in the USA and Canada
by Routledge
29 West 35th Street, New York, NY 10001

Typeset in Goudy by Routledge
Printed and bound in Great Britain by MPG Books Ltd, Bodmin

British Library Cataloguing in Publication Data
A catalogue record for this book is available from the British Library

Library of Congress Cataloguing in Publication Data
Smith, Anna Marie.
Laclau and Mouffe: the radical democratic imaginary / Anna Marie Smith.
Includes bibliographical references and index.
1. Democracy. 2. Radicalism. 3. Laclau, Ernesto. 4. Mouffe, Chantal. Political
science—History—20th century. I. Title.
JC423.S65 1998
321.8′01—dc21 976–53303
CIP

ISBN 0–415–10059–3 (hbk)
ISBN 0–415–10060–7 (pbk)

FOR ZILLAH

CONTENTS

ACKNOWLEDGMENTS

It is my pleasure to acknowledge the assistance of the friends and colleagues who
made this book possible. I would like to thank Bob Gallagher, formerly of the
University of Toronto, and Sue Golding, Greenwich University, for introducing
me to Laclau and Mouffe's work. Juan Maiguashca, York University, generously
volunteered to lead me through an independent study course on Laclau and
Mouffe's *Hegemony and Socialist Strategy* during the spring semester of 1986, when
I was a doctoral student in the Department of Political Science, University of
Toronto. I drew inspiration as well from Frank Cunningham's Contemporary
Political Philosophy seminar that was held at the University of Toronto at the
same time. My deepest thanks to Ernesto Laclau and Chantal Mouffe who were
my Ph.D. advisors and intellectual mentors when I was a graduate student in
Ernesto's Ideology and Discourse Analysis seminar at the University of Essex,
1987–91, and who read and commented extensively on the manuscript.

My writing was influenced by various discussions that were held at the Society
for the Humanities during my fellowship there during the 1995–6 academic year. I
am particularly indebted to Dominick LaCapra for sharing his work on Lacanian
psychoanalysis and to Etienne Balibar for allowing me to attend his seminar on
historicity, power and violence.

Simon Critchley invited me to write this book and remained an encouraging
supporter throughout the project. Lynne Segal, Jeffrey Weeks and Mandy Merck
assisted me with my research on the British Left. Zillah Eisenstein challenged me
to adopt a more sophisticated grammar *vis-à-vis* the complexity of contemporary
social forces and political practice. Patty Zimmerman encouraged me to consider
the contradictory and uneven effects of cultural globalization for democratic
theory. Aletta Norval, Peggy Kohn, Paul Apostolidis, Jeannie Morefield, Jodi
Dean, Nancy Hirschmann, Alison Shonkwiler, Susan Buck-Morss, Dominick
LaCapra, Martin Bernal and Isaac Kramnick read the text and provided valuable
comments. Julie Fendo submitted the final draft to editorial treatment in her
capacity as my research assistant. Judith Butler and an anonymous reader were
especially generous in their detailed critical assessment of the manuscript. Tony
Bruce at Routledge remained a patient and helpful correspondent throughout the

project. I accept full responsibility for the errors and weaknesses that remain in the text.

I would also like to acknowledge the sources of institutional support for this book. My thanks to the Cornell University Humanities Council which provided two grants that allowed me to conduct research in Britain. A faculty fellowship at Cornell's Society for the Humanities, release from the Department of Government to take up that fellowship and a semester of study leave provided by the College of Arts and Sciences at Cornell created favorable conditions for my work. I would also like to thank Verso for kindly granting me permission to quote extensively from the following texts: Ernesto Laclau, *Politics and Ideology in Marxist Theory: Capitalism, Fascism, Populism* (1977), *New Reflections of the Revolution of Our Time* (1990), *Emancipation(s)* (1996), Ernesto Laclau (ed.), *The Making of Political Identities* (1994), Ernesto Laclau and Chantal Mouffe, *Hegemony and Socialist Strategy: Towards a Radical Democratic Politics* (1985), Chantal Mouffe, *The Return of the Political* (1993) and Chantal Mouffe (ed.), *Dimensions of Radical Democracy: Pluralism, Citizenship, Community* (1992).

By dedicating this book to Zillah Eisenstein, I wish to celebrate my love for a wonderful teacher, mentor, straight supporter of lesbian and gay rights, and friend. She is courageously lighting the path so that others may follow.

INTRODUCTION

Laclau and Mouffe's texts should be read as political theory – as an intervention in concrete historical conditions rather than an abstract exercise. In their "Introduction" to *Hegemony and Socialist Strategy*, Laclau and Mouffe locate their critique of Marxist essentialism by referring to the strategic and theoretical "crisis of the Left." Writing in the early 1980s, they note that the traditional leftist forces in Western Europe – leftist political parties and the trade union movement – had lost substantial ground while right-wing forces had gained more legitimacy. At the same time, new autonomous movements had emerged to engage in political struggles that had not been adequately addressed by the traditional left. Feminists, peace activists, environmentalists, lesbian and gay activists, and the movements of people of color had radically redefined the very meaning of leftist politics (1985: 1–5).

Several events have taken place since that time which pose even greater challenges for traditional leftist thought, such as the disintegration of the Soviet Union and its imperial hegemony in Eastern Europe, the unification of Germany, the break-up of Yugoslavia and the war in Bosnia. In the OECD (Organization for Economic Cooperation and Development) countries, the attacks on the welfare state and the trade union movement have continued almost unabated, while the gap between the wealthy and the poor has dramatically increased. At the same time, masses of protestors in Italy, Germany and France have expressed their opposition against the Maastricht Treaty-style cuts in public pensions and health benefits. Although racial and ethnic antagonisms were already prominent in Europe and the United States in the early 1980s, they have escalated even further in the late 1980s and 1990s. The resurgence of identity-based antagonisms cannot be dismissed as "a return of the archaic" or a temporary deviation from an otherwise seamless progression towards liberal democracy's triumphant resolution of political conflict (Mouffe 1994: 106). In virtually every globalizing economy, women are now more overrepresented among the poor than they were only a decade ago. In the less developed countries, debt and currency crises have been used to legitimate severe austerity measures and "free trade" policies that have often led in turn to a decline in popular living standards and to escalating cycles of exclusion and violence.

1

Many other developments have transformed the political terrain in complex ways. During this period, we have seen the Tianamen Square massacre in China, the defeat of the Sandinistas in Nicaragua, the Zapatista revolt in Mexico, and the genocidal war in Rwanda. We have also seen the electoral victories of Bill Clinton and the Congressional Republicans in the United States, Nelson Mandela and the African National Congress in South Africa, Vladimir Zhirinovsky and his ultra-nationalist Liberal Democratic Party in Russia, post-Communist parties in eastern Europe, Massimo d'Alema's Democratic Party of the Left in Italy, Tony Blair's "New Labour" in Britain, and Lionel Jospin's Socialists and Jean-Marie Le Pen's National Front in France. Economic shifts in OECD economies such as the globalization of production; de-industrialization; de-skilling; the substitution of non-union workers for unionized workers; the growth of "freelance," sub-contracted, part-time and temporary contract work; and new worker-management "productivity development" schemes have radically changed the nature of trade union organizing, the traditional backbone of leftist opposition. New political organizations such as ACT-UP (AIDS Coalition to Unleash Power) and women's health groups have been founded while nationalist and transnationalist forms of solidarity have been adapted to suit contemporary conditions.

Laclau and Mouffe describe the new social movements and antagonisms as a "'surplus' of the social *vis-à-vis* the rational and organized structures of society – that is, of the social 'order'" (Laclau and Mouffe 1985:1). The "surplus" metaphor invites a Derridean critique of the supplementarity at work here (Derrida 1973, 1976; Gasché 1986). Will these developments be treated as harmless accidents, irrelevant deviations, and just another data point by a resistant political theory, or will they be recognized as subversive interruptions that demand a radical re-examination of the most basic categories and arguments?

At this fork in the road, Laclau and Mouffe take the second route.

> The new forms of social conflict have . . . thrown into crisis theoretical and political frameworks . . . [that] correspond to the classical discourses of the Left, and the characteristic modes in which it has conceived the agents of social change, the structuring of social spaces, and the privileged points for the unleashing of historical transformations.
>
> (Laclau and Mouffe 1985: 1–2)

The authors argue that nothing less than the "whole conception of socialism" is in crisis: its "ontological centrality of the working class," its notion of "Revolution" as the "founding moment in the transition from one type of society to another," and its utopian dream of a post-revolutionary and post-political society in which a "perfectly unitary and homogeneous collective will" would prevail. From their perspective, the novelty of the "new social movements" does not consist solely in their articulation of new demands. In addition to their politicization of new areas of the social, these movements also establish a somewhat new form of political contestation. Their struggles are irreducibly complex and plural in nature. Because classical Marxism presupposes the existence of "universal" subjects and conceptualizes the social as a "rational, transparent order," it cannot adequately capture these movements' complex negotiations of difference (Laclau and Mouffe 1985: 2).

If the authority of meta-narratives has declined, the revitalization of traditional forms of structural oppression and exploitation and the deployment of new forms of authoritarianism have had devastating anti-democratic effects. Inspired by diverse traditions – Gramscian socialism, liberal democratic discourse on rights and citizenship, post-structuralism, post-analytic philosophy, phenomenology and Lacanian psychoanalysis – Laclau and Mouffe have attempted to produce a political theory that captures the specificity of contemporary antagonisms. The authors also believe that their theory provides a useful framework for the conceptualization of radical democratic pluralist practice, namely the political activism that aims to overthrow oppression and exploitation in all their multiple and hybrid forms.

The authors' work has been the subject of numerous lively debates.[1] Because they have not advanced their anti-capitalist arguments in the traditional forms that many of their critics favor, they have sometimes been mis-read as totally abandoning socialist politics altogether. The interpretation of their writing is sometimes a demanding task for the student of social and political theory, for it often requires extensive knowledge of the various traditions that Laclau and Mouffe appropriate.

I was first introduced to Laclau and Mouffe's work when I was a graduate student at the University of Toronto in the mid-1980s. It was taken for granted within my circle of friends, colleagues, mentors and most of my teachers that we all shared a commitment to some form of socialist struggle. As a young girl growing up on the edge of the Canadian wilderness in northern Ontario, my first image of wealth had been that of an alien American invasion, personified by tourists who loudly demanded pristine lakes and forests even as the pollution from American-owned mines and US-sourced acid rain devastated the environment. For all its political ambiguity and its erasure of the local elite's accountability, the prevailing populist discourse had constructed an antagonistic divide between the American multinational corporations and the Canadian urban political elite on the one hand and the local workers, rural poor and Native American communities on the other, such that that opposition had appeared as an obvious fact of life, rather than a far-fetched idea.

Living in Toronto during the Reagan years, I was exposed to the Canadian Left's critique of global capitalism and American imperialism.[2] My teachers, mentors and friends participated in numerous projects, including the social democratic politics of the Canadian New Democratic Party, the pro-Sandinista solidarity movement, socialist-feminist union solidarity work, the alternative arts community's anti-censorship campaign, the struggles of the immigrant communities to obtain access to English-as-a-Second Language training, the campaign of the Dene people to stop non-renewable resource development in the Northwest Territories, a joint project by native peoples and environmentalists against the logging of an old growth forest in northern Ontario, demonstrations against the homophobic and racist abuse of police power, and a number of feminist and gay struggles that ranged in orientation from radical feminism to anarchistic cultural politics. As leftist Anglophones in eastern Canada, we were also influenced to varying degrees by the rise of Québec nationalism and official bilingual discourse.

In our circle of graduate students and activists, the real question was not, "Should we be socialists?" but, "What kind of socialists should we be?" Heated discussions about Laclau and Mouffe's *Hegemony and Socialist Strategy* took place. One group denounced their discourse as neo-conservative surrender, a second dismissed it as impenetrable post-structuralist waffle, while a third hailed their work as one of the most important advances in contemporary leftist theory. In the intervening years, I have completed a doctoral degree under Laclau's supervision; conducted research on British politics, racism and homophobia; taught my first students; and worked as an activist in various feminist, gay and pro-union campaigns in Thatcher's Britain and Clinton's America. Based on these diverse experiences, I would give my full support to the latter assessment.

My first aim in this text is to make the strongest possible case that Laclau and Mouffe's texts constitute a ground-breaking contribution to radical democratic pluralist theory. In pursuit of this goal, I have engaged in what I hope is a useful exegesis of their work, supplemented by critical analysis, reading "against the grain" and reconstruction. In my discussions of Laclau and Mouffe's texts, I will bring parenthetical remarks and implicit arguments to the fore. For the sake of clarity, I will add a new theoretical formulation to their discourse, namely the distinction between structural positions and subject positions. I will discuss the most controversial aspects of their arguments, and indicate where the authors' theoretical shifts have introduced tensions into their discourse.

Second, I will attempt to demonstrate the extent to which Laclau and Mouffe's anti-essentialist intervention in the Marxist tradition has been preceded and accompanied by parallel critiques in feminist theory, race theory and lesbian and gay studies. In their best moments, all of these different anti-essentialisms recover the most promising elements in their respective traditions and re-articulate them together with a radical politics that is based on the recognition of plural democratic differences. Anti-essentialist criticism has already been enhanced by appropriations from the socialist tradition; the intellectual work that is influenced by what is called "British cultural studies" (Hall 1980, 1988a, 1988b, 1990, 1993; Hall *et al.* 1978; Gilroy 1982, 1987, 1993) is but one example. In the interest of promoting further dialogue, I will use texts from the anti-essentialist feminist theory, critical race theory and lesbian and gay studies traditions as a source of theoretical inspiration for my own analysis of the authors' work.

Laclau and Mouffe emerged out of political and intellectual environments in Argentina and Belgium/France respectively in which Marxism constituted the most authoritative meta-narrative (Laclau 1990a: 197–204; Fraser and Nicholson 1990: 23; Dean 1992: 49–50). In their earlier texts, they rightly assumed that much of their audience – like our small circle at the University of Toronto – was already firmly committed to leftist politics. In these moments, their critique of Marxist essentialism is implicitly situated within a leftist political horizon, namely the belief that some form of socialism is necessary – albeit insufficient in itself – for democratization.

Today, of course, their audience has changed tremendously. Their younger readers were educated during the Reagan/Bush/Clinton and Thatcher/Major era, and many of them associate all forms of socialist politics with Stalinist anachronisms. Further, in our post-1989 context, the meaning of "democratization" has been diluted, such that it often signifies nothing more than consumerism, free market policies and the most superficial liberal-democratic electoral reforms. At the same time, major thinkers such as Rorty assert that all we need to do today is to expand the community of "we liberals" and to set it to work in bringing out the potential that is already present within existing liberal institutions. Such an analysis tends to conflate key concepts such as economic liberalism and liberal democracy (Daly 1994: 186; Critchley 1996: 23).

With this context in mind, it may be useful to revisit the classic democratic socialist arguments about the linkage between democratization and the anti-capitalist struggle. I will locate Laclau and Mouffe's theory of radical democratic pluralism in Chapter 1 by contrasting their approach with the liberal democratic, neo-conservative, and socialist perspectives. I will also introduce the most important theme in their work, namely the image of the democratic revolution as a subversive force that can be spread throughout the social in the form of an infinite series of contingent recitations. From this perspective, democratization is understood not as a set of superficial reforms, but as the struggle to institutionalize a radical democratic pluralist imaginary.

In Chapter 2, I will discuss the Gramscian roots of Laclau and Mouffe's theory, with a special emphasis on structural positioning and the interpretative dimension of social identities. Having examined the ways in which identities operate, I will turn to an exploration of Laclau and Mouffe's post-structuralist theory of identity formation in Chapter 3. Chapter 4 will feature Laclau and Mouffe's interventions in the debates between liberals, communitarians and postmodernists. In Chapter 5, I will discuss the contributions by contemporary feminist theorists and the authors to the conceptualization of power relations, hegemony, equivalence and difference. Finally, I will offer, by way of a conclusion, some remarks on the implications of the authors' approach for theorizing multicultural difference.

1

RETRIEVING DEMOCRACY

The radical democratic imaginary

Laclau and Mouffe contend that radical democracy is the best route towards progressive social change for the Left today. As we will see, radical democracy embraces many aspects of the socialist tradition. Radical democracy also appropriates the most progressive moments of the liberal democratic, anti-racist, anti-sexist, anti-homophobic and environmentalist traditions as well. As Mouffe argues, "The objective of the Left should be the extension and deepening of the democratic revolution initiated two hundred years ago" (1992a: 1). These appropriations are complex and reconstitutive in nature. Radical democratic pluralism does not recognize a theoretical division of labor between these traditions: it does not simply add socialism's economic agenda to liberal democracy's political principles. It values, for example, the Marxist critique of liberal politics (Brown 1995: 14) and seeks to respond to pluralist concerns about the effects of central planning.

From the authors' perspective, the "democratic revolution" is much more than a series of historical events. Laclau and Mouffe consider it instead as the very condition of possibility for the radicalization of social resistance. Citing Foucault, they recognize that wherever there is power, there is resistance, but they also recognize that resistance can take many different forms. They argue that it is only in specific historical contexts that resistance becomes political in the sense that it begins to aim not only to oppose a specific instance of domination but to put an end to the entire structure of subordination itself (Laclau and Mouffe 1985: 152–3).

Referring to the politics of contemporary social struggles, Laclau and Mouffe write,

> There is therefore nothing inevitable or natural in the different struggles against power, and it is necessary to explain in each case the reasons for their emergence and different modulations that they adopt. The struggle against subordination cannot be the result of the situation of subordination itself.
>
> (1985: 152)

Politicized resistance, then, is discursively constructed; subversive practices never automatically follow from the simple fact of exploitation and oppression. The authors' central argument is that a resistance discourse only becomes politicized insofar as the democratic revolution is reappropriated and redefined in specific historical conditions and transferred to the social site in question. Each of these recitations (in the Derridean sense (Derrida 1988)) introduce innovative and contextually specific new meanings into the democratic tradition and yet simultaneously preserves a non-essentialist trace of previous articulations such that every moment of democratic struggle to some extent stands on historically prepared ground.

The ability of the oppressed to imagine the complete overthrow of their oppressors depends upon the circulation, radicalization and institutionalization of democratic discourse.

> Our thesis is that egalitarian discourses and discourses on rights play a fundamental role in the reconstruction of collective identities. At the beginning of this process in the French Revolution, the public space of citizenship was the exclusive domain of equality, while in the private sphere no questioning took place of existing social inequalities. However, as de Tocqueville clearly understood, once human beings accept the legitimacy of the principle of equality in one sphere they will attempt to extend it to every other sphere of life.
>
> (Laclau and Mouffe 1990: 128)

Lefort has similarly argued that democratic discourse on human rights can incite remarkably different forms of emancipatory struggles. Writing in the late 1970s, Lefort was inspired by both the 1968 popular protests in France and the struggles of Chinese and Soviet dissidents. He rejected the view that was, at that time, predominant among the leaders of the French Left. The latter assumed that the subject of rights is by definition the possessive and atomistic individual of capitalist society; they therefore concluded that demands for human rights are ultimately bourgeois and reformist in character (Lefort 1986: 242–3). Lefort insisted instead that rights should not be regarded as if they were already fully established institutions with fixed meanings, and that notwithstanding its origins in bourgeois liberal discourse, the concept of human rights can be enormously expanded.

The struggles for human rights have always been open-ended: in the nineteenth and twentieth centuries, subjects with a long history of struggle such as workers, peasants, slaves and the colonized took on new identities – as trade union members, citizens, anti-colonial nationalists, anti-imperialist internationalists, and so on – as they demanded rights in innovative ways. New subjects also emerged – women, racial/ethnic minorities within nation-states, peace activists, environmentalists, lesbians and gays – and framed their rights-based claims in language borrowed from previous struggles. By its very nature, the whole project

7

of securing official recognition for human rights remains contested and incomplete. This is even more true today as reactionary forces continue to gain strength in many contemporary political formations and threaten to empty the emancipatory content out of the "rights" that they claim to uphold. Lefort calls human rights the "generative principles of democracy" for it is through the promotion of an "awareness of rights" – the dissemination of democratic discourse to new areas of the social, the radicalization of the concept of human rights, and the institutionalization of democratic principles – that disempowered political subjects can win their struggles for recognition (Lefort 1986: 260).

Laclau and Mouffe's position *vis-à-vis* the subversive effect of the democratic revolution can be clarified by examining their distinction between relations of subordination and relations of oppression. In the former, a social agent is subjected to the will of another, but does not see the subordinating agent as someone who blocks her from fully realizing her identity. In the latter case, the social agent is also subjected to the will of another, but she recognizes that that relation of subordination is indeed an antagonistic one, for she believes that that relation is stopping her from developing her identity. To achieve this profound shift in her perspective, she must have access to the tools that allow her, first, to envision a world that lies beyond subordination and to imagine what she could become in that alternative space, second, to analyze the ways in which she has become caught up in and thwarted by the relation of subordination, and third, to grasp the possibilities for collective struggle to overthrow the entire subordinating structure. As an example of this difference, Laclau and Mouffe point to the fact that women have been subjected to male authority for centuries, and have engaged in many forms of resistance against that authority, but that that relation of subordination was transformed into a relation of oppression only when a feminist movement based on the liberal democratic demand for equality began to emerge (1985: 153–4).

In another illustration, they consider the differences between the workers' struggles that have sought limited reforms as opposed to those that have challenged the entire capitalist system (1985: 156–8, 167–8). Their point is that in itself, the experience of subordination does not guarantee that the subordinated social agent will develop a radical perspective *vis-à-vis* her subjection. The subordinated agent only becomes radicalized when she finds a compelling political discourse that gives an effective account for her condition, provides her with the critical tools that she needs to join with others in constructing an alternative world, and shows her how the entire subordinating structure might be overthrown through collective struggle. It is precisely a radicalized interpretation of the principles of liberty and equality that can interrupt relations of subordination in this manner. Radical democratic discourse thereby creates the discursive conditions in which even the most normalized forms of subjection can be viewed as illegitimate and the elimination of subordination can be imagined. As we will see in Chapter 4, democratic discourse is also marked by an irresolvable tension, for there will always be some degree of incompatibility between liberty claims and equality claims. For Laclau and Mouffe, however, this tension is not a fatality but a vital resource for radical democracy.

As mere ideas, "liberty" and "equality" do not change anything. Democratic discourse cannot exert this interruption effect upon relations of subordination until the democratic imaginary becomes embodied in norms and institutions.[1] The extension of democratic principles into new spheres of the social[2] did not take place until actual democratic struggles won some concrete strategic ground through political struggle. Political struggle does nevertheless depend in part on the ability to imagine alternative worlds. Laclau and Mouffe locate the first significant advance of liberal democracy in the French Revolution, for it was in this moment that the *ancien régime* was displaced by a new order whose political legitimacy was based on nothing other than the "rule of the people" (1985: 155).

As the ideas of liberty and equality were given a material life by becoming embodied in more and more political practices and institutions, it became possible for increasing numbers of people to take up a democratic imaginary that allowed them to envision their worlds differently.

> This break with the ancien regime, symbolized by the Declaration of the Rights of Man, would provide the discursive conditions which made it possible to propose different forms of inequality as illegitimate and anti-natural, and thus make them equivalent as forms of oppression.
>
> (Laclau and Mouffe 1985: 155)

The authors depict the democratic principles of liberty and equality as a "fermenting agent." Once they were institutionalized in one context, these principles were spread to other sites with an accelerating chain-reaction effect (1985: 155). Referring again to Tocqueville, Laclau and Mouffe state that "It is not possible to conceive of men as eternally unequal among themselves on one point, and equal on others; at a certain moment, they will come to be equal on all points" (1985: 156).[3] Hence the multiple appropriations of democratic discourse: nineteenth-century English workers drew inspiration from the French Revolution, abolitionists cited the American Constitution, and suffragettes combined the myth of a morally pure feminine nature with Enlightenment ideals. American civil rights leaders of the 1960s borrowed from various sources: the Anglo-American liberal democratic tradition, radical religious discourse, anti-racist and anti-imperialist resistance, and socialist discourse. Contemporary feminists, progressive lesbians and gays, environmentalist activists and radical trade union leaders in the United States now fashion much of their political discourse out of elements borrowed from the civil rights movement.

The success of these circulations, appropriations and radicalizations of the democratic imaginary depends largely on historical conditions. The new social movements, for example, have brought a whole new field of demands onto the political agenda in the 1960s and 1970s. They owed much of their effectiveness to the ambiguous effects of the commodification of social life, the rise of the interventionist state, and the expansion of mass communication (Laclau and Mouffe 1985: 159–71). Because the extension of the democratic revolution depends in part on the contingencies of historical conditions, its extension into new areas of the social is not guaranteed (Laclau and Mouffe 1985: 158, 168). Instead of proceeding in definite stages or unfolding according to a single logic, democratic struggles are shaped by local conditions, historical peculiarities and the uncertainties of political contestation. As we now witness the rise of the new right, the neo-conservatives, and the religious right, along with the resurgence of many types of sexism and racism, we also have to consider the possibility that much of the liberatory and egalitarian potential of the democratic revolution may be eviscerated as these forces attempt to impose their own reactionary definitions of "liberty" and "equality."

Laclau and Mouffe's conception of radical democratic pluralism can be further clarified through an exploration of the work of leftist theorists who have attempted to construct a new hybrid democratic theory through the "retrieval" of the most progressive aspects of the liberal democratic and socialist traditions. Like the "retrieval" theorists, Laclau and Mouffe argue that the liberal-democratic definition of human rights is open to contestation: just as the unfixity of this definition is now permitting various right-wing redefinitions, that same unfixity also allows for radical democratic appropriations (1985: 176). Mouffe asserts that Macpherson became a key figure in contemporary political theory precisely through his work on the radical potential of liberal democracy (1993b: 102). In the following section, Macpherson's political theory and the "retrieval" tradition will be discussed. The hybrid and complex character of both the liberal democratic and socialist traditions, as well as the illegitimacy of the neo-conservative alternative, will then be considered. An initial sketch of radical democratic pluralist strategy and the processes through which imperfect democratic societies can be radically democratized will be offered. Finally, it will be argued that the mere addition of extra elements to an otherwise unchanged Marxist theory would be insufficient for radical democratic pluralist thought.

The contested meaning of liberal democracy

Macpherson, like Laclau and Mouffe, argues that democratic theory must be taken beyond its liberal-democratic origins (Macpherson 1973). These limits are, in a sense, internal to liberal democracy, for they stem from irreducible tensions that are present in the very foundation of this tradition (Cunningham 1987: 141–202; Golding 1992: 3–18; Green 1985). Liberal democracy marks a liberatory break with the traditional hierarchies of pre-Enlightenment society: it defines the individual as an equal and rational self-determining agent and it attempts to construct socio-political obligation on the basis of consensual contracts. For example, Locke's critique of feudal obligation and his theory of government by the consent of the people (Locke 1963) are extremely valuable for radical democracy. Although Locke's Eurocentric view of the indigenous peoples of the

Americas is unacceptable, his defense of individual rights can be mobilized wherever discrimination and exclusion are bolstered by theories of natural, social and moral hierarchies.

For Locke, however, the defense of market relations and the defense of individual rights and freedoms are inextricable. Indeed, the predominant definition of liberal democracy combines Locke's contract theory with Smith's *laissez-faire* bourgeois economics (Watkins and Kramnick 1979: 11). The individual proper to liberal democracy is supposed to possess a specifically instrumentalist type of rationality and a fundamental interest in the acquisition of more and more goods. Because liberal democratic theory is based on what Macpherson (1962) calls "possessive individualism," it portrays the infinite competition for scarce goods, the institution of private property, the class divisions that necessarily follow from these conditions, and the social contract that preserves the class-divided society from self-destruction, as natural and inevitable (Golding 1992: 4–5). As we will see below, a liberal democratic order can be entirely compatible with the perpetuation of non-class-based forms of domination as well.

In short, liberal democracy begins with an egalitarian and freely self-determining conception of the individual, but ultimately tolerates and even promotes the formation of a highly inegalitarian social order. John Stuart Mill's vision of a society that is governed by "the people" and that secures the conditions necessary for every individual's realization of their own capacities, is an especially promising moment in the liberal democratic tradition (Macpherson 1977: 1). Macpherson nevertheless contends that even Mill's ethical liberalism does not resolve the tensions between egalitarianism and domination. Like Locke, Mill expresses various ethnocentric views that are problematic. Further, Mill does not pay sufficient attention to the fact that individuals will be truly free to develop their capacities only after the relations of exploitation and oppression that structure modern societies are fully dismantled. Following Macpherson's lead, the task of contemporary radical democratic theory is to "retrieve" the most progressive moments of the liberal democratic tradition and the most democratic moments of the socialist tradition and to bring them together in a fusion that is suited to contemporary political conditions.

Progress towards radical democratic pluralism would necessitate a radical transformation of capitalism. Such a transformation would have to address the unlimited accumulation of wealth and power and the private ownership of the means of production that prevail in every capitalist formation, as well as the exploitation of labor that follows from these conditions (Green 1993b: 10). Radical democratization must also involve the elimination of the structural relations of oppression – such as sexism, racism and homophobia – that are often combined with class relations in many complicated ways. Exploitation and oppression are deeply rooted in social relations; they are much more extensive and intensive than isolated moments of bigotry. In structural relations of exploitation and oppression, the dominant group achieves its power through the disempowerment of the dominated group. Where that asymmetry is institutionalized, the relations of exploitation or oppression become so entrenched that their reproduction does not exclusively depend on individuals' personal attitudes (Cunningham 1987: 114).

One of the achievements of the radical civil rights movement in the United States was precisely the normalization of the idea that racial inequality is the product of deeply embedded social structures (Omi and Winant 1994: 69). Centuries of systematic exclusions based on race – slavery; genocidal policies towards Native Americans; racist immigration, citizenship, and property laws; the *de jure* and *de facto* disenfranchisement of blacks, Latinos, Asians and Native Americans; the super-exploitation of black, Latino and Asian workers; racial discrimination in the banking, insurance and housing sectors; segregated workplaces and education systems; organized violence and so on (Takaki 1993) – have led to the vast over-concentration of racial minorities among America's unemployed and working poor. Consequently, upward socio-economic mobility has been much more difficult for these groups to achieve. In this manner, racial inequality tends to perpetuate itself. Some of the data on inequality in the United States will be examined below. The point here is that inequality should be understood as a structural phenomenon. Once a "playing field" is established that is sharply tilted against an exploited or oppressed group, that inequality will be generally reproduced and extended even if key social institutions operate in a basically unbiased manner, and even if leading decision-makers do not hold prejudicial attitudes.[4]

Neo-conservatism and its socialist critics

In the Western media's coverage of the collapse of the Soviet Union and the Eastern bloc, the political terrain was reduced to a simple choice between two caricatures: the "good" choice, "democracy" – meaning a neo-conservative free market system *à la* Thatcher, Reagan and Friedman – or the "bad" choice, "socialism" – meaning planned centralism, a Stalinist totalitarian state and an imperialist military strategy. The devastating effects of the Thatcherite and Reaganite policies for much of the working class and the poor were forgotten. Alternative definitions of socialism and democracy were also erased during the transitions in the former Soviet bloc; indeed a socialist theory of democracy became oxymoronic. In Friedman's words,

> Fundamentally, there are only two ways of coordinating the economic activities of millions. One is central direction involving the use of coercion – the technique of the army and the modern totalitarian state. The other is voluntary cooperation of individuals – the technique of the marketplace.
>
> (1993: 147)

For the neo-conservatives, an individual's freedom is maximized insofar as the capitalist market in which she competes is freed from government intervention (Green 1993b: 10). However, the capitalist market only "liberates" the individual in a very narrow historical sense. In those cases in which capitalist labor contracts displace feudal arrangements, the worker becomes "free" to participate in the capitalist labor market. In any event, this "liberation" always gives rise to a new loss of freedom. In the capitalist wage-labor contract, those who do not own the means of production are obliged to sell their labor in market conditions that they do not control in order to survive. Because they are systematically subjected to these conditions, workers in the capitalist market are not really "free" agents at all (Marx 1977: 279–80; Macpherson 1962: 48; 1973: 143–56).

The wage-labor contract only appears to be a fair exchange between two freely self-determining, rights-bearing parties who are equal before the eyes of the law. The capitalist effectively forces the worker to labor on the capitalist's terms. Under these conditions, the worker is actually compensated only for a fraction of the value that she produces. Her total earnings for a day's work are, generally speaking, much less than the value that she adds to the product in question during that day. This unpaid value, the surplus value, is concealed by the fact that the worker is paid on an hourly basis. The capitalist does not pay the worker for the surplus value, and – thanks to her exclusive ownership of the means of production – retains control over the surplus (Buchanan 1982: 44). Formal equality in market society is therefore only a mask that conceals the exploitative nature of the relation between the capitalist and the worker. Liberal democratic rights and freedoms are supposed to be universal, but, in actual practice, they may either conceal or – in the case of the unlimited right to private property – actively contribute to class-based exploitation. Further, the political sphere in a liberal society is strategically depicted as if it did not include the economic sphere. When many of our life chances are actually shaped by the ways in which we are positioned within socio-economic structures, we are encouraged in liberal democratic regimes to act as if our lives were determined by our own individual choices (Femia 1993: 32). The "common good" is reduced in a utilitarian manner to the mere sum of individualistic market decisions. Liberal principles can therefore operate as a legitimating discourse: "the 'heavenly' equality of equal political rights [serves] to mask the 'earthly' inequality of the social classes" (Harrington 1981: 14). Finally, the development of capitalism also entails the encroachment of capitalist instrumental rationality into other spheres of the social. Political, social, cultural, economic and familial questions that ought to be considered in ethical terms are settled with reference to market efficiency and individualistic utility (Buchanan 1982: 36–49; Marx and Engels 1976: 433–4; Habermas 1970, 1984, 1987).

Marx's dream of a global workers' revolution has not, of course, been realized. Over the long term, Western economies have become highly resilient in the face of crises. Even though the institutions that once softened the impact of capitalist exploitation (labor legislation, the welfare state, trade unions, redistributive programs and so on) have been weakened, an all-out class war remains highly unlikely. The expansion of globalization has accelerated the already deep divisions between workers. Capitalism has proven that it can endure or even foster connections with authoritarian forms of gender, racial and national hierarchies; it has exacerbated or even invented these differences in order to find new ways to extract super-profits and to keep workers divided and disciplined. As classes have fragmented, non-class socio-political identities – racial, ethnic, sexual, gendered, national, and so on – have proliferated and have sometimes become more prominent than class identities. While the moment of class war becomes more remote, the natural environment has been devastated by the modern technologies that have been developed under capitalism (Braidotti *et al.* 1994).

Where full-scale socialist revolutions have occurred, they have remained isolated in countries with "backward" economies that have proven vulnerable to hostile Western policies. The socialist revolutions faced the internal pressures of scarcities and the external pressures of diplomatic and military aggression from the developed West as the global expansion of advanced capitalism was buttressed by specifically anti-communist foreign policies. Under these conditions, the socialist revolutions gave way to the establishment of perpetual war economies and national-security states (Ahmad 1992: 22–3).

Ahmad lists the key features of Soviet-style authoritarianism: the disciplining of dissent in the name of national security, the military distortions of the domestic economies, the expansion of anti-democratic bureaucratism and the intensification of corruption and nepotism. He estimates, however, that at least some aspects of the Stalinist degeneration of the 1917 Revolution were determined not by Leninist principles, but by the intensive economic and strategic pressures on the regime from foreign powers (Ahmad 1992: 23). Lefort, by contrast, would place greater emphasis on the role of Leninist discourse. For Lefort, Soviet totalitarianism was not produced by a bureaucratic elite that corrupted an otherwise sound political regime. The Bolsheviks' implementation of the Leninist approach to political leadership set the stage for the subsequent exclusion of popular participation in decision-making in post-revolutionary Soviet society. Like Kolakowski (1978), Lefort sees strong continuities between the writings of Lenin and the political practices of the Bolshevik revolutionaries, the rise of a bureaucratic class as a dominant power after the revolution, the abolition of the distinctions between state and civil society, the suppression of popular dissent under Soviet rule, and full-scale Stalinism itself (Lefort 1986).

I will return to the question of Leninist-Stalinist continuities in Chapter 2. For our purposes here, however, it should be noted that Lefort would nevertheless concur with one of Ahmad's conclusions. Ahmad argues that as socialism became equated with Stalinism, the anti-democratic closures thwarted further democratization in two ways. There was no opportunity for the reassertion of democratic forms of socialism within the Soviet bloc. Meanwhile, the anti-democratic reputation of the Stalinist regimes was such that it became extremely difficult to inspire workers in Western countries to engage in the socialist struggle, for Stalinism appeared to be the only viable form of socialism (Ahmad 1992: 24). Today, the Stalinist legacy continues to thwart genuine democratization. Since feminist principles were embraced as state policy and yet badly corrupted under Soviet rule,[5] the current backlash against women's rights in the former Soviet Union can be defended in the name of women's "democratic" "liberation" from "compulsory equality" (Eisenstein 1994: 24–5). Women currently organizing against neo-conservative patriarchal policies and misogynist violence in Eastern Europe and the former Soviet Union tend to distance themselves from the feminist tradition altogether, and to pursue their struggles in the name of "human rights" (Eisenstein 1996: 161).

The socialist revolutions did of course lead to a dramatic improvement in the standard of living for many, and the contribution of the Soviet Union was crucial to the defeat of fascism. Further, the fact that Western countries faced the threat of Soviet expansionism and domestic socialist organizing was certainly an important factor in the Western elites' decision to embrace Keynesian fiscal policies, welfare state programs and civil rights reforms (Hobsbawm 1991: 118–20, 122; Cockburn 1991: 168–9). Indeed, it is no coincidence that the attacks on the democratic gains of the post-war period have been accelerated since 1989. With the disintegration of the Soviet system, neo-conservative capitalist policies have become the "only game in town." Western elites no longer have to consider the relative attractiveness of a socialist alternative for the marginalized populations in the global economy.[6]

It is nevertheless true that the Stalinist socialist regimes wholly betrayed the democratic moments within the Marxist tradition (C. Gould 1981: 49; Harrington 1993: 60–90). While Laclau and Mouffe contend that socialism is a necessary moment within radical democracy, they also insist that socialism in itself can be either democratic or anti-democratic; clearly it is only the democratic moment within the socialist tradition that holds promise for radical democracy (1990: 132, 229–30). The retrieval project, then, has to make distinctions between democratic and anti-democratic moments in both the liberal and socialist traditions. Political activists have to engage in what Laclau and Mouffe call a hegemonic struggle to bring the more democratic moments in these traditions to the fore (1990:132).[7]

At the height of the welfare state, the social democratic parties in Western countries have tended to assume that democracy would be automatically strengthened wherever they gained greater control over the state's bureaucratic institutions and extended the state's networks of power. Social democratic policies sometimes impoverished the concept of democracy as they intensified state control over more and more areas of the social, promoted corporatist solutions to the tensions between capital and labor, and replaced popular democratic mobilizations and civil liberties with eviscerated rituals of representation (Keane 1984; Hall 1988a: 126). In the United States, welfare programs have all too often reduced male recipients to passive consumers and female recipients to pathological clients, disempowered single women with children, institutionalized the feminization of poverty, and left single mothers exposed to the right's moralistic demonizations (Fraser 1989: 132, 144–60).

While socialist revolutions and the social democratic parties generally failed to produce the conditions necessary for the advance of the democratic revolution, the answer certainly does not lie in an unregulated capitalist "free" market. The common equation of the capitalist "free market" with "democratic rights and free-doms" is groundless. The liberal state that emerged in tandem with the shift from feudalism to the capitalist market was originally undemocratic; decision-making authority was vested only in freeborn male property owners. Entire imperialist and colonial systems were shaped by the elites in the emerging liberal democratic Western states. As capitalism developed in the West, liberalism was democratized, but democracy was also liberalized; democracy was neutralized such that it tended to serve capitalist interests (Macpherson 1965: 10; 1977: 65–6). Although the franchise has been formally extended to non-property-owners, women, and racial minorities, the so-called democratic institutions have failed to empower "the people." Market-oriented decision-making in Western countries now takes precedence in more and more areas of human interaction in a manner that is fundamentally at odds with democratic principles (Habermas 1970, 1984, 1987; Buchanan 1982: 40). Throughout capitalist societies, political discourse is profoundly shaped by corporate interests, while dissenting voices are muted, distorted or excluded altogether (Chomsky 1988; Parenti 1993, 1995: 165–78).

Capitalist development therefore tends to promote the dilution of democratic principles and institutions. Capitalism can also be fully compatible with an undemocratic society. Capitalist formations depend upon, perpetuate and some-times even invent complicated networks of exploitation and oppression that are organized in terms of class, gender, race, ethnicity, nationality and global location. The juxtaposition of "successful" capitalist development with military govern-ments in Latin America and authoritarian regimes in Taiwan, South Korea and Singapore is further historical evidence that the advance of capitalism does not guarantee democratization. Insofar as development in Latin America continues to reflect the interests of capital, these countries will remain marked by colonialism, dependence, social fragmentation, exclusions and violence even where dictator-ships have been replaced by liberal democratic governments (Escobar 1992). Deng's free market reforms in China have been twinned with sharply anti-democratic policies. It is also remarkable that many of the leading corporate executives in Hong Kong give their full support to the Beijing government. The shift to capitalist systems in Eastern Europe and the former Soviet Union is currently coinciding with a sharp reduction in women's rights and with a rise in income disparities, poverty, racism, sexism, ethnic hatred, chauvinist nationalism, anti-Semitism, organized crime, corruption, militarism and imperialism.

Meanwhile, there is every sign that inequality in the distribution of wealth in Western societies is increasing on a massive scale. Virtually all income groups enjoyed rising standards of living in the developed countries during the post-war period. With global restructuring, the transnational mobility of capital, special-ization in the Western countries according to comparative advantage in high-technology and capital services sectors, niche marketing, automation, downsizing, de-industrialization, de-skilling, the attack on unions, regressive taxation and welfare program "reforms," the rich are getting richer and the poor are getting poorer at an unprecedented rate.

In the United States, for example, the real incomes of the poorest 20 percent have decreased 17 percent while those of the wealthiest 20 percent have increased 18 percent between 1978 and 1994 (Corn 1995). The richest 1 percent of American households own almost 40 percent of the total national wealth. The top 20 percent of American households own more than 80 percent of the national wealth (Herbert 1995). During the 1980s, 75 percent of the income gains and 100 percent of the increased wealth went to the top 20 percent of American households (*New York Times* 1995). The United States now has the most unequal distribution of income and wealth, and the fastest growing gap between the rich and poor, in all of the developed countries. The American child poverty rate is four times greater than the average for the Western European countries (Bradsher 1995a). One out of every five children in the United States now lives in poverty. Half of the Americans who live below the poverty line are elderly. Between 250,000 and 3,000,000 Americans are homeless, and families with children make up as much as one-third of the homeless (Parenti 1995: 28–9).

All of this data on the distribution of income and wealth in the United States was compiled before the massive reduction in welfare rights took place in 1996–7. Under the new welfare regulations, poor people will be cut off welfare programs in a country whose Federal Reserve is deliberately controlling interest rates to maintain high unemployment. Seven million Americans were already seeking work in 1996, a year in which there were fourteen applicants for every unskilled minimum wage job in an inner city fast food restaurant (Justice For All 1996). The new welfare laws will remove three and a half million children from public assistance by 2001, and will add a million more children to the vast numbers of those already under the poverty line (*The Nation* 1996: 3). This will take place in a country in which over 4,200 babies below twelve months in age already die each year because of low birthweight and other problems directly related to the poverty of their mothers (Cockburn 1996: 9).

Although some middle-class women and blacks have fared relatively well, women, blacks and Latinos remain highly overrepresented among the unemployed and poor. The differentials in median incomes partly reveal these inequalities. The median annual income for black women in 1993 is $19,820, as compared to $22,020 for white women, $23,020 for black men and $31,090 for white men. Family income differentials are even more striking. The median household income for blacks is 58 percent of the median white household income, and this gap has remained constant between 1972 and 1992 (Holmes 1995a). The black and Hispanic workers who had found secure and relatively well-paying jobs were concentrated, for historical reasons, in the unionized industrial manufacturing and government sectors. They were particularly hard hit, then, by the automation, global relocation, downsizing and privatization that transformed these sectors in the 1980s and 1990s (Marable 1983; R.M. Williams

1993; Harrington 1993: 257; Barrett 1988). Racial disparities are even greater when we look at total family wealth instead of income. In 1991, the typical white household was ten times more wealthy than the typical black household (Eisenstein 1994: 183). Compared to whites, African-Americans have a 100 percent greater infant mortality rate, a 176 percent greater unemployment rate, and a 300 percent greater poverty rate (Parenti 1995: 27).

Hispanics are also enormously over-concentrated among the poor in the United States. While median household income rose for every other American ethnic and racial group in 1995, it dropped 5.1 percent for Hispanics. This average decline was experienced by both the new immigrant and the American-born Hispanic groups. Although the median household income for blacks actually rose between 1989 and 1995, it dropped 14 percent for Hispanics. Between 1992 and 1995, white median family income increased by 2.2 percent to $35,766; black median family income increased by 9.9 percent to $22,393; while Hispanic median family income decreased by 6.9 percent to $22,860 (all figures are expressed in 1995 dollars.) The poverty rate among Hispanics surpassed that of blacks for the first time in the mid-1990s. While Hispanics represented 16 percent of the total American population living in poverty in 1985, this figure increased to 24 percent by 1995. Almost one out of three Hispanics was considered poor in 1995;[8] the poverty rate for the Hispanic population was therefore three times greater than that for non-Hispanic whites (Goldberg 1997).

The increase in the prevalence of female-headed households is related to the sharp decline in earnings for young men with an educational level of a high school diploma or less (Holmes 1995b). As men with low levels of education are now much more likely to be holding jobs that pay poverty wages than they were in the 1970s (R.M. Williams 1993: 85–6), they are much more reluctant to form stable households with the mothers of their children. As a result, female-headed households are highly overrepresented among all households that fall below the poverty line (Eisenstein 1994: 183). Forty-four percent of single mothers remain below the poverty line and two out of three adults living in poverty are women (Parenti 1995: 27).[9]

Although neo-conservatives equate the growth of the capitalist "free" market with freedom, equality and democracy, the evidence suggests that capitalist formations depend on exploitation and coercion, foster inequality, and either neutralize democracy or tolerate fundamentally anti-democratic conditions. Again, at its most promising moment, liberal democratic theory suggests that every individual has an inalienable right to engage freely in the development of her own unique human capacities. Socialists, however, are correct in their assertion that fundamental rights and freedoms cannot be secured in a society that is structured according to the dictates of capitalist relations of exploitation. With Macpherson, Laclau and Mouffe contend that we should appropriate these insights from liberal democratic and socialist thought and combine them together to construct a new approach to democracy.

Socialism as a necessary moment within radical democracy

Capitalism, by its very nature, systematically denies large sections of the popula-tion access to the resources necessary for self-determination. Those who are disempowered under capitalism – the workers and the unemployed who do not own the means of production – are locked in exploitative conditions not, as Herrnstein and Murray (1994) argue, because of some sort of psychological, intel-lectual or genetic abnormality on their part, but because of the institutionalized structures of inequality that are integral to the capitalist system. Brown contends that Laclau and Mouffe have not given sufficient emphasis to their critique of capitalist exploitation.

> While thinkers such as Bowles and Gintis, Laclau and Mouffe, and the analytical Marxism school are certainly critical of capitalism's inequities, they are less concerned with capitalism as a political economy of domina-tion, exploitation, or alienation, precisely those terms by which the problem of freedom is foregrounded as a problem of social and economic power and not only a matter of political or legal statutes. It is as if the terrible unfreedom and indignities attendant upon "actually existing socialisms" of the last half-century persuaded such thinkers that free enterprise really is freer than the alternatives, that alienation is inherent in all labour, and that freedom, finally, is a matter of consumption, choice, and expression: an individual good rather than a social and political practice.
>
> (Brown 1995: 13)

For their part, Laclau and Mouffe do state that the socialist struggle to overcome capitalist exploitation is a necessary but not sufficient condition for the advance of the democratic revolution: "Every project for radical democracy implies a socialist dimension, as it is necessary to put an end to capitalist relations of production, which are at the root of numerous relations of subordination" (Laclau and Mouffe 1985: 178). Brown nevertheless rightly indicates that the authors have not fully developed the political economy implications of their position. In what follows, I will attempt to respond to Brown's challenge by outlining the radical democratic perspective on political economy.

The socialist demand for the radical transformation of the fundamentally inegalitarian socio-economic structures that are integral to every capitalist forma-tion should be seen not as a rejection of the democratic revolution, but as an internal moment within its general extension to new areas of the social. Liberal democratic theorists from Mill to Dahl have addressed the tensions between democracy and economic inequality (Green 1993b: 9; Mill 1972: 210–11, 216, 276–92; Dahl 1956: 113, 126, 137, 139–40; 1982: 108–37, 170–87; 1989: 108–14). Rousseau held that liberty cannot exist without equality and defined equality such that it would preclude the development of exploitation (Rousseau 1973: 204). Some of the French Revolutionists believed that the true realization of the revolution's aims – "liberty, equality and fraternity" – depended not only on securing formal legal equality for every citizen but on establishing some sort of basic equality through the redistribution of wealth as well (Watkins and Kramnick 1979: 43). Indeed, Marx himself was greatly influenced by the democratic discourse of the Enlightenment and the French Revolution. The Marxist image of society as divided into two totally encompassing camps locked in a decisive struggle, the workers versus the capitalists, is derived from the revolutionary struggle between "the people" and the *ancien régime* (Laclau and Mouffe 1985: 156). The Marxist demands for economic equality and human freedom from the tyranny of the capitalist system were adaptations of the liberal democratic demands for political equality and freedom.

Capitalist societies only allow for the self-development of the privileged few. The small minority that does gain access to the resources necessary for self-development only does so thanks to the exploitation and oppression of the majority. Marx envisioned, by contrast, a society in which every individual would have a truly equal right to realize freely her own potential (Marx 1975a; Elster 1989: 140; Wood 1981: 53). Marx and Engels explicitly defined communism as a society in which "the free development of each is the condition for the free development of all" (Marx and Engels 1969: 127). For C. Gould and Mostov, not only is it not true that socialist theory is anti-democratic; the socialist conception of the collective control over the means of production – a collective control that would empower diverse individuals – is a necessary condition for the realization of democracy (C. Gould 1981: 51–4; Mostov 1989: 212). While Marx was highly critical of liberal democracy's false promise that it alone could deliver genuine rights and freedoms, he advanced his critique of liberal democracy in the name of democracy itself. Both Marx and Engels held that democracy is the highest possible form of political organization (Harrington 1981: 12; Avineri 1970: 35–6, 47).

Harrington insists that it is Luxemburg, rather than Lenin, Trotsky or Stalin, who captures the spirit of Marx's democratic theory. Luxemburg argues that "it is the historic task of the proletariat when it seizes power to replace bourgeois democracy with the creation of socialist democracy [,] not to do away with any kind of democracy" (Harrington 1981: 18). Socialism should not, therefore, be seen as a struggle that is opposed to democracy *per se*; socialism should be viewed instead as a struggle that aims to complete the democratic project that was begun in the liberal democratic revolutions of the eighteenth and nineteenth centuries (Hunt 1980: 17). As such, Laclau and Mouffe's support for the contemporary movements on the Left that attempt to appropriate, deepen and expand liberal-democratic principles is entirely consistent with their inclusion of the socialist struggle within radical democracy (1985: 176).

If liberty is broadly defined as the capacity for genuinely free self-development, and equality is similarly defined as the equal right to pursue self-development, then the condition of possibility of liberty and equality is free and equal access to the material resources that are necessary for self-development. Furthermore, the individual's right to self-determination entails the right to participate in the collective determination of all the social activities in which that individual is engaged, including economic relations. Only a socialist transformation of the capitalist system would bring about these conditions. Progress towards socialism would entail, for example, a large-scale transformation in property ownership and the decision-making authority that flows from such ownership. In a truly socialist society (as opposed to the authoritarian bureaucratic collectivist societies that called themselves "socialist"), everyone would enjoy access to the basic material resources that are needed for the exercise of individual freedoms. It would establish a "floor" – everyone would receive sufficient opportunity for work, income, education and security – and a "ceiling" – no class would be able to accumulate so much wealth that it could opt out of the public provisions for ecological management, security, transport, military and policing, and education by substituting its own private goods (Connolly 1995: 81). Equal access to material resources would take away the economic weapons that are currently used by the privileged to maintain the undemocratic status quo, and would provide those individuals who wished to challenge an oppressive familial, cultural, social or political situation with the means to do so (Cunningham 1987: 124–5).

The meaning of the socialist transformation of capitalism has changed a great deal since Lenin's day. Contemporary leftists now generally recognize that economic decisions in our complex societies cannot be made solely by a central command structure. The combination of democratic participation, some degree of central planning, extensive state intervention, substantial redistributive programs and a highly regulated market would facilitate efficient decision-making, consumer choice and the decentralization of power, without reintroducing the capitalist problems of structural inequality and social costs.

The real debate among leftists now revolves around the question of the balance between different types of economic institutions. Some theorists, such as C. Gould, insist that democracy necessitates the total displacement of private property in favor of collective ownership and workers' self-management. They would allow only for a free market in the exchange of commodities (C. Gould 1981: 56–8). Others, such as Bay, insist that an ideal society would establish a regulated sphere of private property ownership and market relations and would allow individuals to accumulate the social privileges that would flow from relations in that sphere. Regulation of the market would be determined by majority rule while the primacy human rights would be absolute (Bay 1993: 292–4).

In Nove's "feasible" socialist economic model, state- and co-operative-owned property would predominate and only small-scale private ownership would be allowed. The economy would be managed according to the democratic decisions of the people. Individuals would be free to choose the nature of their work and their location within the state, cooperative and private entrepreneurial sectors (Nove 1983: 197–230). Following Nove, other theorists have proposed models of "market socialism" that would combine state management, worker cooperatives, small-scale entrepreneurism, income supplements and progressive taxation (Blackburn 1991: 223).

21

Connolly outlines an egalitarian program that includes a steep progressive tax and extensive state subsidization for what he calls inclusive consumption. Exclusive consumption takes place wherever more popular access to a good leads to a decrease in its value for those who already enjoy access to it; an increase in the private costs incurred because of its use; higher social costs; and larger per capita state expenditures either for subsidizing the good or for addressing the socio-ecological problems that are caused by its use. Connolly cites automobile-centered transportation systems, single-family suburban housing policies, and high-technology, profit-driven medical systems as examples. Wilderness management programs that are designed to suit the interests of the very wealthiest outdoors enthusiasts would also fit into his category of exclusionary goods. With inclusionary goods, by contrast, an increase in popular access brings about an increase in its private value and a decrease in its social costs. State subsidies should therefore be directed towards inclusionary goods such as rapid transit systems and universal health care programs rather than their privatized counterparts (1995: 81–5).[10]

Walzer contends that free market relations should not necessarily be ruled out, but that no one should be allowed to exercise "market imperialism" by converting private wealth into political influence and social privilege (1993: 244). Elson suggests that the best way to check the social costs of the market, such as inequality, exploitation and disenfranchisement, would be to expand the rights of citizens to include the rights to basic goods and services, and the rights to participation and accountability (1991: 311). Indeed, environmentalist activists in the United States are currently seeking to amend the Constitution to enshrine the right to live in a clean environment, thereby addressing one of the market's "externalities." Democratization would also require extensive measures to check the rise of technological, scientific, medical, legal, administrative and security (police, secret service and military) elites, such that the newly democratized economic sphere would not be allowed to deteriorate into bureaucratic authoritarianism (Harrington 1981: 19–21). Miliband contends that the best way to check the authority of these elites would be to promote "popular power" at multiple sites outside the state (1991: 15).

For all their disagreement on the specific details, there is a strong consensus among leftists today that real progress towards democracy would require fundamental social change – including the democratization of the economy such that basic economic decisions would reflect the will of the people rather than the will of the most powerful. The aim here should be to work towards a combination of different economic institutions that would best suit the structural changes necessary for the progress of democratization in a specific historical context. In every case, however, many of the same basic problems will have to be addressed, namely the greatest possible decrease in the exploitation of labor, the democratization of resource allocation decision-making, the redistribution of wealth, and reforms that would block the conversion of economic wealth into political and social privilege, and that would limit the market's oligopolistic tendencies.

22

Radical democratization would also have to address the urgent problem of environmental destruction. As I will discuss in Chapter 3, one of Marx's approaches to history entails a stagist theory in which capitalist property relations would eventually become a fetter on the productive process. Miliband notes that this prediction has not been borne out by history. He nevertheless maintains that the capitalist system has "come to be a fetter upon the most beneficent use of the immense resources it has itself brought into being" (1994: 13). The productive process has to be radically transformed such that it begins to serve humane and ecological ends rather than the dictates of profit (Miliband 1994: 13).

Brown cautions that an exclusive emphasis on the redistribution of goods can impoverish leftist politics; the pragmatic focus on feasible goals in the present should not be allowed to displace more fundamental aims, such as the transformation of political subjectivity and the radical democratization of power (1995: 5). Laclau and Mouffe would also add the following warning note to these discussions. The rules and norms that lay the foundations for radical democracy will always have to be re-examined in the light of new conditions and struggles. For Laclau, the very conception of a universal blueprint for radical democracy is a contradiction in terms.

> In order for the demands on which the socialist myth has been based to regain validity and acquire new historical possibilities, it only needs them to be inscribed in a discourse different from that of "social management" – by which we mean an abstract universality that must be embodied. But this means moving in the opposite direction to the discourse of eschatological universality.
>
> (Laclau 1990a: 77–8)

In the eschatological dimension in Marxist thought, it is assumed that the socialist revolution would resolve all fundamental antagonisms, give birth to a whole new human being and establish a power-free social space. Eschatological Marxism also claims that the working class is the only subject that can emancipate all of humanity from virtually every form of domination, because it alone is destined to become a universal subject, a pure human essence without a trace of particularism (Laclau 1996a; Balibar 1994: xv; Aronson 1995: 91–7). For Laclau and Mouffe, these eschatological assumptions are dangerous illusions. They insist that we should imagine radical democratic pluralism as inciting an infinite series of contestations instead. Following Lefort, the authors contend that an "empty space" at the center of a truly democratic society would always be preserved (Laclau and Mouffe 1985: 186–8). In Lefort's terms, democracy in modern societies thrives on the contradiction between its two founding principles: power rests with "the people," but the site of popular sovereignty must remain "an empty place, impossible to occupy, such that those who exercise public authority can never claim to appropriate it" (Lefort 1986: 279). In other words, "the people" must rule in a modern democratic society, but it is self-destructive for a democratic society to allow political actors and institutions to define shared values, common ends and the identities of the citizen in a substantive and permanent manner.[11] Democracy is destroyed wherever this tension is canceled out.

Radical democratic theory rejects teleologies, "scientific" predictions and eschatological prophecies. Radical democratic pluralism requires a fallibilist approach that abandons every kind of prediction (Miliband 1991: 29). This does not mean, however, that Laclau and Mouffe endorse the view that anything is possible, that every social formation is utterly unique and monadically isolated, and that there are no discernible institutionalized continuities that structure the social across time. The authors do in fact provide tools that we can use to assess power relations at a given moment in time and across different genealogical moments. Their theory does allow for a certain degree of generalizing descriptions and estimations about future probabilities. Because contingency always limits and interrupts the operation of necessity, however, prediction in the full sense is impossible; indeed, the strategic dimension of every prediction-claim should be revealed.

In this sense, Laclau and Mouffe's position echoes Luxemburg's argument that a "one-size-fits-all" plan for socialism is a contradiction in terms, and that no social movement should operate as if it did in fact have exclusive access to such a plan. Luxemburg was active in the German socialist movement until her death in 1919. A critic of both Bernstein's revisionism and the Bolsheviks' despotism, she held that socialists should state what they are against in specific and practical terms, but should only offer general descriptions of their alternative societies. Taking issue with Lenin, she declared that "socialism, in its very nature, cannot be decreed, introduced through ukases [edicts]" (Harrington 1981: 18). Luxemburg rejected the Leninist vanguard party approach to revolution, arguing that unless the revolution encouraged dissent and maintained democratic institutions such as elections, the right to free speech and freedom of assembly, it would lose its popular energy and degenerate into a bureaucratic dictatorship. Instead of imposing a vanguard leadership from above, Luxemburg believed that socialists ought to sustain and to encourage the workers' self-organized revolutionary energy during strikes and uprisings. For Luxemburg, it is only through the workers' own praxis, their concrete experience in constructing a new society, that they will liberate themselves from their past and achieve a higher form of cultural existence and morality (Wright 1986: 87, 107; Löwy 1981: 73).

For all her opposition to dogmatic theory, the predominance of scientific socialism in Luxemburg's day was such that she herself subscribed to the view that the collapse of capitalism was objectively necessary. Ultimately, she could only think of politics in terms of the class struggle (Wright 1986: 45–6; Laclau and Mouffe 1985: 11–12; Kolakowski 1978: 61–97). While she did not reject the concept of the dictatorship of the proletariat, she nevertheless insisted that this leadership had to involve – in an open and profoundly democratic manner – the workers as a mass movement. Against the authoritarian tendencies that were already emerging during the first years of the Soviet Revolution, she asserted,

"Freedom only for the government supporters, only for the members of the Party – however numerous they may be – this is not freedom. Freedom is always at the very least freedom for those who think otherwise" (Löwy 1981: 74).[12] Luxemburg followed other socialists in making a clear distinction between bourgeois democracy and socialist democracy, but she saw the latter as preserving the freedoms that had been won for the workers under bourgeois democracy and expanding them to include new freedoms that had not been possible for them under capitalism (Löwy 1981: 75).

We can capture some of the independent spirit that thrives in Luxemburg's discourse in the form of a warning. We may become dangerously seduced by leaders who claim that thanks to their "scientific knowledge," they can grasp historical "necessities" and predict exactly how a progressive struggle should unfold. These leaders would impose rigid political programs and restrict democratic contestation out of the arrogance that arises from the misuse of theory, when they ought to remain conscious of their epistemological limitations. Further, theory must be consistently defined and redefined with reference to the concrete experiences of the disempowered as they struggle against domination, rather than conjured up in a magical space that has been separated off from the complexities of concrete political contestations. I will return to this theme, with reference to Gramsci's conception of organic philosophy and common sense, in Chapter 2.

Laclau and Mouffe's argument also echoes Foucault's bio-power theory. The space for democratic contestation must always be preserved within the democratic struggles themselves, for even the most "progressive" leaderships can deteriorate into some form of authoritarianism. This potential for authoritarian reaction – through the disciplining of deviance, the normalization of specific values, and the neutralization of oppositional forces – is permanent and universal, for it is inscribed within every institution's structure. Further, because the potential for authoritarian reaction is always embedded within institutional structures, it is prior to individuals' intentions; even the best-intentioned individuals may find themselves caught up in the disciplinary regulation of democratic differences.

The limitations of socialism for radical democracy

While Laclau and Mouffe do recognize that the socialist struggle against capitalist exploitation is a necessary moment within radical democracy, they nevertheless sharply differ with Marxist theory in many respects. As I noted briefly above, the social has become divided along both class and non-class lines; classes have fragmented and new identities have emerged that criss-cross class lines. Laclau and Mouffe contend that the socialist struggle should not be understood as the single struggle that will, by definition, bring all forms of subordination to an end, or as the single struggle that ought to subsume all other democratic struggles under its leadership. Although it is of course true that capitalist exploitation is linked with other forms of oppression, these linkages are so complex and contradictory that significant aspects of imperialism, sexism, racism, homophobia and other forms of oppression would remain intact even after a socialist revolution (Laclau and Mouffe 1985: 178).

Laclau and Mouffe's radicalization of democratic discourse envisions both the revitalization of the socialist struggle against capitalism and the promotion of the struggles of the democratic new social movements: "urban, ecological, anti-authoritarian, anti-institutional, feminist, anti-racist, ethnic, regional [and] sexual minorities" (1985: 159). The authors call for the construction of a specific form of solidarity between these different democratic struggles. They insist that the radical democratic pluralist form of unification would bring movements together through articulation while simultaneously preserving their autonomy. They propose complex processes of democratization as each progressive movement would renegotiate its identity by incorporating the others' demands, and by forging temporary blocs according to the tactical conditions at hand, but without ever imposing the disciplining leadership of a preselected dominant group over the emerging historical bloc as a whole.

While socialist theory provides a powerful analysis of the incompatibility between genuine progress towards democracy and capitalist relations of exploitation, it cannot adequately capture every facet of domination and inequality. Class analysis sheds some light on different types of sexism, racism and homophobia, but it does not always detect the specificity of these structures (Omi and Winant 1994: 24–35; Hall 1980; Gilroy 1982: 276–314; 1987: 15–42; Cose 1993; Eisenstein 1979, 1994; Barrett 1988; Rowbotham *et al.* 1981; Sargent 1981). Capitalist formations shape and are shaped in turn by non-class-based forms of oppression. We are never actually confronted with nothing but capitalism; similarly, sexism, racism and homophobia never appear in isolated form. We experience, instead, contextually-specific hybrid formations that emerge out of the combinations of these forces. The theories that attempt to predict – without sufficient attention to contextual specificity – exactly how capitalist exploitation will combine with other forms of oppression are therefore problematic.

Some feminists argue, for example, that sexism and capitalism combine together such that the cost of the reproduction of labor is kept low. Their basic argument is that women, in their familial roles as mothers and spouses, are socially, legally and culturally pressured to perform unpaid domestic labor. From this perspective, women's unpaid labor subsidizes capital, for the labor units purchased by capital are performed not by machines but by individual workers. Adult workers not only had to be reared until they were old enough to become full-time wage-earners, but they also usually return after every shift to their familial homes for their food and shelter. Child-raising, meal preparation, the cleaning and repair of clothes, home cleaning and so on constitute the domestic activities through which labor is reproduced. Feminists such as Hartsock contend that the control and seizure of the goods produced by women through their domestic labor – their unpaid childrearing and housework labor – is the foundation of women's oppression (Hartsock 1983: 291).

26

These relations of oppression do not, however, apply evenly to all women. Men certainly do not directly appropriate the value that is generated through domestic labor, childbearing and childrearing in lesbian households as a matter of course. The gendering of the household structure itself is irrelevant in the relation between capital and the domestic reproduction of labor: capital benefits equally from the value that is generated by lesbian households and gay male households alike. In addition, nothing in the relation between the household and capital would be affected by a woman capitalist's purchase of controlling shares of a factory. The assumption that women are universally positioned to perform their family's unpaid domestic labor is also problematic with respect to class and race differences. Domestic workers relieve their women employers of much of their patriarchally-allocated housework and childcare burdens. Women of color are overrepresented among domestic workers, while white women are overrepresented among their bourgeois employers. We should of course recognize that there are cases in which the reproduction of labor model is in fact helpful. However, even if we find that the model is appropriate in the majority of cases, we cannot assume that we have discovered a universal rule for the combination of capitalism and sexism.

Universal rules for the combination of capitalism and racism are equally problematic. In some contexts, such as the employment of newly arrived Afro-Caribbean and south Asian immigrants in the lowest paid sectors of the British labor force from the mid-1950s to present (Sivanandan 1982), it is clear that capitalists have reaped super-profits by practicing race-based job segregation and wage differentiation. It is also often the case that capital does not hesitate to utilize, incite or even invent racial differences among the workers to maintain workplace discipline (Higginbotham 1992: 260; Takaki 1993). However, analyses of racism that focus exclusively on super-exploitation and job segregation can overlook the salience of the racial solidarities that span class divisions.

Omi and Winant contend that the relation between race and class in the United States is so complex that no general descriptions can be offered. The sectoral differences within the labor market "overlap and cut across racial lines of division" (1994: 34). Where a distinct black bourgeois culture is consolidated, the black middle class may nevertheless remain symbolically and structurally linked to the black working class. The educational and job opportunities that have made the success of some middle-class blacks possible depend on the mobilization of the entire black community's voting power. The public funding for the positions held by black professionals in the government and educational sectors has often been provided because black voters have successfully demanded improved services for the black community as a whole (1994: 28). Against the theories that prioritize class differences over racial solidarities and imply that cross-class race-based mobilizations are expressions of "false consciousness," Omi and Winant conclude that "race and class are competing modalities by which social actors may be organized. . . . 'Class unity' might prevail at one moment or on one terrain, while racial conflict might rule the day on another" (1994: 32, 33).

27

In other cases, the structural linkages between the different class sectors within a minority community do not become the basis for cross-class racial/ethnic solidarities. Some theorists have suggested that the class differences within the black community are more important in terms of shaping interests and identities than cross-class commonalities based on race (Miles 1984; Wilson 1978). Cultural critics have noted that black and post-colonial middle-class intellectuals have sometimes embraced cultural nationalism without adequately taking class differences into account (Gilroy 1993: 32–3; Ahmad 1992; Spivak 1997: 478–9), or without preserving the critical force of anti-colonial politics (Shohat and Stam 1994: 38). A cross-class racial/ethnic solidarity will only be effective insofar as it is meaningful in a practical sense for individuals who occupy different positions in socio-economic structures. I will return to this problem of theorizing the combination of identities and power relations in my discussion of Laclau and Mouffe's conception of articulation in the following chapters.

Class-centered analyses are also limited in terms of the light that they can shed on homophobia.[13] This is not to say, however, that lesbians and gays are extraordinarily wealthy. American right-wing groups have portrayed gay men as a homogeneous wealthy group and have cynically used the data about the incomes of gay male up-market magazine subscribers to support their claims. Gluckman and Reed, by contrast, point out that lesbians and gay men are actually located in every income bracket, occupation and poverty program (1997: xii). Lesbians and gay men pay the price of homophobic exclusions in the form of job losses, promotion denials, and discrimination in housing and health care. Recent studies have found that lesbians, gays and bisexuals tend to earn less than their heterosexual counterparts. One study found that after controlling for education, age and other relevant factors, gay men earned between 11 and 27 percent less than similar heterosexual men. As for lesbians, some studies indicate that there is relatively little difference between the average incomes of lesbians and straight women, while others suggest that lesbian households are overrepresented among the very poor, and that individual lesbians earn as much as 30 percent less than similar heterosexual women (Badgett 1997). Lesbians are also confronted with the same gender gap as our heterosexual sisters; women earn on average 70 percent of men's income.

These findings make sense on an intuitive level. Traditional familial ties play a key role in various aspects of the reproduction of wealth – such as access to higher education, family-based career networking, financial gifts, personal loans, entrepreneurial investment capital, the inheritance of estates, financial support during a career crisis or unemployment, and so on – and lesbians and gays are often excluded from our traditional families. In the face of extreme bigotry, gay men, and, to a lesser extent, lesbians, often choose migration to urban centers that contain supportive subcultures over career-oriented transitions. While in theory a gay male household could benefit from its doubling of the gendered wage differential, discrimination against individual gay men often cancels out this privilege altogether. Finally, lesbian households are, on average, much worse off than their heterosexual counterpart. Even if both members of a lesbian couple are fortunate enough to escape sexual orientation-based economic discrimination, they will still have to contend with job discrimination, "glass ceilings" and "mommy tracking" as women and as actual or potential mothers.

The difficulties in capturing homophobia and heterosexism within a class-centric perspective stem from the fact that there is no singular functional relation between capitalist development, the formation of sexual identities and the politics of sexual regulation. Weeks recognizes that sexuality has been influenced by the rise of capitalist forces, but contends that the effects of capitalism on sexuality have been complex and even contradictory. In nineteenth-century England, for example, tensions often emerged between the interests of evangelical moral campaigners and the capitalists who wanted to put men, women and children to work in the same factory. Divisions in popular opinions on prostitution, birth control, abortion, marriage, divorce and homosexuality emerged and persisted between the classes and within the same class (Weeks 1981: 19–33; 1985: 22–5). At other moments, the linkages between sexuality and class are more straightforward. Anxieties about the sexual practices of racial minorities and immigrants, for example, continue to be used as a normalized site of intensive social control, leading to the intensification of state intervention in the personal lives of poor women of color (Spillers 1987; Eisenstein 1994; Fraser and Gordon 1994; Lubiano 1997).

Where industrialization and urbanization tended to introduce a separation between economic activity and kinship systems, the opportunity for the emergence of sexual minorities and the consolidation of distinct socio-cultural subcultures became much more pronounced (Gluckman and Reed 1997: xiii). At the same time, however, persistent gendered and racial differentials in income and wealth meant that these developments were not always equally available for women and racial minorities. The commodification of more and more areas of social relations has also had an ambiguous effect. For example, the dramatic expansion of consumer markets and the relative improvement of the standard of living for most Westerners in the post-war period have provided the conditions for the emergence of both the pornography industry and the contemporary lesbian and gay commercial subcultures. While the largely sexist pornography industry has done little to advance genuine freedoms, the lesbian and gay commercial subcultures have provided the sexual liberation movement with extremely valuable spatial and financial resources for political mobilization (Weeks 1985: 22–5).

For all its complicated relations with capitalism, homophobia remains a powerful structure of oppression that systematically rewards those who conform to the heterosexual nuclear family norm and punishes those who deviate or even merely appear to deviate from that norm. Lesbians and gays are widely exposed to discrimination in employment, housing and government services without governmental protection. People with AIDS who cannot afford expensive drug treatment programs are left to die, and programs to stop the spread of HIV are underfunded because AIDS has been equated with the "immorality" of homosexuality. Children are routinely taken from loving homes solely because of their parents' homosexuality. Lesbians, gays, bisexuals, transgendered individuals and those who are merely suspect-homosexuals are subjected to cultural exclusion, intimidation, harassment, violence and even brutal murder. Our relationships and families are not recognized by our employers, insurance companies, school systems, legislators, courts, income tax agencies, immigration officials and military forces. The attack on lesbian and gay rights has become a central part of the new right's agenda (Smith 1994b, 1997b). The entire homophobic system of rewards and penalties is so extensive that virtually every married adult's participation in the officially sanctioned family is actually a coerced practice rather than a truly free choice (Rich 1993; Halley 1989, 1993).

Democratic anti-racist, -sexist and -homophobic discourses are often dismissed by class-centric socialists as mere "identity politics"; it is implied that compared to the "hard" issues that flow from economic inequality, these are "soft" issues. (It should be noted that this type of socialist discourse itself engages in a misogynist and homophobic abjection of the feminine.) For those people who are subjected to discrimination, job segregation, wage differentials, political disenfranchisement, environmental pollution, right-wing smears, police bigotry and vicious hate crimes, there is nothing "soft" or illusory about non-class-based oppressions. Many socialists in both Europe and the United States already support the anti-racist struggles to defend the rights of immigrants; the pro-multicultural and pro-affirmative action campaigns; the feminist struggles against rape and for abortion rights; the various campaigns against the religious right; the struggles against AIDS and for lesbian and gay rights; and the campaigns to protect the environment. There is no reason why the linkages between leftist forces and these struggles should not be deepened; or why they should not be joined together with the struggles for the rights of workers in a global economy and for the rights of welfare recipients and the unemployed in the face of neoconservative policies.[14]

In the end, the prominence of cultural elements within workers' struggles, and the anti-capitalist character of many democratic movements, may make the entire distinction between class-based and non-class-based struggles increasingly irrelevant (Laclau and Mouffe 1985: 167). For example, the Zapatista movement in Mexico, with its indigenous, rural, peasant/worker, socialist, feminist, anti-state and anti-free trade dimensions, defies categorization in these terms. In any event, the Left can only assert itself as a compelling and effective source of democratic resistance to the extent that it thoroughly integrates anti-racist, anti-sexist, anti-homophobic and environmentalist values into socialist discourse.

Towards a definition of radical democratic pluralism

As I have noted above, political economy themes have not been given a prominent place in Laclau and Mouffe's texts. On the basis of their specific remarks and their theoretical horizon, we can nevertheless construct the radical democratic pluralist approach to these issues. In a radical democratic society, there would be equal access not only to the material resources necessary for self-development, but also to meaningful participation in social, cultural, political and economic decision-making. The radical democratization of existing state structures and social formations would require a profound redistribution of power and a complete dismantling of the structures that institutionalize inequality, including capitalist exploitation, sexism, homophobia and racism. Today we are also confronted with the rise of transnational corporations and the global restructuration of investment, production and marketing (Barnet and Cavanaugh 1994; Bennis and Moushabeck 1993). This is not to say that there is anything inherently progressive in familiar, "local" or small-scale institutions, but that radical democratization would ultimately require economic transformations and progressive forms of political solidarity on a transnational level.

Radical democratic theory must retrieve the most progressive aspects of the liberal democratic and socialist traditions while moving beyond their limitations. In addition to liberal democracy's basic values of freedom and equality, radical democracy must retrieve from this tradition the concepts of civil liberties and individual self-determination and self-development. For all of Marx's own attempts to achieve a Hegelian reconciliation between the most positive aspects of individuality and community in a post-capitalist communist society (Avineri 1970: 33, 34–7; Elster 1989: 151; Marx 1975a: 350), many critics argue that he failed to value non-class-based forms of solidarity, human rights, plural conceptions of the good and the permanence of democratic contestation (Femia 1993: 65; Bowles and Gintis 1986: 18–20; C. Gould 1981: 49; Sypnowich 1990: 167; Schwartz 1995: 21–4, 104–45). While it is true that liberal democracy has often been intertwined with capitalist development, these historical precedents are contingent. For Laclau and Mouffe, the radicalization of the most promising moments of the liberal democratic tradition is entirely possible. Indeed, once the liberal democratic principles of freedom, equality and democracy are radicalized, they can be used to weaken capitalism itself (Cunningham 1987: 158–9).

These liberal democratic principles therefore have to be both retrieved and radicalized. Eisenstein contends, for example, that we need to transform the liberal feminist conception of the right to privacy. A radicalized approach to privacy would, first, dismantle the interventionist machinery of the state where it pursues authoritarian moralistic and domestic security agendas. But it would also reverse the trend towards state privatization by expanding individual rights to include social rights and by reinvigorating the conception of public responsibility. Eisenstein rejects the shrinkage of the right to privacy to its current status as the right for wealthy women to obtain an abortion through privately insured or financed health care. A meaningful right to privacy would entail universal access to abortion, contraception and childbearing for all women, poor and wealthy alike. It would also embrace the rights of lesbians and gays to organize their personal lives according to their own values without interference or the discriminatory subsidization of heterosexuality on the part of the state. A genuine right to privacy would not just shelter the individual from state interference in the "private" sphere; it would also entail the right to live in conditions in which everyone has equal access to the basic resources necessary to make meaningful choices in that protected sphere (Eisenstein 1994: 174–5).

Laclau and Mouffe's original contribution to democratic theory – and the specificity of what they call "radical democratic pluralism" – consists in the way in which they combine two apparently contradictory goals together: unity and autonomy. The authors' fundamental concern is that the imposition of the wrong kinds of unity can limit the democratic potential of the social movements in question[15]. Laclau and Mouffe call for the kind of political strategy that can achieve unity and preserve autonomy at the same time – that is, a radical democratic pluralist hegemonic strategy. They argue that it is only by conceptualizing unity in terms of hegemonic articulation that the goal of unifying different movements becomes compatible with the goal of preserving their autonomy (Laclau and Mouffe 1985: 166–7, 178, 181–3, 191). I will discuss the concepts of articulation and hegemony with greater precision in the following chapters. At this point, however, the following outline of their argument can be offered.

Laclau and Mouffe want to promote the type of unification of democratic movements that would allow for effective solidarity without asking any individual movement to pay the price of tokenism, co-optation and assimilation. No single struggle should be allowed to impose its agenda over all of the others. While each struggle should learn from the others – it should share political values and tools, engage in collaborative strategies, and reform its identity as it takes on board the democratic demands of the other progressive struggles – it should also continue to develop its own distinctive worldview and pursue its own projects. A leading struggle may emerge; as we will see, Laclau and Mouffe call this the "nodal point" in the radical democratic "hegemonic bloc." Even where this occurs, however, the leading struggle will be so deeply affected by its negotiations with other progressive struggles that its philosophy, program and tactics – its very identity – would be reshaped in the process.

In this sense, each of the democratic struggles would constantly reconstruct their identities through a democratic process of mutual education with the others. This process could not, therefore, be characterized as the formation of a coalition between pre-constituted interest groups. It would take the form instead of continuous negotiations that give rise to new hybrid identities and temporary blocs. Insofar as these negotiations were successful, democratic values would take hold within movements, circulate among different movements and radiate out into new areas of the social. We would witness the further promotion of democracy within each of these struggles and within their corresponding communities, as democratic wisdom would be transmitted across multiple sites. The difficult lessons that are learned in the course of actual political struggles – such as the dangers of charismatic and vanguardist leaderships, the importance of ensuring equal representation to women in decision-making, the value of examining racial privilege and racial exclusion, the continuing relevance of class analysis, the discriminatory character of heterosexism, and so on – would be traded back and forth across heretofore uncrossable boundaries. It should also be noted that this "politicization of identities" presupposes a vibrant civil society that is relatively free from total regulation by the state. In a totalitarian context, democratic forces would have to "de-politicize" identities – in the sense of freeing them from the grip of state apparatuses – before this deeper politicization could take place (The Chicago Cultural Studies Group 1994).

The authors summarize their conception of radical democratic pluralism in the following terms:

> Pluralism is *radical* only to the extent that each term of this plurality finds within itself the principle of its own validity, without this having to be sought in a transcendent or underlying positive ground for the hierarchy of meaning of them all and the source and guarantee of their legitimacy. And this radical pluralism is *democratic* to the extent that the autoconstitutivity of each one of its terms is the result of displacements of the egalitarian imaginary.
>
> (Laclau and Mouffe 1985: 167)

For Laclau and Mouffe, the irreducibly plural character of the social must be preserved, even as democratic struggles combine to fight authoritarianism. Plurality and diversity are not problems to be overcome; the promotion of those differences that do not contradict liberty and equality is the very condition for the expansion of the democratic revolution (Laclau and Mouffe 1985: 166).

This argument could be extended further. The diversity among democratic differences must be affirmed as a good in itself; minority groups should never be asked to pay the price of cultural self-destruction through assimilation and disciplinary neutralization in exchange for inclusion, legitimacy and recognition. Genuine "tolerance" must mean that minority groups are granted access to the material resources that they need to preserve their rights and to promote their distinct democratic differences. Genuine "multiculturalism" must mean not only the addition of minority democratic values, but also the opening up of the values held by the majority to the minorities' democratic critique, and the construction of a new set of shared community values through negotiation. Immigration programs that rate the eligibility of an applicant on the basis of their conformity with white Western middle-class standards; military policies that promise lesbians and gays inclusion only insofar as we keep our sexual orientation a secret; university structures that add women's studies or black studies courses to the curriculum without addressing sexism and racism on campus; electoral reforms that extend suffrage to women and people of color while job segregation and "glass ceilings" ensure their over-representation among the unemployed, the poor and the homeless; health care "reforms" that ban abortion funding for women on welfare; elections in a Bosnia that remains "ethnically cleansed"[16] and elections in a

Russia that conducts brutal civil war against its own people, would all fail this basic democratic pluralism test.

Laclau and Mouffe do not, of course, endorse an unlimited promotion of autonomy. They insist that progressive struggles must be united to the extent that they reshape their identities with respect to the others' demands (Mouffe 1996b: 247). They also impose strict conditions on the value of difference for radical democracy. Difference should be celebrated as a positive good, but only insofar as difference does not promote domination and inequality (Mouffe 1992a: 13). This qualification has several implications. Every social movement will have many different political variants, for the political value of a movement is not naturally determined by its structural location, but by the way in which it combines different political values together (Laclau and Mouffe 1985: 168–9). Laclau and Mouffe would reject, for example, Gitlin's and Hobsbawm's argument that environmental politics are inherently "universalist" in contrast to the inherent "particularism" of race, gender and sexuality politics (Gitlin 1995: 101; Hobsbawm 1996: 45); ecological demands can be phrased in either reactionary or progressive terms. Protection for the environment can be defined, for example, in a racist manner. Some environmentalists have failed to respect the land claims of the aboriginal peoples, while others have embraced population control for the poor in developing countries[17] and immigration control in the developed world as policies necessary for the protection of the ecology from excessive pressure. Environmentalists can also define their struggle in an anti-capitalist manner, such that it primarily targets corporate profiteering. For radical democratic pluralism, only those fragments of the social movements that uphold democratic principles should be valued as progressive differences.

Furthermore, reactionary social elements commonly appropriate the discourse of civil rights movements in their demands for the protection of their "special ways of life." Again, respect for autonomy should be extended only to those groups and movements that value liberty and equality. Demands for multicultural programs that would preserve the cultural symbols of the pro-slavery American south, and demands for affirmative action for right-wing religious extremists, should be dismissed as fraudulent claims. For Laclau and Mouffe, the political meaning of environmentalism, civil rights and every other social struggle is open to contestation; the task for the Left is to engage in a political battle to bend their meaning in a radical democratic pluralist direction.

Radical democratic pluralism attacks all forms of domination and holds disciplinary normalization in suspicion; it takes aim at anti-democratic economic institutions, state apparatuses, social structures and cultural practices alike while it works with the democratic elements that are scattered throughout the social; it welcomes democratic forms of diversity, activism, innovation and dissent; and above all, it seeks to deepen and to broaden the advance of freedom and equality. The task for radical democratic pluralism is "to struggle against autocratic power in all its forms in order to infiltrate the various spaces still occupied by non-democratic centers of power" (Mouffe 1993b: 94). The fact that we are now at a great distance from genuine democracy is sobering but not devastating for radical democratic theory and practice. The achievement of close approximations to radical democratic pluralism is both feasible and desirable. Imperfect democracy should always be valued over an even more imperfect democracy, for the greater the degree of democracy, the greater the degree of freedom, and an increase in democracy always creates favorable conditions for greater democratization in the future (Cunningham 1987: 55, 60).

Radical democratic pluralist moments

Laclau and Mouffe acknowledge that much of their thinking about the value of autonomy is derived from Gramsci. Gramsci argued that because power had been dispersed across many different institutions and social sites in modern Western societies, counter-hegemonic forces should not concentrate their attack in a single front against a single seat of power, but should engage in a wide variety of struggles (Laclau and Mouffe 1985: 178). In this sense, the autonomy principle has a pragmatic aspect. A "top-down" leadership that imposes disciplinary normalization upon a variety of progressive struggles according to its own abstract program would not benefit from the contextually-specific wisdom that the locally-situated groups have developed. (I am using the concept of a "local struggle" here and elsewhere not to refer to geographic limitations of a given movement, but to emphasize its particular focus on a contextually-specific antagonism. A transnational women's organization for peace in Bosnia would be a "local struggle" in this sense.) Negotiation between the leaders and the led would ensure that this wisdom would be put to work. Further, the preservation of plurality and autonomy among the elements within the counter-hegemonic bloc would create the space for the sort of innovation in tactics and organizational structures – a kind of decentralization and "flexible specialization" – that every movement needs in order to respond effectively to the specificity of hybrid antagonisms.

Support for Laclau and Mouffe's position can also be found in classic liberal texts. Mill, for example, contends that democracy ought to preserve the space for individual liberty against the tyranny of the majority (Mill 1972: 68). Contemporary democratic socialist theorists, such as Cunningham, similarly insist that a truly democratic society would both foster communal forms of solidarity across differences and protect "the autonomy of people to pursue a variety of goals" (Cunningham 1987: 194).

Laclau and Mouffe's promotion of autonomy also brings to mind the radical critiques of assimilation and co-optation that can be found in the works of Fanon (1968, 1986), Baldwin (1985), Malcolm X (1965) and the later Martin Luther King, Jr (1968, 1991). These writers argue that when well-intentioned "liberal supporters" only offer their support for anti-colonial or anti-racist groups insofar as the latter conform to white Western values and traditional political standards, their actions can be just as reactionary as that of the colonial powers and the

35

segregationists. Laclau and Mouffe's autonomy argument is especially reminiscent of Baker's work with the Student Non-violent Coordinating Committee (SNCC). Under Baker's direction, SNCC developed a system of decentralized grass-roots empowerment rather than a charismatic leadership. Since the mid-1960s, SNCC's philosophy has been influential for many strands of the civil rights, student, feminist, environmentalist, lesbian and gay, anti-AIDS and anti-breast cancer movements, thereby circulating Baker's radical ideas to more and more activist communities (Payne 1989).

It should be noted, however, that Laclau and Mouffe intend their work to be read not only as a theoretical argument, but also as an accurate description and diagnosis of contemporary leftist politics. Many of their remarks about leftist political practice are highly critical, especially with respect to the autonomy principle. Referring to the new social movements, for example, they state that "The Left, of course, is ill prepared to take into account these struggles, which even today it tends to dismiss as 'liberal'" (1985: 164). They refer to the "traditional dogmatism" of the Left that has led to the dismissal of liberal democratic struggles as superstructural epiphenomena (1985: 174). They conclude that if the Left "wishes to succeed in founding a political practice fully located in the field of the democratic revolution and conscious of the depth and variety of hegemonic articulations which the present conjuncture requires," then it will have to undergo a radical transformation in its political imaginary, namely a complete shift away from foundationalist thought (1985: 177).

Although this description and diagnosis may be appropriate for the socialist thinkers whose work is examined in *Hegemony and Socialist Strategy*, some critics would disagree with their analysis of contemporary leftist activism in Britain. (I am focusing here on the British Left, for the latter was one of the most important political points of reference for Laclau and Mouffe during the early 1980s, when they were writing *Hegemony and Socialist Strategy*.) Segal, for example, cites the new political struggles of the 1970s as important departures from the closures that characterized the traditional Left. Further, she asserts that many of these movements nevertheless saw themselves as elements united in a broadly defined socialist struggle (Segal 1989; 1991).

The historical record of the contemporary British Left is ambiguous on these points. On the one hand, Segal's interpretation usefully directs our attention towards a whole range of significant leftist projects that flourished in the 1970s. This period saw the continuing activism of the peace movement, shop stewards and local union action committees, and black community groups, as well as the emergence of militant tenants' and squatters' groups; welfare rights groups; ecological struggles; mental patients' groups; feminist groups; gay liberationists; artists' projects; anti-apartheid and Third World solidarity groups; student activists and anti-racist/anti-fascist coalitions.[18] Leftist intellectuals also participated in the enormous expansion of progressive cultural projects involving theater productions, alternative newspapers, specialist journals and film and television productions (Barnett 1986).

Many of these projects formed alliances with the traditional Left – the trade union movement and the Labour Party – while developing a non-class-reductionist approach and maintaining their autonomy.[19] Some of these alliances between popular movements and the traditional Left became especially effective at the local government level and the Greater London Council in the 1980s, giving rise to municipal socialist experiments with innovative policies that often democratized social service delivery. Where these reforms were successful, municipal socialism earned a great deal of popular support. With its new principles for political action – recognition of autonomous groups, operation at multiple sites of oppression, and rejection of vanguardism – the independent Left did in fact make some progress towards the realization of radical democratic pluralist ideals (Massey *et al.* 1984; Segal 1991; Osborne 1991; Weir and Wilson 1984; Gilroy 1987).

The lively and often irreverent pages of the feminist magazine, *Red Rag* (1973), document the birth of a new wave of anti-reductionist socialist feminist thought and activism that took place during the 1970s. The journal's writers called for the expansion of feminist and socialist solidarity through strike support for women workers; the organization of women workers such as night cleaners and nursery school staff; collective bargaining tactics that aim to lift working women out of poverty and to establish maternity rights and affirmative action programs; and trade union support for childcare, abortion rights, and campaigns against domestic violence. These feminists certainly did not envision solidarity as the absorption of their struggle into the traditional Left. *Red Rag's* contributors preserved a critical distance as they took the traditional Left to task for its masculinism and anti-feminism. New advances in feminist theory were also made; Rowbotham's writing, for example, juxtaposed socialist and feminist values with a critique of economism, class reductionism, and vanguardism. Her work remains exemplary for its emphasis on historical specificity and the irreducibly multiple character of social forces (1981).

This same period saw the launch of *Gay Left: A Gay Socialist Journal.* The journal's gay male editorial collective aimed to advance the Marxist analysis of homosexual oppression and to promote an understanding in the gay male community of the links between sexual liberation and socialism. Where feminists were affirming that the "personal is political," radical lesbians and gay men were also embracing the slogan, "Out of the closets and into the streets." The *Gay Left* collective, however, believed that gay politics had to extend far beyond counter-cultural resistance and personal affirmation to address institutionalized forms of inequality. Unlike the feminists and gay women who participated in the sexual liberation movement, leftist gay men were directly confronted with the contradictions of the gay male subculture. In their more anarchistic moments, gay male sexual liberationists had "dropped out": that is, they had turned away from an engagement with mainstream institutions to found their own alternative communes and to experiment with non-monogamy, cross-dressing and soft drugs. Meanwhile, the expanding commercial gay male scene (pubs, bars, clubs, large discos, saunas and bath-houses) and the gay male popular press were creating a vital space for the consolidation of a vibrant and increasingly autonomous community, but those same enterprises largely preserved capitalist values and posed little challenge to sexism both inside and outside the community.

Following the lead of socialist theorists such as Engels and Kollantai, the earlier Gay Liberation Front (1970–73), and contemporary socialist feminists, the *Gay Left* collective emphasized a Marxist analysis of the patriarchal family's role in the economic and ideological reproduction of capitalist relations. Journal articles also constructed analogies between the treatment of gay, women and black workers. Strategically, the journal attacked the assimilationist politics of the Campaign for Homosexual Equality. It also criticized the labor movement for its anti-democratic tendencies, its reformist orientation and its failure to embrace women's and gay issues. Collective members called for the radicalization of gay politics and the formation of gay caucuses in trade unions and shopfloor movements. The journal documented the formation of lesbian and gay workers' groups among teachers, social workers, journalists, printworkers and others, and the participation of lesbians and gay men in strike pickets and anti-fascist rallies (*Gay Left* 1975–80; Weeks 1977: 185–237).

One of the more innovative leftist political projects that attempted to combine the goals of unity and autonomy was Big Flame, a revolutionary socialist party founded in the late 1970s. It aimed to work with existing progressive struggles and to create mass organizations among the working class without reproducing the dogmatism and authoritarianism of the sectarian Left. Big Flame specifically pledged to preserve the independence of its allies within the women's movement, black organizations, gay groups, youth groups, and the trade union rank and file, and to learn from their struggles. One of their pamphlets states, "Only the oppressed groups themselves can adequately analyze and understand their own oppression. For this reason, we accept both the organizational and the political autonomy of oppressed groups" (1981b). Its approach stood in sharp contrast to that of the sectarian Left, for the latter used every available opportunity to take over progressive groups and to redefine the groups' agendas according to their particular programs.

Big Flame developed a detailed critique of the co-optation of the trade union leadership and concrete proposals for trade union democratization. While other socialist organizations merely aimed to replace trade union leaders with their own leaders, Big Flame emphasized the importance of direct education and the empowerment of the rank and file membership. Because it recognized that racism and sexism could not be defeated solely through workplace-based struggles, Big Flame called for the creation of linkages between the trade union rank and file and progressive social struggles. Its attention to gender and race was so well sustained throughout its socialist analysis of Callaghan's and Thatcher's assault on the working class that its program integrated commentary on issues as diverse as childcare, domestic violence, maternity rights, race- and gender-based job segregation, immigration controls, fascism and homophobia into its positions on unemployment and de-industrialization (1981a; 1979).

Perhaps the difference between Segal and Laclau and Mouffe is one of emphasis. If we look at the remarkable achievements of these important political projects, they certainly do stand out as important experiments in radical democratic pluralist practice. On the other hand, however, the alliances between the grassroots independent Left and the traditional Left were never successfully transformed into articulations. Although significant democratizing gains were made at the local government level, in grassroots Labour Party activism, and in the structures of the progressive trade unions, the mainstream Labour Party kept its patriarchal, paternalistic, bureaucratic, monocultural and anti-grassroots tradition largely intact. Much of the traditional Left, in other words, never fully renegotiated its identity in the light of the independent Left's demands (Massey *et al.* 1984; Weir and Wilson 1984). Segal further notes that when orthodox Marxist members of the Communist Party and conservative members of the Labour Party did champion the movements of women and racial minorities during the later 1980s, they did so only to bolster their attack on their enemies within the labor movement and the militant Left (1989: 26–7).

Laclau and Mouffe are therefore at least partially correct in their assessment; the leftist leadership did ultimately remain stubbornly opposed to the new movements' innovative political approaches. Segal's critique nevertheless reminds us that the failure of the independent Left to transform socialist politics in Britain was due not only to the theoretical orientation of the traditional Left, but also to factors that lay beyond the control of both the emerging movements and the entrenched leftist leadership. Economic recession, combined with the Conservative government's abolition of the Greater London Council, its overall assault on local government autonomy, and its victories against organized labor also contributed to the decline of the independent leftist movements in the 1980s.

The question of supplementing Marxism

As we have seen, Marxist critics have rightly pointed out that the most progressive aspects of the liberal democratic tradition – such as the individual's right to self-development – are incompatible with the perpetuation of capitalist relations of exploitation. Some have even argued that socialism – as opposed to Stalinist forms of bureaucratic collectivism – necessarily entails democracy, and that democracy necessarily entails socialism. Radical democratic pluralists, however, have expressed concerns about socialist theory's inadequate attention to difference. Anti-racists, feminists and queer theorists have pointed out that Marxist class analysis fails to provide an adequate framework for understanding the structural relations of racism, sexism and homophobia. This does not mean, however, that we ought to develop isolated analyses of each of these different forms of oppression and then merely add them one by one to the analysis of class exploitation. A theoretical model that starts with abstractions – a set of socio-political relations artificially isolated and removed from a complex historical formation

39

– and then proceeds to "reconstruct" the social formation by adding several abstractions together, will always be inadequate. Each set of relations – class, race, gender and sexuality, and so on – is fundamentally shaped by its historically specific interactions with other sets of relations. We cannot assume that one set of relations, such as class relations, is necessarily more fundamental than all of the other structures. In capitalist formations, class will always be relevant, but the ways in which class actually interacts with race, gender and sexuality will be contextually specific.

Radical democratic pluralist theory must provide the tools that would allow democratic activists who are engaged in the struggles against capitalist exploitation, sexism, racism and homophobia to map out the context of those struggles, namely the given configurations of power relations. We should, however, acknowledge the fact that democratic activists are already engaged in this important work; radical democratic theory needs to learn from their activism and to keep pace with their valuable innovations. In any event, radical democratic pluralist theory cannot stop short with a model based on "scientific" abstractions, however elegant they may be. What is needed is a theory of social structures and identity formation that explores the complex ways in which the multiple forms of exploitation and oppression intersect, overlap, combine together, shape one another and contradict one another. Attention must be paid to both genealogical continuities and to historical specificities. Power relations are never totally dispersed; they are always concentrated in various institutional centers. At the same time, the irreducible differences between the various centers of power will always preserve some degree of tension between them such that no single system of power will emerge. Similarly, radical democratic pluralist theory cannot suggest that any one subject or struggle will be able to embrace the demands of virtually every democratic movement. There are, nevertheless, concrete possibilities for effective forms of democratic solidarities across enormous differences; indeed, the advance of radical democratic pluralism depends precisely on these articulations.

It is at this juncture that we can begin to grasp the role of anti-essentialist theory in the advance of radical democratic pluralism. As we saw above, some of Marx's sympathetic critics fault him for giving inadequate emphasis to individuality, pluralism and human rights in his vision of a democratic post-capitalist society. It is of course true that Marx intended only to provide a provisional outline of the transition to socialism. He held that his provisional outline could only be filled in as human knowledge developed further and that it was therefore impossible to predict exactly what a socialist order would look like (Wood 1981: 53–4).

It may be tempting to argue that radical democratic pluralist discourse should merely take Marx's historical materialist theory as its basic foundation and then add to that foundation a supplementary plan for the formal guarantee of human rights in a post-revolutionary society. Even with this approach, however, tensions would remain between the resulting theory and the task of moving towards a radical democratic pluralist society. The shortcomings of Marxist discourse are so fundamental to its central structure that they cannot be overcome through secondary additions. Marxist discourse privileges class as the primary form of social agency and capitalist exploitation as the primary form of domination. It is, in this sense, an essentialist discourse that cannot grasp the irreducible multiplicity of oppressive power relations; only an anti-essentialist discourse can perform this task. The radical democratization of contemporary societies depends upon the advance of struggles against both class exploitation and non-class-based oppressions as they are experienced today in their historically specific hybrid forms. Progress towards radical democratic pluralism would be halted in a social order that overcame capitalist exploitation but left structural oppressions such as racism, sexism and homophobia intact. Even more important, the intertwining of these forces is so extensive that the advance of the struggle against class exploitation often depends upon the advance of the democratic struggles that address non-class-based oppressions.

Anti-essentialist theory can help us to think through these hybridities and historical specificities, and it can also help theorists to catch up with the innovative political practices that democratic activists have already deployed. Anti-essentialism is not in itself a panacea against authoritarianism. Anti-essentialism is, on its own, politically indeterminate; the right has proven its ability to borrow anti-essentialist formulations to great effect.[20] A complete break with the essentialist moments of the socialist tradition is nevertheless crucial to the construction of radical democratic pluralist theory.

2

ESSENTIALISM, NON-ESSENTIALISM AND DEMOCRATIC LEADERSHIP

From Lenin to Gramsci

For Laclau and Mouffe, radical democratic pluralist theory must appropriate the most progressive moments of the socialist tradition while subverting its essentialist moments. The authors argue that nothing less than the "whole conception of socialism" is in crisis: "the ontological centrality of the working class," the very notion of "Revolution" as the "founding moment in the transition from one type of society to another," and the utopian dream of a post-revolutionary and post-political society in which a "perfectly unitary and homogeneous collective will" would prevail (Laclau and Mouffe 1985: 2). Because essentialist Marxism presupposes the existence of "universal" subjects and conceptualizes the social as a "rational, transparent order," it cannot adequately capture the complex negotiations of difference that are crucial to radical democratic pluralism (Laclau and Mouffe 1985: 2; Mouffe 1993b: 12).

The authors' critique should be read as a *post*-Marxist – rather than an *anti*-Marxist – strategy. As we saw in Chapter 1, they do recognize that progress towards genuine democratization requires, in part, the advance of the socialist struggle in some form. They nevertheless admit that their critique of essentialism amounts to a radical break with the Marxist tradition. Further, the authors would not accept the displacement of essentialist Marxism for another type of foundationalist discourse. Unlike the "post-Marxism" of MacKinnon, who substitutes gender reductionism for class reductionism and women's consciousness for proletarian consciousness (1989), Laclau and Mouffe's post-Marxism takes the form of an anti-foundationalist theory of politics.

Because Laclau and Mouffe's intervention in Marxist theory is shaped by their commitment to radical democratic pluralism, they do not take aim at essentialist class theory merely because foundationalist discourse has fallen out of fashion in contemporary intellectual circles. As we will see in Chapter 4, the authors reject many aspects of "postmodern" theory as well. Their concern is, rather, a practical one. Essentialist theory tends to construct a political horizon in which authoritarian practices are legitimated and radical democratic pluralist negotiations of difference are foreclosed. It is for this reason that the radical democratic pluralist project must be based on anti-foundationalist epistemological and ontological presuppositions. The authors' analysis of Leninist discourse brings the logic of this connection between essentialist logic and the potential for authoritarian practice to the fore (1985: 48–65). Gramsci's political theory, by contrast, is a valuable example of a socialist discourse that attempts to develop a more democratic conception of leadership precisely by moving away from essentialist closures. Leftist politics have obviously changed enormously since the days of Lenin and Gramsci. Their discourses nevertheless remain relevant today, for they can clarify our contemporary debates on political leadership, unity, autonomy and democracy.

The democratic potential in Lenin's theory of hegemony

In the development of his theory of hegemony, Lenin contends that in the extraordinary conditions of Tsarist Russia, liberal-democratic reforms – political campaigns that socialists had previously associated with the bourgeoisie – should be taken up by the revolutionary proletariat. To understand why Laclau and Mouffe find promise in this idea, we need to review some aspects of Marxist theory. According to a very basic reading of Marx's famous *Preface to a Contribution to the Critique of Political Economy*, society as a whole is supposed to progress from lower to higher stages. A new development in the productive forces – say, for example, the introduction of a new technology or production method – tends to come into conflict with the existing property relations. Marx believed, for example, that feudal relations became increasingly obsolete as industrialization progressed. This conflict blossoms into a full-scale social revolution in which a whole new set of property relations become predominant, and, as this occurs, a corresponding transformation in the superstructure – the state apparatus, socio-cultural life and the legitimating ideologies – also takes place (Marx 1969a: 503–4). We will return to this key text below and in Chapter 3. For my purposes here, it should be noted that within the terms of this historical model, liberal democratic reforms in the superstructural political sphere are supposed to be introduced once capitalism displaces feudalism and the bourgeoisie displaces the aristocracy.

It is assumed, then, that the working class emerges as the transition from feudalism to capitalism takes place, and that the revolutionary proletariat will operate on a political stage in which liberal democratic institutions are already fully established. Tsarist Russia, however, did not fit this model. Capitalist class relations had developed but elements of feudalism persisted as well, and the transition to a liberal democratic regime had not even begun. Plekhanov and Axelrod advanced the extraordinary argument in 1883–4 that because the Russian bourgeoisie was so weak, and the grip of the autocratic regime on the political terrain was so restrictive, the working class would have to join in the battle for liberal democratic reforms against the feudal Tsarist order (Anderson 1976–7: 15; de Giovanni 1979: 261). Lenin extended their argument further, calling for the proletariat not only to join in this battle, but to take the lead. Lenin, of course, retained Marx's critique of liberal democracy as a self-contradictory tradition. Although liberal democratic reforms were viewed by Lenin as a necessary condition for the socialist revolution, they would eventually be replaced by socialist institutions.

In the end, however, Lenin does not stray very far from traditional Marxism. Even as the workers' movement takes up the demands that are supposed to "belong" to the bourgeoisie, and even as it enters into alliances with other social forces such as the peasants or the anti-Tsarist democratic movements, the basic constitution of the working class is supposed to remain absolutely the same. Leninist theory suggests that class interests are constructed exclusively at the economic level. The workers are supposed to become a subject – the working class – purely through their positioning within the relations of production. They are supposed to become "the working class" through their common structural positions as the individuals who – because they do not own the means of production – are obliged to sell their labor power to the capitalists. All other facets of their identity – their nationality, ethnicity, race, gender and so on – are supposed to be secondary to their "authentic" subjectivity. Further, the ways in which they interpret their structural positions are supposed to follow directly from their structural positioning itself. Any degree of deviation in this correspondence between structural positioning and interpretation is wholly illegitimate and – to the extent that proper leadership is exercised – corrigible.

According to Lenin, then, classes are defined in terms of their pre-discursive objective interests. Their political relations with other subjects are supposed to be purely superficial; they are supposed to have no effect whatsoever on their constitution as a subject. A workers' organization, for example, might form coalitions with a peasant movement, or a peace movement, or an anti-censorship bloc of students and intellectuals, but it is supposed to retain the same fundamental identity throughout this entire process. Lenin depicts the political and the economic as separate spheres, with the economic as foundational and the political as the mere stage upon which the prefabricated interests of the classes are played out.

In other words, Lenin posits class as the "essence" of identity: class is the element that makes a subject what it truly is, the element that gives the subject its "authentic" interest. A person who is structurally positioned as a worker is supposed to have an "authentic" interest in the revolutionary overthrow of capitalism, while her bourgeois counterpart is supposed to have an "authentic" interest in the perpetuation of capitalist exploitation. From this perspective, subjects who may appear to be radically different – such as workers who differ in terms of race, nationality or gender – but who share the same class "core" by virtue of their common structural positions *vis-à-vis* property relations, ought to have their shared class interests as the principle of their being. Non-class elements are, in metaphysical terms, "accidents": they are supposed to remain strictly external to the formation of the subject's "authentic" interests.

Lenin's essentialist approach to class has its origins in Marx's own writings. In the *Communist Manifesto*, for example, Marx and Engels argue that capitalism would eventually lead to the polarization of the social into two great classes. Each class would become so homogeneous that age and gender differences between various members of the same class would become irrelevant (Marx and Engels 1969: 115). The experience of exploitation for the workers from different nation-states would become increasingly uniform; workers in different countries would gradually develop similar interests such that they could be united in a single global movement. The bifurcation of the social along class lines would be so far-reaching that even the worker's relationship with his or her sexual partner, children and family would become a specifically worker-identified relationship which would "no longer [have] anything in common with the bourgeois family-relations." The worker is ultimately supposed to reject any cross-class solidarities based on "law, morality, religion" for the latter are but "so many bourgeois preju-dices, behind which lurk in ambush just so many bourgeois interests" (Marx and Engels 1969: 118). Marx and Engels conclude that the workers have "nothing of their own to secure and to fortify; their mission is to destroy all previous securities for, and insurances of, individual property" (1969: 118).

Furthermore, Marxist theory privileges the revolutionary proletariat: the liber-ation of all of humanity from domination is supposed to be a necessary consequence of the proletariat's overthrowing of capitalism. The revolt of the workers neces-sarily entails the abolition of private property and the transition to the utopian society in which all power relations would be canceled out and overcome. Marx himself later questioned the polarization thesis, introduced a much more complex conception of subjectivity, and offered contradictory remarks on the relation between the economic and the political (Harrington 1993: 21). Some contempo-rary theorists such as Cohen (1978: 73) have nevertheless returned to Marx's essentialist formulations.

Laclau and Mouffe demonstrate that in certain moments, Lenin's text strains against its own essentialist limitations. Lenin departed from a narrow conception of the role of the Social Democratic Party to insist that the Party ought to work with the wide range of forces that stood opposed to the Tsarist regime. For Laclau and Mouffe, this moment of Lenin's theory of hegemony "entails a conception of politics which is *potentially* more democratic than anything found within the tradi-tion of the Second International" (Laclau and Mouffe 1985: 55).[1] Because of the peculiar historical circumstances in Russia, Lenin decided that the Party ought to fight religious persecution, to denounce the Tsarist regime's treatment of the students and intellectuals, and to support the peasants (Kolakowski 1978: 388).

Lenin's reassessment of socialist strategy begins with an analysis of the contin-gent historical conditions in Russia at the turn of the century (Lenin 1989). If it were developed fully (and here we depart from Lenin altogether), this pragmatic and contextually specific approach would become a political theory that would reject essentialist dogma and would grasp the complexity of power relations and the plurality of the social. Instead of imposing teleological or "stagist" theories of history, the historical specificities of a given formation would be recognized. The essentialist conception that the subject is fully constituted in the economic sphere and merely plays out a predestined role in the political sphere would be abandoned. While Marxist theory positions the working class as the sole agent of revolution, this new theory would recognize that "revolutionary legitimacy is no longer exclusively concentrated in the working class," such that the democratizing potential of other subjects would be recognized (Laclau and Mouffe 1985: 56). With the weakening of class essentialism, the ground would be prepared for a complex negotiation of differences – between theory and practice, between the leaders and the led, and between the different democratic struggles themselves.

In the terms introduced in Chapter 1, Lenin's conception of the type of unity between the different elements in the struggle against the Tsarist regime is closer to that of a coalition, rather than a hegemonic bloc. Again, the identities between the members of a coalition are not altered by their interactions with other coalition members; the renegotiation of their identities and interests does not take place. The transformative character of the linkages between the different elements in a hegemonic bloc is absolutely crucial to the advance of radical democratic pluralism, for it is only when these linkages work in this way that democratic forces can be circulated, extended and deepened. With reference to multiculturalism, for example, the issue is not simply the inclusion of minorities; it also entails the structure of their inclusion. Will the minority groups merely be added to the coalition, or will their inclusion entail a radical reconstruction of the majority identity? A thoroughly colonized fragment of a minority group can always be found that would create the appearance of diversity in the form of tokenistic inclusion. What is needed is the release, circulation and expansion of radical democratic pluralist forces, and that can only occur where unity does not mean that the least powerful members of a bloc will be subjected to assimilation, neutralization and dogmatic discipline.

Lenin's vanguard party theory

In these terms, Lenin took a very specific approach to coalition building, for he insisted that the Social Democratic Party ought to play a vanguard role in leading the anti-Tsarist struggle. The socialist theorists of the Second International were confronted with the fact that many workers acted in ways that contradicted their "authentic" interest in revolution. Following the lines of Marx's own elitism (Marx and Engels 1969: 120), Kautsky argued that the workers had to be brought to revolutionary consciousness by a force originating outside the class, namely a bourgeois intelligentsia that possessed a scientific grasp of history (Kolakowski 1978: 42–3, 53; Laclau and Mouffe 1985: 19–20). Lenin was even more pessimistic; he believed that the Western workers' revolutionary potential was becoming neutralized as they embraced trade unionist reformism within bourgeois institutions. He concluded that if the workers were left to themselves, they would not only fail to develop a socialist consciousness, they would naturally fall prey to bourgeois trade-unionist ideas and to anti-revolutionary leadership. For

Lenin, the overwhelming power of bourgeois ideology was such that there were only two choices: either the Party had to intervene by any means necessary to direct the workers towards proletarian consciousness, or the workers would be swept up by reactionary bourgeois ideology. Lenin decided that the Party had to bring the workers to their "authentic" consciousness, and that this required in turn an all-out war against what he called the bourgeois tendencies that threatened to divert the class from its true revolutionary calling (Lenin 1989: 97–8, 106–7, 108–9; Wright 1986: 105, 108; Kolakowski 1978: 386–7).

Lenin argued that the revolutionary Party therefore could not accept any direction whatsoever from its grassroots worker membership. The Party had to become a vanguard leadership that made political decisions based solely on objective knowledge and scientific theory. Intellectuals who "correctly" understood the Marxist laws of history were the true embodiment of proletarian consciousness, regardless of their own class position, for their scientific theory was the only legitimate guide for political decision-making (Kolakowski 1978: 391). Lenin optimistically predicted that the distinction between the Party intellectuals and the workers would eventually disappear, but only after the workers had in fact developed the revolutionary interests that the leadership had assigned to them in advance. The Party could always claim that it alone had access to the true interests of the workers, regardless of what the workers actually thought about the Party. Far from entering into a dialogue, the Party leadership was allowed to regard the workers as an "obstacle, an immature state to be overcome" (Kolakowski 1978: 391). Laclau and Mouffe conclude that the Leninist notion of a vanguardist leadership "postulates a clear separation within the masses between the leading sectors and those which are led" (1985: 55).

Leninist theory also rules out plural perspectives. Where other Russian socialists argued that without open debate, the socialist movement would become "ossified," Lenin insisted on the necessity of a single doctrine. Critics who questioned scientific Marxism and the inevitability of the socialist revolution were dismissed by Lenin as bourgeois thinkers (Lenin 1989: 75, 90). Lenin held that the development of multiple factions was "unhealthy, since in principle only one group could be in possession of the truth at a given time" (Kolakowski 1978: 392). Lenin launched a full-scale attack on "factionalism" in 1921, arguing that the Party could not afford to indulge in "the luxury of studying shades of opinion." He further declared, "We must make it quite clear that we cannot have arguments about deviation and that we must put a stop to that" (Kolakowski 1978: 514).

Lenin later reassessed his position on the trade union movement and admitted that it could play a valuable role in the revolutionary struggle. He nevertheless remained a harsh critic of trade union independence (Kolakowski 1978: 513). Only those political practices that were brought under the direction of the Party leadership could further the revolutionary cause. Indeed, the road to revolution – as interpreted by the Party – provides a moral compass for virtually every social practice: "everything which serves or injures the Party's aims is morally good or bad respectively, and nothing else is morally good or bad" (Kolakowski 1978:

516). Art, literature, law, political institutions, democratic values, religious ideas and philosophies were evaluated solely in terms of their relationship to the class struggle (Kolakowski 1978: 383).

The Party imposed itself, from above, as the true center for all forms of anti-Tsarist protest (Kolakowski 1978: 388). As the workers' movement constructed new alliances with emerging social forces, these alliances were seen as "necessary and yet transitory steps in pursuit of [the workers'] class objectives" (Laclau and Mouffe 1985: 56). Lenin strongly opposed Martov's proposal that the Party remain a loosely structured mass organization open to any individuals who "worked under the guidance and direction" of a Party organization (Kolakowski 1978: 393). For Lenin, the development of the Party as a loosely-knit ensemble of highly autonomous groups would be utterly counter-productive; the Party had to be built in a completely top-down manner. Dismissing Martov's model as "false 'democracy,'" Lenin insisted that the Party ought to establish strict membership rules and ought to maintain absolute control over all of its sub-organizations (Kolakowski 1978: 394).

There is some disagreement on the extent to which Leninism laid the foundation for Stalinist authoritarianism. Kolakowski claims that "there is absolutely nothing in the worst excesses of the worst years of Stalinism that cannot be justified on Leninist principles, if only it can be shown that Soviet power was increased thereby" (Kolakowski 1978: 516). Blackburn remarks that many militants were attracted to Lenin's cult of Party organization and discipline in the context of the Tsarist "incoherent autocracy." They judged the Bolsheviks' ruthless methods for seizing power against the background of brutal historical conditions, including the carnage of the First World War, the harsh conditions that the war created for the masses, and the urgent problems of massive famine, epidemics, civil war and foreign invasion (Blackburn 1991: 189–90). In any event, many of the first steps towards Stalinism – the fusion of the Party and state, the lawless suppression of pluralism in civil society, the ban on opposition within the Party, the manipulation of elections and usurpation of the Soviets, the deployment of militaristic strategies to safeguard the regime and the displacement of small-scale production by central management – all took place in the first few years of the revolution.

Blackburn insists that Lenin himself did grasp, perhaps even more than Marx, the complex character of politics and economics, and that he did argue in some specific moments that political organizing must be to some extent autonomous. Lenin allowed for a degree of self-determination for Finland and the Baltic states, while some aspects of worker self-management, the autonomy of educational institutions and a free press survived well into the mid-1920s. However, by the time that Lenin began to express explicit warnings about the excessive authority of the new Soviet bureaucracy, it was far too late (Blackburn 1991: 189–90, 195). Where Lenin demanded total loyalty on the part of the Party member, Stalin extended that principle to every citizen. Lenin's ideal of a disciplined Party became Stalin's ideal of a disciplined society, and suppression of dissent within

48

the Party was expanded into a full-scale campaign of terror against actual, potential and imagined seats of opposition throughout the Soviet Union (Blackburn 1991: 196).

The Communist regimes that were established under Stalinist rule differed in many respects, but they all shared two basic features: an economy dominated by state ownership and control, and a political system in which the Communist Party monopolized authority. Dissent was censored and those social forces that were not controlled by the state/Party were repressed. The regimes also promoted a sort of simulacra pluralism. A wide variety of institutions were established that appeared to address a wide range of socio-cultural concerns, including women's rights. These institutions did not, however, promote the formation of a vibrant civil society that nurtured oppositional discourse. The socio-cultural institutions actually reinforced the regime's totalitarian grip over the social at every turn, for they were fully integrated into the state-Party system (Miliband 1991: 7; Lefort 1986: 290–1).

The "scientific" approach to history and politics in the socialist tradition leads to disastrous results. To the extent that socialist activists believe that their Marxist principles constitute a science, they will ignore the importance of democratic dialogue with others. For scientific Marxists, the success of the "correct" political practice is guaranteed by "correct" theory, for theory is supposed to predict the future course of history (Wright 1986: 48). Either they will place a "quietist" trust in the necessity of historical forces to deliver "the people" automatically from false consciousness to their "authentic" interests, or they will embrace the "vanguardist" assumption that the deviation of the exploited from their "authentic" interests requires the disciplining intervention of a revolutionary leadership. Where scientific Marxism does recognize that the worker does not automatically possess a revolutionary consciousness, the worker is regarded as a revolutionary in embryonic form, and the Party is considered as the only agent that can properly bring that embryo to maturity (Kitching 1994: 7–8).

The "scientific" approach to activism – that of a theoretically enlightened elite bringing a deluded mass to its "authentic" consciousness in a top-down manner – can also be found in the feminist, anti-racist, lesbian and gay, and environmentalist traditions as well. The problem of vanguardism does not reside exclusively in the socialist tradition; it emerges in all types of political activism. If democratic activists consider their principles as a fallible and contextually-specific position that owes its coherence to a historical horizon, rather than the necessary corollary of an objective truth; and if they abandon foundationalist categories such as "authentic" identities and objective interests, then they will tend to value democratic dialogue, the exchange of activist wisdom between movements, and mutually constitutive negotiations between the leaders and the led. It should also be recognized that we can find many examples of vanguardist leadership on the right as well. Right-wing religious fundamentalist leaders in the United States, for example, do not hesitate to speak in the name of the true "moral interests" of the American people and to dismiss their democratic critics as the victims of a spiritual "false consciousness."

Gramsci versus Lenin: philosophy and common sense

Gramsci's response to the fragmentation of the working class and the rise of trade union reformism differed sharply from that of Lenin. Inspired by the example of the Turin workers' council movement of 1918–20, Gramsci favored the type of unification for working-class organizations that empowered the grassroots and preserved each group's specific character and autonomy (Wright 1986: 87). He argued that a counter-hegemonic leadership should be constructed out of "organic" popular traditions and value systems that are specific to a given historical formation, rather than imposed from above in the form of abstract scientific theory. The targets of counter-hegemonic struggle should include not only the state apparatus and the economic structures, but socio-cultural institutions as well, for cultural struggle is integral to socialism (Bobbio 1979: 39).

For Gramsci, democracy is not merely a mechanism, but a "force to be released" through the mobilization of "the people" (Wright 1986: 74). The task of organic socialist activism is to achieve this mobilization by harnessing the most promising fragments of popular traditions. Radical democratic hegemony aims to construct a new collective will that is capable of institutionalizing its alternative conception of the world in the form of new state apparatuses, economic relations, social structures and cultural practices (Bobbio 1979: 39, 40).

Gramsci argued that counter-hegemonic leadership should be democratic in both its aim and its actual practice. Kautsky accepted a "stagist" Marxism in which democratic demands were regarded as inherently bourgeois. For Mouffe, Gramsci's position is closer to that of the "young Marx" for whom democracy is a "terrain of permanent revolution begun by the bourgeoisie [and] concluded by the proletariat" (1979b: 174). Gramsci insisted on the "unfixed" political meaning of democratic demands: the socialist struggle had to take democratic demands back from the bourgeoisie, radicalize them, and fuse them into the socialist project.

In Laclau and Mouffe's post-structuralist terms, Gramsci treats each ideological element or political demand like a "floating signifier" (1985: 113). A demand for civil liberties, for example, does not have an intrinsic meaning outside of a concrete historical situation. It could be shaped in a pro-capitalist ("free speech for corporate lobbyists") or an anti-capitalist ("freedom of assembly for striking workers") manner; its actual value will depend on its precise definition in a specific historical context. Even where a given political demand has been so thoroughly claimed by one political group such that that group's definition of the demand appears to be the only possible definition, alternative definitions are always logically possible. If the hegemonic bloc has to some extent incorporated the democratic demands of popular sectors into its collective will, the counter-hegemonic intellectuals must enter into a direct ideological struggle to represent themselves as the only leaders that can respond to these demands (Mouffe 1979b: 197). Political struggle therefore entails not only the incorporation of a wide range of demands into a new historical bloc, but also the deployment of strategic attacks against the dominant bloc's discourse. The principle of unity that holds the dominant bloc together must be attacked, such that the defining grip of the dominant bloc over its constitutive elements – movements, campaigns, values and symbols – can be loosened. As these elements become more open to redefinition, they can be re-articulated with the counter-hegemonic struggle.

In a Gramscian sense, the actual probability of the successful institutionalization of an alternative definition depends on the configuration of power relations in a given historical context. The prevailing meaning of the demand for racial equality, for example, is not derived from anything intrinsic to the concept itself. It reflects, first, the contemporary balance of power between the political forces in question – such as the conservatives who strive to normalize an anti-affirmative action "equality of opportunity" definition versus the radicals who support a conception of substantial equality; second, the prevailing meanings of contiguous and analogous terms – gender equality, class equality, the equality of citizens, and so on; third, the trace-effects of meanings that have prevailed in the past; and, in some cases, the extent to which the term in question has been overtly or covertly articulated with popular demonizations. Clearly we are at a great distance from scientific Marxism, for whom the success of a strategy is supposed to depend on its correspondence with "correct" theory.

Gramsci rejects Lenin's conception of a distinction between "scientific" theory and the everyday discourse of workers at the grassroots level. For Gramsci, a historical formation has an overarching epistemological effect – like the horizon in phenomenology or Foucault's "episteme" (1970) – such that every discourse within that formation shares the same basic "conception of the world" (Mouffe 1979a: 8). An apparently abstract philosophy will have much in common with an everyday discourse if both are located within the same formation. Philosophy, then, should not be treated as an absolutely separate level of thought that obtains a superior rationality to that which is found in everyday discourse. Given his Hegelian influences, Gramsci insists that philosophical discourse cannot exist outside a historical context (Gramsci 1971: 326; Hegel 1957). "The philosophy of an historical epoch is, therefore, nothing other than the 'history' of that epoch itself" (Gramsci 1971: 345). Every world view is a "response to certain problems posed by reality, which are quite specific and 'original' in their immediate relevance" (1971: 324). Even when a philosophical discourse pretends to exist apart from history, it actually draws the set of problems that it addresses from its specific historical conditions.

Gramsci claimed that "all men are philosophers" (1971: 323) in the sense that everyone participates in the formation of a more or less coherent worldview that in turn shapes practical activity (1971: 344). Gramsci explicitly criticized, for example, Croce's argument that religious faith was appropriate for the masses since only an elite group of superior intellectuals could develop a truly rational conception of the world (1971: 132). Gramsci did admit that popular religious mobilizations tended to leave the masses immersed in a "primitive" form of common sense discourse. He envisioned, however, socialist mobilizations that would educate the masses and raise them to a "higher conception of life" (1971: 332–3).

The intellectuals should even strive to produce a new intellectual cadre by training individuals who were themselves part of the masses (1971: 340). This pedagogical relation, however, should flow in both directions, for the intellectuals must learn valuable lessons about the specificity of historical conditions from the masses' local traditions. If the intellectuals' philosophy can teach the masses to achieve a higher form of rationality in their worldview, the masses' everyday discourse can make the intellectuals' philosophy historically relevant (1971: 350, 352). Gramsci was able to insist on the reciprocal pedagogical exchange between the intellectuals and the masses precisely because he grasped the rational character of the masses' everyday discourse.

No individual participates in a common-sense discourse that is so narrowly solipsistic, particularistic and ahistorical that it cannot become the basis for dialogue across differences. Through the development of her worldview, every individual expresses her identity as a social being. "In acquiring one's conception of the world one always belongs to a particular grouping which is that of all the social elements which share the same mode of thinking and acting" (Gramsci 1971: 324). Although Gramsci is sharply critical of what he calls "irrational superstitions" and narrowly-defined "provincial" perspectives, he maintains that common-sense discourse has a "healthy nucleus" or "good sense" (1971: 328).

Gramsci's expansion of the concept of rationality laid the groundwork for a theory of political practice that is based on a fundamental respect for common-sense discourse. Intellectuals and activist leaders should look for the wisdom that has been accumulated through traditions of local resistance against domination in even the most eccentric everyday discourses. If a folklore tale, for example, is understandable for at least one other person in one other place and time in the sense that she knows "what to do with it" – if, for example, she knows how to read the tale's constellation of animals and spirits as an analogy for social structures and historical phenomena – then that tale is a coherent philosophical discourse. African-American resistance, for example, has often drawn on folklore tales as a political resource in this manner (Hurston 1978).

The recuperation of local wisdom for radical democratic pluralism is not, however, a straightforward operation. There is nothing inherently progressive in a popular tradition simply because it is popular; to paraphrase a famous marketing slogan, the fact that "billions have been served" is not in itself a sufficient political guarantee. Indeed, many popular traditions are profoundly anti-egalitarian and anti-democratic. One of the principles that radical democratic pluralism borrows from liberal democracy is the concept that democratic minorities must be protected against the tyranny of anti-democratic majorities. At the very least, however, a dialogical engagement with popular traditions will force an intellectual leadership to reassess its theoretical framework with respect to the specificity and hybridity of the structures of oppression and exploitation that prevail in a given historical formation.

Gramsci was not purely "spontaneist," for he did not accept the validity of the people's everyday discourse simply because it was popular. He held that the intellectuals had to subject the masses' common sense to a democratic and socialist critique, to bridge the particularities between disparate groups, and to raise the masses' worldview to a higher, more universal form of rationality (1971: 198–9). While the intellectuals test the discourse of the masses, the intellectuals are tested in turn by the masses and by the historical situation (1971: 346). The best theory is not just popular; it must resonate with the masses and provide them with compelling solutions to their everyday problems, but it must also move them to engage in democratic and socialist struggles (1971: 326, 341). The new worldview that the intellectuals construct through their negotiations with the masses acts as the ideological "cement" (1971: 328) that unifies the dispersed democratic fragments into a single collective will or historical bloc (Hall *et al.* 1977: 51).

Intellectuals should not see themselves as the privileged agent that discovers the truth outside popular struggles and then carries it to the people. They should instead see themselves as strategists who "organize consent" (1971: 125–35, 259) by raising to a more coherent level the fragments of good sense that are already implicit in local everyday discourse. Where theory does not fit the actual material conditions, it is theory that should give way: "it is not reality which should be expected to conform to the abstract schema" (1971: 200). In a particularly suggestive metaphor, Gramsci states that the intellectuals' relation to the masses is analogous to the "whalebone in the corset" (1971: 340). Here the masses are compared to passionate feminine bodily excess, the surplus voluptuous flesh that fills out the potential of otherwise abstract forms, but ultimately needs the addition of a cyborg apparatus – the Party – to achieve a practical shape. It is true that Gramsci often positions the "masses" as an unruly otherness that is so dependent upon the intellectual elite for discipline and rational thought that if it were left to its own devices, it would remain trapped in spontaneist, "primitive," fragmentary and above all particularist discourse (1971: 152–3, 155, 328). When measured against Leninism, Gramsci's respect for the historical rationality of common-sense discourse nevertheless comes to the fore. I will return to the problem of Gramsci's residual elitism and to the theme of universalism and particularism in the Conclusion.

The constitution of the subject through ideological struggle

Gramsci's displacement of Lenin's scientific rationality with his conception of historical specificity allows his theory to attend to many political dimensions that have been neglected in Marxist theory. He firmly rejected the reductionist conception that the superstructural sphere – the sphere of social relations, cultural practices, state structures, ideologies and so on – was thoroughly determined by the economic base. Kautsky, by contrast, viewed political relations and ideological discourses as "epiphenomena," or mere reflections of the underlying economic structure (Mouffe 1979b: 174). With his rejection of Kautsky's epiphenomenalism, Gramsci concluded that we cannot dogmatically determine the meaning of democratic struggles with reference to their relations to the class struggle. The workers' movement should instead enter into ideological struggle to redefine the democratic movements and to win them over to its side (Mouffe 1979a: 17). Gramsci did maintain that ultimately the political terrain would take the form of two great historical blocs standing in opposition to one another, and that these two blocs would be defined in terms of their class-based leadership, namely the leadership of the proletariat and the bourgeoisie. He nevertheless regarded the two blocs as complex unities or collective wills; he even saw class struggle itself as "complex relations of forces" (Mouffe 1979b: 180). Above all, Gramsci maintained that the socialist struggle would not succeed in its counter-hegemonic strategy merely by relying on the dictates of scientific theory. It would have to engage in the complex game of redefining democratic struggles and the most promising popular elements, and then integrating them into a hegemonic socialist bloc.

Gramsci's strategic approach remains relevant today. Radical democratic activists in the United States, for example, are constantly attempting to counteract the right's appropriation of the American democratic tradition with alternative constructions. When the neo-conservatives suggest that affirmative action contradicts the Fourteenth Amendment, or the religious right invokes the myth-ical constitutional right of American employers to discriminate against lesbian and gay workers, democratic activists do not remain silent; they enter the fray and offer oppositional constructions of these American political values. When the anti-immigrant forces depict America as a white-English-only space, radical activists respond with a vision of a multicultural and hybrid America. This is not to endorse a full-scale "alternative patriotism"; the historical sedimentations of American nationalism are such that a radical democratic pluralist American patriotism has become almost an oxymoron. This is only to note that wherever authoritarianism advances its agenda by appropriating traditions and symbols, radical democratic activists respond by attempting to rescue the progressive elements that can be found in those institutions and to transform that potential into concrete political tools.

In the development of his theory of hegemony, Gramsci drew inspiration from the same text that reductionist Marxists cite in defense of their epiphenome-nalism, namely Marx's *Preface to a Contribution to the Critique of Political Economy* (Gramsci 1971: 365; Texier 1979: 56–7). Marx argues that the economic struc-ture of society constitutes the "real foundation on which rises a legal and political superstructure and to which correspond definite forms of social consciousness," and that "it is not the consciousness of men that determines their being, but, on the contrary, their social being that determines their consciousness" (Marx 1969a: 503). This passage has, with some justification, been widely interpreted as an endorsement of the view that the political is merely a reflection of the economic base.

In a later passage, however, Marx offers an epistemological comment.

A distinction should be made between the material transformation of

the natural economic conditions of production, which can be determined with the precision of natural science, and the legal, political,
religious, aesthetic or philosophic – in short, ideological forms in which
men become conscious of this conflict and fight it out.

(Marx 1969a: 504)

The "conflict" to which Marx refers is the contradiction between the forces of
production and the relations of production, the contradiction that in this text
operates as the "motor of history" (Marx 1969a: 504). The text is profoundly
ambiguous. It could be read as an affirmation of the negative meaning of
"ideology" as that which is not scientific and as that which conceals social contradictions. Further, the passage could be made compatible with the argument that
although some philosophical, legal and political discourses are ideological insofar
as they are opposed to science, not all of these discourses are necessarily ideological. Finally, it is asserted here that individuals become conscious of the "conflict"
through the work of "ideological forms"; it is not stated that only ideological
forms can play this role. It remains possible, then, that non-ideological discourses
could also contribute to this process (Larrain 1981: 9–10).

Marx's main argument, namely that ideology should be understood negatively
as that which is unscientific and conceals social contradictions, is therefore barely
interrupted by this methodological aside. In any event, this fragment inspired
Gramsci as he asserted that humans can only have a mediated relation to the
movement of great historical forces. Although Gramsci had to reconstruct Marx's
text by memory during his imprisonment, he seized on this passage and concluded
that "'man acquires consciousness of social relations in the field of ideology'"
(Gramsci 1971: 138; Texier 1979: 57). For Gramsci, then, "ideology" is not a
simple tactical tool that can be used by the bourgeoisie to delude the workers.
"Ideology" plays a constitutive and epistemological role: it is through ideological
struggle that the terms that define the political terrain are constructed (Gramsci
1971: 365). "Ideology" also has ontological effects, for where an ideology
resonates with the masses, it takes on a "psychological" validity: it organizes
humans into groups, constructs group members' concrete sense of shared interests, and stages the groups' struggles (Gramsci 1971: 377). "Ideology" not only
provides the mediating element through which basic conflicts are grasped; it also
sets up the defining framework for political battles (Przeworski 1985: 69).
Although Laclau and Mouffe abandon the concept of "ideology" because of its
residual connections to the reductionist base/superstructure model (Laclau
1990a: 89–92), they nevertheless appropriate Gramsci's argument about the positive role of ideology in their constructivist conception of identity formation.

Structural positions, subject positions, identity and antagonism

From Laclau and Mouffe's perspective, a fully constructivist theory of identity formation must go much further than those Marxist theories that merely recognize that political discourse can affect the formation of interests or that it can play a secondary role in the reproduction of social structures. For the authors, discourse is prior to identity formation in the sense that identity is wholly constructed through discourse. Their embrace of constructivist theory has been widely criticized. Hall argues, for example, that his position differs from that of Laclau and Mouffe insofar as he does not believe that "just anything can be articulated with anything else." He asserts that every discourse has specific " 'conditions of existence' which, although they cannot fix or guarantee particular outcomes, set limits or constraints on the process of articulation itself." Hall insists that although historical formations are contingent, they can be "deeply resistant to change" (Hall 1988a: 10).

Laclau and Mouffe would, however, agree that in the context of a particularly entrenched hegemonic project, the possibilities for subversive interventions and re-articulations in a given social formation would in fact be limited. They do not hold that politics has become a game in which everything is equally possible and every position has equal value. They speak extensively about the ways in which political strategies must always be deployed in specific contexts and recognize that relations of domination may prevail in those contexts (Laclau and Mouffe 1985: 149–94). Laclau also situates his more recent arguments about subjectivity within broader considerations about the processes of sedimentation, normalization and institutionalization (Laclau 1990a). By way of a response to Hall's criticisms, and in the interest of clarifying Laclau and Mouffe's theory, a distinction that is already implicit in their work will be brought to the fore, namely the distinction between structural positions and subject positions.

Like all radical theories, radical democratic pluralist theory rejects the neo-conservative assumption that individuals freely choose their identity and freely utilize socio-economic networks and institutions to shape their material conditions according to their preferences. In the case of class, for example, radical democratic pluralist theory recognizes that in capitalist formations, those individuals who do not own the means of production must become workers; they must sell their labor according to conditions that are not of their choosing in order to survive. We could say, then, that an individual is structurally positioned within hierarchical social, cultural, political and economic systems by forces and institutions that are prior to her will.[2] Further, these structural positions shape the individual's life chances, for they situate her within the relatively stable networks of power relations that shape the distribution of material resources. The masses of the poor and the homeless in the United States are not impoverished because of their low motivation, faulty self-esteem or inferior intelligence; their condition should be explained instead in terms of historical patterns of exploitation and oppression. The same holds true with respect to race and sex. In a racist and sexist society, no one chooses to be positioned as white, black, Latino/a, Asian, mixed race, male, female and so on; one finds oneself "always already" positioned by forces and institutions within a discursive field that is never wholly of our choosing. (I will critique the biological determinist conception of race and sex in Chapter 5.)

Following Gramsci, we could argue further that no one experiences her structural positions within the social in a direct and unmediated way. It is only through political discourses that we experience the ways in which we are positioned within social structures. In the metaphorical terms provided by psychoanalysis, we could say that discourse provides the imaginary framework through which we interpret the symbolic order into which we are thrown (Bellamy 1993: 28). This process is contingent: there is no guarantee that one specific discourse will defeat all its rivals and become a predominant interpretative framework. The struggles between discourses to become predominant interpretative frameworks do tend to reflect the configuration of power relations in a given historical moment, but they are so complex that we cannot predict their exact outcomes. Some discourses may, given the strategic terrain, be more likely to become compelling frameworks, but none of them – not even the ones that seem to "reflect" predominant social structures – are utterly guaranteed to succeed. In any event, no individual can choose to stand outside the totality of interpretative frameworks; our fundamental dependence upon the interpretative function of discourse is written into our very human condition.

Laclau argues, for example, that an individual's class structural position becomes coherent for her through some specific and compelling political discourse (Laclau 1990a: 9, 16). We could imagine the way that this might work for different workers on the same assembly line in an American factory. One worker might be influenced by neo-conservatism. She might believe that her position as a worker results from the fact that she made a greater effort in life than her neighbors on welfare. She might think that the corporate executives and the corporate shareholders owe their positions to luck, hard work, corruption, nepotism or maybe a combination of these and other factors. The second worker might be influenced by right-wing religious fundamentalism. She might claim that her neighbors on welfare are living lives of sinful sloth and sexual immorality, and that her own industriousness is a reflection of her Christian way of life. She might even believe that the executives' and shareholders' relatively better fortune is in part the result of God's will. The third worker might be influenced by leftist leaders and the progressive wing of her trade union. She might believe that her position as a propertyless worker results from systematic exploitation, that she has in this sense much in common with her neighbor on welfare, and that the executives and shareholders won their positions thanks to the better opportunities that were systematically provided for them from birth onwards in a basically inegalitarian social order.

These imaginary examples are already too abstract, for the interpretative frameworks described here do not have racial, gender, national and other elements blended fully into them whereas actual interpretative frameworks are always irreducibly multiple, complex and even contradictory. Political subjects may think one thing, state another, and act in yet another manner altogether.

Perhaps their basic principles are reinterpreted in unpredictable ways whenever they are applied in specific circumstances; or perhaps their conscious affiliations are haunted by unconscious fixations and aversions. With these reservations in mind, we can nevertheless assert that an individual's sense of her structural positions – the way that she lives in her structural positions and responds to them – is shaped not by the mere fact of the structural positions themselves, but by the subject positions through which she lives her structural positions.[3] Furthermore, the meaning of each subject position is constituted with respect to its differential relations with the entire system of subject positions. I will return to the relational character of subject position formation below and in Chapter 3.

This argument sets Laclau and Mouffe's constructivism entirely apart from essentialist identity theory. An essentialist approach ignores the constitutive role of mediating political discourse, and assigns to the individual an "authentic" interest that is supposed to flow directly from her structural position. Hence propertyless workers are supposed to have an "authentic" interest in the socialist struggle to overthrow capitalism, just as women in sexist societies are supposed to have an "authentic" interest in the feminist struggle, and so on. Where individuals do not actually act in accordance with their putative "authentic" interest – where workers vote for conservatives, women reject feminism, racial minorities oppose affirmative action, and so on – the essentialist diagnosis is that they are caught in the grips of false consciousness and require firm leadership to guide them towards their "authentic" interests.

The essentialist approach does not pay sufficient attention to the specificity of these individuals' interpretative frameworks. There may be some very good reasons why a woman finds a particular anti-feminist interpretation more compelling than a feminist one in a given moment, and these reasons should be taken into account during the reconstruction of a more effective feminism. Laclau and Mouffe do not pursue the question of identity formation with the aim of piercing ideological distortions to arrive at the authentic subject. False consciousness theory assumes that we can stand in an objective position outside political discourse in order to establish the distinction between objective interests and ideological illusion. For Laclau, not only is it impossible for us to occupy such a position, this promise is itself an ideological illusion (1996i).

Laclau and Mouffe define "subject positions" as "points of antagonism" and "forms of struggle" (1985: 11). We will see in Chapter 3 that each subject position is constituted through its differential relations with other subject positions, in the form of equivalential and antagonistic relations at a given moment in time, and in the form of the "iterated" traces of genealogical precedents. At this point, however, we need to explore what a subject position does. Adding another element to Laclau and Mouffe's theory, we could say that a "subject position" is like an "identity" in the following sense. A "subject position" refers to the ensemble of beliefs through which an individual interprets and responds to her structural positions within a social formation. In this sense, an individual only becomes a social agent insofar as she lives her structural positions through an ensemble of subject positions that makes sense to at least one other person in one other time and place.[4]

The relationship between subject positions and structural positions is often quite complex. Consider, for example, a white heterosexual bourgeois woman, living in a social formation characterized by highly stabilized structural hierarchies and yet a relative openness with respect to the availability of different interpretative frameworks. Her racialized, gendered, sexual and class structural positions are in this case largely determined by the social formations into which she is "thrown," and it is largely her structural positions, rather than her free will, that shape her life chances. At the same time, her subject positions, the ways in which she lives her structural positions, will tend to be somewhat more vulnerable to political intervention and even the accidents of personal circumstance. That same individual could live her structural positions through subject positions such as liberal anti-racist Catholicism; socialist environmentalism or neo-conservative anti-feminism. In a social formation with stabilized structural hierarchies and a relatively closed set of normalized interpretative frameworks, however, a singular and rigidly defined set of subject positions will tend to operate as the only coherent interpretative frameworks through which structural positions are lived. This is often the case, for example, in religious fundamentalist communities or in strong nationalist movements.

Strictly speaking, we cannot speak of a "false" subject position in the same way that some Marxists refer to "false" consciousness. Laclau asserts, for example, that workers take on radicalized identities solely because of the intervening effects of political discourses that come from outside the relations of production as such (Laclau 1990a: 9, 16). Their identities do not emerge as a direct result of what I am calling their structural positions. We can refer to our working definitions of political values and suggest that in a given set of circumstances some subject positions will tend to have more democratic effects than others; radical democratic pluralist activists make these sorts of practical assessments all the time. The identity of the leftist worker in our imaginary factory, for example, expresses principles that are clearly quite close to radical democratic pluralism, while the principles expressed in the identities of the neo-conservative and the religious fundamentalist clearly oppose this project.

The term "class" becomes problematic wherever it is used indiscriminately to refer to both of these facets of subjectivity, structural positions and subject positions. One is more or less assigned a class structural position within stable capitalist structures; as we saw in Chapter 1, there is very little class mobility in capitalist societies. All of our three workers – the neo-conservative, the religious fundamentalist and the leftist trade union supporter – are being exploited through their wage labor contracts, and, because their life chances are profoundly shaped by their working-class structural position, it is very unlikely that they will ever escape this condition. But we must recall that when we group individuals together by virtue of their shared structural position alone, we are actually referring to theoretical categories, and not to actual social agents who perform concrete social practices. In Marxist theory, for example, we use economic categories to depict the capitalist relations of production – the bourgeoisie/proletariat relation – and actual social actors only appear in this model insofar as they are the "bearers" (*Träger*) of this structure (Laclau 1977: 163; 1990: 9). Commenting on Althusser's conception of interpellation, and using the term "ideology" where he would later substitute "political discourse," Laclau states,

> *Individuals*, who are simple bearers of structures, are transformed by ideology into *subjects*, that is to say, that they live the relation with their real conditions of existence as if they themselves were the *autonomous principle* of determination of that relation.
>
> (1977: 100)

In the abstract Marxist model, we reduce the members of a workers' movement, in all their historical specificity and contradictory desires, to nothing but a group that sells its labor power to capitalists. Some degree of abstract theoretical reduction is of course necessary; it is only through some type of conceptualization that we can describe, for our practical purposes, the ways in which different individuals are affected by the systematic and hierarchical distribution of life chances. The pragmatic and anti-positivistic aspects of theory should be underlined at this juncture. Theoretical models never correspond perfectly to the concrete world; there will always be some element of materiality that exceeds our theoretical grasp, for the real ultimately cannot be reduced to the concept (Laclau and Mouffe 1990: 107–9). Against positivist social scientists, Laclau and Mouffe would therefore argue that the search for falsifiable claims about social structures is futile.

This does not mean that all theoretical formulations are therefore utterly useless. Wittgenstein says, for example, that a sign-post may be read different ways, or that we may have different ideas about what being "on time" means, but that these imperfect forms of communication may nevertheless work well enough in most circumstances, in the sense that they usually fulfill their specific purposes. The inevitable absence of exactitude in a concept does mean that it is "unusable" (1958: 39–42). As Quine insists, vague terms sometimes rescue communication from failure (1960: 127). The question for theory, then, is not whether it perfectly corresponds to the real, for the real cannot be reduced to the concept. We should consider instead whether or not our necessarily imperfect theoretical concepts work well enough for our particular practical purposes. As for a definition of our practical purposes, we can turn to Marx's famous declaration, "The philosophers have only *interpreted* the world, in various ways; the point, however, is to *change* it" (1969b: 15). From this perspective, then, we can say that one theory such as radical democratic pluralism offers a better description than another – say neo-conservatism – on the grounds that it tends to be more useful in describing and inciting concrete struggles towards progressive social change. For all their inevitable failure to reduce the real to concepts, our theoretical arguments can sometimes serve our pragmatic purposes well enough in specific circumstances.

We might also note in passing that this approach sets Laclau and Mouffe apart from critical theory as well. For the authors, we can only evaluate a particular social and political theory with reference to a political horizon. With this perspectival approach, Laclau and Mouffe reject the immanence principle in critical theory, namely the claim that we must be able to find an element of critique within social reality itself (Honneth 1994: 256). The authors also distance themselves from the scientific Marxist argument that theory ought to be unified with practice in the sense that theory should allow us to grasp the objective truth about the world that is unfolding before us. Insofar as Marx believed that he had captured the logic of history, he depicted the commitment to the socialist struggle as an objectively necessary position (Aronson 1995: 42, 44). For radical democratic pluralist theory, we inhabit a world in which contingency always threatens to interrupt even the most institutionalized social order. Every time that we attempt to apprehend the logic of social structures, there will always be some irreducible remainder that exceeds our grasp. This implies that the commitments that are possible for us can only be moral and normative, rather than objectively necessary; we can no longer comfort ourselves with illusions about the objective necessity of any political position.

It should nevertheless be emphasized that the claim that we interpret power relations discursively does not contradict in any way other claims regarding the material effects of power relations, namely that the humans who are caught up in what we call exploitative and oppressive relations actually do experience pain and suffering. The point is altogether a different one, namely that our attempts to grasp those experiences through theoretical concepts will always be more or less inadequate, and that we can only assess our theories on the basis of pragmatic tests – the tests of their practical effects *vis-à-vis* the incitement of subversive resistance. I will return to the theme of the discursive constitution of the social in Chapter 3 in the context of my discussion of Saussurean linguistics.

In concrete historical settings, actual subjects get caught up in solidarities that never neatly correspond to theoretical categories. They come together through their practices and build up some sort of collective social agent – such as a social movement – that is meaningful to them only insofar as they share a common subject position or identity, that is, a common interpretation of their structural positionings. It is their identity – and never their common structural positions alone – that operates as the principle of their political solidarity.

This implies, for example, that we cannot assume solely on the basis of empirical data about income levels, wealth and job classifications that class is a meaningful axis of identification. We have to look instead for the ways in which individuals respond in a concrete way to class-oriented discourses that conceptually organize their experience (Scott 1988: 56–7). Workers' movements do not, therefore, merely describe an existing state of affairs.[5] Nor do workers' movements merely appeal to a fully formed, albeit dormant, subject. Like all movements, workers' movements are performative: they have to bring the resisting subject into being. Movements may work with fragments and traces of previous solidarities, but they never simply deliver into existence an embryonic subject that matures according to its own unfolding logic. Social movements' political discourses are constitutive rather than epiphenomenal. Social movements offer critical frameworks that allow the exploited to interpret their experience, and thereby provide them with "forms of social consciousness based on common terms of identification and . . . the means for collective action" (Scott 1988: 94). To the extent that their incitements to identification are successful, exploited individuals collectively take up the "anti-exploitation/anti-capitalist" subject position.

Given the fact that every iteration introduces deviation, there will always be variations in the identities that the workers' movement incites. Every social movement's discourse is overdetermined; the discourse of every specific workers' movement is a "mélange of interpretations and programs" that is tactically built up in a contextually-specific manner (Scott 1988: 61). In this sense, every workers' movement will always incite hybrid worker identifications that are articulated in complex ways with other identifications. In some cases, a worker identity might be constructed in terms of the citizen/foreigner difference, while, in other cases, symbols such as "family values," "technology," or the "environment" might play a crucial role.

The idea that class structural positioning does not immediately give rise to a class-defined subject position is of course highly problematic for traditional Marxists. In the *Communist Manifesto*, for example, Marx and Engels contend that capitalist society will inevitably polarize into "two great hostile camps," the bourgeoisie and the proletariat. They further argued that these two great classes, by virtue of their different relation to the means of production, will ultimately pursue the interests that are proper to each of them as a class and thus will engage in a total class war. Rephrased in the terms introduced here, Marx and Engels' argument is that there is no difference between structural positions and subject positions, and that it is the economic structural position that determines the being of every social agent. In one of his richest texts, *The Eighteenth Brumaire*, Marx still constructs the French peasants as an embryonic class that would progress towards maturity as soon as the proper material conditions emerged (1978: 608).

And yet, even in the *Manifesto*, we can detect the presence of a supplementary element that is introduced into the account of the revolutionary proletariat's maturation, namely the intellectuals' intervention. While material conditions, such as the massive concentration of workers in huge factories, their de-skilling and their pauperization, create favorable conditions for the emergence of a revolutionary proletariat, the Communist Party's leadership is necessary in the last instance. It is the Communists, as opposed to other workers' leaders, who are capable of formulating the most advanced expressions of the interests of the workers' movement as a whole (Marx and Engels 1969: 120). Paradoxically enough, the Communists include among their number certain "bourgeois ideologists." The latter is a "small section of the ruling class [that] cuts itself adrift [from the bourgeoisie] and joins the revolutionary class." No mere opportunists, these particular "bourgeois ideologists" "have raised themselves to the level of comprehending theoretically the historical movement as a whole" (1969: 117). With these remarks, Marx and Engels note an extraordinary exception to their principle of objective class interests; some of the "ideologists" of the Communist movement will come from the bourgeoisie. Against his own highly deterministic schema, then, Marx recognizes that the development of the proletariat's identity as a revolutionary class always requires some type of political intervention. Commenting on *The Eighteenth Brumaire*, Balibar concludes, "the revolutionary polarization does not *directly* develop from the existence of classes, but rather from a more complex process (Althusser would call it overdetermined) whose raw material is composed of mass movements, practices and ideologies" (1994: 144). We could argue, in this respect, that Laclau has not rejected Marx's discourse altogether, but has freed the supplementary logic that was already at work in Marx's own texts – namely the constitutive role of political intervention – from the essentialism that prevails therein.

Subject positions, "habitus," antagonism and practice

If the process of identification with a subject position tends to orient the social agent in question by providing an interpretative framework, we should note that this framework never takes the form of rules that command total obedience. We can only state that subject positions tend to incite certain practices. Creative reinterpretations of the subject position's interpretative horizon within specific contexts, rather than perfectly predictable conformity, are the norm. Borrowing freely from Bourdieu, we could say that relatively stable and enduring forms of identification with a subject position construct an orientation towards practice that is not unlike a "habitus." Bourdieu defines "habitus" as a durable disposition towards a set of goals; the "habitus" tends to incite regularized practices, but without ever producing perfect obedience to rules. Further, the social agent who is caught up in this process of identification with a specific subject position may or may not be conscious of that process, and may or may not develop a fully conscious grasp of the goals that correspond to that subject position (Bourdieu 1977: 72).

Unlike Bourdieu's "habitus," subject positions may or may not be durable; their relative fixity depends upon the contingencies of political struggle. It should also be noted that where Bourdieu's conception of the relation between the "habitus" and the social structure is defined in deterministic terms, such that the possibility of subversive iteration is foreclosed, his theory becomes problematic (Jenkins 1992: 79–82; Butler 1997a: 134–63). My position is closer in this respect to that of Fish. In his commentary on the parol evidence rule, Fish contends that although every institution fails to constitute a closed totality governed by an absolutely functionalist logic,[6] it can nevertheless exercise a significant structuring effect on the social. Although the rule that extrinsic evidence may not be introduced to contradict the explicit terms of a legally binding contract is not actually upheld in practice, it nevertheless works in concert with a whole set of background moral

assumptions and thereby sets the rhetorical agenda for acceptable legal argumentation (Fish 1994: 151–6). In a Wittgensteinian sense, then, rules are always
imperfect, but they often work "well enough" for our pragmatic purposes. The question then becomes who gets to decide what passes the "well enough" test, and the
answer ultimately shifts our attention towards hegemonic power relations.

The analogy between a subject position and a "habitus" is, however, suggestive
in many other respects. Like a subject position, a "habitus" does not fully determine practices, for it merely disposes the subject to perform certain acts. The
subject's actual performance of those acts will be influenced by the structural
limits of the social field in question (Jenkins 1992: 78). Instead of considering
identification with a subject position as a process that guarantees a perfectly
predictable conformity, then, we should think in terms of its incitement of what
Bourdieu calls "regulated improvisations" (Bourdieu 1977: 8, 11, 15, 21). And,
against rational choice theory, we should recall that the social agent's negotiation
between her orientation towards practice and the structural limits that she faces is
never a fully conscious process. Not only does she necessarily have an incomplete
awareness of the way in which she has become caught up in an array of subject
positions, her identifications are both driven and interrupted by the unconscious
in unpredictable ways.

This distinction between structural positions and subject positions is important for it is social agents with a common identity – and not merely individuals
who share common structural positions – who engage in political action. Think of
white women and women of color working together; cross-class unities within
communities of color; or transnational solidarities between the North and South.
These solidarities become possible insofar as the individuals in question get
caught up – consciously and unconsciously – in a shared subject position or a
shared worldview. It is only on the level of theoretical abstraction that it is legitimate to group individuals together on the basis of common structural positions
rather than subject positions. The first question for political strategy, then, is this:
how can more democratic forms of solidarity be organically promoted so that
more and more people will live their structural positions in increasingly democratic, egalitarian and radical pluralist ways, such that they are incited to take up
critical perspectives and subversive practices?

Once again, we have to caution against a voluntarist interpretation of Laclau
and Mouffe's theory. They do not hold that although individuals are more or less
"thrown" into structural positions that are not of their choosing, they are free to
select their interpretative subject positions from an infinite à la carte menu of
possibilities. Laclau and Mouffe situate the networks of subject positions with
respect to hegemonic power relations. Hegemonic discourses construct "horizons
of intelligibility" that "delineate what is possible, what can be said and done, what
positions may legitimately be taken, what actions may be engaged in, and so
forth" (Norval 1996: 4). Often what counts as an "available," "intelligible," or
"compelling" subject position is shaped by the power relations that structure a
given political terrain. As Norval argues with respect to apartheid discourse,

"imaginary horizons, far from being merely superstructural phenomena, served to delimit the sphere of the thinkable, setting the boundaries within which all social practices, including capitalist production, had to find their place" (1996: 27). The study of the cultural intervention by the intellectuals who are associated with a specific social movement, for example, should be based on a precise map of the prevailing horizons (Norval 1996: 52).

The task of promoting more democratic forms of solidarity, then, has to begin with an analysis of the prevailing networks of power relations and political horizons. In social formations that enter into a crisis moment, the processes of subject formation can become much more fluid and vulnerable to political interventions. This does not mean, however, that all identities are equally possible in a given historical moment. In a logical sense, there is an infinite number of ways in which an individual could interpret a single structural position. In an historical sense, however, some interpretations will have more credibility than others thanks to the ways in which they draw upon already normalized common-sense ideologies and traditions of domination and resistance, and thanks to their embodiment within authoritative institutions. The discursive interventions that are central to the formation of identity are not, therefore, random phenomena. They must operate within the field of political forces that prevail in a particular historical conjuncture. Those forces may be highly unstable – as is the case during an organic crisis (Gramsci 1971: 275–6) – or they may be highly stabilized.

Even in the latter case, however, there is always some opportunity for the reconstruction of identity through political intervention. While a given hegemonic configuration may construct extensive mechanisms that promote its reproduction, such as the assimilation of potential rebels and the incitement of false resistances, no formation ever obtains the status of a perfectly closed totality in which all differences are always already neutralized. The possibilities for the failure of total closure are endless. Perhaps taboos, censorship, and abjection end up promoting the forbidden; perhaps the regime's legitimation discourse incites the formation of a cadre who is dangerously committed to the regime's principles and who therefore begins to press the regime to fulfill its own promises; perhaps the iteration of standard practices in changing contexts introduces new and subversive values; perhaps an oppressed minority gains symbolic and material strength from political sources that are located outside the context in question; or perhaps the incitement of conformity always depended on the demonization of certain social enemies, and that process begins to crumble when the demonizations in question are interrupted by a series of displacements. Faced with these developments, the imaginary corresponding to a hegemonic discourse might shift in unpredictable ways, or it might enter into a full-scale crisis as it fails to "fulfill its function of interpellating subjects into stable, 'normalized' forms of identification" (Norval 1996: 27). As the effects of contingent – albeit conditioned – struggles, the formation of subject positions is therefore somewhat indeterminate: through historical analysis, one can suggest a probable outcome, but no reliable prediction vis-à-vis the successful emergence of a particular form of political solidarity can be given in advance.

Laclau and Mouffe's Gramscian attention to the organic character of effective ideological interventions also should not be understood as an endorsement of historicist "expressive totality" theory. Like Lukács, Laclau and Mouffe argue that we cannot draw up an abstract model that will help us to determine which political interventions will be more effective than others; we can only make estimations about effectiveness with respect to analyses of historically specific conditions. The resemblance between their approaches, however, ends here. Lukács holds that for every historical epoch, a single worldview will tend to define the social, and the social will take the form of a "totality." For Lukács, virtually every aspect of the social is integrally connected in a closed system that embraces not only the forces of production, the relations of production, the state and the legal system, but cultural expression and class consciousness as well (Barrett 1991: 22–6). Laclau and Mouffe contend, by contrast, that every social formation remains an incomplete totality (Laclau 1990a: 89–92).[7] Where Lukács' expressive totality approach holds that there can be only one effective form of discursive intervention at a given moment in time – namely the general worldview that corresponds to the specific formation in question – Laclau and Mouffe argue that we will always find a plurality of discourses competing with one another to provide an effective framework for the construction of popular identities. Further, even where Laclau and Mouffe adopt the Gramscian conception that effective discourses must appropriate some elements from already normalized traditions, they do not imply that political struggles are in this respect always already trapped within the fixed limits of traditions. We should not take Marx too literally when he writes that "the tradition of all the dead generations weighs like a nightmare on the brain of the living" (1978: 595). In logical terms, there are an infinite number of possible variations on traditional discourses; ideally, the potential for novel iterations is limitless. In strategic terms, some of these variations will be accepted as plausible or legitimate more readily than others, according to the ways in which political struggles define the limits of the "normal" political terrain, but no single variation ever enjoys the guarantee of success in advance.

A radical democratic pluralist struggle in our imaginary factory would have to include a strategy to undermine the credibility of the neo-conservative and religious fundamentalist interpretative frameworks so that the first two workers could be won over to the radical democratic pluralist side. But – and here is the crucial difference with the Leninist approach – that strategy would begin first with the concrete study of the neo-conservative, religious fundamentalist and leftist discourses as they are actually received by our three workers. Radical democratic pluralist activism would attempt to grasp the ways in which democratic and anti-democratic discourses actually resonate – or fail to resonate – with "the people" in specific historical circumstances. Further, it can be useful to map out the relational systems of difference and equivalence that obtain between discursive elements, for these systems are constitutive for each individual subject position. Perhaps the religious fundamentalist discourse responds to anxieties about sexuality and gender when leftist discourse has been too silent on these issues. Perhaps a Perot-style neo-conservatism speaks to the American workers' xenophobic fear of foreign workers when leftist discourse has not engaged energetically enough with the issues of immigration and racism. Perhaps all of these points are salient, but they are exacerbated by the fact that the corporate media has stifled leftist alternative messages and the American electoral system is overwhelmingly dominated by corporate interests. Perhaps our third worker, the progressive trade unionist, was won over to the radical democratic pluralist side by workers' campaigns that opposed free trade and supported the Canadian-style single-payer health care plan.

Clearly we could not arrive at any of these findings without careful and sensitive concrete research. The radical democratic pluralist activist would proceed not by imposing an abstract image of the workers' "authentic" interest, but by waging a war on the level of the "politics of meaning": by borrowing already popular elements, redefining them in a radical democratic pluralist manner, and fusing them together in a leftist interpretation of the workers' condition. When Laclau affirms that there is no necessary connection between an individual's location in class structures and her formation as a subject, he does not dismiss the possibility of a radicalized workers' struggle. On the contrary, Laclau's Gramscian theory places an enormous emphasis on the political interventions that are needed to radicalize the exploited and the oppressed.

It is only when an exploited individual begins to live her relation with capital as an antagonistic relation – that is, as a relation that is denying her identity, as something that is blocking herself from realizing what she regards as her true potential and stopping her society from becoming an ideal social order – that she is transformed into a worker who is ready to engage in subversive collective resistance (Laclau and Mouffe 1985: 125; Laclau 1990a: 18, 126). An antagonistic construction of identity is in itself politically ambiguous. Connolly asserts, for example, that given the fact that the drive to achieve a fixed identity always fails to achieve its goal, we remain vulnerable to the lure of demonization. This is especially the case when we attempt to ground identity in religious, biological or rationalist arguments. In these conditions,

A powerful identity will strive to constitute a range of differences as *intrinsically* evil, irrational, abnormal, mad, sick, primitive, monstrous, dangerous, or anarchical – as other. It does so in order to secure itself as intrinsically good, coherent, complete or rational and in order to protect itself from the other that would unravel its self-certainty and capacity for collective mobilization if it established its legitimacy. This constellation of constructed others now becomes both essential to the truth of powerful identity and a threat to it. The threat is posed not merely by *actions* the other might take to injure or defeat the true identity but by the very visibility of its mode of *being* as other.

(Connolly 1991: 66)

An antagonistic perspective may, nevertheless, become an extremely important resource for resistance. As we saw in Chapter 1, a relation of subordination will only be transformed into a relation of oppression insofar as the social agent's worldview is radicalized by democratic discourse. It is only when subordinated individuals are inspired by radical democratic pluralist demands for freedom and equality that they can begin, first, to imagine what they could become in an alternative democratic world; second, to see the ways in which power relations are antagonistically blocking them from pursuing that path of self-development; and third, to construct possible avenues for collective resistance that would radically transform the entire capitalist system to make way for the realization of their alternative vision. As they become radicalized, their alternative world ceases to be compatible with the current world; instead of thinking merely in terms of piecemeal reform within the current formation, they construct their alternative as a distinct imaginary.

Borrowing from psychoanalytic theory, we could say that subjects are constituted through the process of identification with subject positions. This psychoanalytic analogy allows us to insist on a principle which is fundamental to Laclau and Mouffe's conception of agency: identities are centered on lack. Social agents constantly come up against the limits that are posed by the material effects of their structural positionings, and they are constantly searching for political discourses that provide explanations or legitimations for their experiences of these limit-effects. We will never arrive at a final identity, an ensemble of subject positions that would offer an interpretative framework that would operate as a perfect explanatory discourse. The limiting material effects of our structural positionings will always exceed the explanatory frame provided by our identities. As such, every subject remains somewhat alienated and restless, for she can never be "at home" in her largely determined structural positionings. This universal condition is of course differentiated with respect to authority and historical conditions: the more empowered the social agent, the more they will have access to resources that allow them to make their alienation more bearable; and the more a social formation disintegrates into an organic crisis, the more every social agent will be driven to seek out new identities. We can nevertheless maintain that the whole process of identity formation always remains incomplete, for it always fails to resolve the subject's fundamental drive to be "at home" in her given structural positionings. As such, every process of identity formation – even for the most empowered, and even in the moments of greatest social stability – remains somewhat open to interruption and contestation.

With this approach, politics is not a power game between already fully constituted subjects; political struggles are primarily struggles to produce subjects (Mouffe 1979b: 171,186; Przeworski 1985: 47, 66, 70; Althusser 1971; Bellamy 1993: 28).[8] Many of the individuals who are thrown into the structural position of the exploited do not see themselves as "workers" at all. They may be interpreting their structural positionings through patriotic, racial or gendered subject positions first and foremost; usually, they participate in solidarities that displace radicalized identities. Our neo-conservative factory worker might live her class structural position through her American patriotism first and foremost, such that she tends to identify primarily with cross-class xenophobic and imperialist solidarities. Our religious fundamentalist might see the world in terms of the division between the saved and the damned rather than the bourgeoisie and the proletariat.

Even where we have a popular workers' movement that seems to have sprung directly from the simple fact of the members' common structural positioning, we have to recognize the invisible work that has been done by political discourses to create their solidarity. A worker whose political orientation is defined chiefly by neo-conservative views may become radicalized by her participation in a strike, as her trade union deploys radical democratic pluralist arguments for a broad-based anti-capitalist solidarity. But it is also possible that she will become radicalized in other ways as well. She might be compelled to reinterpret her structural positioning as a worker in an antagonistic manner by the black community's response to racist police violence. She might become inspired by feminism while struggling to obtain childcare and then begin to live her class structural position through a feminist perspective. Again, radical democratic pluralist discourse is like a "fermenting" agent: the more it circulates throughout the social, the more it can inspire radicalized resistance, and it does so by providing a radicalized interpretative framework for the structural positions into which we are "thrown."

Clearly, workers in capitalist formations need much more than a shift in their identity; they also need access to institutional resources. The views of many of the workers who decided to go on a hunger strike after being locked out for over two years at the Staley corn-processing plant in Decateur, Illinois, were already quite radical. Citing the civil rights movement and Gandhi, Dan Lane, one of the hunger strikers, declared, "A person has certain rights, which are undeniably connected with his being as a person. One of those rights is to his body, to determine what his body does, and what is done to his body" (Frank and Mulcahey 1995). The radicalization of a group of workers can only bear fruit for the labor movement and for radical democracy as a whole if their rights to unionize, to engage in collective bargaining, to strike without being replaced by strike-breakers, and to respect other workers' picket lines in a single industry – regardless of the ways in which corporations break up work sites and internationally relocate production – are recognized in law and upheld in practice. The union-busting activities of Staley and Caterpillar in Decateur, or the Gannett and Knight-Ridder newspaper publishers in Detroit, or the corporations operating the maquiladoras[9] on the Mexican side of the US–Mexican border, can only be stopped through profound reforms in labor laws and their implementation (Glaberson 1995; Bacon 1995).

The identity of the exploited and the oppressed is nevertheless one of the crucial factors in the fight to democratize our societies, for every identity acts as a horizon within which a set of political practices becomes thinkable, and different identities tend to incite different acts of resistance. The reactionary forces in

America are already well aware of the importance of identity formation; hence the bitterly fought "culture wars" and the censorship of socialist discourse. Wherever reactionary forces gain authority, they always do so in part because they have made strategic gains in cultural struggles. Reactionary forces always aim to promote those subject positions that make it possible to live one's assigned structural positions within relations of domination as if they were legitimate, natural and necessary. Reactionary forces also always aim to silence, to exclude, or to colonize those political discourses that make it possible to experience one's assigned structural position within relations of domination as unjust, unnecessary and alien. With respect to identity formation and the corresponding incitement of resistance, everything depends on the availability of political discourses that can operate as credible and organic frameworks for the interpretation of everyday experience. Because political horizons play this crucial role, every effective struggle has to have a cultural dimension; it has to engage in the battles for power within key cultural institutions such as governmental agencies, the education system, global multi-media corporations, and so on.

The social is "open" in the following sense: even the most powerful reactionary forces cannot fully anticipate the ways in which their strategies will backfire and produce unintended and unpredictable consequences. During the Cold War, for example, the civil rights leaders were able to use the prevailing anti-Soviet American patriotic discourse to promote the anti-racist struggle. Homophobic medical panics can actually promote homosexuality by bringing homosexual discourse into official and popular sites. A sexist attack on a figure such as Hillary Clinton might mobilize popular sympathy for her. The vicious misogynist, homophobic and anti-Semitic strategies of the religious right do not always succeed, in spite of this movement's enormous authority; sometimes the religious right's extremism actually backfires quite badly.

In some cases, a discourse of social control may, in its attempt to define the boundaries of the social imaginary, unintentionally incite the formation of subject positions that in turn open up the possibility for interruption and subversion. The neo-conservative repeal of welfare rights, for example, includes measures that force able-bodied welfare recipients to work in return for their benefits. This policy shift institutionalizes the extremely reactionary idea that the majority of welfare recipients have become a permanent "underclass," and that they only have themselves to blame for their impoverished condition. The term "underclass" signifies the black and Latino inner-city populations in the United States; it is widely alleged that the "underclass" is locked in a culture of dependency thanks to its own inferior work ethic and the overly generous character of the welfare state (Reed 1990; Fraser and Nicholson 1994). This construction conceals the structural shifts in the American economy, such as automation, globalization, deregulation, tax cuts and social spending cuts, that have made it increasingly difficult for people with a high school education or less to earn a livable wage while the wealthy benefit from record profits. The "workfare" programs are therefore supposed to symbolize the extremely reactionary concept

70

that America's massive poverty is actually caused by a lack of individual initiative on the part of the poor, and that the only obligation for the larger community is to promote the work ethic and to restore the strict discipline of the market.

It is highly unlikely that any of the neo-conservatives who designed the workfare programs anticipated their politicizing effect for the participants. Since most welfare recipients actually move back and forth between low-wage non-unionized employment and welfare, the mere experience of holding a regular job will have little impact on their lives. They are not receiving the kinds of training in these programs that could actually assist them in finding a job that pays a livable wage; nor are governmental agencies deploying job creation programs on a meaningful scale. The "workfare" participants will therefore probably return to the low-wage employment/welfare cycle at the completion of their program. The punitive discourse surrounding the program constructs the participants as publicly shamed demon-figures on a welfare chain gang. It is nevertheless the case that the workfare programs bring otherwise isolated welfare recipients together in public spaces, and locate them, as the cleaners of streets and parks, in positions that are analogous to that of unionized workers. Some workfare participants have borrowed union discourse to redefine themselves as legitimate workers, and have begun to demand their rights through collective action. Given their situation, they will continue to lack access to the resources necessary to achieve significant social change. This is, nevertheless, an instance in which the deployment of a technique of social control inadvertently creates favorable conditions for the construction of oppositional subject positions.

Laclau and Mouffe argue, in sum, that although the discursive fields in contemporary Western societies are largely structured by capitalist, sexist, racist and homophobic forces, there always remains some limited and context-specific possibility for subversive resistance. Against Althusser, then, they would say that in those societies that remain defined in some minimal way by the democratic revolution, we never arrive at a situation in which a ruling force can become so authoritative that it can totally impose its worldview onto the rest of the population. Althusser's totalistic "teeth gritting harmony" between what he calls the "repressive official apparatuses" and the "ideological state apparatuses" (1971: 150) is never fully established.

Subject positions, then, are constructed by more or less institutionalized political discourses, and their formation is arbitrary in the sense that no individual's structural positioning guarantees identification with a particular political discourse. A relatively stabilized subject position provides a collectively shared framework for the interpretation of a given set of structural positions. The struggle to construct subject positions – the struggle to provide compelling frameworks through which structural positions are lived – never takes place in a vacuum. That struggle is profoundly shaped, although never fully determined, by the prevailing configuration of authority in key official and popular institutions.

Subject position formation influences political practices, and political practices constitute, through regimented iterations over time, social structures. Every specific subject position tends to incite a more or less corresponding set of beliefs and practices. Once a struggle to radicalize and to democratize the ways in which a group lives its structural position as workers gains ground, we would, in ideal conditions, expect those workers to engage in broader and broader forms of solidarity with the exploited and the oppressed. We would also expect them to pursue increasingly democratic goals through increasingly democratic means.

Further, because there is never a simple predetermined correspondence between structural positioning and subject position formation, and subject positions become effective through interpellation and identification, rather than the awakening of a preconstituted dormant essence, subject position formation always opens up the possibility of complex, unintentional and unpredictable processes of transitivistic (mis-)identifications. Consider, for example, the number of daughters who became successful because they thought that the encouraging words expressed by their parents but intended for their brothers were meant for them. Or consider the ways in which analogical forms of identification structure the popular response to films, such that a black man suffering from racist insults could take comfort by cheering for the Indians in a Western (Shohat and Stam 1994: 351). Democratizing social forces possess the same sort of unpredictable potential. In an ideal case, democratization would touch the lives of more and more people, leading in turn to the expansion of democratic forces at many sites in the social. To the extent that the democratic forces gained strategic ground, key institutions, such as the system of elected representatives, government administrations, the media, private corporations, the education system, familial structures and so on, would become more and more democratized as well. These structural changes would not only provide more hospitable conditions for the development and circulation of radical democratic discourses. They would also affect the forces and institutions that locate individuals in structural positions in the first place: fewer and fewer people would be locked in exploited and oppressed structural positions. In short, shifts in subject positions may contribute to the political practices needed to bring about shifts in the formations that produce structural positions, just as innovative speech acts might bring about a change in the rule structure of a language. This analysis raises many questions about resistance; I will address the themes of power, hegemony and resistance in greater detail in Chapter 5 and the Conclusion.

The distinction that I have made between class as a structural position and class as a subject position – the collectively shared interpretation through which a structural position is actually lived – should be extended to non-class identities as well. Like class structural positioning, racial structural positioning is largely determined for both whites and people of color. This is clearly the case for those individuals who are read as racially "other." Consider, for example, the predicament of Plessy, the complainant in the 1896 Supreme Court case, *Plessy* v. *Ferguson*, that established the separate-but-equal doctrine. A mixed-race man, Plessy, did not regard himself as black, but his own opinion had no bearing on the matter; as far as the Louisiana laws of segregation were concerned, he was black.

Fanon's narrator, to take another example, also has no choice; pinned down by the white child's categorizing observation, he becomes the object of the racialized gaze:

"Look, a Negro!" . . . In the train it was no longer a question of being aware of my body in the third person. In the train, I was given not one but two, three places. . . . I am being dissected under white eyes, the only real eyes. I am *fixed*.

(1986: 12–16)

Individuals who are read as white also cannot opt out of racializing structures in a voluntaristic manner; we are thrown into a powerful network of structural relations that more or less secures our enhanced access to resources. Every white person in a racist society is structurally positioned as racially privileged; she may be able to abandon some of that privilege through principled anti-racist practices, but she will never be able to stop the process by which white privilege is conferred onto her through her individual actions alone. Shohat and Stam comment,

No one should be ashamed of belonging to the identity categories into which they happen to have been born, but one is also accountable for one's active role or passive complicity in oppressive systems and discourses. . . . No one need perpetually apologize for the crimes of remote ancestors, but it would also be a crime to ignore benefits accrued over centuries, especially when those benefits "bleed into" contemporary situations of structured privilege.

(1994: 344)

However, the ways in which a white person interprets her experience of her whiteness – the ways in which she lives with and responds to her white privilege – do not flow directly from her whiteness itself. A white person may, for example, live her whiteness through a racist religious fundamentalism, an anti-racist liberal feminism or an anti-racist progressive worker's solidarity. Gilroy, quoting rap artist Rakim, puts it this way: "It Ain't Where You're From; It's Where You're At" (Shohat and Stam 1994: 344).

Racism has become so hegemonic that many whites live their whiteness through some type of racist subject position without being aware that they are doing so. In a similar manner, many men live their gender, many heterosexuals live their sexuality, and many capitalists live their class unconsciously through reactionary political frameworks. In this way, they never experience the fact that goods flow to them by virtue of their structural positions as an abnormal or problematic phenomenon. All that is required for subject position formation is the development of a shared interpretation of a common structural position; self-conscious awareness of this process may or may not occur. Indeed, psychoanalytic theory would insist that the moment in which a subject achieves total mastery

73

over the entire complex ensemble of subject positions through which she organizes her experience remains infinitely postponed. The reactionary apparatuses of racism, sexism, heterosexism and capitalism often work precisely to foreclose awareness of the mediating effects of political discourse for both the exploiter and the exploited, the oppressor and the oppressed. We often assume that there is nothing but "nature" at work in the most concentrated sites of power in the social.

The implications of the anti-essentialist post-Marxist approach to subjectivity and political leadership are enormously important. If, following Lenin, we assume that social agents possess identities or "interests" that are already automatically constituted through their structural positionings, and that a privileged leadership can fully grasp those positionings through scientific concepts, then it becomes necessary to think in terms of an elitist vanguard Party-type leadership. Again, such a leadership enjoys a privileged access to knowledge of the subject's true interests, thanks to its objective theory of history, and can intervene – even in the name of democracy itself – to correct the led wherever they deviate from their putative predestined course of action by any means necessary. If, on the contrary, the anti-essentialist approach is taken, then the formation of identity is viewed as a contingent and context-specific process. Where a contradiction emerges between the leaders' theory of what the led should be doing and what the led are actually doing, the leaders must consider the possibility that it is the led who are correct and that it is their own theory that is mistaken. Even where an identity emerges that is clearly anti-democratic, such as a specific form of a populist racist whiteness, radical democratic leaders should try to find out why that particular identity became compelling at a given time and space and not some other identity. All popular identities and practices – even the ones that are the most repugnant to a radical democratic pluralist – are the effects of political discourses that must be providing some sort of convincing answer to the problem of interpreting the experience of structural positioning.

Popular identities are not, in short, the effects of total irrationality, a complete absence of knowledge, a failure of cognition, or the devious machinations of the corporate media. In this sense, they must never be dismissed out of hand as irrelevant chimeras. Popular discourses must be valued as weathervanes or signposts that allow the organic intellectual leaders to map out the configuration of power relations and cultural struggles that obtain in a given formation. Once these maps are drawn, the leaders will be much better equipped to offer effective counter-interpretations of experience than they would be if they relied upon abstract theories of history alone. More important, they will be democratically situated vis-à-vis the masses: they will begin their interventions in popular discourse by looking for the rationality – however unfamiliar, obscure, or even anti-democratic – that is embodied in popular identities.

Post-Marxism and Lacanian theory

There are many important continuities between Laclau and Mouffe's approach to subject position formation and Žižek's (1989) and Salecl's (1994) Lacanian theory of ideology. Žižek and Salecl would agree that individuals cannot immediately apprehend the ways in which they are located within the symbolic order, and that they live their structural positions through phantasmatic frameworks. From a Lacanian perspective, every explicit political discourse is supported by a hidden fantasy structure. A political discourse can become compelling not just because of what it explicitly says, but also because of its concealed responses to our unspeakable desires, or more precisely, because of its ability to teach us how to desire in the first place. Our openness to the constitutive effects of phantasmatic frameworks is, according to Lacanian psychoanalysis, inscribed in the human condition itself. Because we continually encounter the traumatic experience of the interruption by the real in the symbolic order, we are constantly driven to seek compensation for that trauma in the phantasmatic realm, for only the latter offers us a fully sutured conception of the social.

An apparently neutral technocratic discourse about governmental budgetary restraint, for example, might be supported by racial and sexual fantasies that are either concealed or referred to in heavily coded ways. A subject might speak as if her support for the massive cuts in welfare programs were motivated purely by her neo-conservative principles. Žižek and Salecl, however, would encourage us to look behind her affirmation of individualistic values for the implicit phantasmatic operation of this discourse. Perhaps she has accepted the racist and groundless assumption that there is an "epidemic of teenage pregnancy" – which, in the United States, is a code for the threat of uncontrolled fecundity of poor black and Latina women – and believes that the welfare system rewards "irresponsible promiscuity." Perhaps her support for the restriction of welfare benefits is motivated in this manner by her fears about the expansion of a multicultural America in which the white "middle class" would have less power. In short, a given subject position may become compelling not solely because of the relative attractiveness of an explicitly affirmed set of beliefs, but also because of the ways in which underlying fantasies about threats to the social order have become attached – in a contingent manner – to those beliefs. When the linkages between apparently "legitimate" beliefs and unspeakable fantasies are solidified, an extremely influential political force is set into motion. Counter-discourses have to attend to this underlying phantasmatic structure. The attack on the rights of the poor in the United States, for example, cannot be countered through the recitation of statistics and direct appeals to rationality alone. Democratic activists have rightly taken on the whole issue of racist and sexist imagery in the fight against the right-wing anti-welfare campaign.

While these aspects of Lacanian theory are highly suggestive, it should be noted that there is a tension between Žižek's conception of ideology and the Gramscian approach to historicity. Scott argues that Lacanian theory "does not permit the introduction of a notion of historical specificity and variability" (1988: 39). LaCapra similarly contends that although Žižek rightly criticizes reductive contextualization, "he runs the risk of an equally reductive hypostatization and leveling of problems" (1994: 206).[10]

Žižek does not resolve this crucial problem; he offers a purely formal model of the relationship between trauma, fantasy and desire. For Žižek, any fantasy could provide the crucial suturing effect at a given moment. From his perspective, the predominance of one fantasy over others, the emergence of new fantasies and the decline of older ones are purely random phenomena. When Žižek argues that a dominant discourse relies on anti-Semitism and the figure of the corrupt Jew to patch over its inconsistencies and gaps, he cannot explain why a particular type of anti-Semitism is prevalent in a given moment, or why it is anti-Semitism and not racism, sexism or homophobia that does this work.[11] From a Gramscian perspective, the practical effect of a political discourse will always depend to some extent on its historical traces, the ways in which it resonates with already normalized traditions. Further, patterns of normalization and problematization of popular discourses are never random events but reflect the complex fields of power relations that obtain in a given formation.

In his more recent theoretical writing, Laclau has moved closer to Žižek's Lacanian formulations (Laclau 1990a; 1994; 1996d; Laclau and Zac 1994). Laclau contends that because the subject is a subject of lack, she is caught in an endless and impossible search for completion and is thereby driven to perform an infinite series of identifications. Although each identification seductively promises to deliver completion, it necessarily fails to constitute a complete identity, for in the process of becoming a human subject, one necessarily abandons the originary condition of completion as one enters into language. Laclau contends that it is the impossible return to unity and completion in a formal sense that the subject seeks through her identification with a subject position.

> Identification presupposes the constitutive split of all social identity, between the *content* which provides the surface of inscription and the *function* of identification as such – the latter being independent of any content and linked to the former only in a contingent way.
>
> (Laclau and Zac 1994: 35)

According to this analysis, it is primarily the formal character of a political discourse that makes it a compelling site of identification. "One approves of the Law because it is Law, not because it is rational. In a situation of radical disorganization there is a need for *an* order, and its actual contents become a secondary consideration" (Laclau 1994: 3).

In a moment of organic crisis, one becomes acutely aware of the dislocation in the structure, in the sense that one has "an 'experience' which makes visible the ultimate contingency of all forms of identification" (Norval 1996: 13). Craving order, we become extremely vulnerable during a crisis to political discourses that promise to restore coherence first by offering themselves as myths – concrete readings of the otherwise unintelligible crisis – and later by offering themselves as imaginaries – horizons of intelligibility. Laclau's central argument is that there is nothing in the materiality of an organic crisis or a dislocation in the structure that predetermines which political discourse will prevail in this manner. At the center of a crisis – where we might expect an embryonic substance that will reveal itself as the necessary solution – there is actually nothing but a radical indeterminacy, emptiness or lack. The moment of dislocation in the structure is not just a weak point; it is a radical absence.

In Laclau's terms, this process of becoming caught up in one identification rather than another is a "decision" that is taken in the (non-)space in which the structure has failed, for our choice is ultimately contingent, rather than determined in advance. The subject is partially "self-determined" in the sense that it is "condemned" to take a decision in conditions that Derrida describes as the "ordeal of the undecidable" (Laclau 1996c: 53). This moment of "self-determination," however, should not be understood as a voluntarist expression of a preconstituted interest, for it is produced out of a fundamental absence, namely the failure of the structure to constitute fully the being of the subject. Laclau asserts that the "subject equals the pure form of the structure's dislocation, of its ineradicable distance from itself" (1990a: 60). The subject never exists as a fully self-conscious actor who can stand back from her historical embeddedness, obtain total clarity about her condition, and instrumentally select one alternative among many according to her already-determined set of preferences. As Nietzsche puts it, " 'the doer' is merely a fiction added to the deed" (1969: 45). Nor is the subject merely the vehicle of an omnipotent historical force or all-encompassing totality, such that all of her decisions are always already determined. Laclau's argument can be read, then, as a critique of voluntarism, historicism and functionalism. To the extent that Laclau's position is integrated with the conceptions of the historical trace and overdetermination, it does not collapse into a relativist agnosticism; I will return to this problem in Chapter 3.

The selection of one political discourse instead of another in the condition of undecidability is therefore analogous to identification in psychoanalysis, rather than the decision in rational choice theory. If one selection prevails over another in the context of an organic crisis, then that decision is contingent; there is nothing that wholly guarantees that another identification could not have prevailed in its place. With identification, we construct an analogy between political decision-making in undecidable conditions and the struggle of Lacan's infant in the "mirror stage" to make sense of its chaotic world. Traumatized by the unbearable experience of dislocation, we search for some sort of organizing framework that makes our experience bearable. Lacan's infant (mis-)takes the image in the mirror as its own self, and the lure of the mirror image that facilitates this substitution consists precisely in its framed and stabilized character. The infant thereby achieves the sense of itself as a coherent totality, but only through (mis-) identification with an external image that remains irreducibly "other." In this manner, dependence on otherness, alienation, transitivism and paranoiac knowledge are written into the very principle of our subjectivity (Lacan 1977: 1–7;

Muller and Richardson 1982: 5–34). From a Lacanian perspective, there is no subject with fully formed desires prior to the decision; there is only a deep anxious need for order. One political discourse will tend to prevail over others, then, to the extent that it effectively promises to provide a "minimum of consistency" (Žižek 1989: 75) in an otherwise chaotic terrain.[12]

Understood from a psychoanalytic perspective, the "subject" is not the same as "subject positions." With the psychoanalytic concept of the subject as a subject of lack, we have the principle of the impossibility of identity, for "every identity is already in itself blocked" (Žižek 1990: 252). With subject positions, by contrast, we emphasize the ways in which identity plays an interpretative, mediating role – albeit in necessarily imperfect and incomplete forms – in the incitement of certain practices in specific historical contexts. As Norval contends, an emphasis on both dimensions is needed. Subject position theory without the principle of the impossibility of identity could become just another version of functionalism, while the psychoanalytic concept of subjectivity on its own tends to disregard the ways in which social agents are constructed within historically specific networks of power relations (Norval 1996: 64).

With the emphasis on Lacanian theory in his later work, Laclau has shifted away from his earlier post-structuralist conception of the "articulation" of "floating signifiers." I will deal with the concept of articulation at length in Chapter 3. At this point, articulation can be loosely defined as follows. Political discourses attempt to give new meaning to key signifiers such as "freedom" or "democracy," as they struggle to become the interpretative frameworks through which we live our structural positionings. In *Hegemony and Socialist Strategy* (1985), Laclau and Mouffe argue that these struggles over meaning take the form of articulation. "Floating signifiers," the political concepts that are open to redefinition, are given new meanings as they are combined with other concepts in novel ways. Every articulation is always partial, such that the meaning of these signifiers is never fixed once and for all. However, even when the effects of past articulations are weakened, they are never totally lost; every signifier bears the traces of past articulations (1985: 113). Those traces are more akin to Derrida's "minimal remainders" than essences, in the sense that they never play a fully determining role (Derrida 1988: 51–2). The non-determining presence of those traces in every signifier that is available for articulation nevertheless means that it is never purely empty, never purely open to the assignment of just any meaning. With the concept of the articulation of "floating signifiers," Laclau and Mouffe achieve a remarkable synthesis between the Gramscian and post-structuralist approaches. Their argument about the non-essentialist historical continuities that consistently reassert themselves in unpredictable ways across contingent repetitions draws on both the Gramscian conception of historicity and the Derridean (non-)concept of *différance*.

The tension between Laclau's earlier and later work can be explained in part with respect to the different arguments in Lacanian and post-structuralist theory on the question of structure, the failure of closure and repetition. While both

Lacanians and post-structuralists would agree that every structure – that is, in the respective terms of these two theories, a symbolic order or a discourse – is never completely closed, they disagree on the "structurality" of that openness. For Lacanians, it is the real that constantly interrupts every structure and yet compels the identifications that build up identity-effects and give rise to partial social formations. For Derrideans, by contrast, a structure attempts to spatialize a semantic field. A structure aims to achieve totality-effects; it strives to appear and to operate as if it did have a fixed center and an unbroken ring of borders at its circumference. To the extent that this process is successful, the discourse in question actually does begin to have structuring effects; the signifier that poses as a center becomes a defining point for contiguous elements, its apparent boundaries begin to exercise border effects, and so on. Deconstruction aims precisely to demonstrate the concealed processes that simultaneously make this spatializing effect possible, and yet fundamentally and necessarily open every structure to différance: the movement of difference that cannot be domesticated (Gasché 1986: 143–7). Deconstructive criticism may decenter structure, for example, by showing its hidden dependence on multiple centers; its secret constitutive relation with what is outside the boundaries; its consistent subversion of its own rules as each of its repetitions introduces irreducible differentiation; and so on.

For our purposes here, we should note that these two arguments differ in one crucial respect. The real is utterly unsymbolizable; as such, we cannot grasp via any *historical* logic the relations between the different moments in which the real interrupts the symbolic order. From Žižek's perspective, each of the traumatic moments in which the real erupts in history are, in a formal sense, equivalent and substitutable (1989: 50). Butler suggests that for Žižek, "what is historical and what is traumatic are made absolutely distinct; indeed, the historical becomes what is most indifferent to the question of trauma" (1993: 202).[13] It could be further argued that the Lacanian tendency towards formalistic arguments and transhistorical laws flows precisely from this quarantining of historicity. Butler contends, "Žižek's rendition of the real presupposes that there is an invariant law that operates uniformly in all discursive regimes to produce through prohibition this 'lack' that is the trauma induced by the threat of castration, the threat itself" (1993: 205).[14]

By contrast, post-structuralists insist on the "structured" character of the failure of structure. While deconstruction, like psychoanalysis, holds that a series of moments in which closure becomes impossible cannot be grasped in fully positive terms, it does nevertheless describe these closure-failures as imperfect repetitions. One moment in which closure fails will not only compel a reasserted attempt to achieve closure, it will also partially construct the conditions for the next failure. The contingency that characterizes these transitions – from failure to closure attempt to new failure – is such that we cannot predict exactly how they will proceed, but we can retroactively describe the traces or family resemblances that cut in and out of these moments, and suggest various possibilities for future iterations.

In Butler's commentary on Laclau's Derridean conception of articulation, she writes, "to take up the political signifier... is to be taken into a chain of prior usages, to be installed in the midst of significations that cannot be situated in terms of clear origins or ultimate goals" (1993: 219). Further, Butler describes this chain of citations as an "iterable practice that shows that what one takes to be a political signifier is itself the sedimentation of prior signifiers" (1993: 220). Each citational moment reworks the signifier, mobilizing the "phantasmatic promise" that was integral to past citations – namely the promise to deliver order and completion – and yet simultaneously reconstructing those past articulations such that the signifier also promises " 'the new,' a 'new' that is itself only established through recourse to those embedded conventions, past conventions, that have conventionally been invested with the political power to signify the future" (1993: 220). Butler agrees with Žižek that the subject is never coherent and self-identical because it is founded on a series of exclusions – refusals, repudiations, repressions, abjections, and so on – and that every political signifier will necessarily fail to deliver on its promise of order and completion. She nevertheless differs with him on the historical character of that failure.

> The "failure" of the signifier to produce the unity it appears to name is not the result of an existential void, but the result of that term's incapacity to include the social relations that it provisionally stabilizes through a set of contingent exclusions. This incompleteness will be the result of a specific set of social exclusions that return to haunt the claims of identity defined through negation; these exclusions need to be read and used in the reformulation and expansion of a democratizing reiteration of the term.
>
> (1993: 221)

Butler therefore acknowledges the openness of the structure while insisting on the historical specificity of the instances in which the failure of completion takes place. Further, this approach does have concrete implications for democratic political practice. Butler is, in a sense, calling for the interpretation of what Gramsci would call the organic character of constitutive exclusions and the deployment of that historicizing interpretation in the construction of counter-articulations.

The non-essentialist repetition principle – what Derrida calls "iteration" (1988) – and the concept of political signifiers in current articulations as always bearing the non-determining traces of past articulations, has been relatively de-emphasized in Laclau's recent work. In a co-authored article published in 1994, Laclau and Zac state that "terms such as 'the *unity* of the *people*', the '*welfare* of the *country*', and so forth, as something that antagonistic political forces claim to ensure through totally different political means, have to be necessarily empty in order to constitute the aims of a political competition" (1994: 37). Like Žižek, Laclau and Zac contend that the content of a political discourse is almost irrelevant, for it is really the formal framework of a political discourse that makes it compelling for "the people." Various political signifiers may appear to operate differently, but they are all "empty signifiers," blank spaces whose organizational form – and not its content – compels phantasmatic investments. From a Lacanian perspective, those investments are made not because the signifiers have specific meanings that resonate organically within a given context, but because the "empty signifiers" promise to deliver jouissance, the primal unity and completion that was foreclosed at the entry into language. The (impossible) lure of a return to jouissance, which restimulates profound longings in the interpellated subject, is therefore the key to the power of a given political signifier (Butler 1993: 191, 199, 209). Laclau's Lacanian shift is in this respect a departure not only from post-structuralist theory, but also from the Gramscian tradition, for Gramsci insists that a political discourse will only resonate with "the people" insofar as it organically resonates in some way with popular traditions.

One of the hallmarks of Laclau's early work is precisely his Gramscian attention to historical specificity. In his influential article, "Towards a Theory of Populism," for example, Laclau notes that opposed forces often appeal to the same political symbols: Tupac Amaru has been evoked by both guerrilla movements and the Peruvian military government; the symbols of Chinese nationalism were deployed by Chiang-Kai-Shek and Mao Tse-tung; and German nationalist symbols were used by Hitler and Thälmann. Laclau cautions, however, that

> popular traditions are far from being arbitrary and they cannot be modified at will. They are the residue of a unique and irreducible historical experience and, as such, constitute a more solid and durable structure of meanings than the social structure itself.
>
> (1977: 167)

Laclau does not, however, completely reject the post-structuralist and Gramscian approaches in his more recent work. He maintains, for example, that political signifiers can only offer themselves as empty surfaces of inscription for new articulations to a certain extent: "imaginary signifiers forming a community's horizon are tendentiously empty and essentially ambiguous" (1990a: 65). If the contents of a political discourse are of "secondary consideration" in contrast to their formal characteristics (Laclau 1994: 3), this implies that they still retain some significance. A hegemonic discourse must be more than the formal embodiment of order itself; it must offer some compelling concrete alternative vision of the social.

> This does not mean, of course, that any discourse putting itself forward as the embodiment of fullness will be accepted. The acceptance of a discourse depends on its credibility, and this will not be granted if its proposals clash with the basic principles informing the organization of a group.
>
> (Laclau 1990a: 66)

Many interesting questions could be addressed in future research within this theoretical horizon. Exactly how are the boundaries of "credibility" established in a specific historic formation? If both the form and the content of rival political discourses matter, what can we say about the limits of hegemonic practice?

Perhaps the best way to approach these problems would be via a recuperation of the Gramscian emphasis on historicity and concrete empirical research. With respect to her own study on apartheid discourse, for example, Norval contends that the Afrikaner community's world was thrown into crisis through the 1930s and 1940s by a drought, the Depression, rapid urbanization and the Second World War. Various Afrikaner discourses that expressed different nationalist, religious and racial elements competed with one another to become the new hegemonic discourse. One of the key factors in this rivalry consisted precisely in the ways in which each of these discourses resonated with residual Afrikaner traditions (1996: 65–6).

Norval's argument can be usefully illustrated with reference to McClintock's account of the mobilization of Afrikaner nationalism in the years leading up to the apartheid era. McClintock examines, for example, the conservative Afrikaners' staging of the "Second Trek," the 1938 re-enactment of the 1838 migration, in which Afrikaners fled from British rule, rejected slave emancipation and massacred the Zulus at Blood River. Citing Benjamin, McClintock contends that archaic images can become potent elements within popular commodity spectacles insofar as they are redefined, paradoxically enough, to identify precisely what is new in the contemporary moment, while simultaneously granting free rein to reactionary nostalgia. For McClintock, it was precisely the trek's double-faced historical logic that gave it a tremendous organic force.

> Unlike socialism, then, the *Tweede Trek* could evoke a resonant archive of popular memory and a spectacular iconography of historical travail and fortitude, providing not only the historical dimension necessary for national invention but also a theatrical stage for the collective acting out of the traumas and privations of industrial decline.
>
> (1995: 376)

Although Lacanian theory usefully draws attention towards the formal aspects of identification, it must be supplemented by a Gramscian approach to historicity. Competing articulations never work on a signifier as if it were a blank space; every floating signifier has some meaning – albeit one that is always open to subversive recitation – insofar as it bears the fading traces of past articulations. The effectiveness of a political discourse, in other words, is not merely a question of its formal characteristics. It is entirely possible that a highly ordered, consistent and organized discourse that was supported by devastating demonizations would absolutely fail to incite popular identifications if it assigned meanings to key terms such as "freedom" and "democracy" that did not resonate in any way with organic traditions.

The Lacanian and Gramscian approaches are not totally opposed to one another. Gramsci argues that the formal character of the intellectuals' intervention – the way that the intellectuals bring greater coherence and universality to fragmented popular discourse – is central to hegemonic strategy. Both Lacanians and Gramscians would agree that there is no single discourse that is predestined to act as the single hegemonic solution to an organic crisis. Gramscians insist that there has to be some degree of continuity between a hegemonic discourse and the partially normalized traditions that make up the discursive formation in question, but that continuity is not analogous to an essentialist repetition with a predictable trajectory. Again, the type of repetition that is proper to a series of articulatory moments in time is similar to the imperfect and unpredictable continuity that is found in Derridean iterations (1988), Wittgenstein's family resemblances (1958), and Foucauldian genealogy (1977, 1979, 1980b). Present articulations must resonate with normalized traditions to become effective, but they also introduce novel redefinitions of those traditions at the same time.

In this sense, both the Lacanian and Gramscian approaches share the assertion that we cannot predict with exact certainty which discourse will emerge out of a given crisis as hegemonic. Unlike the Lacanians, however, the Gramscians attend to both the form and the content of competing discourses. By searching for organic traces, Gramscians can reconstruct the genealogical, non-essentialist logic that is displayed by a series of articulations. Like the Derrideans, Gramscians insist on the historically structured character of structure failure. Finally, Gramscians can construct historically specific maps of institutionalized power relations and the residual effects of the crumbling traditions that make up the background for any organic crisis. On that basis, Gramscians can suggest, in a limited manner, various probable outcomes. Because Lacanians remain exclusively concerned with the formal characteristics of identification, they cannot do so.

3

SUBJECT POSITIONS, ARTICULATION AND THE SUBVERSION OF ESSENTIALISM

As we have seen in Chapter 2, Marx and Engels treat class as the essence of every socio-political identity in their *Communist Manifesto*. Where there are variations between different subjects who are supposed to belong to the same class, these differences – nationality, race, ethnicity, gender, and so on – are not supposed to affect their class "core." Class is supposed to be constituted solely with reference to that subject's relationship to the means of production. According to traditional Marxist theory, one working-class group's objective interest should ultimately be the same as that of another working-class group, regardless of the other differences between them. These non-class differences, then, are supposed to be secondary and external. In technical terms, they are non-constitutive accidents, for they are nothing but superficial differences that can be added or subtracted from the subject without transforming the subject's true being and its objective interests in any way. A boundary is therefore supposed to exist between class and non-class differences such that class is protected from the latter's effects. Other essentialisms take the same form. Gender, race or nationality, for example, can be considered as the subject's essential "core" in other theories.

Saussurean linguistics

Laclau and Mouffe's subversion of essentialist identity theory is based on Saussurean linguistic theory. For the authors, Saussure provides a radical ontology precisely because of his exclusively relational theory of value (Laclau 1990a: 207). Saussure rejects the referential theory of language which suggests that objects are already given to us as coherent entities. According to the referential theory, humans merely assign a name to each object or idea; different language-using communities might choose different names, but the relationship of every community to the totality of objects is basically the same. Saussure holds that a linguistic sign unites a concept and a sound-image – a signified and a signifier – rather than a thing and a name (Saussure 1966: 66). The relationship between the signified and the signifier is arbitrary. The first and rather banal implication of the arbitrariness of the sign is that one signifier could easily be replaced by another signifier for the same signified. "Sister" and "sœur" both function equally well as signifiers for the concept "sister"; the signified in itself does not in any way suggest which combination of sounds or written marks ought to be used as its signifier.

Saussure's principle of the arbitrariness of the sign also implies that each language system "articulates" reality (1966: 10). It is through language that the objects that are meaningful for us are constructed. Each language divides up, categorizes, and makes coherent the totality of objects that is used by its corresponding language-using community. We can only grasp objects insofar as we do so through the structures that are provided for us by language. The articulation of reality is arbitrary in the sense that nothing in extra-linguistic matter motivates this process (Saussure 1966: 113). There is nothing in "nature," for example, that determines where we should place a boundary between "green" and "blue," or "hill" and "valley." Language therefore not only constructs contingent linkages between the signifier and the signified, it also constructs the signifieds themselves in a process that is entirely independent of the extra-linguistic. When we move from one language to another, then, we are not merely substituting new labels for the same objects, we are, in a sense, leaving the totality of objects that is proper to the first language and entering that of the second. Although there is always some degree of overlap and translatability between these language-specific worlds, every language constructs its totality of objects in a distinct manner (Culler 1986: 32–3).

Where Derrida and other post-structuralists claim that there is "nothing outside the text," they are referring explicitly to these Saussurean principles (Culler 1988: 148; Johnson 1987: 14). Laclau and Mouffe similarly contend that the social is coextensive with the discursive, and that the extra-discursive has no constitutive effect on the world as we know it (1985: 105–14). None of these theorists is denying the mere existence of extra-discursive matter; this is not a return to Berkeley's idealism. But extra-discursive matter is formless and therefore cannot be grasped by us; we only have access to the objects that are constructed for us through the mediating articulation work of language. Individual discourses can become objects for us. We can, for example, study a discourse or we can consider a discursive formation – an ensemble of discourses that are combined together in a given context – as an object as well. We must nevertheless grasp individual discourses and discursive formations through the frameworks that are provided by other discourses.

The discursive is the totality of discourses taken as a whole. The discursive, then, is not one object among many, it is the theoretical horizon that constitutes the being of objects as such (Laclau 1990a: 105; Laclau and Mouffe 1990: 103–4). Indeed our very attempt to delimit the totality of possible meaningful objects for us by gesturing towards an extra-discursive sphere of utterly unthinkable matter is impossible, since we are necessarily using discourse to do so (Butler 1993: 31). Even our conception of "nature" is itself discursively constructed in that our knowledge of natural phenomena is given to us through historically specific theoretical discourses (Kuhn 1962; Feyerabend 1993; Haraway 1991). Following Wittgenstein's concept of the "language game," Laclau and Mouffe include written documents, speech, ideas, concrete practices, rituals, institutions, and empirical objects (insofar as they are meaningful for us in a given context) within their conception of the discursive (Laclau and Mouffe 1985: 108; Wittgenstein 1958).

With the principle of arbitrariness, Saussure asserts that meaning is exclusively constituted through the relational differences that obtain within a language. In one of his famous examples, Saussure considers the meaning of the pieces in a chess game. The knight piece by itself means nothing to the chess player outside the game for its value as a chess piece is constituted solely within the game; "it becomes a real, concrete element only when endowed with value and wedded to it" (1966: 110). The meaning of the chess piece depends on its position on the board in relation to the other pieces, and on the rules of the game as a whole (1966: 88). If a piece were lost from a set, it could be replaced by an equivalent piece from another set, or even by a bit of wood or a piece of paper. The only thing that matters in these substitutions is that "the same value is attributed to it" (1966: 110).

In other words, the chess piece has no positive meaning when it is considered apart from the chess game. The fact that it is made of wood, plastic or paper is irrelevant to its value in the game itself. The linguistic sign, like the chess piece, has no positivity in isolation from the linguistic system, for its meaning is constructed exclusively in terms of the differences between itself and the other signs in that system.

> In language there are only differences *without positive terms*. Whether we take the signified or the signifier, language has neither ideas nor sounds that existed before the linguistic system, but only conceptual and phonic differences that have issued from the system.
>
> (Saussure 1966: 120)

This argument does not merely amount to the claim that linguistic signs are different from one another, in the sense that no two signs are exactly the same. It implies instead that if we took a sign and subtracted all of the effects that its relations with other signs have had on its meaning, it would be purely meaningless. Saussurean linguistic analysis, then, examines the sign as it is constituted exclusively through its differential relations with other signs in a linguistic system.

Saussure privileges the synchronic analysis of language – the study of a linguistic system at a single moment in time – over diachronic analysis – the study of the evolution of that system over time. This privileging, however, does not imply that Saussure's theory is ahistorical. Culler argues, to the contrary, that Saussure developed a profoundly historical theory of language. "If there were some essential or natural connection between the signifier and signified, then the sign would have an essential core which would be unaffected by time or at least would resist change" (1986: 46). The arbitrariness of the sign also does not allow for individualistic voluntarism. A language is a system of social conventions that facilitates communication between individuals. Saussure compares language to a "social bond" and to a "storehouse filled by the members of a given community through their active use of speaking" (1966: 13). Analysis of the linguistic acts of an individual apart from a language community can only provide an incomplete and artificial conception of that language: "For the realization of language, a community of speakers [masse parlante] is necessary" (1966: 14, 77).

Articulation, equivalence and difference

From Laclau and Mouffe's perspective, political identities are analogous to Saussure's linguistic signs. Like Saussure, they reject a referential theory of identity in favor of an exclusively relational theory. Political discourses and identities are wholly constituted through articulation, which they define as "any practice establishing a relation among elements such that their identity is modified as a result of the articulatory practice" (Laclau and Mouffe 1985: 105). An articulation consists of the transformative combination of two or more discursive elements. As we saw in Chapter 1, for example, socialism is not necessarily democratic, but a socialist project can indeed become democratic insofar as it is articulated with – that is, transformed through its combination with – democratic discourse.

In Chapter 2, we considered an imaginary example in which three different individuals live their structural positions as workers through the neo-conservative, religious fundamentalist and democratic leftist subject positions. Having looked at what subject positions do, we should now consider the ways in which subject positions are constituted. Each of the subject positions are like "floating signifiers": their meaning is never entirely fixed but always remains open to change. The meaning of a subject position is constructed through its differential relations with the other subject positions that are found in a given discursive formation (Laclau and Mouffe 1985: 113).

Following Barker (1981), for example, we could distinguish between two basic types of racism: traditional racism on the one hand, and cultural racism or the "new racism" on the other. While traditional racism explicitly affirms the superiority of the white Anglo Saxon race, the new racism gives its support to the same segregationist politics, but defends the latter as the only public policy that adequately expresses recognition of cultural differences. The traditional racist subject position became meaningful through its differential relations with similar and opposed subject positions, such as social Darwinism, eugenics, and anti-Semitism on the one hand, and universalist humanism on the other. Although traditional racism became a widely accepted discourse in the West through the nineteenth and early twentieth centuries, it did not fix the meaning of racism for all time. A new discourse that opposed racism gained authority, namely cultural relativism. As the latter became normalized, the value of traditional racism changed, for it became largely discredited. Post-colonial racists, however, soon appropriated key elements out of cultural relativism and constructed a new cultural racism. Because their racism mimics the normalized features of cultural relativism, the post-colonial racists were able to pose as anti-racists.

In short, what we have in this example is a complex field of different interpretative frameworks, or subject positions, in which the meaning of each subject position is shaped by its differential relations with the others. The study of the differential construction of a subject position becomes all the more complicated when the constitutive role of absent subject positions is taken into account. A taboo, for example, might preclude the explicit articulation of a signifier – this may be the case, for example, where abject feminine, homosexual or racially "other" signifiers are concerned – but that may not prevent it from shaping the meaning of other signifiers in an invisible manner. Discourse analysis cannot stop short at the interpretation of the subject positions that a discursive formation openly avows; it must always perform genealogies of erasure and archaeologies of silence as well (Sedgwick 1990; Hammonds 1994: 138–9).

Saussure contends that the extra-discursive does not determine the constitutive relations between signs. Laclau and Mouffe similarly insist that there is nothing that is meaningful or has being for us outside the discursive. Extra-discursive matter has brute existence but remains fundamentally unknowable for us. We can say nothing positive about pure matter; it is so utterly formless that it even defies description. Again, our discursive attempts to distinguish between the discursive and the extra-discursive become impossible, for we inevitably resort to discursively-constituted concepts to refer to the extra-discursive (Butler 1993: 31).

In the examples presented in Chapter 2, we considered different subject positions in isolation. In actual political situations, identity is always overdetermined in the psychoanalytic sense. Overdetermination entails not only a plurality of causal factors, but also a certain degree of irreducibility. A dream, for example, is the product of condensation whereby various different unconscious elements are merged together such that they give rise to a single manifest sequence. However, even if we could isolate each of those constitutive elements, we could not say that their combination necessarily produced this specific dream, for their mutually constitutive convergence could have produced several other meaningful sequences as well (Laplanche and Pontalis 1973: 292–3). The identity of an individual, group or movement is also in this sense a product of condensation: it is always the product of an irreducible plurality of subject positions. Insofar as the coherence of that plurality is always context dependent, every identity is at least potentially precarious. Each ensemble of subject positions is like an incomplete linguistic system: the value of each subject position is shaped by its relations with the others, but always remains open to the constitutive effects of new differential relations.

Consider, for example, the two sides in the affirmative action debate in California during the mid-1990s. The pro-affirmative action side includes civil rights organizations, people of color community organizations, feminist groups, progressive trade unions and the AFL-CIO, student groups and small leftist organizations. On the anti-side, we have the Republican Party, neo-conservatives who oppose what they call "special rights" and "preferential treatment," anti-feminists, racists who oppose the advance of people of color in any shape or form and xenophobes who see affirmative action as an incentive for non-white immigrants to settle in California. Insofar as these groups form two opposed blocs, the following analysis can be suggested. On each side of the debate, the different subject positions are articulated together to form a chain of equivalence (Laclau and Mouffe 1985: 127–9). To the extent that we are dealing with articulation – and not just a superficial coalition – the value of each subject position in the chain is shaped by its relations with the others. Perhaps trade union militancy or radical feminism, for example, would become more multicultural as these subject positions were brought into closer negotiations with progressive anti-racist subject positions during the pro-affirmative action campaign. Ultimately, hegemonic articulation would occur on both a conscious and unconscious level, as anti-racism began to operate as a compelling overarching framework for identification for anti-racists, trade union militants and radical feminists alike. Wherever different subject positions are symbolically located together in opposition to another camp, such that their meanings are subsequently transformed by their overlapping identifications with partially shared sets of beliefs, then we are dealing with an articulated chain of equivalence. We should note, however, that a chain of equivalence never dissolves into a singular homogeneous mass; the differences between the subject positions in question are always to some extent preserved.

Taking the chain as a whole, we could say that its identity is constituted by its differential relation with other chains. The meaning of the "pro-affirmative action" movement is defined by the antagonism between itself and its opponent, the "anti-affirmative action" camp. Actual struggles are, of course, extremely complex. Every subject position bears the residual traces of past articulations, and is always being articulated into many different chains of equivalence at the same time. As progressive feminism is active in the pro-affirmative action campaign, its meaning is also being shaped in its campaigns on abortion, sexual harassment and rape, breast cancer, the war against poor women and so on. Further, the negotiations between the different subject positions within one chain of equivalence can be extremely complicated. As I will discuss below, one position, the "nodal point," can emerge as the position that is predominant in the sense that it has the greatest effect in reshaping the meaning of the other positions in the chain.

This is one logic of the social, namely the logic of equivalence (Laclau and Mouffe 1985: 129–30). Wherever social forces tend to become organized in terms of an antagonistic relation between two great chains of equivalence, we can describe that form as the logic of equivalence. In some contexts, political forces that have become stabilized in terms of a logic of equivalence representation will be displaced by other forces attempting to impose a logic of difference counter-representation. A struggle to manage difference will ensue, and its dimensions will always remain beyond the conscious grasp of the social agents in question. At some moments, political forces attempt to construct the social as an antagonism-free system of subject positions, and subjects find themselves caught up in a corresponding set of identifications.

When the Republican Presidential 1996 campaign, for example, learned during the summer of 1996 that many voters had been offended by the extremism of the religious right, they attempted to adopt a complex strategy to manage the differences at hand. Within the Party, every effort was made to accommodate the extremist demands of the Christian Coalition into the official Party platform. In this moment, the Republican Party constructs America according to the logic of equivalence, as an all-out war between "good" and "evil." When addressing audiences outside the Party, however, Dole attempted to take the moral high ground and to construct the Republican Party as a site in which Americans from all "walks of life" were welcome and respected. Explicit extremist language about abortion and gay rights was almost completely dropped from Dole's public discourse, and he waited until his defeat was certain before emphasizing his anti-affirmative action and anti-immigration positions. Women, people of color and the handicapped were prominently featured in the Party's convention and campaign materials. In this second moment, "America" is no longer represented as two great warring camps; it is depicted instead as a peaceful system of different subject positions. For Laclau and Mouffe, this second representational form is the logic of difference (Laclau and Mouffe 1985: 130).

These two logics limit one another (Laclau and Mouffe 1985: 129–34). No political force can sustain a "total war" construction indefinitely; at some point, the antagonism will either dissolve or be suppressed, and at least some of the subject positions that were formerly at war with one another will be effectively reconstructed as elements within an antagonism-free system of differences. This might occur through some degree of genuine resolution of the antagonism, co-optation, assimilation or the splitting of a subject position into new fragments. On the other hand, it is impossible to suppress antagonisms indefinitely in order to maintain a construction of a social field as a peaceful system of differences. The Christian Coalition, for example, is heavily invested not only in the defeat of the Democratic Party, but in an antagonistic construction of "America." At some point, the Republican Party's "big tent" approach and back-room deal-making will alienate key players on the religious right, and they will leave the Party to join movements in which they will be able to wage blatantly right-wing extremist political campaigns. Dole's campaign ultimately failed, and it did so in part because its linkage between neo-conservatism and religious fundamentalism remained exposed as a fragile and opportunistic coalition. The campaign therefore could not construct Dole's agenda as a coherent worldview that would operate as a compelling site for popular identifications.

Anti-essentialism and political assessment

As we have seen in Chapter 2, the reductionist tendency in the Marxist tradition maintains that democratic demands of all types and in all cases are fundamentally bourgeois in nature. This thesis is one of Laclau and Mouffe's primary targets, and their critique is entirely sound. The reductionist approach would decide, in abstraction, whether environmentalist demands would further either the interests of the revolutionary proletariat, or those of the capitalist bourgeoisie. Based on this abstract decision, it would construct a fixed political strategy with respect to environmentalist demands well in advance of actual engagements with concrete environmentalist politics. This sort of reductionism is equally flawed where racial or gender principles are substituted for class principles. When lesbian and gay rights are dismissed in advance by heterosexual people of color as an inherently "white thing," or anti-censorship demands are rejected in advance by feminists as capitulations to the patriarchy, they are reproducing the same sorts of illegitimate reductionism that we can find in the Marxist tradition.

What Laclau and Mouffe insist is that when we are dealing with democratic demands, we will not know in advance exactly how they might be articulated with other political discourses, and how they might be open to alternative definitions. Environmentalism could be articulated with either reactionary concepts such as the protection of private property rights and the eugenicist management of population growth, or progressive elements such as the defense of indigenous people's rights and an attack on corporate greed. Its political meaning cannot, therefore, be decided in advance. Similarly, the demand for lesbian and gay rights could be phrased such that they would bring progress for only wealthy white male conservatives, or it could be shaped to contribute to the liberation of all individuals, including heterosexuals, from coercive familial situations. And an anti-censorship demand might be constructed either as an assault against progressive sexual harassment procedures, or as a defense of feminist free speech. We cannot make these distinctions without looking at the concrete situation; theories that decide the political value of a democratic demand in advance cannot be reconciled with radical democratic pluralist principles.[1]

As to the descriptive features of a democratic group's membership and leadership, the situation is more complicated. Laclau and Mouffe rightly reject the argument that the "authentic" interests of a social agent can be determined with reference to their structural location. There is nothing "inauthentic" about blacks, women, gays or workers who embrace conservative and even anti-democratic values. Instead of charging them with false consciousness, we would prefer to say that radical democratic pluralists have the better moral positions and arguments.

Laclau and Mouffe's argument that there is no necessary connection between an individual's structural position and their subject position should not be extended beyond this point. It is in fact often appropriate to include in an assessment of a group's politics an analysis based on the descriptive features of its membership and leadership. An organization that claims to pursue democratic goals but actually maintains an exclusionary leadership structure, such that members of dominant social groups – whites, males, heterosexuals, the bourgeoisie and so on – always prevail in that organization, and minority members are either excluded altogether or included in merely tokenistic roles, is acting in a manner that contradicts its stated goals. We do not need to retreat to reductionist logics or essentialist categories of authentic consciousness to make this point, for leadership and membership structures are material expressions of an organization's common-sense ideology. At the same time, it remains entirely possible that a group with a leadership composed predominantly of women, people of color, queers or workers could indeed promote reactionary politics; reactionary fragments can always be found within any disempowered group. In this sense, the assessment of the representation of the disempowered in leadership positions is but one part of a contextually-specific analysis for a given movement. What we need is a both/and approach: an analysis of both the movement's leadership and membership structures, and an analysis of the political concepts that are fused together in the construction of the movement's democratic demands.

The political assessment of a democratic movement's politics must also include an analysis of the movement's response when the material effects of its practices deviate from its stated intentions. Because every movement makes history in conditions not of its choosing, it cannot always control the ways in which its practices are reappropriated by other forces. The anti-choice Pope appropriates feminist language; a conservative political group co-opts civil rights arguments; a powerful corporation persuades trade union members to contribute to its corporate strategy. A feminist organization may try to close a red-light district down, only to find that its efforts are assimilated into the reactionary social control agendas of a racist police force and profit-driven urban developers. To the extent that a movement is democratic, it will abandon dogmatic predictions about the success of its strategies, remain vigilant about unintended effects and co-optation, and act quickly to redefine its strategies where necessary. A movement can only maintain this sort of mobile approach to political strategizing insofar as it promotes vigorous debate and critique within its own ranks.

For Laclau and Mouffe, the meaning of every subject position remains arbitrary in the Saussurean sense. Even the most naturalized subject position that is defined through a relatively stable field of differential relations with other positions is open to subversive redefinition. Subject positions, like signs, may appear to be natural – they may appear to have, by necessity, only one possible meaning – but this is merely the effects of hegemonic normalization. As Culler puts it, "the more powerful a culture, the more it succeeds in having its signs taken as natural" (1986: 108). Laclau and Mouffe's semiological approach to the constitution of subject positions, in which Saussure's principle of arbitrariness is extended to identity formation, prompts the analyst to look for concealed power, namely the forces of institutionalization, behind every apparent "nature."

Laclau and Mouffe's semiological approach can be somewhat difficult to grasp because it contradicts much of our common-sense understanding about identity. In our everyday discussions, we usually presume that the individual is the basic unit of analysis, and that the individual has already been assigned definite characteristics at birth, such as race, gender and sexuality, and that there are "natural" and "unnatural" ways to express these assigned characteristics. If, however, it can be shown that these apparently "natural" identities have a history, and have different meanings across different contexts, then their "natural" status becomes suspect.

Semiology, genealogy, sexuality and race

This point can be clarified further with reference to the use of genealogical methodology in contemporary lesbian, gay and bisexual studies. Genealogy is an "effective" history, a radical contextualization that seeks to clarify the conditions of possibility for identity formations that are specific to a given time and place (Foucault 1977: 154; Connolly 1991: 181–4). Sexuality historians who have taken up this paradigm – Rubin (1984), Weeks (1977, 1981, 1990), Foucault (1977, 1980b), Halperin (1990), Chauncey (1990), Vicinus (1993), Almaguer (1993) and others – have demonstrated that "sexuality" has not remained an essentially unchanged field of subjects, practices and norms throughout history. Indeed, "sexuality" carves out a specific area of concerns and anxieties which, strictly speaking, only makes sense in modern Western contexts. The historicization of apparently universal categories such as "heterosexual," "homosexual" and "lesbian" allows us to problematize contemporary value systems by demonstrating the fragility of the norms that are taken for granted as transcendental rules.

An imaginary critic of Laclau and Mouffe, however, might grant the historicity and contingency of sexual subject positions without abandoning essentialist theory with respect to other types of subject positions. Indeed, homophobic discourse is often centered on the idea that otherwise "normal" people can be "made" homosexual through the illegitimate promotion of homosexuality. Homophobic bigots and leftists alike often maintain that sexuality is unusual in that, unlike other identities, it is socially constructed. Laclau and Mouffe would respond by insisting that all subject positions are arbitrary in a Saussurean sense. This does not mean that all oppressive and exploitative forces work in exactly the same way, but that we can use the same ontological and epistemological presuppositions in our explorations of these different discourses. Support for this argument can be found in the theories of Hall and Gilroy on racial formations.

Hall contends that a racialized social field is not the direct expression of an underlying economic structure. From his perspective, capitalism and racism intertwine with one another in complex, contradictory and mutually constitutive ways, and the subject positions through which we live our class and race structural positionings mutually constitute one another through specific articulations. Hall suggests that in contemporary Britain, "race is . . . the modality in which class is 'lived', the medium through which class relations are experienced, the form in which it is appropriated and 'fought through'" (Hall 1980: 341). Similarly, economic crises in America are widely interpreted through racialized discursive frameworks, such that an assault on "unmarried teenage mothers" – again, a code for blacks and Latinas – is accepted as a legitimate solution to the national debt. Racialized subject positions can "cross over" in that they can serve as frameworks for the interpretation of both racial and class structural positioning. In an abstract sense, virtually any subject position could play this role, but Hall is referring to the specific conditions in post-colonial Britain, in which racialized ways of thinking have become deeply woven into official and popular discourse. Hall concludes that instead of using universal categories and trans-historical theories to analyze race and racism, we should investigate the "specific conditions which make [racial or ethnic] distinction[s] socially pertinent, historically active" (Hall 1980: 338).

The dimensions of Hall's articulation approach can be clarified with reference to the work of Sedgwick, Crenshaw and Alarcón. Sedgwick contends that although gender and sexuality are inextricable in concrete instances, they can be imagined as "two distinct axes" (1990: 30). She recognizes that different identities "mutually constitute one another," but argues that "there is always at least the potential for an analytic distance between gender and sexuality" (1990: 30). From Hall's perspective, gender, like race, is always so thoroughly constituted in and through its relations with other positions that treating it as an isolated entity – even in theoretical discourse – becomes an abstract exercise with little pragmatic value. This does not mean that comparative research on different racialized and gendered formations is utterly impossible, but that we can only expect to discover family resemblances and genealogical tendencies from these studies, rather than transcendental rules.

In her intervention in American legal discourse on sexual and racial harassment, Crenshaw argues that sexism "intersects" with racism such that the wrongs suffered by women of color are often different in form from the exclusions and injuries that affect men of color and white women. Since existing jurisprudential traditions tend to think in terms of black male and white female complainants, the courts' inability to accommodate the intersectional perspective virtually guarantees the erasure of the experience of women of color (1992). Given her limited aim, Crenshaw does not take issue with the fact that litigation in these areas is structured by other problematic assumptions, such as the primacy of an individualistic approach to injury and the idealization of the white masculine middle-class condition (Brown 1995: 61). For our purposes, however, it should be noted that Crenshaw's intersectionality metaphor implies that these two "roads," racism and sexism, form an "intersection" – racialized sexism or gendered racism – at only one position in the social "map," namely in the condition of women of color.

Hall's articulation metaphor, by contrast, suggests instead that racism and sexism are more akin to three-dimensional force-fields than to intersections. Their mutually constitutive combination has implications for every position within the discursive formation in question. The identity of white males, for example, could be affected by the combination of racism and sexism. In lynching, white males position themselves not only as superior to women and superior to blacks, but as chivalrous "protectors" of "their (white) women" against the black male "sexual predators." White males' assaults against women of color, and the economic and political motivations for their attacks on black men, are thereby erased. In a factory with white and black women workers, to take another example, all the workers may be paid the same wage, but the white women may be paid a "symbolic wage" by being placed in the cleaner, safer and less physically-demanding jobs. In this case, the factory management would be attempting to incite a "lady worker" identity among the white women that would set them apart from their black women co-workers. In these and many other cases, the articulation of racism and sexism have implications for the identities of both women of color and virtually every other subject who is caught up in the same formation.

Alarcón would also take issue with the ways in which Crenshaw's intersectionality theory leaves the whole question of constitutive intra-gender conflicts unaddressed. In her critique of feminist standpoint epistemology (Hartsock 1983), Alarcón notes that Women's Studies research often merely appropriates material about women of color without considering the ways in which a radical integration of their discourse would require feminist theory's transformation. In this case, the failure to extend the articulation approach facilitates the erasure of white women's accountability, as white femininity is represented as if it emerged solely out of a simple binaristic gender relation.

> The inclusion of other analytical categories such as race and class becomes impossible for a subject whose consciousness refuses to acknowledge that "one becomes a woman" in ways that are much more complex than in a simple opposition to men. In cultures in which "asymmetric race and class relations are a central organizing principle of society," one may also "become a woman" in opposition to other women.
>
> (1990: 360)

Following Hall, Gilroy also rejects the view that racial discourse can be understood from a universalist perspective. Against traditional Marxist theories of race, in which race is always reduced to epiphenomena determined by economic relations,[2] Gilroy argues that the relation between race and class should be understood as a "complex syncretism." Gilroy's conception of syncretism is quite similar to Laclau and Mouffe's definition of articulation: race and class combine together in a mutually constitutive relation that produces a contextually specific hybrid formation that nevertheless retains genealogical traces and non-essentialist resemblances to contiguous formations. Like Hall, Gilroy advocates a historicizing approach to the study of racial solidarities (Gilroy 1987: 17, 27–38). He concludes that race is a "political category that can accommodate various meanings which are in turn determined by struggle" (Gilroy 1987: 38). With their meaning established only within particular syncretisms, racial signifiers are in themselves "elastic" and "empty"; they become signifiers only through "ideological work" (Gilroy 1987: 39). Unity across the complex differences that mark the trans-Atlantic African diaspora remains possible, but that unity must be constructed within specific strategic conditions: resistance against the racisms of slavery, colonialism and post-colonialism.

Shohat and Stam would concur; they point out that the very form of syncretistic hybridity is politically available for radically different articulations.

> As a descriptive catch-all term, "hybridity" fails to discriminate between the diverse modalities of hybridity: colonial imposition, obligatory assimilation, political cooptation, cultural mimicry and so forth. Elites have always made cooptive top-down raids on subaltern cultures, while the dominated have always "signified" and parodied as well as emulated elite practice. Hybridity, in other words, is power-laden and asymmetrical.
>
> (1994: 43)

For his part, Gilroy locates his discourse in opposition to both the ethnic absolutists and the post-modern relativists (1993: 31–2, 80–1, 99–103). White ethnic absolutists construct fantasies of a homogeneous and timeless Western identity that ignores both the hybridity that has always been a central characteristic of whiteness (Smith 1994b: 132) and the fictitious character of the attempts to Aryan-ize the origins of Western civilization in ancient Greece (Bernal 1987). Black ethnic absolutists question the "authenticity" of the black popular cultural projects that combine traditional African elements with Western influences or construct alternatives to the black heterosexist patriarchal family. For Gilroy, hybrid diasporic cultural formations are continually undergoing transformations as blacks in the present moment reinterpret the past to serve their current strategic needs and desires. Against the ethnic absolutists, he argues that hybrid cultural projects should not be dismissed out of hand. He demonstrates, for example, the ways in which complex appropriations from African, black Caribbean and African-American sources take place in black British popular culture (1993, 1987). Indeed, the very structure of the racisms to which Africans have been subjected has incited this continual syncretistic activity. Slave traders uprooted different African peoples and forced them to endure the horrors of the "middle passage" across the Atlantic. Their subsequent owners then separated the slaves that belonged to the same linguistic groups in order to frustrate the slaves' rebellion. Preservation of a black culture and a tradition of resistance in these conditions, then, was already a syncretistic operation. This sometimes involved not only the articulation of different African traditions, but also the integration of indigenous native American traditions as well.

While Gilroy recognizes the possibility of legitimate syncretisms, he opposes cultural theories that uncritically celebrate each and every form of appropriation. He argues that the latter approach has not always achieved an adequately critical stance, for it has been "insufficiently alive to the lingering power of specifically racialized forms of power and subordination" (1993: 32). Gilroy explicitly reserves, for example, the right to assess the work of contemporary black hip-hop artists on the basis of their gender politics and their positions *vis-à-vis* racial representations and commercialism (1993: 84–5). Instead of grounding his assessments on a fixed conception of racial authenticity, however, he consistently returns to contextual analyses that consider new racial syncretisms against the background of their structural conditions. A black cultural project, then, should not be regarded as a spontaneous construction that can be invented and reinvented according to a subject's every whim; it should be understood instead as the product of social practices and the "outcome of practical activity" (1993: 102). As we will see in the following chapters, Gilroy's critical stance is remarkably similar to the position of Laclau and Mouffe. Where Gilroy distances himself from both ethnic absolutism and post-modern voluntarism, Laclau and Mouffe deploy a non-essentialist and yet critical approach to difference.

The analogy between Saussurean signs and identities is therefore relevant for both sexual differences and racial differences, even though the latter are often regarded as ahistorical, natural and fixed. As long as identity formation is seen as the mere addition of already constituted individuals or as the addition of "natural" groups together in simple coalitions, the complexity of contemporary political practices will never be grasped. Political discourse does not merely reflect the interests that are already constituted at the structural level; the subject positions through which we live our structural positionings are wholly constructed through the differential relations within political discourses.

The hybridizing effect of articulation occurs throughout the social, between and among subject positions and social structures alike (Laclau 1977: 42). As we have seen in Chapter 1, for example, capitalist exploitative relations are always intertwined with other oppressive relations such as racism or sexism. A given economic structure might entail complex relationships between different sectors, such as a so-called "backward" peasant sector and a "modern" industrial sector. According to traditional Marxist theory, these sectors are organized in terms of distinct modes of production; qualitatively different property relations and class relations are supposed to obtain in each one. In some cases, however, the constitutive relations between these sectors play a prominent role. The industrial sector may depend on the peasant sector for the reproduction of the labor force at low costs. Perhaps the workers in the industrial factories can afford to work for the low wage offered by the capitalist because their families live on peasant plots and engage in subsistence farming. The peasant sector may depend on the industrial sector for the cash needed for input investment. The money for the seeds, fertilizer and insecticide used on the family plot may come from the wages that are earned by the family member working in the factory. In these cases, we have a formal distinction between the two sectors at the level of traditional Marxism's abstract theory, but at the level of the concrete formation, we have a complex relationship of interdependence between them. Where essentialist theory cannot grasp this sort of interdependence, the articulation metaphor brings the irreducible complexity of overdetermination to the fore.

Nodal points and subject positions

While Laclau and Mouffe's subversion of essentialism begins with their

97

appropriation of Saussurean linguistics, they introduce several important departures from this theoretical framework. First, Laclau and Mouffe recognize that although subject positions are constituted through their differential relations with each other, some of the differential relations between the subject positions have more force than others. A single subject position may, in a particular context, become privileged such that the meaning of other subject positions becomes increasingly defined through their relations with that position. Borrowing the Lacanian conception of the "point de capiton," Laclau and Mouffe call this privileged position a nodal point. The nodal point in a given formation increasingly acts as one of several discursive "centers" (Laclau and Mouffe 1985: 112). The nodal point tends to exercise a totalizing effect on contiguous positions such that they partially lose their floating character and "become parts of the structured network of meaning" (Žižek 1989: 87).

In essentialist theory, essence plays this totalizing role. Essentialist class theory, for example, defines social movements in terms of their structural class position. Nodal points differ from essences in many ways. No one can predict with exact certainty which subject position will become primary in any particular historical moment. If – to paraphrase Hall – racial subject positions offer "the modality in which class is 'lived' " in some contexts, in other contexts sexual subject positions may be the modality in which race is experienced, class-oriented subject positions may be the modality in which gender is experienced, gendered subject positions may be the modality in which national identity is experienced, and so on. Gilroy remarks, for example, that in contemporary Western nation-states, identifications with subject positions that are structured in terms of "nationality, ethnicity, authenticity and cultural integrity" are widely used as "a means to make political sense of the world," and that it is these identifications, rather than class-based ones, that are now ubiquitous (1993: 2). He further argues that racial discourse is now so thoroughly defined in terms of gender and sexuality that "gender is the modality in which race is lived" (1993: 85). In any event, the primacy of a specific nodal point is always temporary; the privileged status of one subject position could always be interrupted by new articulations. While some unusual discursive formations may tend to be organized around a single and relatively stable nodal point – such as a nationalist discourse that has achieved an unusual degree of predominance and stability – most will be organized around a complex constellation of multiple and shifting nodal points.

Laclau and Mouffe also depart from Saussurean linguistics in their conception of the construction of a formation's boundaries. Saussure, for example, takes the unity of a community of language users for granted. He simply assumes that a language-using community is a harmonious and naturally bound collective entity. He ignores power hierarchies within the community and he provides no account for the construction of the community's constitutive exclusions. Further, Saussure tends to consider a language at a given moment in time as a complete and closed system, and defines the relations that obtain in that moment between the signs as necessary relations. There is no moment in Saussure in which the Lacanian conception of the subject as a subject of lack is affirmed. For Laclau and Mouffe, by contrast, the social never takes the form of a complete system or a closed totality, identities are never completely constituted, every formation always remains vulnerable to subversive interruption, and the moment of final articulation is never obtained (Laclau 1990a: 90–1). This allows Laclau and Mouffe to insist, once again, on the contingency of articulation, and on the possibility of subversion even in the case of the most normalized articulations.

There is some degree of tension between Laclau and Mouffe's terminology and the implications of their theory. Although the term "position" itself suggests a fully defined space, Laclau and Mouffe argue that articulation can only produce partially fixed subject positions. Subject positions should be regarded as somewhat fluid processes rather than fixed interest groups (McClure 1992: 121). Again, concrete historical identities never fully correspond to the theoretical categories that we use to analyze structural positionings. A worker's experience of her position in the capitalist wage labor contract is mediated by the interpretative work that is performed by her identity, the ensemble of overdetermined subject positions through which she lives her structural positionings. In actual political relations, then, we never meet groups of people who are neatly divided up according to the theoretical categories that we use to discuss structural relations in our social theories. Actual workers have a much more complex principle of identity than is anticipated in traditional Marxist theory, for they are positioned at "points of intersection of a multiplicity of relations and contradictions articulated by class practices" (Laclau 1977: 11).

Laclau is quite close in this respect to Balibar who contends that

> there is no "ideal type" of classes (proletariat and bourgeoisie) but there are *processes* of proletarianization and embourgeoisement, each of which involves its own internal conflicts (which I shall, for my part, following Althusser, term the "overdetermination" of the antagonism): in this way we can see how the history of the capitalist *economy* depends on *political* struggles within the national and transnational space.
>
> (Balibar 1991c: 11)

McClure, citing the feminist theory of De Lauretis (1987), similarly argues that the logic of articulation implies that there are no actual political subjects which correspond to abstract structural categories. "No subject, in sum, is simply gendered; there are no 'women' *simpliciter*, already constituted as a bound political group with necessary common interests, already given as a political category" (McClure 1992: 122). The fact that we never actually encounter subjects that correspond to abstract structural categories does not, of course, imply that anyone can be anything they want to be. All workers interpret their exploitation through the framework constructed by an overdetermined ensemble of subject positions, such that their identities are formulated through the mediating effects of political discourses. This does not mean, however, that an individual worker can step outside her exploited structural positioning at will, for, as a propertyless worker in a capitalist society, her life chances have been shaped to a great extent in advance.

The return of essentialism in "anti-essentialist" socialist theories

Many apparently non-foundationalist theories actually become incoherent as they attempt to combine incompatible arguments together. Fuss argues that much of social constructionist theory commits this error. Constructionist discourses sometimes appear to escape essentialism through their insistence on the historically specific character of identity: "constructionists take the refusal of essence as the inaugural moment of their own projects and proceed to demonstrate the way previously assumed self-evident kinds (like 'man' or 'woman') are in fact the effects of complicated discursive practices" (1989: 2). Where essentialists interpret differences as the effects of a pre-discursive "nature," constructionists perform genealogical analyses that reveal the political relations that are concealed within that "nature."

Fuss contends, however, that constructionists "often work with uncomplicated or essentializing notions of history" (1989: 3). She points out that constructionists can often appear to accommodate plurality without really departing from the essentialist tradition. Constructionist feminist theorists, for example, may recognize that they should speak of plural groups of "women" rather than a singular universal category, "woman." They may nevertheless take for granted the primary relevance of sexist structures and gendered subject positions for all of these different women. All women, however, would only share the exactly same structural positioning if they were located in a social formation in which gender social structures were absolutely isolated from other social structures. This is never the case in actual history, for the sexisms that define our life chances are always overdetermined with other structures, such as capitalism, racism, homophobia and so on. White women and women of color, for example, are positioned differently insofar as sexisms are hybridized through their articulation with racism. Further, even if we were referring to some women who shared similar structural positionings within overdetermined formations, we would find that they interpreted their structural positionings through different subject positions. Given these conditions, it is never legitimate to presume that a solidarity among all women already exists in embryonic form and only needs to be brought to maturity through the invocation of universal women's interests.

Again, we can say that some subject positions are more progressive in a radical democratic pluralist sense than others, but we cannot say that one is more or less "authentic" than another. Workers should not be viewed as "embryonic revolutionaries" who possess an "authentic" interest in socialism; their solidarity with a socialist struggle has to be produced through organic and democratic political interventions. The same is true for the relation between women who occupy an oppressed structural position in sexist formations. In Gramscian terms, feminist movements have to "organize their consent"; they must offer feminist subject positions as compelling frameworks through which women's oppression can be lived. As many feminist leaders have already recognized, the successful pursuit of this goal requires close attention to the overdetermined character of sexism. The hybrid combination of sexist structures with other structures mean that some women are more privileged than other women; effective democratic feminist organizing fully recognizes that women who are positioned differently in terms of race, class and sexuality do not have the same access to material resources.

Fuss insists that what appears to be a challenge to essentialism in constructionist theory often amounts to a mere "displacement" of essentialist terminology while the underlying essentialist presuppositions are kept intact (1989: 4). Although Fuss's critique is useful in this respect, her argument can be enriched by integrating an analysis of power relations into her anti-foundationalism. After demonstrating the insufficient degree of pluralization in various feminist theories, it would be useful to examine the strategic conditions in which women's movements have in fact constructed compelling feminist subject positions and have actually made progressive feminist solidarities meaningful for many different women.

Following Fuss, we should consider theories that appear to mark a significant departure from essentialism, but actually reintroduce essentialism. Some Marxist theorists, such as Hall in his earlier work, argue that the clearest calls for close attention to historical specificity, and some of the strongest warnings against the imposition of universal theoretical rules – that which social science calls "methodology" – on empirical cases, can be found in the work of Marx himself.

Hall cites a passage in *Capital*, Vol. III, in which Marx discusses the different ways in which surplus labor is extracted in various political formations, including the peasant society, the slave-based or plantation-based economies, and the "Asian" formation in which the state operates as both landowner and sovereign.[3]

> The specific economic form in which unpaid surplus labour is pumped out of the direct producers determines the relationship of domination and servitude, as this grows directly out of production itself and reacts back on it in turn as a determinant. On this is based the entire configuration of the economic community arising from the actual relations of production, and hence also its specific political form. It is in each case the direct relationship of the owners of the conditions of production to the immediate producers – a relationship whose particular form naturally corresponds always to a certain level of development of the type and manner of labour, and hence to its social productive power – in which we find the innermost secret, the hidden basis of the entire social edifice, and hence also the political form of the relationship of sovereignty and dependence, in short, the specific form of the state in each case.
>
> (Marx 1981: 927)

101

Marx allows for some degree of reciprocal determination – the relationship between the rulers and ruled does react back on the economic sphere – but the determining effects of the political on the economic are always secondary to the primary effects of the economic on the political. In this moment, Marx reproduces the determinist closures that can be found in his *Preface to a Contribution to the Critique of Political Economy* (1969a). For Hall, the "materialist premise" expressed by Marx in this passage is that political formations are "grounded in their material conditions of existence" (Hall 1980: 322).

This "materialist premise" in Marx's discourse is complemented by a second premise, namely the "historical premise." Hall notes that Marx continues this passage by immediately qualifying his remarks.

> This does not prevent the same economic basis – the same in its major conditions – from displaying endless variations and gradations in its appearance, as the result of innumerable different empirical circumstances, natural conditions, racial relations, historical influences acting from the outside, etc., and these can only be understood by analyzing these empirically given conditions.
>
> (Marx 1981: 927–8)

According to this second premise, the simple imposition of an abstract model upon a specific empirical situation is illegitimate. Commenting on another passage in *Capital*, Hall argues that the "specific forms of [political and ideological structures] cannot be deduced, *a priori*, from this [economic] level but must be made historically specific 'by supplying those further delineations which explain their *differentiae sp[ecificae]*' " (Hall 1980: 322).

In this early text, Hall contends that empirical research ought to be guided by both premises. In a more recent work, he adopts a post-Marxist view and rejects the conception that the political is determined by the economic base (Hall 1988a, 1990). For my purposes here, however, it should be noted that the conception of "difference" in the passages cited above is entirely compatible with essentialist closures. Retaining the logic of the materialist premise within his "historical premise," Marx reduces differences to "variations and gradations" in the "appearance" of economic formations whose "main conditions" remain basically "the same." Marx's call for attention to difference is, in these passages at least, a very weak one that is already subordinated to economic reductionism in the very moment of its articulation. For Laclau and Mouffe, economistic reductionism is highly problematic because it assumes that the economic is a self-regulating sphere that determines the rest of the social. Economic reductionists may admit that the political influences the economic, but they would only say that the political does this after it was determined by the economic in the first place.

Laclau and Mouffe find traces of economism in some of the most promising Marxist theories. After underlining the tremendous democratic potential in

Gramsci's theory of hegemony, for example, they point to his return to class reductionism.

> For Gramsci, even though the diverse social elements have a merely relational identity – achieved through articulatory practices – there must always be a *single* unifying principle in every hegemonic formation, and this can only be a fundamental class.
>
> (Laclau and Mouffe 1985: 67)

In other words, for all his emphases on the contingency of political struggles, Gramsci attempts to preserve Marx's idea that identity will ultimately have a class principle. For all his sophistication, Gramsci ultimately thinks of politics in terms of a binary struggle between two "natural" subjects: the proletariat and the bourgeoisie.

Althusser's discourse also juxtaposes anti-essentialism with essentialism. Laclau and Mouffe regard Althusser's theory of overdetermination as an extremely useful analogy for the conceptualization of identity. The theory of overdetermination suggests that identity is constructed exclusively on a symbolic terrain; like Saussure's rejection of a referential theory of meaning, overdetermination implies that there is no underlying plane of literal meanings that imposes an external necessity upon the constitutive relations within the symbolic order (Laclau and Mouffe 1985: 97–8; Žižek 1994: 52; Laclau 1977: 51–80). Althusser nevertheless restricts the anti-essentialist possibilities that are inherent in this theory with his insistence that the political is determined in the last instance by the economic (1971). For Laclau and Mouffe, the Althusserian conception of the "relative autonomy" of the political does not in the end offer a decisive alternative to theories of strict determination.

On voluntarism and relativism

A rigorous theory of the relation between the political and the economic cannot have it both ways. It must either hold that the political is structured in terms of the logic of necessity or that the political is structured in terms of the logic of contingency. With the logic of necessity, we can anticipate the fundamental character of social structures according to laws that are supposed to hold true for each and every case. Future determinations are necessary, for they are nothing but the unfolding of the potential that exists in the present. According to this approach, once the theorist has correctly grasped the nature of the present, she is supposed to be able to predict future configurations with perfect accuracy.

With the logic of contingency, by contrast, we cannot do so. This is not to say that once we theorize politics in terms of the logic of contingency we arrive at a voluntaristic position, namely that the social is so utterly devoid of all structures that all outcomes are equally probable and history becomes the product of individual wills, or a relativist position, namely that all outcomes are equally valid.

A theory that rejects the logic of necessity would only arrive at a voluntarist and relativist position if and only if it were perfectly ahistorical as well.

> It is always possible to distinguish between the just and the unjust, the legitimate and the illegitimate, but this can only be done from within a given tradition, with the help of standards that this tradition provides; in fact, there is no point of view external to all tradition from which one can offer a universal judgement.
>
> (Mouffe 1993b: 15)

Again, for Laclau and Mouffe, the democratic tradition has been one of the most important ethical horizons in modern society. The principles of equality and liberty are deeply embedded in our social institutions (Mouffe 1993b: 35). The democratic tradition is by definition an open-ended one in which contestation about the very meaning of key terms is inevitable. Slavery and the official exclusion of women have been considered perfectly compatible with the meaning of "democracy" at different points in time. We now generally accept that these elements are incompatible with "democracy," but we do so only because contingent political struggles gained substantial strategic ground and institutionalized their values such that they became integrated into the taken-for-granted background knowledge that structures the democratic tradition. Some of us would also like to normalize the idea that capitalist exploitation and contemporary forms of racism and sexism are incompatible with "democracy"; to do so, we will have to engage in further struggles to redefine the democratic tradition's horizon. In any event, terms such as "democracy," "liberty" and "equality" will never become purely empty, or wholly available for new articulations, because they will always bear the traces of past articulations.

In this sense, we could only arrive at a truly voluntarist and relativist theory if we supplemented our basic assumption that nothing outside the discursive determines articulations with the further assumption that all of the articulations, identity formations, social structures and political struggles from the past have absolutely no influence whatsoever on articulations, identities, structures and struggles in the present. All outcomes would in fact be equally probable and equally legitimate, since every moment in time would be like a perfectly blank slate. In this case, we would be not only unable to predict with exact certainty which subject positions would prevail as nodal points, we would be utterly unable to say anything about the probable forms of identity formation and the underlying social structures as well. History would then appear to take a perfectly voluntarist form as the product of individual wills that seek their atomistic ends without encountering any structural limits. We would also be unable to give any coherent explanation for our preference for one future outcome as opposed to others.

Laclau and Mouffe cannot be rightly charged with voluntarism, for they understand the subject as the subject of a "lack," rather than a fully self-conscious actor who is capable of standing back from her historical embeddedness, assessing her situation with total clarity, and then instrumentally choosing between alternatives according to her given set of preferences. Further, they certainly do not treat the present moment like a blank slate in which all outcomes are equally probable. They fully retain the radical, anti-individualist conception that every individual's life chances are profoundly shaped by the ways in which she is thrown into structural positions that are never wholly of her choosing. To say that subject positions are not directly determined by structural positions but are constructed through political struggle by mediating political discourses is not to deny the materiality of social structures. Laclau carefully distinguishes between the infinite set of logical possibilities and the limited set of historical opportunities.

> [The] internal ambiguities of the relation of representation, the undecidability between the various movements that are possible within it, transform [the relation of representation] into the hegemonic battlefield between a plurality of possible decisions. This does not mean that at any time everything that is logically possible becomes automatically an actual political possibility. There are inchoate possibilities which are going to be blocked, not because of any logical restriction, but as a result of the historical contexts in which the representative institutions operate.
>
> (1996c: 50)

The idea that an individual can choose freely to transcend her structural positionings is nothing less than absurd when considered in the light of the everyday experiences of oppressed peoples. In the introduction to her critical analyses of slavery's brutal interruption of African kinship relations, and of the 1965 Moynihan Report's demonization of African-American women's power, Spillers writes,

> Let's face it. I am a marked woman, but not everybody knows my name. "Peaches" and "Brown Sugar," "Sapphire" and "Earth Mother," "Aunty," "Granny," God's "Holy Fool," a "Miss Ebony First," or "Black Woman at the Podium": I describe a locus of confounded identities, a meeting ground of investments and privations in the national treasury of rhetorical wealth. My country needs me, and if I were not here, I would have to be invented.
>
> (1987: 65)

Similarly, Eisenstein cites the case of Pamela Obron, a black woman contractor. Obron describes the various obstacles that she encountered in her attempt to establish her own construction company: " 'The white men look at you and see a black. The black men look at you and see a woman.' " Eisenstein remarks, "Of course, she is both. White men deny her womanhood while distancing her as black; black men deny her their similarity of race while distancing her as a woman" (Eisenstein 1994: 216).

Laclau and Mouffe also do not argue that just any subject position may become a nodal point through which other subject positions tend to be defined. They hold that every articulation is performed upon subject positions that are partially floating and yet already marked by traces of past articulations, and that articulations become more influential insofar as they are institutionalized and integrated into the social formation's very horizon. Using this principle, for example, we could say that the prevailing racist interpretations of post-industrial economic dislocation do not come out of nowhere. Effective racist demonizations work on a historical terrain that has been already prepared for them. They draw, for example, on similar and already normalized interpretative frameworks, such as other racisms; post-imperial narcissism, megalomania and paranoia; xenophobia and jingoistic nationalism; anti-Semitism and so on. A novel racism advances insofar as it exploits the opportunities that have been created by the integration of similar discourses in economic, political, social and cultural institutions. In Gramsci's terms, to be effective, an ideology must be organic: it must resonate with "popular" traditions.

What Laclau and Mouffe insist is that all traditions are open to new articulations, or what Gilroy would call syncretisms, and that the structured innovations that can be introduced within a tradition can be so unusual that they cannot be predicted with exact certainty. By embracing the logic of contingency, Laclau and Mouffe only abandon positivist prediction and theoretical meta-narratives; they certainly do not abandon the critical practices of analyzing asymmetrical social structures and tracing traditions, institutionalizations and genealogies altogether. Their theory of hegemony can in fact be used to detect the social structures that, in spite of their incomplete nature, do indeed create specific limits for political practice. From their perspective, we can use contextually-sensitive genealogical studies to suggest that in a specific moment, some forms of identity formation will – thanks to their family resemblances with already institutionalized identities – probably offer more compelling interpretative frameworks than others.

Where some individuals do believe that "each individual is responsible for her own success or failure," or that "anyone can succeed if they try hard enough," these opinions are largely the effect of power relations. Some individuals may indeed act as if they operated on a terrain in which individual will is sovereign; as if anything were possible. This does not, however, prove that an individualist and voluntarist interpretation of history is correct; it only demonstrates the extent to which hegemonic formations can covertly naturalize a specific range of possibilities, such that this limited set of structured outcomes begins to pass itself off as an infinite number of freely chosen results.

> For discourse to materialize a set of *effects*, "discourse" itself must be understood as complex and convergent chains in which "effects" are vectors of power. In this sense, what is constituted in discourse is not fixed in or by discourse, but becomes the condition and occasion for a further action. This does not mean that *any* action is possible on the basis of a discursive effect. On the contrary, certain reiterative chains of

discursive production are barely legible as reiterations, for the effects they have materialized are those without which no bearing in discourse can be taken. The power of discourse to materialize its effects is thus consonant with the power of discourse to circumscribe the domain of intelligibility.

(Butler 1993: 187)

This is, of course, often the case with neo-conservative pro-free-market discourse, for the latter always tries to pass off the limited range of life chances for each individual – especially for exploited individuals – under capitalism as the very expression of human freedom. As neo-conservative discourse is reiterated in multiple cultural sites and its horizon of intelligibility is exercised more and more effectively throughout the social, the narrow range of differences that are possible under capitalism will increasingly appear to exhaust the totality of possible outcomes.

As for relativism, Laclau and Mouffe do not hold that we can ever occupy a space in which all arguments would be equally valid. Coles contends that the ethical argument for democratic engagement with others "as others" – an engagement that would rule out totalitarian assimilation and disintegrationist separatism – is "painfully lacking" in Laclau and Mouffe's work (1996: 380). In this respect, it is crucial that the authors' attention to historicity is brought to the fore. If the present moment were a blank slate such that all normative commitments would always have to be reconstructed from scratch, then we would have no grounds for arguing that one position is better than another. For Laclau and Mouffe, the enduring character of traditions of oppression and resistance means that political wisdom is in fact handed down through time across generations of democratic activists.

Why prefer one future over another? Why choose between different types of society? There can be no reply if the question is asking for a kind of Cartesian certainty that pre-exists any belief. But if the agent who must choose is someone who *already* has certain beliefs and values, then criteria for choice – with all the intrinsic ambiguities that a choice involves – can be formulated.

(Laclau 1990a: 83)

As Gilroy insists, traditions are marked by syncretistic appropriations and various discontinuities, but the preservation of a "changing same" – what Derrida (1988) would call iteration – that makes the construction of solidarities across difference, time and space possible is inevitable.

The work of transmitting political wisdom over time – even as it shifts in meaning with every contextually-specific citation – is carried out through subject position formation; it is through the latter that traces of past political discourses are preserved and "regulated improvisations" become possible. Hall makes precisely this point as he refers to the American civil rights movement.

Could one imagine the civil rights struggle of the sixties without the long traditions of black struggle that historically go back at least as far as the beginning of slavery? And yet, is there anybody here who wouldn't want to describe the civil rights movement as a movement that produced new black subjects? But new black subjects – now, what is that "new" then in the light of the tradition? Would it have happened without the tradition? Absolutely not. Where would traditions of struggle, where would the accumulated knowledge, where would the expectivity of human values that kept people going in dark days, where would that have come from if there hadn't been languages and historical traditions of one kind or another that sustained them across times? That sustained human beings in their lives of struggle across time – and yet the particular way that black people occupied that identity, lived that identity, and struggled around it, produced something which had never been seen before.

(1997: 293)

Some aspects of liberal feminist discourse, to take another example, are now thoroughly normalized. We cannot find a significant political bloc today in a liberal democratic regime that would claim that it is impossible to decide whether or not women should have the vote. The principle of suffrage rights for women has been normalized to such a degree that it has become embedded deep within a wide range of subject positions through which gender is interpreted. In liberal democratic regimes, feminists and anti-feminists alike generally take this principle for granted. Other aspects of feminist discourse, such as the conception that all women have the right to control their own bodies and therefore ought to have access to contraception, abortion and the choice to conceive, are more controversial; these feminist elements are not as widely integrated into the subject positions through which gender is lived. As Daly contends, the opposition between the antagonistic discourses on AIDS (is it a non-moral virus or divine retribution for sin?) and on abortion (is it a woman's reproductive right or murder?) cannot be resolved with reference to utterly neutral facts. When we take a position on these issues, we are necessarily making a value judgment (Daly 1994: 179).

Further, we can and in fact do arrive at temporary solutions to impossible conflicts between competing value claims by citing political traditions. And we select some traditions rather than others insofar as we have found – consciously and unconsciously – that they can offer identifications that are compelling and effective enough in our current predicament. As Hall points out, this process always takes place in a strategic and antagonistic context. "Identification means that you are called in a certain way, interpellated in a certain way: 'you, this time, in this space, for this purpose, by this barricade with these folks'" (1997: 292). In our citations, we redeploy the moral judgments that are constitutive of those traditions, even as we introduce a small degree of innovation in their meaning.

Again, this does not mean that convention fully determines our moral judgment, for each political horizon has to be interpreted with respect to new problems, and, as the context of each application of the horizon shifts with each new case, the possibility of a somewhat novel redefinition of the horizon emerges. To the extent that we identify with a single political tradition, it tends to dispose us towards a certain range of judgments, but it never resolves our moral dilemmas for us in advance. Obviously, the situation becomes even more complex as we identify with an overdetermined ensemble of political traditions.

At a more "micro-social" level, our interpretations of terms such as "justice" or "equality" within the democratic tradition take on greater specificity and refinement as we are located within specific roles in different social spheres. We have, for example, standards for determining whether a parent is competent in the sense that he or she respects the rights of his or her children; we would use somewhat different standards to assess the human rights competency of a police officer or a prison guard. Because we are always already positioned within specific social roles that are shaped by conventional standards, and because those standards are shaped in turn by a more or less shared political horizon, we never occupy an "originary position" in which we are utterly incapable of making judgments.

> Since those who are embedded in local practices – of literary criticism, law, education, or anything else – are "naturally" heirs of the norms and standards built into those practices, they can never be without (in two senses) norms and standards and are thus always acting in value-laden and judgmental ways simply by being competent actors in their workplaces. The post-structuralist characterization of the normative as a local rather than a transcendental realm, far from rendering ethical judgment impossible, renders it inevitable and inescapable. Antifoundationalist thought, properly understood, is not an assault on ethics but an account of the conditions – textual and revisable, to be sure – within which moments of ethical choice are always and *genuinely* emerging; it is only if ethical norms existed *elsewhere* that there would be a chance of missing them, but if they are always and already where you are they cannot be avoided.
>
> (Fish 1994: 39)

We never arrive at a moment in which every choice has equal value for us, for the subject positions through which we grasp our choices always bear traces of past political struggles within them. A theory of normative decision-making is therefore not only compatible with Laclau and Mouffe's conception of the contingency of articulation, it is integral to that formulation.

The critique of economism

To return to Laclau and Mouffe's critique of economism, they insist that the logic of contingency is incompatible with the logic of necessity. A theory such as Althusser's that is supposed to combine "relative contingency" with an "ultimate necessity" simply reproduces the logic of necessity in a new guise.

> If the economy is an object which can determine any type of society in the last instance, this means that, at least with reference to that instance, we are faced with a simple determination and not overdetermination. If society has a last instance which determines its laws of motion, then *the relations between the overdetermined instances and the last instance must be conceived in terms of simple, one-directional determination by the latter.*
>
> (Laclau and Mouffe 1985: 99, original emphasis)

Laclau and Mouffe conclude that the economic can only determine the rest of the social if it satisfies three conditions. First, there can be no political subject which is not defined in terms of its location in the class struggle, and each class must be constructed exclusively at the level of the economic structure. Classes may appear to be superficially differentiated due to the effects of political relations, but these effects must remain secondary and accidental. Second, each class must possess "objective interests" that follow directly from that class's structural position in the relations of production. Third, the economic must be a sphere that is prior to the political. The political may affect the economic, but only after the economic has determined the political.

The authors demonstrate that these first two conditions are theoretically and politically impossible. With the development of contemporary forms of capitalist accumulation and the proliferation of multiple political antagonisms, the social will never become polarized into two great, all-encompassing classes. The condensation of all political interests into class interests will never take place. As we noted in Chapter 1, Marx and Engels proposed that capitalist development would cancel out the differences between different workers (Marx and Engels 1969: 109–19, 121). Marx himself abandoned the polarization thesis; he stated in his *Theories of Surplus Value* that the bifurcation of the social into two great classes was not going to unfold (Harrington 1993: 21). Capitalist development through the nineteenth and twentieth centuries has actually exacerbated and even invented intra-class differences based on skill, employment sector, union status, employment status, race, gender, nationality and citizenship (Laclau and Mouffe 1985: 81–2).

Given the complex segmentation, fragmentation and – in some cases – disintegration of the working class, the assignment of a single set of objective interests to all workers has become an increasingly abstract exercise. Again, every social structure is overdetermined, and there is no necessary linkage between an individual's structural position in the relations of production and the subject position through which she lives in and reacts to her structural positioning. Cross-class solidarities based on nationally-, racially-, ethnically-, gender- and sexually-constructed subject positions are so common, and make so much sense in light of the complex nature of contemporary politics, that very few contemporary theorists continue to dismiss them as exceptions and distortions. Laclau and Mouffe state that "in order to advance in the determination of social antagonisms, it is necessary to analyze the plurality of diverse and frequently contradictory positions, and to discard the idea of a perfectly unified and homogeneous agent, such as the 'working class' of classical discourse" (Laclau and Mouffe 1985: 84).

The third condition that must be satisfied if the economic is to have a determining effect on the social involves the primary character of this sphere. In the originary moment of the formation of the economic, the effects of political relations must be wholly absent. Citing Hume, Clegg states,

> A genuinely causal relation will only hold between things or events which are entirely discrete or separate from one another in space and time but which share a contingent or contiguous relationship. Effects must be distinct from causes: they cannot be at all implicated as the same phenomenon but must be rigorously separate in actuality, in conceptual distinction and in logical relation.
>
> (1989: 41)

The theory of economic determination therefore cannot be valid unless that which is determined – the political – is entirely distinct from the determining sphere – the economic – in its originary moments.

When we study actual historical formations, however, we are confronted with complex formations in which political and economic relations have always been inextricable. Laclau quotes Balibar's argument that the imposition of universal categories such as "the economic," "the legal" and "the political" onto historical research about different modes of production is highly problematic. Abstract theoretical categories such as "the economic," "the juridical" or "the political" do not correspond neatly to the actual spaces that are meaningful for us within social formations (Laclau 1977: 78). A theory of determination must illegitimately suppress the complexity, specificity and interdependence that obtains in actual political-economic relations. In Laclau and Mouffe's terms, economic determinist theory holds that "[the] laws of motion [of the economic] must be strictly endogenous and exclude all indeterminacy resulting from political or other external interventions – otherwise, the constitutive function could not refer exclusively to the economy" (Laclau and Mouffe 1985: 76). The authors contend that any theory that attempts merely to minimize the relative influence of the economic on the political cannot avoid the problem of economic reductionism – the reduction of extra-economic phenomena to mere effects of economic relations.

Paggi, quoting de Felice, asserts that "the starting point of Gramsci's thought is the rediscovery of the economic sphere 'not only as the production of goods, but also of social relations' " (1979: 123). How exactly should this relation of interdependence between the economic and the "superstructural" social, political and cultural relations – an interdependence that obtains in the economic's originary moment –

be specified? Even the most reductionist Marxist theory already acknowledges that the political affects the economic, for political ideologies contribute to the reproduction and legitimation of economic relations (Mepham 1979).

If we can find a necessary interdependence between the economic and the political in the very originary moment of economic formation, then it is no longer possible to describe the relation between these moments as one of determination. Further, the entire image of a clear boundary between the economic and the political will have to be rejected as a problematic metaphor. Our attention, then, should be drawn towards the temporal and spatial aspects of the determination claim: can economic relations be established in a purely non-political space in the first instance, and does the interpenetration of the economic and the political across the boundary that is supposed to divide the two spheres really take place only after the moment of determination? If so, then the essentialist theory of economism would be valid. If, on the other hand, political relations are necessarily intertwined with economic relations in the latter's origin, then the relation of determination becomes impossible. In this case, the political would operate like a Derridean supplement (Derrida 1973: 88–104; 1976: 141–64; Gasché 1986: 205–12; Staten 1984: 111–60); the political would be constitutive of the economic.

At the heart of this problem lies the nature of the "productive forces": the means of production and labor power. Again, Marxist theory holds that a class is supposed to be defined exclusively in terms of its relationship to the means of production. In a capitalist formation, the capitalist owns the means of production, while the worker merely owns her own labor power. Although the worker is a "free" participant in the labor contract, she is obliged to sell her labor power to a capitalist, according to the capitalist's exploitative terms, in order to survive. The economic property relations that establish who owns the means of production and who does not own capital and is therefore obliged to sell her labor power are called the relations of production.

From a Marxist perspective, the prevailing form of the relations of production is never accidental; it "corresponds" to the development of the productive forces. As Marx writes in his *Preface to a Contribution to the Critique of Political Economy*,

> In the social production of their life men enter into definite relations that are indispensable and independent of their will, relations of production which correspond to a definite state of development of their material productive forces. The sum total of these relations of production constitutes the economic structure, the real basis on which rises a legal and political superstructure and to which correspond definite forms of social consciousness.
>
> (Marx 1969a: 503)

For Marx, the contradiction between the productive forces and the relations of production is so central to the development of the social formation as a whole that it operates as the "motor of history."

112

> At a certain stage of their development, the material productive forces
> of society come into conflict with the existing relations of production. . . .
> From forms of development of the productive forces these relations turn
> into their fetters. Then begins an epoch of social revolution. With the
> change of the economic foundation the entire immense superstructure is
> more or less rapidly transformed.
>
> (Marx 1969a: 503–4)

This passage in Marx's *Preface* has been interpreted in many different ways by
Marxist scholars. Harris outlines what he describes as the "most straightforward"
interpretation. Within a given mode of production, such as feudalism or capitalism, there is a correspondence between the forces of production and the
relations of production, and, in turn, a correspondence between the relations of
production and the legal, socio-political and ideological superstructure. This
correspondence is guaranteed by the primary status of the productive forces. The
development of the productive forces – innovations in the production process,
the utilization of new technologies and energy sources, the education of the
workers, and so on – is supposed to be the absolute origin of change for the entire
social formation. This development of the productive forces is supposed to be
purely non-political in nature; as I will point out below, this is a crucial aspect of
Marx's argument. "The development of the forces of production *leads to* a contradiction between them and the relations of production . . . and the intensification
of this contradiction *leads to* the breakdown of the existing mode of production
and its superstructure" (Harris 1983: 179). Cohen agrees that Marx believed that
the productive forces were primary, and further argues that the productive forces
actually remain primary to this day in determining the actual course of human
history (Cohen 1978).[4]

Laclau and Mouffe take an entirely different approach. First, they question the
logic of Marx's argument based on his own conceptualization of the productive
forces. Second, they consider whether the development of the productive forces
does actually obey an endogenous set of laws. The key point here is that the productive forces include both the means of production and labor power. Labor power is a
peculiar commodity in two senses: it produces more value as its own use-value is
being consumed, and it does not passively yield its use-value to the person who
purchases it. If the capitalist purchases a piece of machinery, she may have to go to
great lengths to make that commodity yield its use-value. In the case of her
purchase of a unit of labor power, however, she has to deal with the fact that the
labor unit remains attached to a social agent who has the capacity to perform
political acts of resistance. There is, in short, a huge qualitative difference between
attempting to extract use-value out of a machine, and attempting to extract use-
value in the form of a labor unit from a worker who has the capacity to engage in an
entire range of complex practices. In organizing the productive process, the capitalist has to anticipate the workers' potential for political resistance.

According to the primacy of the productive forces thesis in Marxist theory, the productive forces become more and more efficient in a purely non-political, technical, and "spontaneously progressive" manner. Historically, however, the capitalist effort to extract use-value from labor has necessarily introduced a political aspect into the heart of the production process. The development of production technologies has always been deeply intertwined with the development of social control technologies. In some contexts, production technologies that divide up workers according to different specializations or replace workers through automation have not been driven by economic considerations alone, for they have also been deployed to block the workers' attempts to organize collectively and to engage in industrial action. Indeed, workers are sometimes segregated according to race, gender, nationality or religion in order to promote a "divide and rule" discipline, and production processes are shaped accordingly. At various moments, workers' resistances have brought about entire shifts in the application of new technologies and in regimes of capitalist accumulation. The "post-Fordist" trend towards the decentralization of production, for example, has been pursued not only to improve the sensitivity of the production process to various shifts in demand, but also to break up organized masses of workers. The capitalists' anticipation of workers' resistance is so thoroughly integrated into production planning that the very conception of "efficient" technology always includes a disciplining dimension (Laclau and Mouffe 1985: 78–80).

Where, according to Marxist theory, we are supposed to have a purely non-political development of economic efficiency and technical progress at the level of the productive forces, we have instead a "politics of production." In this sense, the political is necessarily interwoven into the economic at its very founding moment; the political is a constitutive supplement, rather than a determined effect, of the economic. That which is supposed to be in the determined "outside" superstructural sphere, namely political struggle, can be found at the heart of the supposedly determining "inside" sphere, the development of the productive forces in the economic base. Given the necessarily inextricable relation between the economic and the political in the very origins of the productive forces, the economic cannot satisfy the condition of originary autonomy.

Unlike many other critics of economism, Laclau and Mouffe do not undermine the primacy of the productive forces thesis in order to make way for yet another autonomy thesis, namely the argument that economic relations and class antagonisms have virtually no effect on the political sphere and the state. As Balibar points out, the latter argument merely reintroduces the liberal dualisms, state/civil society and politics/economics (Balibar 1991c: 3). Marx's critique of these dualisms constitutes one of the most important contributions from the Marxist tradition for radical democratic pluralism; that critique is preserved in Laclau and Mouffe's deconstruction of economism.

Laclau and Mouffe's theory also does not completely reject class analysis and economic theory altogether. Radical democratic pluralist theory cannot abandon the Marxist critique of capitalist exploitation precisely because capitalist relations, in all their hybrid forms, continue to block the genuine democratization of contemporary societies. Instead of discarding the Marxist critique of capitalism, Laclau and Mouffe are calling for the decentering of class, and for the recognition of the fact that the economic never exists as an autonomous and self-regulating sphere. In some cases, solidarities based primarily on class-oriented subject positions may indeed operate like a nodal point, as precarious micro-centers within a social formation. Even in those cases, however, their predominance would be partial and temporary, structural relations of class exploitation would remain articulated with other structures, and the subject positions through which exploitation is lived would be overdetermined as well.

4

SELF-DETERMINATION, COMMUNITY AND CITIZENSHIP

The debate between the liberals and communitarians has waxed and waned over the last few years. Some theorists such as Rawls and Sandel have changed their positions somewhat in response to their critics, while others such as Walzer, Young and Kymlicka have attempted to offer a fresh perspective. The questions that have been raised in the course of this debate concerning the relations between the individual and her communities, the dominant group and minority groups, and traditionalists and dissenters, remain central concerns. I will argue that Laclau and Mouffe's position does not fit into either the liberal or communitarian camp. While it is true that their intervention is fashioned out of concepts that are borrowed from both the liberals and communitarians, Laclau and Mouffe's theory of radical democratic pluralism breaks new ground.

Self-determination and community: the liberals and the communitarians

Rawls' liberal theory is best understood as a response to utilitarianism. Utilitarians hold that justice consists in that which produces the greatest aggregate happiness among the individual members of society. For liberals, utilitarianism is problematic because it reduces society to the mere sum of individual utilities. Like Kant, they contend that empirical principles, such as utilitarianism's measurement of utility, are not fit to serve as the basis of moral law. Utilitarianism does not recognize that the individual is a rational choosing self who is always prior to the ends that she pursues at a given moment. Human freedom depends on the individual's ability to stand back from her impulses and reassess her true ends through rational deliberation. The individual must therefore be seen as an independent, autonomous and rational rights-bearing subject, rather than the sum total of her fleeting desires. Utilitarianism's agnostic approach to ends goes too far for the Kantian liberals, for it makes no distinction between those routes to aggregate happiness that respect human rights and those that do not. The majority's domination of a minority could be considered the best course of action if it produced enough pleasure for the majority.

As a Kantian liberal, Rawls prioritizes individual rights and freedoms.

Individuals must be respected as ends in themselves; they must never be sacrificed to the whims of the powerful. For Rawls, the best way to secure this fundamental respect is to privilege individual rights over all other principles, including that of the common good. His basic argument is that it is only from a position that is neutral with respect to the common good that the primacy of individual rights can be preserved. The citizen, from Rawls' perspective, is a rights-bearing individual who pursues her own self-interest within a minimal set of limits. Rawls strikes a balance between the protection of individual rights and egalitarianism by removing only those inequalities that disadvantage the least favored. The "social primary goods" – liberty, opportunity, income, wealth and the bases of self-respect – are to be distributed equally, or only unequally insofar as that inequality benefits the least advantaged. Individual rights cannot be sacrificed for the common good, nor can they be constructed on the basis of any substantial good. The individual cannot be obliged to perform public service, for such an obligation would illegitimately interfere with her personal liberty (Rawls 1971; Sandel 1984; Kymlicka 1990).

Invoking Aristotle's conception of citizenship and Hegel's critique of Kant, the communitarians question the liberals' individualism and their prioritization of individual rights over the common good. The communitarians argue that we cannot perceive our status as political persons without referring to our role as citizens and participants in the life of a political community, and that we cannot justify political frameworks without some reference to common goods and ends (Sandel 1984: 5). Because the self is at least partly constituted by the individual's bonds with others, these relations cannot be treated as instrumental means to an individualistic end. Every identity is developed through dialogical relations between the individual or social group and its communal others (Taylor 1992: 31–2). Further, some of these bonds take the form of allegiances and obligations that are inherited by virtue of the ways in which the individual is positioned *vis-à-vis* her community's traditions. Socio-political relations therefore cannot be treated as if they were freely chosen in a voluntaristic manner. Further, the assertion that each individual's network of social bonds is constitutive of identity should be understood in both an ontological and moral sense. Allegiances and obligations are implicit in our social bonds; we construct moral horizons out of these principles (Sandel 1982: 150). These horizons never dictate a specific outcome or demand perfect obedience, but they nevertheless create basic reference points from which the individual navigates her way through moral problems.

The communitarians do of course agree with the Kantian liberals insofar as the latter attack utilitarianism's characterization of the individual as the mere sum of her desires. For the communitarians, however, the Kantian liberals' critique of utilitarianism results in the illegitimate detachment of the individual from her political community. From the communitarians' perspective, it makes no sense to speak of the rational deliberations of an isolated individual, for the individual and her goods are shaped by the roles that she plays in a specific community, and the goods that are valued in her specific community are shaped in turn by the latter's particular moral tradition (Sandel 1984: 5–6; MacIntyre 1981). The self is not atomistic but a situated communal self whose ends are always shaped by communal allegiances, obligations, traditions and values. Where Kantian liberals construct philosophical worlds of universal maxims, in which the individual is stripped of her socially-acquired moral compass, the communitarians dismiss those worlds as ideal spaces that do not help us to understand actual historical conditions. Rawls' stripped self in the original position becomes, for the communitarians, a non-self.

The communitarians insist that there would be no contradiction between individual liberty and the obligations of the citizen in an ideal state. The individual only realizes her self-determination insofar as she participates fully in deliberation about the public good. This implies, in turn, that the best regime cannot be neutral with respect to values. Given that good deliberation requires an individual who has developed civic virtues, such as recognition of the importance of public service and respect for the rights of others, then the best polity would be one in which individuals were encouraged to cultivate these virtues. The neutral regime favored by the Kantian liberals cannot safeguard individuals' genuine freedom precisely because "it cannot sustain the kind of political community and civic engagement that liberty requires" (Sandel 1996: 24).

For the communitarians, each member of a community is always morally oriented with respect to communal traditions. As a member of a household, a movement, a community or a nation at a specific historical moment, one is always more or less positioned within their respective narratives. Every individual is in this sense a bearer of a tradition: she inherits a set of communally- and historically-determined debts, obligations, rights and privileges. If, for example, the individual is placed in the role of the citizen, then her good must consist, at least in part, in the good that is proper to a citizen. If, furthermore, citizenship in her nation-state has been historically won through the violation of the rights of others, then she inherits not only a set of citizenship rights, but also an obligation to the peoples who have suffered that violation (MacIntyre 1981; Sandel 1982: 150; 1984: 6). An individual may owe special responsibilities to "members of those communities with which [her] own community has some morally relevant history, such as the morally burdened relations of Germans to Jews, of American whites to American blacks, or of England and France to their former colonies" (Sandel 1996: 15). When the Kantian liberals describe social duties as obstacles to individual liberty, their communitarian critics respond by invoking the principle of republican citizenship, namely the idea that individual liberty can be maximized through public service and the prioritization of the common good over the pursuit of individualistic interests (Skinner 1992: 217).

Laclau and Mouffe reply to the liberals and communitarians

With the liberals, Laclau and Mouffe caution against the imposition of a substantial conception of the common good. They would agree with Berlin, for example, when he asserts that human values are so irreducibly plural that they cannot be

118

reconciled in the form of a substantive common good (Berlin 1984: 29–34). Laclau and Mouffe also share Rawls' view that the plurality in individuals' conceptions of their own good is a good in itself. Different individuals should be given the freedom to determine and to pursue their own good. Where others offer us opinions as to what our good should be, their views should never be raised above the status of advice (Rawls 1971). Laclau and Mouffe would prefer Rawls' skepticism about our ability to know the good of the other over Sandel's optimistic claim that insofar as we are members of the same community and therefore bound together by a shared discourse, we can substantially reduce the opacity between us (Sandel 1982: 172). Where the communitarians represent political debate as a peaceful and benevolent conversation between friends in which one's best course of action is determined through harmonious dialogue (Sandel 1982: 181), Laclau and Mouffe would invoke the Foucauldian principle of the ubiquity of domination and resistance in all discursive situations.

Furthermore, Rawlsian liberalism combines its pluralistic perspectivism on the question of the good with a prioritization of individual rights. It maintains that in a well-ordered society, citizens ought to hold the same principles of right and the same principles by which conflicting claims are heard and decided. Here perhaps Laclau and Mouffe are lacking. After advising us not to place all our hopes in institutionalist solutions, they offer neither substantially developed alternatives nor extensive comments on specific debates about rights. Laclau and Mouffe do establish several limitations to their autonomy principle. They insist that each progressive struggle ought to reconstruct its identity with respect to the others' demands (Mouffe 1996b: 247). Further, they maintain that difference should be celebrated as a positive good, but only insofar as difference does not promote domination and inequality (Mouffe 1992a: 13). From this perspective, the right to self-determination for all social groups must be upheld, except where the exercise of that right stops a traditionally disempowered group from achieving equality. Laclau and Mouffe would not extend autonomy rights, for example, to a dominant group that wanted to trump the equal rights claim of a subordinate group in the name of the preservation of its special way of life. The authors clearly state at many junctures that radical democratic pluralism does not tolerate domination in any form; as such, domination cannot be allowed to advance in the name of self-determination. For Mouffe, an "extreme pluralism" that values all differences equally in an unlimited manner suppresses the political, for it blocks us from recognizing the ways in which some differences are constructed as relations of subordination (1996b: 246–7).

Mouffe is nevertheless right to take issue with some aspects of Rawls' argument. Against Rawls, she maintains that pluralism is not just a given condition that has to be accepted, but is "constitutive of modern liberal democracy" (1996b: 246). The task, then, is not just to cope with the fact of pluralism but to create the conditions in which radical democratic forms of plural differences would thrive. She also takes issue with Rawls' circular argument that "political liberalism can provide a consensus among reasonable persons who *by definition* are persons who accept the principles of political liberalism" (1996b : 250). With this circular logic, Rawls dismisses anti-liberals as unreasonable persons.

Mouffe explicitly accepts one aspect of Rawls' argument, namely his insistence that a just society cannot tolerate an infinite diversity with respect to the principles of political association. How could a just society, for example, provide infinitely tolerant conditions for fascists? For Mouffe, however, Rawls deals with the problem of setting the appropriate limits to pluralism by resorting to exclusionary definitions of rationality. Rawls himself admits that rational agreement with respect to religious and philosophical doctrines is impossible, but suggests that we can relegate our inevitable disagreements on these issues to the private sphere, such that we will be able to obtain a reason-based consensus in the public sphere. Mouffe, by contrast, insists that when we struggle to define the boundaries of legitimate and illegitimate political principles, we are engaging in profoundly political struggles that cannot be resolved by appeals to neutral rational standards. Rawls' ideal image of a society in which political contestation has been overcome, or at least greatly minimized, also leaves no legitimate space for dissent. Dissenters in his best society would be "irrational" or "unreasonable" persons. Mouffe's concern is that without the preservation of a legitimate space for genuine dissent, the unpredictable harms that could be caused by even the most apparently progressive institutions would not be revealed and addressed (1996b).

Against the Kantian liberals, Laclau and Mouffe share with the communitarians the conception of the political subject as a socially-positioned self – the product of the articulation of multiple subject positions that are in turn inscribed within diverse social relations (Mouffe 1993b: 97). Insofar as each subject position preserves within itself traces of past articulations even as it is transformed through articulation, it brings with it elements of previously sedimented shared traditions. Taken together, the traces accumulated by the ensemble of subject positions create a somewhat open and flexible moral horizon. As an incomplete horizon, it cannot supply a substantial answer to specific moral questions, but it can at least provide a framework for deliberation. If we can always assume that every individual is situated with respect to multiple social solidarities through her positioning within common traditions, we can never predict exactly what type of solidarity will prevail. Laclau and Mouffe would agree with the Kantian liberals that a particular commonality is like a contingent "good" in the sense that it may or may not be constructed. However, where the Kantian liberals are content to designate commonality as a good that may or may not be chosen, such that that choice remains the product of an inscrutable accident, Laclau and Mouffe would insist upon the constitutive effects of the strategic conditions in which competing movements and social forces struggle to define the community.

Laclau and Mouffe therefore agree with the communitarians insofar as the latter replace the Kantian liberals' tendency towards arguments based on abstract universalist hypothetical conditions with their explicit recognition of the community- and tradition-specific character of the individual's positioning. They nevertheless sharply oppose the communitarians in many respects. Communitarians envision a rational succession of institutionalized moral frameworks, as a new framework wins legitimacy and displaces the old one only insofar as it provides better explanations of the previous framework's failures and incoherences – better, that is, according to the standards of the previous framework – and furnishes new solutions (MacIntyre 1983: 591). Power relations are virtually absent from this account. For Laclau and Mouffe, by contrast, political struggle is ubiquitous; the very notion of a power-free moral standard – however "rational" it may appear – is impossible. Laclau and Mouffe do not return to the Thrasymachean position, namely that justice is simply the will of the strongest. Power does nevertheless shape the rules of legitimation and the determination of the contexts in which those rules obtain (Lyotard 1984: 47).

Where one moral argument prevails over another – where slavery, for example, becomes widely understood as an unacceptable condition – it does so thanks to political struggle, a process that redefines the very standards by which moral arguments are assessed. Political struggles are precisely contests about moral standards; changes in moral standards are never the straightforward products of a tradition's rational unfolding. Values are determined in struggle and embodied in traditions of struggle; they are tested and re-articulated in conditions of struggle. The pragmatic demands of a people in struggle are such that values are always subject to some degree of redefinition. What people of color and anti-racists need to include in the definition of racism, for example, has shifted to some degree in the America of Reagan, Bush and Clinton, and yet retains many aspects from the older concept of racism under slavery, imperialism and "Jim Crow" segregation.

The communitarian claim that each individual is located within a community and that that community's traditions operate as a moral horizon for her is also problematic. For if every tradition is constructed, passed down through generations, interpreted and reapplied in conditions of struggle, then it is by definition always multiple in character. As Berlin insists, the ends within a single tradition – even if we could assess those ends from a single common perspective – are plural and can never be harmonized (1984: 29–31). In actual history, political ends are never assessed from a single common perspective. There will always be clashes between different traditions and within a single tradition. The vigorous debate in the United States on affirmative action is a case in point: all sides in the key cases (*Bakke* v. *University of California* 1978; *Richmond* v. *Croson*, 1989; *Metro Broadcasting* v. *FCC* 1990; *Adarand Constructors* v. *Peña* 1995; and *Hopwood* v. *Texas* 1996) cite the same passages in the American Constitution, but offer radically different interpretations of such basic concepts as "equality," "racial classification" and "compelling governmental interest."

The problem of conceptualizing the relation between the individual and her community positionings is centered on the definition of the principle of self-determination. For Kymlicka, Kantian liberal theory does not actually construct the individual as an atomistic entity. It does, however, reserve for the individual the right to question the beliefs, values and traditions that have become normalized within one's community. Individuals may find themselves thrown into specific social roles, but they are not fully defined by those roles. The liberals contend that they should be allowed to challenge any of the moral obligations that follow from their communal memberships. It is only with this fundamental freedom of choice that the individual can pursue a meaningful life. The liberals' insistence on the construction of a state that is neutral with respect to the common good arises precisely from this concern. For the communitarians, by contrast, the common good is supposed to operate not as a reflection of individual preferences but as a standard by which individual preferences are evaluated. Where the liberals believe that the moral individual should ask herself, "Who should I become?" the communitarians would like her to attempt to discover who she already is by virtue of her social positionings. From the communitarians' perspective, the individual can interpret the meaning of her roles, but she cannot reject them altogether as worthless, for in the end, there is no self that is prior to the totality of one's positions in the community (Kymlicka 1990: 204–15).

The communitarians therefore tend to remain silent on the following question: if we did grant that the community's tradition should operate as a moral horizon, what would we establish as the moral obligations of those peoples who have been systematically exploited and oppressed within that tradition? Hegel, for example, allowed that in a corrupt regime, the outlaw who opposed her community's traditions could become a moral hero. It should be noted, however, that his heroic outlaw figures, such as Socrates and Jesus, belonged to ancient communities. Hegel maintained that ultimately, morality can only be achieved within a communal setting, for it is only the community's traditions that can give definitive content to the individual's decisions. A subject who finds herself in a transitional period in which historical rationality has become corrupted must resort to her own individualistic deliberation. Hegel assumed, however, that modern nation-states were generally progressing towards the realization of an increasingly rational morality. His faith in that progress was such that he believed that the modern individual ought to determine her moral views with respect to her community's way of life in all but the most extraordinary conditions (Hegel 1953: 39–43; Taylor 1975: 376–8).

Hegel badly mis-judged the predominant moral traditions in contemporary Western societies. If we follow the critiques by contemporary revolutionaries such as Malcolm X (1965), the later Martin Luther King, Jr. (1991, 1968), and Angela Davis (1981), then the concern of the Kantian liberals about the individual's right to self-determination remains well founded. The communitarians' solution to the traditions of exclusion, namely the simple inclusion of the previously excluded, misses the point. Systematic forms of oppression such as racism are not necessarily accidental to a communal tradition; they are often constitutive of their basic principles. Further, the communitarians ignore the morality of radical rebellion: militant workers; revolutionary blacks, Latinos, indigenous peoples and other oppressed racial/ethnic minorities; feminist women; radical queers and many others find their moral paths precisely by denouncing their assigned social roles within traditional communities as worthless and by entering oppositional

122

moral universes. Kymlicka concludes that what is needed in our diverse and historically exclusionary societies is not heightened conformity with communal traditions but the empowerment of the oppressed to define their own aims (1990: 226, 229).

Kymlicka's emphasis on the enduring presence of social structures of domination is crucial. From Laclau and Mouffe's perspective, both the liberals and the communitarians ignore the impact of power relations and overdetermination when considering communal obligations and the right to rebellion. The communitarian call for respect for the authority of tradition is obviously problematic. The liberals' suggestion that the individual should stand back from all of her positionings and deliberate about their legitimacy is also impractical. Such a totally asocial self would have no reason to make any choices. If we examine actual practices of contemporary rebellion, however, we can observe the ways in which every individual and group is always situated with respect to multiple traditions and their corresponding moral obligations. A subject gains the ability to loosen the grip that a corrupt tradition exerts over her identity only to the extent that an oppositional tradition provides her with the solid ground from which rebellion becomes possible. In Laclau and Mouffe's post-structuralist terms, it is through the discursive interruption of a "constitutive outside" that the democratic revolution is extended and politicized resistance becomes possible. Every social formation is destabilized by its "constitutive outside": the antagonistic otherness that simultaneously operates as its defining principle and lethal enemy (Mouffe 1994: 107–10).

In some cases, destabilization effects can become transformed into useful tools for resistance discourse. When the black power movement, for example, identified the myth of an inclusionary liberal democratic America as a lie, and sought to radicalize the masses of African-Americans *vis-à-vis* the moral bankruptcy of the existing political and economic system, they drew upon numerous oppositional traditions, such as African-American anti-racist resistance, global anti-colonial struggles, the socialist tradition, and the most radical moments in the liberal democratic tradition itself. Progressive black nationalists did not reject dominant American values in order to enter an amoral world, and they did not step back from all moral traditions into a blank space in order to deliberate. On the contrary, they struggled to situate their revolutionary program as the embodiment of oppositional traditions (Malcolm X 1965; Marable 1991; Brown 1992). In this, and many other similar cases, the democratic revolution can be advanced by radical disobedience to hegemonic values and by articulating new moral principles. Those alternative principles are not conjured up out of thin air according to an individual's voluntaristic whim. They are drawn from a "constitutive outside" – the marginal and even "foreign" traditions of resistance that have survived in the shadows cast by the hegemonic value system.

Radical democratic pluralist theory therefore both borrows and departs from the liberal and communitarian traditions. Communitarian theorists rightly reject the claims of universal rationality; they favor instead a conception of morality and rationality that is specific to particular historical traditions and communities.

Like communitarianism, radical democratic pluralist theory is based on a commitment to egalitarianism; the overcoming of domination, exploitation and oppression; and to the supersession of the atomism, instrumentalism and alienation that is specific to capitalism. Radical democratic pluralism, however, is also fundamentally committed to a liberal pluralist vision of the social in which multiple individual goods would be valued and the right to self-determination would be upheld. Communitarianism recognizes the specificity of morality and rationality for each particular community, but insufficiently values diversity within a single community or tradition, and fails to address adequately the ways in which systematic patterns of oppression can become central to a community's "way of life." Finally, both the liberals and the communitarians do not pay sufficient attention to the role of overdetermination: the fact that every individual is positioned *vis-à-vis* an irreducible plurality of communities and traditions, and that every resistance is fashioned out of the traces of oppositional traditions.

Partial accommodations of plurality: MacIntyre, Sandel and Young

MacIntyre, Sandel and Young all offer various solutions to the problem of accommodating the principles of equality, self-determination and the common good. MacIntyre explicitly recognizes that every individual plays a whole set of different roles within her specific tradition-bound community. He then insists, however, that her community's "narrative repertoire" contains a unity narrative for her: a story that gives her complex life an intelligible unity. This unity narrative is in turn granted tremendous precedence: what is good for the individual is determined by the story that gives her life its unity (MacIntyre 1981). From Laclau and Mouffe's perspective, MacIntyre's prescriptive unity narrative comes far too close to the substantive common good. In Lefort's terms, the "empty place" at the center of a democratic polity for contestation and renegotiation (1986: 279) is not adequately preserved.

For his part, Sandel also recognizes that each individual has multiple and overlapping memberships within the many different communities that make up society as a whole. There is no "society as a whole" as such; there is only a complex network of relatively inclusive or relatively exclusive communities. Each community makes a specific claim on its members in terms of communal obligations. Sandel not only admits that the heterogeneity of the various communities' conception of the good renders the formation of a common good for society extremely difficult, but also that we cannot determine in advance which conception of the good should prevail in a given context (1982: 146). Sandel nevertheless maintains his communitarian faith in the possibilities of knowing the good of the other and of conducting coercion-free discourse with the other such that this problem can be ultimately overcome through dialogue. In a more recent work, Sandel acknowledges the danger of coercion in a republican communitarian regime. In almost Gramscian terms, he calls for a complex promotion of civic virtues through persuasion, habituation and the encouragement of independent thinking. He also envisions a pluralistic form of deliberation that would preserve multiple interpretations of the good and the space for future contestation (1996: 318–21).

Young constructs a public sphere that would systematically promote the autonomy of different social groups. She contends that "equality as the participation and inclusion of all groups sometimes requires different treatment for oppressed or disadvantaged groups" (1990: 158). Young does not, however, pay enough attention to the fact that each social group is marked not only by difference but also by antagonism. When she defines a social group as an ensemble of individuals who share a common "way of life" (1990: 186), she does not give adequate emphasis to the sharp contestations that obtain within each social group about the definition of its norms. Young's cultural definition of the collectivities that would be granted special rights therefore becomes problematic. Who would determine the proper membership of a racial, ethnic or sexual minority? Whose cultural standards would they use? The risk here is that the whole problem of social control in the name of regulating cultural "authenticity" could be reintroduced. Contestations about rights should take place on a political terrain that is constructed according to the principle of distributive justice, instead of the principle of culturally-defined groups. Given the complexity of contemporary social formations, and the hybrid and overdetermined character of multiple forms of exploitation and oppression, almost all cultural groups contain within themselves relatively empowered and relatively disempowered members alike. Complex mechanisms of distributive justice can deal with claims that arise out of antagonisms within cultural groups, whereas a system that is based on visions of ideal socio-cultural affiliations and homogeneous cultural groups cannot do so.

Mouffe shares Young's concern that different social groups should not have to suppress their specific identity when participating in the "general will." She notes, however, that Young relies upon an essentialist conception of group membership. For Mouffe, Young implicitly assumes that social groups begin to interact with each other only after they have fully formed their identities and interests. Politics then becomes a conversation between fixed actors who pursue their already established goals. Laclau and Mouffe, by contrast, construct the political as the site of identity formation, contestation and renegotiation. These processes always reflect power relations; in the case of a society tending towards radical democracy, they would also reflect the principles of equality and self-determination. Mouffe concludes that Young searches in vain for a conversational mechanism by which heterogeneous groups can be brought together, for she does not make room for the processes through which they renegotiate their identities and demands (1993b: 85–6).

Mouffe's appropriation of Schmitt's "decisionism"

Mouffe structures her intervention in the liberals versus communitarians debate with respect to the "retrieval" agenda outlined in Chapter 1, that is, radical democratic pluralism's attempt to recover and to radicalize the most progressive moments of the democratic revolution. She contends that the political identity which is best suited to the task of promoting radical democratic aims is that of the citizen. Noting that citizenship can take many different forms, she further specifies that the citizen in radical democratic pluralist theory should be seen as a socially-positioned self, rather than an atomistic bearer of rights. With the communitarians, and against Rawls and the Kantian liberals, Mouffe affirms that "a citizen cannot properly be conceived independently of her insertion in a political community" (Mouffe 1992a: 4). Indeed, Rawls himself has moved towards the recognition of the social character of the self (Mouffe 1993b: 45). Further, like the communitarians, Mouffe affirms that each individual is positioned within a moral tradition that provides the framework for her practical reasoning (Mouffe 1993b: 15–16). As such, Rawls' approach, for all its contributions to the concept of distributive justice, is far too limited, for the citizens in his ideal community only have to share common beliefs about the procedural rules by which they regulate their interactions.

Mouffe also agrees with the communitarian argument that the liberals' position has contributed to the impoverishment of public discourse (Mouffe 1992b: 230). Insofar as the liberals have succeeded in relegating normative problems to the private sphere, they have abandoned public debates on these issues to instrumentalist and religious fundamentalist reasoning. This development has exacerbated the tendencies towards a "not-in-my-backyard," isolationist and even segregationist disavowal of social responsibility among wealthy whites. For example, legal, political, spatial and economic insulation from the decaying inner cities and impoverished rural areas has become the hallmark of upward mobility in the gated communities and exclusionary suburbs of America. Connolly also points out that the liberal neutralist attempt to remove contentious moral debates from the public agenda only contributes further to political alienation, for such a limitation "rules out most of the considerations that move people to present, defend, and reconfigure their identities in public space" (1991: 161). With the communitarians, Mouffe contends that radical democratic pluralism must preserve some conception of civic duty, social obligations and the common good (1993b: 38).

The liberal formulation that allows for an infinite plurality of values in the private sphere is problematic in many respects. Rorty, for example, promotes the formation of an unrestricted private sphere in which individuals could freely pursue their interests without interference from public institutions. Mouffe notes that this attempt to quarantine unrestrained plurality within the private sphere would fail to address the complex ways in which the private and the public spheres are intertwined together throughout the social. Further, Rorty's approach leads him to reject any political strategy that would attempt to articulate the struggle for individual autonomy with social justice concerns (Mouffe 1996a: 2–3).

Rorty's private/public distinction does not, however, perfectly reproduce the traditional division between the domestic sphere and the official political sphere that has been rightly subjected to extensive feminist criticism. With his distinction,

Rorty seeks to separate out the projects that are devoted to the autonomous constitution of the self from those that take justice and the suffering of others as their central concern (Critchley 1996: 21). In any event, such an arrangement could abandon disempowered individuals to exploitation and oppression, for there is no aspect of an individual's pursuit of autonomy which does not directly or indirectly involve relations with others. Daly insists – against Rorty – that democratic struggles have to interrogate the private/public distinction, and that relations of domination in the private sphere need to be "publicized," that is, "put into political question and opened to regulatory forms of social intervention" (1994: 190). Daly concludes that the advance of radical democracy depends not on the quarantining of unlimited difference within a carefully circumscribed private sphere, but on the "active multiplication . . . of public spaces; spaces which are different from, and more diverse than, the formal liberal public space of elections, separation of powers and universal law" (1994: 191).

While Mouffe advances these criticisms of the liberals, she nevertheless warns that communitarian visions of a *Gemeinschaft* type of unified community can be dangerous. The organic community, organized around a single set of moral values and a substantive idea of the common good, will never adequately respect pluralist differences between the micro-communities within the community and between the individuals within each micro-community, nor will it accommodate the complexity of each individual's membership in a plurality of micro-, macro- and transnational communities. For Mouffe, the communitarian tendency towards the organic community should be checked by the liberals' protection of the individual from the imposition of a specific and substantial conception of the good life. The space of radical indeterminacy – Lefort's empty space at the center of modern democratic society (1986) – must be preserved, for it is crucial for the development of unassimilated pluralist difference (Mouffe 1992b: 227). For Mouffe, the binding force that serves as the political horizon for a highly complex collectivity of citizens should be provided by the democratic tradition. As such, we should strive to encourage respect for the values of democracy, equality and freedom, rather than a substantive idea of the good (Mouffe 1992b: 231).

As we have seen in Chapter 1, Laclau and Mouffe understand the democratic revolution as the recitation and institutionalization of egalitarian, democratic and pluralist principles in new social contexts. In Mouffe's terms, this struggle revolves around citizenship, for the radicalization of citizenship creates the conditions necessary for substantial and progressive social change. Laclau and Mouffe's vision can be compared with that of Marshall, who argues that citizenship's egalitarian force comes into conflict with class inequality. In its earliest stage of development, when citizenship is defined merely in terms of civil rights, it exercises a "profoundly disturbing, and even destructive" impact upon feudal status hierarchies, but tends to leave capitalist class inequalities intact (1964: 85, 87). As citizenship is expanded to include political rights (universal suffrage, effective representation, and so on) and social rights (the "absolute right to a certain standard of civilization which is conditional only on the discharge of the general

127

duties of citizenship" (1964: 94)), its egalitarian force is transmitted throughout more and more areas of the social. Marshall himself notes that although the extension of social rights does not necessarily equalize incomes or abolish class differences, it does provide for the "general enrichment of the concrete substance of civilized life" (1964: 102).

The logic of Marshall's own text resists the elevation of his argument to a universally applicable rule. He notes that the enhancement of social rights through the mobilization of increasingly egalitarian political rights coincided in turn-of-the-century Britain with economic and cultural developments that narrowed the gap between the classes (1964: 96, 116). Further, Marshall cites macro-economic planning, national housing policies, public education investment, welfare state programs and the National Health Service as concrete instances of the working-class' social rights gains (1964: 93, 100–15). Today, in post-Thatcherite Britain, these very institutions are massively under-funded and face even greater cuts, while the American welfare state has always been relatively incomplete (Quadagno 1994). Insofar as these constitutive historical contingencies are woven into the model, Marshall's argument cannot be infinitely extended to other cases. The lessons that we can learn from the operation of citizenship in Britain's imperial industrial period, and in British democratic socialism's heady post-war days, may be limited where our contemporary conditions are concerned; they will certainly be limited where those conditions are defined in terms of the neo-conservatives' evisceration of the liberal democratic tradition.

It is entirely appropriate, then, that Mouffe's vision does not take the form of a complete blueprint for a new society; there will always be extensive debate on the meaning of freedom and equality and on the boundaries between the private individual's liberty and the citizen's obligation, and every general theory will have to be reconsidered to some extent in the light of historical contingencies. By its very nature, the democratic tradition is "heterogeneous, open and ultimately indeterminate" (Mouffe 1993b: 17). Mouffe allows for productive and unlimited contestation on the central questions that continue to haunt the democratic tradition, namely, how can the principles of democratic participation and solidarity be reconciled with the principle of defending diversity, and how can we move towards a more egalitarian society without sacrificing individual freedom? At the same time, Mouffe insists that the irresolvable tension between the logics of egalitarian democracy and pluralistic difference can serve as a vital resource. With every failure to resolve that tension, the political terrain remains recalcitrantly indeterminate and the space for undomesticated dissent is preserved (1994: 111).

At this juncture, Mouffe turns to a problematic source, namely the work of Schmitt. Schmitt was an outspoken anti-liberal jurist for the Third Reich who gained Hitler's favor in the early 1930s by advocating temporary dictatorship (Lilla 1997: 38). Schmitt's key essay, "The Concept of the Political" (Schmitt 1976), was motivated by his profound concern that the liberal pluralist state permitted an excessive amount of destructive activities. He believed that radical political movements were exploiting the Weimar state's tolerance of political difference to advance their anti-state causes (Schwab 1976: 12–16). For Schmitt, the liberal pluralist dream of multiple interest groups engaging in peaceful contestation for resources was a dangerous myth. In an argument that was later taken up by the fascists, Schmitt asserted that political regimes had to come to terms with the fact that political actors bent on fighting their foes to the death could emerge in any human society (Schmitt 1976).

Schmitt defines "the enemy" as

> the other, the stranger; and it is sufficient for his nature that he is, in a specifically intense way, existentially something different and alien, so that in the extreme case, conflicts with him are possible. These [conflicts] can neither be decided by a previously general norm nor by the judgement of a disinterested and therefore neutral third party.
>
> (Schmitt 1976: 27)

Citing Hobbes, Schmitt maintains that every single actor who is engaged in an antagonistic conflict constructs itself as the only group that has the capacity to grasp the truth, the good and the just (1976: 65). Further, there is no identity without antagonism. A group of people only become a unified and coherent subject to the extent that they share a common enemy. In his *Glossarium*, Schmitt writes, "Tell me who your enemy is and I'll tell you who you are" and "*Distinguo ergo sum*" (Lilla 1997: 40). Because each collective combatant is situated within what we could call – to borrow from Foucault – its own distinct "truth regime," and the friend–enemy groupings constitute decisive affiliations with respect to the individual members' moral orientation, peaceful settlement through rational deliberation on the basis of shared principles is utterly impossible (1976: 38).

The friend–enemy antagonisms therefore remain nothing but strategic conflicts; sometimes they can only be settled by total war.

> Each participant is in a position to judge whether the adversary intends to negate his opponent's way of life and therefore must be repulsed or fought in order to preserve one's own form of existence.
>
> (Schmitt 1976: 27)

Schmitt's "decisionism" consists in his definition of the political as the moment in which the specific dimensions of the friend/enemy antagonism are constructed. Friend/enemy evaluations are mobile and context-dependent processes; today's friend might become tomorrow's enemy.

For Schmitt, liberalism dangerously negates the political. Instead of distinguishing correctly between the "real friend and real enemy" and acting accordingly (Schmitt 1976: 37), liberalism masks fundamental antagonisms by representing mortal enemies as benign economic competitors or as mere intellectual adversaries.

But insofar as liberal pluralism pretends that radically antagonistic groups can be brought together under a regime of common political principles and made to engage in constructive competition – when they actually regard each other as mortal enemies – liberal pluralism allows utterly destructive forces to conduct stealthy anti-state campaigns. Finally, Schmitt ominously insists that the state alone should possess the ultimate authority to distinguish between friends and enemies, and he explicitly includes both external and internal foes within the "enemy" category. Schmitt was effectively declaring that the Weimar state had to abandon what he regarded as its suicidal constitutional neutrality, to distinguish clearly between its friends and enemies, and to launch a decisive attack against the latter.

Schmitt contends that because liberal pluralism fails to grasp the constitutive character of collective identities, and fails to recognize that the principle of these collectivities may be utterly antagonistic, it necessarily attempts to "annihilate the political as a domain of conquering power and repression" (Mouffe 1996c: 22; 1993b: 122–3). Schmitt insists that where antagonistic "friend"/"enemy" blocs emerge, consensus can only be achieved through the exercise of power and exclusion rather than power-free rational discourse (Mouffe 1993b: 123; 1996c: 22; 1993a). Laclau and Mouffe similarly contend that liberal democratic discourse often illegitimately reduces the terrain of the political to a debate about procedural questions. For radical democratic pluralism, by contrast, the political consists in the struggles to hegemonize the social; that is, in the struggles to reconstruct the social and its subjects through the institutionalization of democratic and egalitarian worldviews. Where antagonistic conflicts prevail, the clash between opposing worldviews may make appeals to common principles impossible. Even where antagonisms are more or less suppressed, and the social is almost perfectly constituted as a peaceful system of differences, exclusionary power relations continue to play a key role. I will return to a more detailed account of Laclau and Mouffe's theory of hegemony, equivalence and difference in Chapter 5.

Like Schmitt, Laclau and Mouffe argue that because we will never be able to occupy a space that is beyond power, every political decision will necessarily entail the exclusion of alternatives; a power-free rational consensus is simply impossible. We can only provide temporary and context-specific solutions to political contestations, and every institutionalized solution will at some point threaten to reverse democratic gains through bureaucratization and new forms of domination. The only way that we can check against this development is to insist on the limitation of our ability to resolve political problems once and for all, and to insert the principles of incompletion and permanent contestation right into the very core of our democratic ideals. I will return to this theme in the Conclusion.

In a practical sense, Laclau and Mouffe's antagonistic conception of politics – their insistence that we will always have antagonistic conflicts that cannot be settled through rational dialogue alone – can shed a great deal of light on contemporary political problems. Rational debate on the basis of shared principles can sometimes work; antagonisms are by no means ubiquitous. In some cases, however, combatants emerge who view the "other" as blocking their very identity and stubbornly position themselves within utterly opposed moral traditions. What can be said, for example, about the possibility of rational dialogue between the lesbian and gay community and the religious right that preaches the extermination of our people? These fanatics represent the liberal democratic tradition as a sinister threat to nothing less than human civilization itself, for they believe that lesbians and gays are engaged in a genocidal campaign against humanity, and that we are merely using principles such as human rights and the separation of the church and state to spread our "sickness" and "evil." These people are deadly serious and have already committed numerous criminal acts of violence against peaceful lesbians and gays. Their belief in perverts' conspiracies is so profound that they cannot be reached through rational debates or appeals to liberal democratic principles. Some of their leaders cynically adopt pseudo-liberal democratic language to gain entry into mainstream politics, but their appropriations signal their political acumen, rather than the triumph of liberal democratic rationality.

Radical democratic pluralist forces must engage in multiple battles when we are confronted by the religious right, anti-abortion terrorists, right-wing militias, fascist anti-Semites, white supremacists, reactionary nationalists and the like. We need to isolate the hard-core extremists in these movements from the rest of society by strengthening liberal democratic institutions within the state and civil society. We need to ensure that the human rights of all citizens are respected, but when these extremists commit crimes, we have to insist that the state steps up its surveillance, containment and punishment of the offenders. Hard-core right wingers cannot be reached by rational dialogue that is conducted in liberal democratic terms because they stubbornly remain situated within a moral universe that is totally opposed to the liberal democratic tradition.

With Laclau and Mouffe, I would also agree that the ideal of a power-free rational dialogue on the basis of shared principles is always at least somewhat problematic, even in those cases in which such extreme antagonisms are absent. Mouffe strongly disagrees with the Habermasian conception that we ought to have as our regulative ideal a conflict-free social in which every antagonism would have been already resolved once and for all (1992a: 13; 1993b: 8, 115). Habermas proposes an ideal model of the social in which instrumental rationality, economic interests and power relations would be strictly quarantined, such that practical and communicative rationality could operate in an uncontaminated lifeworld (1970, 1984, 1987). In order to avoid some of the most common misinterpretations of readings of Habermas, we should underline the fact that this model is a "regulative ideal". Habermas is certainly not saying that we have already arrived at this ideal, and nor is he saying that it is necessary or even possible for us to obtain this goal (Mouffe 1994: 112). His argument, on the contrary, is that we make our best moral judgments when we act *as if* his model were indeed a model of the perfect society in which the good life would be possible, and *as if* we could obtain this perfect goal. Habermas is asking us, in a

131

sense, to use his vision of an ideal society in order to diagnose contemporary society's failure to construct the conditions for democracy, freedom and equality.

There are cases in which Habermas' argument that instrumental rationality should not be allowed to encroach upon the lifeworld is extremely valuable. When conservative policies regarding immigration or health care, for example, are defended on the grounds of economic efficiency, progressives should respond not only with studies that demonstrate the economic benefits of immigration and public health initiatives, but also with moral arguments about a developed nation-state's obligations. Ultimately, however, Laclau and Mouffe are right when they contend that Habermas' dualism – his bifurcation of the social in his ideal model between a power-saturated and a power-free space – is impossible. For Mouffe, Habermas searches in vain for a viewpoint "above politics from which one could guarantee the superiority of democracy" (1996a: 4). With Rorty, she insists that we ought to abandon the attempt to find politically neutral premises, premises that could be justified to anyone, that would serve as the foundation for a universal obligation to defend democracy. We ought to acknowledge, instead, that democratic principles only constitute one possible language game among many others, and that every argument that we could construct in defense of democratic principles will be effective and coherent only within the limits of specific contexts (Mouffe 1996a: 4).

Rorty admits that Western institutions cannot be defended merely on the grounds that they are "rational." From his perspective, we should not assume that anti-liberals will embrace liberal democratic principles to the extent that they become "less irrational." For Rorty, the task of moving an anti-liberal towards liberalism consists neither in rational persuasion, nor in teaching individuals to make proper use of their mental faculties, but in the incitement of sympathy and other solidarity-oriented sentiments. As Mouffe notes, this argument places Rorty on the side of Derrida, against Habermas, on the question of the Enlightenment. Habermas contends that the democratic values of the Enlightenment can only be defended and extended through the assertion of rationalist philosophical foundations. Rorty and Derrida, for their part, share Habermas' commitment to the democratic project, but insist that their anti-foundationalist critiques of rationalism do not contradict that project. Notwithstanding Rorty's skepticism concerning the practical role of philosophical discourse (Rorty 1996a), pragmatism and deconstruction may even help us to grasp the logic of vitally important democratic strategies in the indeterminate context of contemporary politics (Mouffe 1996a: 1).

Laclau and Mouffe do not regard the impossibility of resolving all antagonisms through the dialectical canceling out of power relations or the total quarantine of conflict as a fatality for radical democratic pluralism. From their perspective, the infinite character of conflict is an absolutely vital resource for the perpetuation of the democratic revolution.

To negate the ineradicable character of antagonism and aim at a universal rational consensus – this is the real threat to democracy. Indeed, this can lead to violence being unrecognized and hidden behind appeals to "rationality," as is often the case in liberal thinking, which disguises the necessary frontiers and forms of exclusion behind pretenses of "neutrality."

(Mouffe 1996b: 248)

If a progressive transformation of society actually did take place, and we succeeded in establishing a network of economic, political, social and cultural institutions that would begin to dismantle the exclusions that are central to capitalist exploitation and sexist, racist and homophobic oppressions, we would still be faced with a tremendous political problem. Even the most apparently progressive principles and institutions that we could establish in this moment might endanger liberty and equality in the future, for their meaning will change in new contexts in unpredictable ways.

This unpredictability is due in part to the fact that every rule is open to subversive interpretations in new contexts. The unstable character of a polity's population also introduces the possibility of various unforeseen outcomes to the extent that immigrants, refugees and heretofore non-participating citizens are brought into the political process through massive mobilizations. Unpredict-ability is further introduced insofar as the unmasterable dimension of the unconscious comes to the fore. Perhaps apparently progressive identifications with radical values in the present are haunted by investments from the past, and the ambiguous effects of that which has been lost will only become clear in the future. An individual may account for his resistance against state censorship in libertarian terms, for example, but because he has unconsciously equated the expansion of the censorious state with feminist social engineering, and mourns his lost manhood, he may ultimately pursue a strongly misogynist form of anticensorship activism. Further, to the extent that his sense of loss remains unbearable, it will remain extremely difficult to make him aware of his misogynistic politics. Another person may be drawn to environmentalism with apparently good intentions, but, in the midst of actual political work, she may actually demonstrate that that identification was partially shaped by her racist abjection of urban life. Or we could have a gay man whose devotion to the inclusion of gays in the military and the legality of gay marriages is motivated not only by a concern for civil rights, but also by anxieties produced by traumatic exclusions from American national culture and his own family, such that he tends to embrace an uncritical, bourgeois and patriarchal patriotism.

Further, personal loyalties and desires play a complicated role where identification with political ideals is concerned; this condition is ubiquitous among all types of political activists. One identification may prevail over others because a charismatic figure embodies the political principles in question. In some cases, the triangular dimension of identification will play a conscious or unconscious role. Identification with a set of principles or a movement may be shaped by one's

133

desire to become worthy in the gaze of the Other; in this sense, it is the Other for whom we are performing our identifications (Žižek 1989: 105,106,108). Again, the complex dimensions of identification make our decision-making vulnerable to the interruption effects of the unconscious, and dependent upon our unmasterable relations with otherness. It is precisely because we can never master identification, and we can never predict the effects of our present strategies, that we need to preserve a space for legitimate contestation. Only in this condition could a democratizing social formation nurture those forms of resistance that would identify the ever-changing face of domination, and agitate for new alternatives.[1] I will return to this theme in the Conclusion.

A dangerous degree of unpredictability is of course introduced wherever a hegemonic formation so thoroughly translates itself into a social imaginary that almost any element that adopts its logic is immediately legitimized. Many of the most progressive American and European intellectuals, for example, viewed eugenics as a positive development for everyone, since the policies in question – non-consensual sterilization, forced adoption, coercive medical experimentation, racist immigration policies, segregated blood banks, the use of soldiers from the "lowest orders" to fight in doomed military campaigns, and so on – were framed by Darwinian analogies with competent plant and animal husbandry. Leading politicians who were already favorably disposed towards social engineering, social planning and public health policies were also especially receptive to these ideas. "Eugenic programs resulted from the 'best' scientific opinion of the time, the 'best' medical opinion, and many were ordered and carried out in the democracies with the best of intentions" (Pfaff 1997: 23). Even after the Nazis brought eugenics into disrepute, several eugenics programs were deployed in mainland United States and Puerto Rico during the post-war period, and forcible sterilizations continued until they were officially banned in 1973 (Pfaff 1997).

Mouffe's argument that radical democratic pluralism must construct mechanisms that preserve a space for contestation is therefore entirely sound. Her work, however, enters into a problematic terrain when she appropriates Schmitt's concepts about the limits of liberalism without paying enough attention to the political location of Schmitt's critique. She notes that Schmitt joined the Nazis in 1933 (Mouffe 1993b: 121). Schmitt also held a university position in Berlin between 1933 and 1945, edited an important legal journal during this period and became an enthusiastic legal counselor for the Third Reich (Schwab 1976: 3; Lilla 1997: 38). He fully embraced anti-Semitic ideals, and remained utterly unapologetic about his collaboration for the rest of his life (Lilla 1997: 38–44). For her part, Mouffe does recognize that it was "his deep hostility to liberalism which made possible, or which did not prevent, his joining the Nazis" (Mouffe 1993b: 121). Further, Mouffe is not the first radical theorist who has found inspiration in Schmitt. Benjamin, for example, acknowledges that Schmitt influenced his early work (Schwab 1976: 4). Aron, Kojève, Taubes, and several writers in the journal Télos, have also borrowed Schmitt's concepts in the development of their radical critiques of liberalism (Lilla 1997: 39).

What are the limitations of legitimate appropriation from fascist sources? Lilla contends, for example, that much of Schmitt's anti-liberalism is thoroughly fused together with his deeply anti-Semitic political theology (1997: 43–4). To what extent can theoretical arguments be separated from the normative commitments that were intertwined with them in their very formulation, such that they can be given a different meaning in new articulations? Even though the teleological argument that a discourse's origin determines its meaning throughout its articulations is vulnerable to deconstruction, we nevertheless need to ask to what extent the traces of the past articulations of Schmitt's discourse continue to thrive in contemporary appropriations. A thorough response to these questions would require detailed genealogical research.[2]

Mouffe's theory of citizenship and Walzer's spheres of justice

While Mouffe values citizenship as an identity that is central to the promotion of radical democratic pluralism, she refuses to impose citizenship as the pre-constituted type of solidarity that would determine all other identities. Individuals should be free to pursue their individual goods in their various spheres of interests, but they should also develop at least a minimal common political identity through their participation in the public debates in which shared political norms and rules are constructed. The democratic principles of equality and liberty are in this sense a peculiar type of common good: they constitute the only common good that can be upheld without contradicting genuine rights to individual liberty and pluralist self-determination (Mouffe 1993b: 46–7). In Mouffe's terms, citizens should be bound together by a collective identification with a radical democratic interpretation of the principles of liberty and equality, for it is the democratic tradition that binds differences in the modern society together (1992b: 236; 1993b: 15–16).

With this approach, the citizen is no longer the passive recipient of rights whose freedom resides in the sphere in which the sovereign remains silent. Further, citizenship becomes the "articulating principle" through which the linkages between each individual's diverse memberships, and the linkages between individuals and micro-communities, are mediated. As an articulation, the constitutive logic works in all directions: citizenship shapes other memberships, but it is in turn shaped by them as well (Mouffe 1992b: 233–5). Again, it is only when the conception of the social agent as pre-constituted and fixed is displaced, and the social agent is conceived as the "articulation of an ensemble of subject positions, constructed within specific discourses and always precariously and temporarily sutured at the intersection of those subject positions," that such an approach to citizenship becomes thinkable (Mouffe 1992b: 237).

Mouffe maintains that her theory of radical democratic pluralist citizenship can actually work in a productive manner, in spite of the tensions that persist between its basic concepts. Mouffe refers at this juncture to Walzer's conceptions of "complex equality" and multiple spheres of justice. Walzer argues that the liberals' and communitarians' description of contemporary Western societies are both partly correct. Although these societies are marked by profound forces of disintegration, they are also characterized by enduring social ties and political traditions. Walzer points to, for example, the appropriation of the liberal democratic tradition by the civil rights movement. Although this tradition can be bent in an almost infinite number of political directions, he contends that it still operates as a unifying horizon across multicultural America. He insists that the best conception of the political subject is that of a rights-bearing, separate, voluntarily associating, freely speaking liberal individual, but maintains that we ought to teach individual selves "to know themselves as social beings, the historical products of, and in part the embodiments of, liberal values" (Walzer 1990: 21). For Walzer, a liberal democratic order operates best when it is subjected from time to time to such a "communitarian correction."

Walzer accepts that in contemporary societies, each individual operates in many different social spheres, and that each sphere has a distinct set of criteria by which the good is determined. Each member therefore has a plurality of goods: "We require many settings so that we can live different kinds of good lives" (Walzer 1992: 99). It would therefore be unjust to impose a singular good and set of criteria onto the whole community. Each social sphere is loosely defined with respect to a specific set of social relations. The individuals who meet through their interactions in one sphere may come from a plurality of cultural traditions, but they nevertheless share a common pragmatic interest with respect to the successful conclusion of relations in that sphere. Again, what counts as "success" depends on the sphere in question: "success" in an economic sphere is of a radically different order than that obtained in a kinship or religious sphere. Because Walzer conceptualizes the social as an ensemble of spheres – loosely defined with respect to practical relationships and pragmatic interests – rather than culturally-defined "ways of life," he is able to avoid the problem of cultural norms that is built into Young's model. Walzer concludes that justice would be achieved insofar as the specificity of the criteria for determining the good is respected within each sphere, and a person who is successful in one sphere is not allowed to accumulate resources that could be used to obtain success in another sphere (1983). For Walzer, some degree of economic inequality is in fact tolerable, but the expansion of inequality into "domination and radical deprivation" through the translation of economic success into trump cards in other spheres should not be allowed (1992: 100).

Phillips objects that Walzer creates such strong boundaries around each sphere that a wrong being committed within one sphere could not be addressed by a discourse that is mostly developed in another sphere (1993: 156–68). While Walzer's primary concern remains the conversion of goods across different spheres, his argument rests on the fairly reasonable assumption that his conversion ban would either prevent the formation of monopolies or oligopolies in a single sphere, or would at least make such concentrations of power more vulnerable to strong challenges (1983: 19, 117). He also readily admits that there is no necessary linkage between a high degree of differentiation in a society and its just character. Tyranny could indeed triumph in an autonomous sphere within a differentiated society (1983: 315). Social differentiation on its own does not automatically give rise to complex equality; progressive social change can only be achieved through democratic struggle at the "local" level in each sphere and at the over-arching level of citizenship. Further, Walzer maintains that appropriate principles of justice should prevail in each sphere. With respect to the capitalist market, Walzer does not merely argue that a gain in the market should not be allowed to become the basis for power in other spheres; he also contends that the principle of free exchange should govern relations within the market sphere (1983: 120–1). Where sphere boundary disputes arise, Walzer rightly suggests that they ought to be addressed in the political sphere, and that the state ought to play the crucial role of sphere boundary guardian (1983: 121–2, 281, 319).

Walzer's conversion ban could in fact create favorable conditions for radical social change. If, for example, relations in the kinship sphere, such as the patriarchal nuclear family and heterosexual marriage, were completely detached from their numerous supports in the state and religious spheres, the lesbian and gay challenges to these institutions would benefit enormously. Walzer anticipates that a shift towards an autonomous kinship sphere would render the family much more fragile and open to democratic challenge (1983: 241–2). Far from embracing an agnostic *laissez-faire* attitude, Walzer insists that an appropriate principle of justice ought to prevail in each sphere, that the boundaries of each sphere should always remain open to contestation, that debates between the discourses that emerge in different spheres should be encouraged, and that interventions by a democratic state are needed to sustain democratic associations within civil society (1993: 319; 1992: 100–1).

Indeed, because the democratization of the state is crucial to the creation of democratic associations, Walzer, like Mouffe, holds that citizenship must be privileged over all other memberships (1992: 104–5). A state apparatus that would enhance radical democratic pluralism could not be neutral. It would have to refrain from undue intervention in various social spheres such that genuine multicultural rights to self-determination would be upheld, but it would also have to promote a specifically democratic form of citizenship in a vigorous manner. Public schools, for example, should be operated in such a way that they reflect the special needs, interests and identities that flourish in the particular communities that they serve. But the schools must also teach children the skills that prepare them to take up civic roles in the larger community, such as respect for diversity and co-operation across differences (Walzer 1983: 223).

Notwithstanding Walzer's substantial contribution to radical pluralist thought, his emphasis on the nation-state as the primary site of political identification suppresses the value of transnational movements and thereby impoverishes the whole concept of democratic citizenship (Connolly 1995: xxviii, 146–9). As a fixed territorial imaginary, the nation-state framework is somewhat obsolete in an era in which transnational capital is becoming more prominent. If we granted, for example, that one's political obligations ought to correspond in part to one's ability to earn a profit from other people's labor, what effective citizenship would we establish for a New York investment banking executive who manages complex international portfolios or a computer software engineer who writes programs in his Colorado home for a German–Japanese-American media conglomerate? New York City taxes people who live elsewhere but work in the metropolitan area on the grounds that they consume public goods and services just like everyone else. Capital, however, often enjoys massive public subsidies through its hidden transnational consumption of public goods and services. What are, for example, the political obligations of wealthy American shareholders in the corporate agricultural sector towards foreign communities when their companies purchase the labor of immigrant farm workers at bargain-basement prices, keep the surplus value from that labor, and then send them back to their home countries, without paying a penny towards the public cost of the reproduction of that labor from cradle to grave – the workers' health care, education, pensions and so on? What are, for that matter, the international political obligations of all wealthy shareholders – regardless of their nationality – in the transnational companies that are reaping super-profits through their exploitation of "Third World" labor? Clearly, there are no simple solutions to these problems, but an exclusive emphasis on nation-state territoriality only renders contemporary political theory increasingly anachronistic. Nation-state-centric theory also virtually erases transnational forms of political activism. The stories of movements such as the Women in Black, an anti-war coalition between Serbian and Bosnian women (Eisenstein 1996: 167–9), Stitch and Madre, American feminist organizations that work with women in Central America (Flanders 1997: 70, 240, 260, 273), and joint American–Mexican labor movements aimed at organizing independent unions in the maquiladora sector (Dillon 1997), are rendered irrelevant by a political theory that conceptualizes political participation solely in terms of nation-state frontiers.

Mouffe argues that Walzer provides one of the best frameworks for conceptualizing radical democratic pluralism's embrace of the simultaneous pursuit of egalitarianism and the preservation of liberty (1992: 7–8). Like Walzer, Mouffe contends that we need to guard against the excessive accumulation of power in one group or in one social sphere. The democratization of the economy and the state should be accompanied by the decentralization of power such that diverse social associations obtain effective decision-making authority (Mouffe 1993b: 100). She further contends that the multiple spheres in the social should not be thought in terms of the traditional private/public distinction, for each sphere has both a private and public dimension. The individual's practices in each sphere are "public" in the sense that they must conform in some minimal way to the rules established by the political regime. In this sense, the regime regulates the "grammar" of the citizen's conduct. These political rules reflect the prevailing hegemonic order; in a radical democratic pluralist society, they would tend towards an ideal point in which egalitarianism and individual liberty would both be maximized. A radical democratic pluralist society's rules would refrain as much as possible from regulating the content of the individual's actions and utterances. The "private" sphere of the individual's choices would thereby be protected from illegitimate "public" intervention (Mouffe 1992b: 237–8).

The "public" rules in a radical democratic pluralist society would enhance the conditions necessary for the promotion of challenges to all forms of domination. Democratizing institutions would never remain agnostic *vis-à-vis* the perpetuation of domination within a specific social sphere (Mouffe 1993b: 84). Again, different social movements working against domination in different spheres should be articulated together such that the various democratic struggles would begin to influence each other. In this manner, a "chain of equivalence" would be formed wherein each struggle would retain its specificity, but would also bear within it the traces of the democratic wisdom found in its sister struggles. A democratic "we" is constructed as this chain is opposed, in a symbolic or actual tactical manner, to a "them": the forces of inequality and domination (Mouffe 1993b: 84–5). If the "we" of the citizens is brought together negatively in this sense – as it stands opposed to the "them" – the "we" also has a positive dimension. Allegiance to democratic institutions and identification with the principles of equality and self-determination must be fostered among the diverse social groups (Mouffe 1993b: 151).

Thinking democratic political struggles in terms of the construction of chains of equivalence also provides a practical means for dealing with the inevitable tension between "equality" and "difference." "Equality" is often misunderstood as the complete elimination of difference. Feminists, for example, have debated whether women should demand rights on the grounds that they are "the same as men," or on the grounds that they are essentially "different from men." Scott remarks that "equality" and "difference" should not be viewed as utterly antithetical. Citing Walzer, she contends that egalitarianism can be considered not as the total elimination of difference, but as the act of temporarily ignoring certain differences for specific purposes in a given situation (Scott 1988: 172–3). In certain cases, we should ignore the differences in the wealth that is held by two different citizens – in voting, for example – in other cases, we should acknowledge that difference as requiring an appropriate remedy – through redistributive taxation and governmental programs. While the logic of egalitarianism ultimately does come into conflict with the logic of diversity, some temporary compromises can be worked out. By conceptualizing democratic struggles as the construction and mobilization of chains of equivalence that would, by their very nature, acknowledge and value difference, Mouffe's theory provides a useful solution to this dilemma.

Furthermore, resistance to domination would ideally take a "grassroots" form. Resistance strategies would seek, first and foremost, to work with the organic philosophies of resistance that are already in motion within the sphere in question, and to use them as a basis for further radicalization. Articulating linkages between grassroots groups would be subsequently promoted. Only when those grassroots forms of resistance had developed and matured to the point that they could take on leadership roles would efforts to coordinate the struggle from the bureaucratic level of state or party agencies be launched. The aim throughout the process would be to enhance mobilization, self-determination and empowerment from below, and to guard against bureaucratization and containment from above.

The radical democratic pluralist approach to the expansion of democratic diversity never stops short at the mere inclusion of a new difference. The best regime would be one in which individuals of different genders, religions, races, ethnicities and sexualities were granted equal rights. Beyond this, however, traditionally disempowered minority groups would also have access to the material means that they need to sustain their particular way of life. As Gutmann contends, "Liberal democratic states are obligated to help disadvantaged groups preserve their culture against intrusions by majoritarian or 'mass' cultures" (1992: 5). Once again, this raises the thorny question of cultural norms and the complex problem of institutionalizing distributive justice in hybrid social formations. Which multicultural programs are genuinely oppositional and which ones are really just pacifying diversions that conceal education cuts? Which kind of lesbian and gay relationships ought to be officially recognized? How exactly should affirmative action programs be designed ? The temporary solutions that we implement will have to be carefully shaped with reference to prevailing historical conditions. The legal disputes on affirmative action in the United States, for example, often turn precisely on the question of what historical data is admissible as evidence, and how the boundaries of the relevant social context should be drawn. We should expect even greater conflict on these issues. In every case, however, fundamental human rights must remain primary. The right to cultural survival – the right to defend, for example, the French language and francophone culture in Québec – must never be given precedence over basic human rights such as gender equality or free speech (Taylor 1992: 58–9).

Kymlicka's contribution to the multiculturalism debate is particularly helpful with regard to the inadequacies of liberalism's neutral state. For Kymlicka, liberal individualists from across the political spectrum have placed too much faith in the individual human rights model. Developed after the Second World War, the latter seeks to protect racial and ethnic minorities by guaranteeing basic civil rights and political rights for every citizen regardless of her group membership. Kymlicka suggests that the human rights model reproduces the liberal democratic solution to religious conflicts. Just as the doctrine of church/state separation bans state intervention on behalf of a specific religious minority, so too does the individual human rights model ban the state from recognizing permanent racial and ethnic differences. In practice, however, the neutral state model has all too often resulted in the subjection of disempowered minorities to the will of the majority. Kymlicka concludes that individual human rights principles must be supplemented by a liberal theory of minority rights (1995).

Under radical democratic pluralism's diversity principle, the democratic demands of the newly included group must be satisfied as much as possible. Further, the democratic impact that is created as the new group's demands are met should be transmitted throughout the social system: the particular identities within that system should be reconstructed and citizenship – the articulating principle that links all of these identities together – should be renegotiated in a more democratic manner. The newly recognized groups should not be treated as the childlike recipients of the established group's generosity; where appropriate, they should be recognized as valuable teachers who can reveal the anti-democratic moments within the established group's tradition and provide alternative solutions.

The democratic critique offered by the newly recognized group becomes all the more valuable to the extent that the established group's tradition has declined into increasingly rigid and ossified forms of closure. Citing Derrida's *L'autre cap*, Mouffe defines diversity in a radically anti-assimilationist manner.

> If we conceive of this European identity as a "difference to oneself," as "one's own culture as someone else's culture," then we are in effect envisaging an identity that accommodates otherness, that demonstrates the porosity of frontiers, and opens up [our identity] to that "exterior" which makes it possible. By accepting that only hybridity creates us as separate entities, it affirms and upholds the nomadic character of every identity.
>
> (1994: 111)

Many practical steps need to be taken to realize the democratic potential of this anti-assimilationist approach. Cultural minorities should generally have access to the resources that they need to sustain their traditions. This does not mean, however, that the state should take a neutral position with respect to a minority's illiberal practices. The rights of a cultural minority end where that group attempts to limit basic human rights and to censor internal dissent. Religious minorities in the United States and Canada such as the Amish and the Mennonites currently enjoy an exemption from laws that impose mandatory education for children on the grounds that such an experience would weaken their communities by opening their children to outside influences (Kymlicka 1995: 41). The state has a legitimate interest, however, in providing for the exposure of every resident child to basic democratic, egalitarian and pluralist values. The religious community leaders should have no power to stop a young adult from choosing to leave the community; nor should they have any power to stop them from accumulating the tools that would help them to make a sound decision in this respect.

If, to take another example, two rival leaderships of an immigrant community emerge, and the first proposes a multicultural curricula for a local public school while the second proposes compulsory sex-segregated schools with a dogmatic religious fundamentalist curricula, then the first proposal must be chosen over the latter. The claim of cultural authenticity and an oppositional stance against Western imperialism should never be allowed to trump basic human rights such as gender equality and liberal democratic principles such as the separation of church and state. It is of course problematic to state this argument in isolation, for the

141

risk is that it will be used to perpetuate the myth that the West is inherently pro-democracy and that the worst threats to democracy come from outside the West. If we take the pursuit of radical democratic pluralism seriously, we will in fact find that some of the most serious attacks against the democratic revolution are coming from predominantly Western sources, and that non-Western traditions can become effective resources for progressive social change.

Liberal individualists in university administrations, judicial positions and parliamentary settings alike generally argue that any recognition of group rights will inevitably contradict individual rights and take us down the slippery slope of social disintegration. Once again, Kymlicka provides a useful framework for the consideration of this question. Group rights can be defined as "internal restrictions": the right of a collectivity to limit the freedom of its members in order to safeguard what the group's most influential leaders construct as its "traditional way of life" and "shared values." Group rights, however, can also be defined as "external protections," as the right of a minority to remain free from economic exploitation and political domination by a more powerful majority.

"Internal restrictions" usually contradict human rights and therefore deserve strict scrutiny. If, for example, Irish lesbian and gays are not allowed to participate fully in Irish community events on the grounds that homosexual acts are sinful under Catholic doctrine and Catholic doctrine defines the Irish identity, appropriate state agencies ought to intervene to protect this sub-group from exclusion. "External protection" claims, by contrast, may be entirely compatible with liberal democratic pluralist principles. The endorsement of this principle would not in itself lead to a chaotic situation in which virtually any minority could make virtually any claim. Public policies based on "external protection" claims ought to reflect the relative degree of systemic disadvantage suffered by a given social group, as measured in terms of historical data relating to discrimination patterns, material well-being, the group's position in the cultural market and its ability to participate equally in the political system.

Furthermore, properly crafted policies of this kind, such as those that secure affirmative action for African-Americans, land entitlement for the indigenous peoples, or the survival of the French language in Québec, may enhance individual rights. Kymlicka insists that we ought to understand individual rights as entailing the freedom to develop one's own special talents and to form and to revise one's understanding of the good life. As we have seen, subject positions in Laclau and Mouffe's theory are never constructed in isolation; they only become meaningful through differential relations with other subject positions and with respect to a prevailing political imaginary. Kymlicka similarly contends that individuals can only deliberate and make choices in a meaningful way to the extent that they can situate themselves with respect to viable cultural traditions. Individual freedom is therefore inextricably linked to one's access to cultural resources; the self-determining individual must be able to give concrete content to her identity by locating herself within a vibrant cultural tradition that is not threatened by extreme pressures from a dominant culture. At the same time, individual freedom also entails the right to step back from the cultural space into which one is thrown, and to select alternative moral horizons. An individual's cultural rights therefore also entails the right to engage in vigorous dissent within one's cultural space, to participate in hybridized combinations of multiple cultural traditions, and to move into an alternative cultural space (Kymlicka 1995).

From this perspective, then, multicultural diversity is not antithetical to individual freedom; on the contrary, the protection of the democratic elements in minority cultures from the pressures of the dominant culture is one of the basic conditions for individual freedom. Kymlicka's solution, however, only works where a strong consensus prevails on the question of the minority's membership. The ban on internal restrictions does not necessarily prevent exclusions from the group that receives the external protection benefits. Native peoples, for example, are sometimes divided on the question of membership qualifications in their tribal group, and some of their disagreements turn on gendered definitions of kinship relations.

Minority communities should be granted access to public debates where they can express their critique of the dominant community's culture and political tradition in an effective manner. If a dominant community has decided to grant entry to immigrant populations, it must not be allowed to use these people merely as a source of cheap labor without any regard to their rights and quality of life. Nor should it be allowed to demand total assimilation according to the values of the dominant culture as the price of inclusion. If a dominant community has emerged out of traditions of genocide, displacement and slavery with respect to indigenous peoples, colonized groups and imported slaves, it must acknowledge its substantial political and economic obligations towards the descendants of these peoples. Democratic inclusion must entail a redistribution of material resources from the wealthiest to the poorest, and redistributions should criss-cross the boundaries between the dominant community and the minority communities where necessary. The minority communities' right to self-determination is meaningless without access to resources such as health care, housing, employment, education, majority language training and minority language preservation programs, access to the media and the culture industry, access to political representation, and so on. In some cases, such as that of the indigenous peoples, what is required is not just access to mobile resources but the right to establish self-government and territorial sovereignty as well.

Laclau and Mouffe's critique of the disintegrated society thesis

We have seen that Laclau and Mouffe's radical democratic pluralist theory has, as one of its central concerns, the preservation of autonomy. The logic of autonomy must be mobilized against the logic of assimilation to preserve a genuinely multicultural pluralism. Further, radical democratic pluralism has a differentiated approach to autonomy claims. Autonomy claims that would further empower the traditionally empowered and disempower the traditionally disempowered would be treated as suspect cases. The fraudulent claims on the part of privileged individuals and groups who mimic feminist and civil rights discourse should be exposed. As Marcil-Lacoste argues, all differences should not be equally affirmed, for some differences, such as fascism, are defined in terms of reactionary antagonistic principles. Calling for a differentiated thinking on difference, she contends that some differences already exist and should be preserved, others already exist and should be eliminated, and still others do not yet exist but ought to be brought into being (1992: 138–9). To this, one could add that there is a fourth category of differences: those that do not yet exist and should not be allowed to emerge. Again, it is only at the level of citizenship – Mouffe's nodal point for every counter-hegemonic bloc – that such political distinctions can be formulated (Mouffe 1992a: 13; 1992b: 235).

Having established this pluralist autonomy principle, Laclau and Mouffe specify a limit to its application: the social should not be theorized as if it were disintegrating into a jumble of dispersed fragments that remain closed off from one another. They consistently oppose this "essentialism of the fragments" with their insistence on the ubiquitous nature of overdetermination and articulation (Laclau and Mouffe 1985: 104–5; Laclau 1996e: 59). In this respect, they clearly distance themselves from Baudrillard, for whom the disintegration of the social is so pervasive that virtually every social bond has dissolved, individuals have become isolated particles, and empty discourse and simulation have replaced the circulation of meaning. Baudrillard contends that the "masses" no longer seek values and fully reject the imploded system of political representation. They yearn only for spectacle and participate in the annihilation of culture. Power not only manufactures meaning; it incites the demand for meaning. From this perspective, the alienation of the "masses" is not the effect of their ideological mystification. On the contrary, their indifference and withdrawal into the molecular worlds of the private is their only true form of resistance (Baudrillard 1983). Values, however, are never completely drained out of even the most popular spectacles. We need only consider the American public's fascination with events such as the Rodney King beating, the Los Angeles uprising, the O.J. Simpson trial and the bombing of the federal building in Oklahoma to find evidence of the enduring popular search for values within spectacles.

The distance between Laclau and Mouffe and Lyotard is not as great. Lyotard affirms the complexity of the social: he conceptualizes the social as an ensemble of irreducibly plural language games (1984: 19). Each language game has its own distinct rules of formation, just as every social sphere in Walzer's theory has a specific conception of the good. The individual self is, for Lyotard, not an isolated atom; she is positioned *vis-à-vis* a whole complex web of language games (1984: 15, 22, 25). Like Laclau and Mouffe, Lyotard asserts that there is no metanarrative that can resolve the plurality of discourses into a single, all-comprehending totality (1984: 26–7, 36, 40–1). Lyotard shares with Laclau and Mouffe a suspicion regarding the coercive potential in those moments of Habermas' discourse in which the latter constructs universal consensus as the political ideal. For all of

Habermas' claims that such a consensus could, in ideal conditions, be reached through coercion-free dialogue, Lyotard insists that power relations would always be present, and that progress towards such a consensus would always depend on the suppression of the heterogeneity of language games (1984: xxv, 10, 30, 65–6, 81–2).

Lyotard's rejection of the totalistic aspects of metanarratives, however, leads him to dismiss the possibility of a political practice that would seek to articulate different positions, forces and movements together. He is not altogether agnostic with respect to political values; he speaks out clearly and forcefully against "terror": the condition in which obedience to the rules in a language game is secured solely through brute domination (1984: 63–4). From his perspective, however, the only possible form of governance is temporary and precarious "local determinism[s]" (1984: xxiv, 66). Dallmayr would argue, by contrast, that when it does appear to us that we are caught up in utterly isolated struggles, we may actually be dealing with elements that are situated within a regime that has learned how to conceal its systematic character, rather than atomistic fragments (1993: 102). Lyotard's principle of "local determinisms" cannot adequately address these conditions.

Lyotard is also woefully mistaken when he claims that "most people have lost the nostalgia for the lost narrative" (1984: 41). For all their failures to deliver on their promises of a seamless world, fundamentalist religious, nationalist and totalistic ethnic discourses continue to flourish. Consider, for example, the tremendous success of Patrick Buchanan's religious fundamentalist Republican Presidential bid in 1996 or the vicious nationalism that characterizes not only Slobodan Milosevic's Socialist Party but also significant portions of the Serbian opposition forces as well. We cannot be so enamored with postmodern fashion that we ignore the popular effects of discourses that operate as metanarrative-pretenders; an effective response to the nostalgia for totalistic closure must be offered. Although Lyotard shares with Laclau and Mouffe the view that every institutionalized language game always remains open to contestation, he only advocates practices of interruption, displacement and subversion (1984: 16–17). For Lyotard, the political practices favored by Laclau and Mouffe, such as the construction of alternative identities, progressive institutions and counter-hegemonic blocs, would be so vulnerable to reactionary decline and the coercive suppression of difference that they could never be legitimately deployed in the name of radical democracy.

Laclau and Mouffe's position is closer to that of Derrida in this respect. Deconstruction is often mis-interpreted as an approach that can only affirm the endless play of difference. Derrida contends that post-structuralist theory can account not only for the failure of closure, but also for the necessity of constructing some sort of partial and imperfect closure.

Once it is granted that violence is *in fact* irreducible, it becomes necessary – and this is the movement of politics – to have rules, conventions and stabilizations of power. All that a deconstructive point of view tries to show is that since conventions, institutions and consensus are stabilizations (sometimes stabilizations of great duration, sometimes micro-stabilizations), this means that they are stabilizations of something essentially unstable and chaotic. Thus, it becomes necessary to stabilize precisely because stability is not natural; it is because there is instability that stabilization becomes necessary; it is because there is chaos that there is a need for stability.

(Derrida 1996: 83–4)

Both Laclau and Derrida would contend that the demonstration of both the failure of closure and the paradoxically necessary attempt to achieve this impossible end is on its own insufficient as a political practice. Interruption effects must be thoroughly articulated together with democratic normative commitments and practices that aim to create the institutions necessary to defend and to promote radical democratic difference (Laclau 1996f: 77–8, 87–9; 1996b: 119).

Against Lyotard, Mouffe asserts that radical democratic pluralism must always strive to maintain both the autonomy of social elements and their interconnectedness and mutual transformation. Again, it is specifically the radical democratic pluralist form of citizenship that can play this complex linking role (Mouffe 1993b: 77–8). For Mouffe, any "extreme pluralism" that fails to value the construction of a " 'we,' a collective identity that would articulate the demands found in the different struggles against subordination," dangerously negates the political just as liberalism does with its illusions of neutral procedures and universal rationality (1996b: 247). Citizenship can only become the site of democratic articulations to the extent that it is centered on a firm commitment to equality and human rights. A radical democratic pluralist society would, for example, tolerate the formation of fundamentalist religious communities, but only insofar as the latter did not attempt to impose anti-liberal principles onto the polity as a whole. Religious communities cannot be allowed to construct a form of citizenship that undermines redistributive welfare programs in the name of the work ethic, bans civil rights for gays, violates women's rights to choose abortion and censors the work of radical artists.

All differences cannot be accepted and . . . a radical-democratic project has also to be distinguished from other forms of "post-modern" politics which emphasize heterogeneity, dissemination and incommensurability and for which pluralism, understood as the valorization of all differences, should be total.

(Mouffe 1992a: 13)

Radical democratic pluralism does not, therefore, amount to an infinite tolerance for any difference. Radical democratic pluralism would protect the principle of tolerance for democratic difference precisely by vigorously attacking each and every anti-democratic position. There is nothing contradictory in radical democratic pluralism's lack of tolerance for anti-democratic positions, because radical democratic pluralism must aim to "protect as much as possible the autonomy of people to pursue a variety of goals" (Cunningham 1987: 194). It would promote progressive forms of affirmative action and multiculturalism, for example, while conducting a full-scale assault on racism. Where neo-conservatives take a purely individualist and ahistorical approach and claim that it is impossible to differentiate between democratic and racist recognitions of racial difference, radical democratic pluralism would refer explicitly to historical and group-based data on inequality to support its distinctions.

Pluralism, power and responsibility

With their numerous references to the complex nature of contemporary society, and their embrace of a non-essentialist vision of social change, Laclau and Mouffe may be misread as supporters of the liberal pluralist tradition. For a liberal pluralist theorist such as Schumpeter or Dahl, every individual enters the political arena with a more or less fixed set of interests. She pursues the realization of her preferences by joining an appropriate interest group that competes with other interest groups for political goods. Liberal pluralists generally assume that when a group gains in one moment or in one sphere, it cannot translate its gain into a trump card that ensures its success at other moments or in other places. The power of a small wealthy group, for example, is supposed to be held in check by a poor group because the latter has a larger number of voters. Competing elites are said to check each other's growth in power, such that, over time, power resources are dispersed across multiple sites in the social (Green 1993b: 6). Because she has many different interests, however, the typical individual will affiliate with many different interest groups over the course of her political activity.

The liberal pluralist image of multiple group membership resembles in some small way the radical democratic pluralist conception of the overdetermination of political subjects, but the resemblance goes no further. Liberal pluralist theory is inherently anti-participatory: it reduces the role of the citizen to the periodic selection, through elections, of a set of politicians who make the actual political decisions on behalf of the citizen. The liberal pluralist model therefore reduces democratic participation to voting in a market-like political system. The voter becomes a consumer who chooses among the political goods offered by each party's set of politician-entrepreneurs. Her choices are supposed to be determined by her own possessive individualist instrumental rationality, namely her fundamental drive to maximize her political utility. Again, the interests of the citizen – as a benefit-maximizing possessive individualist for whom the expenditure of energy in political participation may itself become too costly – are assumed to be atomistic and given in advance (Macpherson 1977: 77–86). Radical democratic pluralism, by contrast, envisions participatory mechanisms through which rigid and antagonistic subject positions might be transformed by their democratic interaction with other subject positions.

Liberal pluralist theory also tends to celebrate the dispersal of power and therefore fails to recognize the fact that power resources are in fact monopolized over time by dominant groups (Phillips 1993: 145). Parenti notes that this process is self-perpetuating since "those who enjoy access to resources are best able to parlay such advantages into greater advantages, using the resources they already possess to accumulate still more" (Green 1993a: 189). Contemporary liberal democratic systems may at times operate like the capitalist market in the sense that they often tend towards political "equilibria" or the formation of relatively stable points of consensus among competing elites. Those equilibria points, however, are by definition equilibria that preserve and perpetuate fundamental inequalities, for the "political market" is "oligopolistic" and responds most to those with the greatest "purchasing power," namely the social agents who already occupy the dominant positions in power relations (Macpherson 1977: 86–91). With the neo-pluralists, such as Lowi and Lindblom, Laclau and Mouffe would affirm that in contemporary Western societies, the state is hardly a "neutral referee," for the political "playing field" is fundamentally tilted in favor of large corporations and wealthy individuals (Smith 1990: 316–17). As Bachrach points out, the mainstream elite theory of authors such as Kornhauser, Lipset, Truman and Dahrendorf can serve as a legitimating ideology insofar as it "reflects...a receptiveness toward the existing structure of power and elite decision making in large industrial societies" (Green 1993a: 126). Guinier (1991) and Hero (1992) further argue that the existing pluralist political structures in the United States systematically exclude blacks and Latinos from effective political participation.

Finally, liberal pluralist theory empties the ethical dimension out of the liberal democratic tradition: democracy is defined as nothing but a sphere in which elite groups compete with one another for the power to govern the whole of society. The normative content of Mill's theory – his insistence that a democratic society should strive to maximize every individual's powers to develop her human capacities – is entirely absent from liberal pluralist theory (Macpherson 1977: 78). Democracy is assessed in an extremely narrow and mechanistic way according to a set of procedural criteria such as universal suffrage, free speech, majority rule and free periodic elections. More substantial concerns about the attainment of a truly democratic culture are concealed or brushed aside. Bachrach contends that for mainstream elite theory, "the charge . . . that the common [person] is not given sufficient opportunity to participate in meaningful decision making and is therefore deprived of an essential means to develop [her] faculties and broaden [her] outlook is, under this concept, irrelevant" (Green 1993a: 127). Liberal pluralism defines democracy not as "the conditions under which all legitimate interests can be fulfilled by way of realizing the fundamental interest in self-determination and participation," but as a means for securing compromises between ruling elites (Habermas 1975: 123). To the extent that the liberal pluralist vision of the political is successfully popularized, the fundamentally anti-egalitarian, anti-participatory, and anti-liberatory aspects of the contemporary Western democratic systems are insulated against radical democratic critique (Habermas 1975: 123–4; Phelan 1990: 438).

Liberal pluralist theory therefore does not construct the critical tools that are needed to detect the formation of identities, the rigidification of interests and the monopolization of power (Cunningham 1987: 165). Even Rawls, with his commitment to an egalitarian form of liberal pluralism, cannot overcome the limitations of this tradition. Liberal pluralist theory presupposes a power-free social space in which new differences are merely added to the existing totality. Referring to Rawls' pluralism, for example, Mouffe writes, "Conflicts, antagonisms, relations of power disappear and the field of politics is reduced to a rational process of negotiation among private interests under the constraints of morality" (1993b: 113). Confronted with recalcitrant anti-liberals, Rawls simply asserts that their exclusion from political conversations is a "moral requirement" that is produced by the "free exercise of democratic public reason" (Mouffe 1996a: 10). Consensus, according to the liberal pluralists, is supposed to be achieved through rational discussion – and rational criteria for limiting participation in that discussion – alone. Mouffe points out that the rules that determine what counts as a "reasonable" argument are themselves highly political (1993b: 142–3). Power relations are constitutive of discursive rules and identities; they cannot be ignored. Laclau and Mouffe take subject positions, historic blocs social formations, and hegemonic power relations as their units of analysis, rather than isolated individuals or naturalized interest groups. Laclau and Mouffe contend that power does not come later to the subject; the subject's formation is a response to and an effect of antagonism and hegemony.

Liberal pluralism also fails to uphold radical democratic pluralism's diversity and autonomy principles. Rawls aims to protect plural differences only because he takes the differentiated character of modern society as a "fact" and estimates that the type of state coercion that would be needed to eliminate that difference would be illegitimate. This approach amounts to the mere tolerance of social differences. Radical democracy, by contrast, builds on Mill's conception of self-determination: it takes radical pluralism as "something to be celebrated and valued because it is a condition for personal autonomy" (Mouffe 1993b: 137). Once again, this principle has a material dimension. The commitment to the promotion of democratic pluralism must entail the social obligation to construct the conditions in which self-determination for everyone – and especially for the traditionally disempowered – becomes possible. In the United States, for example, progress towards this goal could only be made after radical changes to the political system and massive redistributions in income, employment, access to education and access to health care took place.

Because power relations are integral to Laclau and Mouffe's radical democratic pluralist theory, their arguments imply that every privileged group has a profound ethical responsibility with respect to rights. Rights are only won through antagonistic conflict; "some existing rights have been constituted on the very exclusion or subordination of the rights of other categories" (Mouffe 1992b: 236). Radical democratic pluralism therefore requires the dismantling of the systems of rights that by their very nature block the democratic and egalitarian claims to justice by those who have been disempowered by those systems. The dismantling of the rights of whites in post-apartheid South Africa to make way for equal rights for blacks and a new democratic constitution is a case in point. Another example would be the debate on "color-blindness" in the United States. Charging that goods ought to be distributed in a "color-blind" manner, some white Americans have described themselves as the victims of affirmative action programs. They argue that the Fourteenth Amendment and the Civil Rights Acts of 1964 and 1965 gave full citizenship rights to African-Americans and that henceforth every racial group should receive exactly the same treatment. Neo-conservative jurists have gone as far as to equate affirmative action with racism (Smith *et al.* 1996; O'Connor *et al.* 1995). Again, a radical democratic pluralist approach to this issue would consider the historical power relations that have obtained between the different racial groups in the United States. Emphasis would be placed not just on isolated hiring and admissions decisions, but on the structural patterns that have led to the dramatic over-representation of blacks among America's poor. Anti-racism would not be simply thought in terms of "color-blindness" but in terms of the structural reforms that are needed to redistribute power to those who have been traditionally disempowered. Under the current conditions that prevail in the United States, recognition of racial difference in the form of well-crafted affirmative action programs would be one important aspect of these reforms (Eisenstein 1994: 39–69).

We have seen in this chapter that Laclau and Mouffe consistently differ with liberal, communitarian and liberal pluralist theorists in the treatment of power relations. Where some communitarians envision an ideal condition in which citizens deliberate on the common good in a coercion-free environment, and progress towards justice is made in each new era as laws and norms become increasingly rational, Laclau and Mouffe insist on the centrality of political struggle. Where liberals contend that the individual has the right to challenge her community's norms, they imagine her doing so from a power-free position outside the social. Laclau and Mouffe argue that each political subject is always situated in overdetermined force-fields that have been produced by multiple normative systems, and that one gains the ability to loosen the grip of one of those normative horizons only insofar as one identifies with a constellation of subject positions within another horizon. Resistance against a dominant tradition cannot come from a blank space; it can only be generated from oppositional traditions. Finally, we have seen that the liberal pluralists, like the neo-conservatives, tend to ignore the ways in which enduring power relations structure contemporary societies. I will consider Laclau and Mouffe's treatment of power relations in more detail in the following chapter.

5

POWER AND HEGEMONY

Laclau and Mouffe's work on power relations constitutes one of their most important contributions to social and political theory. Many of the approaches to power that are central to the political theory tradition are incompatible with the authors' project. As we have seen, radical democratic pluralist theory contends that all identities remain in some way open to contestation. As Bowles and Gintis suggest, the models of social practice that we find in liberal and Marxist theory are generally inadequate in this respect because they specify the contours of social agency in advance, when in fact "individuals enter into practices with others not only to achieve common goals but also to determine who they are and who they shall become as social beings" (Bowles and Gintis 1986: 150). Political struggles do not merely realign already fully-constituted subjects. Every struggle entails the far more profound process of working with partially formed popular identities and reconstructing them according to the values of the warring forces. Laclau and Mouffe have been at the forefront of the effort to develop a theory of power – or, to follow their Gramscian terminology, hegemony – that is appropriate to this specifically post-structuralist conception of identity. In this chapter, I will examine Laclau and Mouffe's approach to power and consider its implications for political practice.

Sex, gender and sexuality

The political implications of this post-structuralist approach to the formation of identity through struggle are often widely misinterpreted. The common misreading of Butler's *Gender Trouble* (1990a) is a case in point. Like Laclau and Mouffe, Butler takes as one of her primary targets the dualistic metaphors that prevail in some types of feminist theory. Where economistic Marxists hold that the economy determines the political, reductionist feminists argue that biological sex is given pre-discursively, and that only gender is socially constructed. Butler appropriates Foucauldian ontological principles to argue that sex is a strategically-constructed fiction whose deployment allows for the extension and intensification of misogynist and homophobic discipline. Wherever it is assumed that it is perfectly natural to divide humans into two simple biological camps, male and female, as if

151

that division had no historical and political dimension, we should look for the operation of underlying authoritarian forces such as sexism and heterosexism (1990a). The claim that sex and gender are the fictional products of political strategies has often been misread as an endorsement of a voluntarist, "anything goes" or "I-can-be-anything-I-want-to-be" approach to identity. If this claim were correct, then any attempt by a constructivist theorist to deal with power would be incoherent.

Butler's constructivist position on sex and gender is well supported by recent feminist research. Many feminists have long argued that theorists such as Chodorow (1978), Hartsock (1983) and MacKinnon (1989) are overly reductionist in their categorization of socio-political subjects in terms of the two biological sexes model.[1] Individuals are of course positioned within social structures – as women, men, feminine, masculine, heterosexual, homosexual and so on – but again, every social structure is overdetermined, and the identity of a subject never flows directly from her complex structural positioning. We never encounter "women" as such in actual history; concrete subjects are produced through the discursive formation of identities. Further, the gendering subject positions that operate as the interpretative frameworks through which complex structural positionings are lived are always overdetermined by other subject positions. A gendered identity is always a hybrid racialized, sexualized and class-oriented construct.

Finally, no subject ever develops an identity that allows her to be "at home" in her structural positions. We can never arrive at a final interpretative framework that would correspond perfectly to a given ensemble of structural positionings such that it would provide an adequate explanation for those structures' effects. Every subject is to some extent alienated from her assigned structural positionings; this condition is shared by the structurally empowered and the structurally disempowered alike. The structurally empowered may enjoy access to material resources that allow them to conceal their alienation or to compensate for it in a more effective manner, but alienation nevertheless remains a universal condition. It is precisely this gap between the interpretative framework that is offered by identity and the effects of structural positionings that drives the individual to engage in an endless search for new identifications.

At the present moment, the hegemonic character of the binary biological sexes model in the developed West is such that virtually every individual is structurally positioned – through medical, legal, economic, linguistic, socio-cultural and other discourses – as either male or female. Scott asserts that this fact derives not from pre-discursive nature, but from the institutionalization of power relations.

> Gender is the social organization of sexual difference. But this does not mean that gender reflects or implements fixed and natural physical differences between women and men; rather gender is the knowledge that establishes meanings for bodily differences.
>
> (Scott 1988: 2)

Scott calls for a critical form of women's history that would investigate "fixed gender categories as normative statements that organize cultural understandings of sexual difference" (1988: 175).

Adams similarly contends that feminist theory ought to challenge the two biological sexes model. Instead of assuming from the start that the world is naturally divided into males and females, we should study the political processes by which otherwise banal material bodily differences are invested with strategic meanings such that they appear to correspond to the two biological sexes model (1979). Nicholson notes that this departure from biologism frees feminist theory to think in radical pluralist terms.

> We cannot look to the body to ground cross-cultural claims about the male/female distinction.... In this alternative view the body does not disappear from feminist theory. Rather, it becomes a variable rather than a constant, no longer able to ground claims about the male/female distinction across large sweeps of human history, but still there is always a potentially important element in how the male/female distinction gets played out in any specific society.
>
> (Nicholson 1994: 83)

The very categorization of human bodies in the supposedly given biological categories, "male" and "female," depends upon the normalizing work of a historically specific political apparatus. As Butler contends, the claim that a given body is one biological sex or the other only appears to be an innocent descriptive claim. Citing Foucault, she states that this supposedly neutral act of biological sex categorization "is itself a *legislation* and a *production* of bodies, a discursive demand, as it were, that bodies become produced according to principles of heterosexualizing coherence and integrity, unproblematically as either female or male" (Butler 1992: 351). Constructivist feminist theory is not sufficiently anti-essentialist if it merely notes the historical specificity of the social construction of gender as it is articulated with other identities. It must further recognize that the myth of a binary biological sex difference is central to sexism and heterosexism. Butler comments that not only is sex positioned as the key to human intelligibility, but that "to qualify as legitimately human, one must be coherently sexed. The incoherence of sex is precisely what marks off the abject and the dehumanized from the recognizably human" (Butler 1992: 352–3).

There is, perhaps, no clearer case of the materiality of the two biological sexes model than that of the treatment of intersexed infants. Fausto-Sterling argues that we should have at least five biological sex categories: male, female, hermaphrodites (who possess one testis and one ovary), male pseudo-hermaphrodites (who possess testes and some female genitalia but lack ovaries), and female pseudo-hermaphrodites (who possess ovaries and some male genitalia but lack testes). She admits that even these five categories are too roughly drawn to reflect the tremendous biological variations that exist between different human bodies. It is estimated that as many as four percent of all newborn babies are born with hermaphrodite and pseudo-hermaphrodite bodies (Fausto-Sterling 1993: 21). Legal and medical institutions respond to this situation not by changing our conception of biological sex to accommodate these bodies, but by changing these bodies so that they fit the myth of binary biological sex categorization. Beginning at a very early age, the intersexed babies are subjected to extensive hormonal and surgical procedures (Fausto-Sterling 1993: 22; Angier 1997). The ethical questions that are raised by this sort of intervention are enormous, and the rights of these infants should be recognized as a feminist priority. The treatment of intersexed bodies also demonstrates the political character of taken-for-granted thinking about sex and gender: as is always the case, "nature" is actually the product of a highly political intervention. Homophobic anxiety is clearly one of the chief motivating forces behind this violent and non-consensual medical assault on the individuals who are born with intersexed bodies. The surgical, pharmacological and psychological construction of the subject's "natural" gender is deemed successful if he or she exhibits heterosexual desire at adolescence (Debonis 1995).

Once an individual is structurally positioned as a "biological" male or female through these medical, psychological, familial and political apparatuses, she is further positioned within gender structures. Again, we find the constitutive effects of contingent political interventions, rather than the mere reflection of an objective "nature." With respect to the law, Adams writes,

> It is not that the law . . . *does* things to women; rather it is a question of women as they are *made* by the law. The law works by constructing a reality that cannot be said to pre-exist the law. What is important are the *means* of representation, for they produce their own effects; it is not a matter of representing a pre-existent reality.
>
> (Adams 1990: 44)[2]

Many different examples from the experiences of working-class women, women of color, women sex trade workers and lesbians who are recognized by official discourse as biological females and yet find themselves structurally positioned outside the normal "woman" category could be offered to support Adams' claim. Because the hegemonic gender structures are overdetermined by racism, heterosexism and bourgeoisification, many "females" have found that they are not always legally and socially included as "women." We could consider, for example, the courts' denial of lesbian mothers' rights to retain legal custody of their children, or the normalization in welfare policy of the idea that poor women do not have the right to conceive a child in the first place. Or we could examine the experiences of working-class women, women of color or prostitutes who have been sexually harassed or raped and yet find that the courts do not take the violation of their rights as seriously as they would for white middle-class victims

(Higginbotham 1992: 258; Morrison 1992; Davis 1981: 172–210). Similarly, we could study the ways in which the payment of a lower wage for third world women in light semi-skilled manufacturing jobs in South-East Asia, the maquiladora region of Mexico, and California's Silicon Valley is justified in terms of their "special nature": they are seen as peculiarly suited to repetitive work, and as naturally content with a standard of living that is much lower than that of their white European and American counterparts (Flanders 1997: 42; Mohanty 1997).

Butler's argument for a constructivist approach to gender also finds support in contemporary literary criticism and psychological research. In some cases, the promotion of gender conformity is profoundly marked by race and class. The incitement of femininity for white middle-class girls is often thoroughly intertwined with racial and class-oriented superiority discourse. Becoming properly feminine – or rebelling against "ladylike" rules – can involve complex encounters with race- and class-differentiated symbols and taboos (Pratt 1984; Martin 1993). Conversely, racist disciplining can take the form of a brutal de-gendering. During slavery, for example, African women were reduced to mere commodities and subjected to torturous conditions that destroyed their kinship relations and personhood (Spillers 1987). In other cases, sexuality operates as the nodal point in gender disciplining. Bem contends that the abjection of same-sex desire is often at work wherever distinctions between "gender conformists" and "gender non-conformists" are made (1993). She notes that by virtue of our dissident sexuality, lesbians, gays, bisexuals, transvestites and transsexuals are subjected to extreme forms of pathologization as "gender non-conformists" (Bem 1993: 167).

Where some feminists assume that individuals are simply "socialized" in a functionalist manner into gender roles that are supposed to correspond to the two biological sexes model, Freudian and Lacanian feminists insist on the precarious and incomplete character of the effects that are generated through identification (Mitchell and Rose 1983: 5–6; Salecl 1994: 116). Founded on lack, the subject always remains troubled by the sense that something at the very core of her being is missing. She is compelled by this fundamental sense of inadequacy to engage in a perpetual search for stability and completion that will always remain beyond her grasp. She is driven to perform an endless series of identifications, but identifications cannot give rise to the formation of complete identities (Lacan 1977; Laclau and Zac 1994). Identifications with subject positions can only produce fragile, unfinished and permanently vulnerable identity effects. These identity effects nevertheless constitute the only bases for stability, coherence and ethical decision-making that the subject can obtain. For psychoanalytic theory, identities always remain incomplete, and compensations for that incompletion always remain somewhat inadequate, because of the paradoxical operation of the unconscious. The unconscious both compels identification and consistently interrupts the identity effects that result from identification. As Rose puts it, "the unconscious undermines the subject from any position of certainty" (1982: 29).

The implications of the psychoanalytic distinction between identification and identity is especially significant in the case of gender. Sex differentiation is constructed through the oedipal complex, but this process does not transform individuals into fully and simply gendered beings who are at peace with their sex assignments and easily take up roles that neatly match the functional needs of broader socio-cultural systems (Brennan 1990: 306–7). After the initial positioning in the phallic phase is forbidden, "the girl will desire to have the phallus and the boy will struggle to represent it. For this reason, for both sexes, this is the insoluble desire of their lives" (Mitchell 1982: 7).

The strategic implications of the Freudian/Lacanian theory of the unconscious are profoundly ambiguous. Men in a sexist society, or whites in a racist formation, or middle-class professionals who expect upward mobility but are faced with downsizing, are constantly confronted with the sense that their actual capacities fall far short of the omnipotence that was phantasmatically promised to them. Some individuals may react to this gap between the promise of omnipotence and their actual experiences of impotence with a self-reflexive critical discourse that could pave the way towards progressive solidaritistic identifications. Individuals who are aware of the structured contingency of their identities may be more likely to react to marginalizing demonizations with suspicion (Connolly 1991: 180). Others, however, may respond with a violent rage towards figures of otherness – such as "castrating feminists," "invading immigrants," "crack-addicted single mothers" or "perverse homosexuals," and so on – and their discourses of demonization might remain almost totally immune to democratic dialogue. Psychoanalytic theory diagnoses the impossibility of full, complete and stable identities as the key to the human condition. It suggests that subjects are necessarily engaged in an infinite search for compensation for their permanent inadequacy, but it cannot predict exactly which phantasmatic or imaginary elements will be temporarily accepted by actual subjects in a concrete context as effective substitutes.

To say that gender and biological sex are both discursively constructed is not to say that they have no material impact on our lives. Sex and gender may be strategic fictions, but these fictions are key elements in the operation of many tremendously powerful institutions and apparatuses. Here an analogy could be offered between post-structuralist feminist thought and critical race theory. Critical race theorists contend that race is wholly discursively constructed. For Gates, race is a "biological misnomer," a "metaphor" and a "trope" (Gates 1985b: 4, 5). Gates' view is supported by recent scientific inquiries that question the "natural" character of racial categories (Holmes 1994; Holt 1994). Appiah concludes that the "biologization of culture and ideology" in racial discourse is purely contingent: "there are no races, there is nothing in the world that can do all we ask 'race' to do for us" (Appiah 1985: 36, 35).[3]

Gates' and Appiah's insistence on the arbitrariness of race can be used as a powerful antidote against the revival of biological racism[4] and against the new racism's "naturalization" of rigid and exclusionary cultural differences (Barker 1981; Balibar 1991b; Smith 1994b; Salecl 1994: 12–14). It should be emphasized, however, that although Gates and Appiah contend that there is no such thing as "race," they are certainly not saying that "there is no such thing as racism." The claim that race is arbitrarily constructed within specific configurations of power relations does not contradict the assertion that racism has become so hegemonic that no one escapes racial structural positioning. Like all authoritarian forces, racism wants to make the contingent processes of racial structural positioning disappear, such that highly political conceptions of racial otherness and whiteness are accepted as "nature" – hence the backlash of conservatives against multicultural and anti-racist curricula. When the conservatives charge that progressive educators are "politicizing the classroom," they are only half correct, for "the classroom" never was a neutral site in the first place. Progressive educators are actually re-politicizing racial, ethnic and national identities precisely by revealing the power relations that operate behind the appearance of unity, necessity and nature.

Higginbotham argues that race, like gender and class, is a social construction: "[Race is a] highly contested representation of relations of power between social categories by which individuals are identified and identify themselves" (1992: 253). For Higginbotham, it is only by grasping the constructed character of race that we can observe the operation of power: the ways in which disciplining strategies advance through racialization, the struggles that take place over racial categorization and racial representation, and the naturalizing concealment of racialization. The rejection of the view that racial differences are pre-discursively constituted allows us to sharpen our analysis of both the ways in which these differences have been constructed in racist traditions and the possibilities for anti-racist resistance. Where we do find discourses in which race appears to operate as if it were a trans-historical and immutable nature, such as Herrnstein and Murray's *The Bell Curve*, we need to pierce the strategic devices of naturalization to reveal the highly political discursive forces that produce this essentialist effect.[5] In this sense, we could say that not only is the constructivist approach entirely compatible with the study of racial power configurations, we cannot even begin to study racial power unless we adopt the constructivist viewpoint.

Constructivism does not, therefore, amount to an "anything goes," "you-can-be-whoever-you-want-to-be" voluntarism. There is no sense whatsoever in the work of Gates, Appiah and Higginbotham that those individuals who find themselves positioned as racially "other" could opt into whiteness simply because the boundary between those two categories has no pre-discursive basis. Racial meanings are "arbitrary" in Saussurean terms because they are not established prior to discourse. However, dominant political forces are interested in the normalization of some racial meanings and the exclusion of others. Because every individual is structurally positioned within discursive fields that are shaped by forces that are to some extent prior to her will, no one can fully escape these structures' limiting effects. Further, because hegemonic social structures condition identity formation – by normalizing some subject positions and excluding others – no one is perfectly free to construct the frameworks through which she lives her structural positionings. Alternative frameworks are never impossible, but their promotion never takes place in a vacuum. The meaning of alternative identities is always to some extent influenced by the meaning of hegemonic identities. Subversive political practices must always wage a complex and sophisticated game of appropriation and redefinition.

Here again we must insist on the lack of total closure in each formation of power relations and the lack of a perfectly functional fit between different formations. Laclau and Mouffe develop this argument in philosophical terms with reference to the Derridean (non-)concept of supplementarity. Because every social formation constitutes itself through its supplementary relation with a constitutive outside, and because it always fails in the end to master its relation with that outside, it remains vulnerable to subversion, for it is constitutionally dependent upon a potentially unruly otherness. This argument can also be phrased in Foucauldian terms. Contemporary forms of power are fundamentally productive: objectification, the regulation of social agency, is achieved through subjectivation, the construction of a mobile subject who is incited to perform self-disciplinary practices. Incitement processes are, however, notoriously complicated. Strategic limitations that originally had regulatory effects may actually have unpredictable enabling effects.

Again, we could point here to the paradoxical domestic effects of foreign policy as an example. When American statesmen proclaimed that the United States was the leader of the "free world" during the Cold War, Martin Luther King, Jr. and other civil rights leaders took advantage of America's official investment in its democratic reputation. At a time when economic, ideological and military wars were being fought to ensure the global hegemony of American capital, images of officially-sanctioned racist violence in American towns and cities were televised across the world, causing profound public relations problems for the American government. Although the Cold War certainly did have a chilling effect on the leftist elements of the domestic civil rights movement, as many anti-racist organizations were banned as "communist" (Marable 1991: 18), America's geo-politically inspired interest in constructing the United States as an exemplary egalitarian space had unforeseen and productive consequences for the cause of civil rights. Racism operated in Cold War America as a hegemonic social structure that exercised an almost omnipotent authority in terms of the naturalization of racial structural positionings and the regulation of the interpretative frameworks through which those racial positionings were lived; indeed, this remains the case today. There are nevertheless moments of "backfiring" and dysfunctional inconsistencies in this and every other apparatus. By their very nature, disciplinary incitements and regulatory apparatuses may produce radically dysfunctional effects; techniques of social control may unintentionally create favorable conditions for the construction of oppositional subject positions; legitimation discourses may inadvertently enable criticism; and overdetermination may keep an apparently closed discursive space open to the subversive influences of "outside" discourses. As such, there is always the possibility that resistance can flourish in the most unlikely situations.

Where Butler's theory has been interpreted as an endorsement of a voluntarist approach to politics, this has only been achieved through the suppression of crucial parts of her discourse. With Butler's claim that gender is "performative," she is not only appropriating Derrida's reinterpretation of speech act theory (Derrida 1988), she is also adding something to his text, namely a political analysis of power relations. For Butler, gender is performative in the sense that the social structures in which we are gendered are nothing but the effect of practices. Further, although Butler affirms that alternative interpretations of given gender structures may give rise to subversive practices, Butler never speaks about resistance as if it took place in a vacuum. Commenting on de Beauvoir, she states, "Gender is the repeated stylization of the body, a set of repeated acts within a highly rigid regulatory frame that congeal over time to produce the appearance of substance, of a natural sort of being" (1990a: 33). Like Martin, Higginbotham, Fausto-Sterling, Bem, Davis, Adams and many other feminist theorists, Butler recognizes the structured character of identity formation. We are all positioned within social structures; notwithstanding their incomplete character, these structures delimit, to a greater or lesser extent, the boundaries of effective resistance in a given historical context. The powerful reactionary forces that are constitutive of oppressive and exploitative structures seek to promote the interpretative subject positions that legitimate those structures, and to exclude the rival interpretative frameworks that threaten to incite subversive practices.

Butler's argument is therefore analogous to that of the critical race theorists and Laclau and Mouffe. Gender, race and class are all strategic fictions in the sense that they are not given pre-discursively, but this does not mean that sexism, racism and capitalism do not exercise actual material effects. The advance of sexism, racism and capitalism depends precisely on the deployment of these normalizing fictions, while resistance depends on the deployment of alternative constructions.

"Methodology," "family resemblances" and the study of power

Given the plurality of possible interpretations of gender, and the always shifting character of gender structures, theories that are based on the presumption of a natural unity among women, or a trans-historical and cross-cultural structure of women's oppression, are problematic. However, this is not to say that we cannot conceptualize the continuities and linkages between different instances of women's oppression. The challenge for feminist theory is to develop analyses of women's oppression that capture institutionalized patterns of repetition without losing sight of contextually specific complexities. Following Laclau's appropriation of Wittgenstein, we could say that social and political theory ought to trace patterns of repetition and institutionalization, but only in the form of non-essentialist "family resemblances" (Laclau 1990a: 21–2, 29, 208–9, 214; Wittgenstein 1958: paras. 66, 69, 185–90; Staten 1984: 13–14, 82). Here the limits of theory must be acknowledged. Strictly speaking, "methodology" is impossible, for the empirical and the transcendental always contaminate one another (Foucault 1970: 318–22; Feyerabend 1993). At best, theory can make us more sensitive to the probability that hegemonic social forces will prevail to a greater or lesser degree in future contexts, but it can never fully predict those configurations. As we study different types of institutions and different discursive constructions of identities, we should expect to find a complicated network of similarities and differences between and among them.

As we saw in Chapter 1, it is impossible to offer universal definitions of the relations between gender and the accumulation of surplus value, or between race and labor market segmentation. It is equally impossible to use a category such as gender to isolate a group of individuals and then offer universal statements about their condition without paying close attention to contextual specificity. The ways in which biological sex and gender structural positionings are overdetermined by other structures may mean that some women are positioned as oppressors and/or exploiters of other women (Alarcón 1990). We cannot, for example, construct a universal account that would explain the ways in which all women and girls are being affected by the globalization of industrial production. We could offer some generalizations, but we would also have to pay close attention to class, national, racial, ethnic, religious and other differences. We also have to anticipate the possibility that different women live their sex and gender structural positionings through antagonistic subject positions. Racially-constructed subject positions, for example, often give rise to intra-gender antagonisms. Where intra-gender antagonisms exist, feminist solidarity can only be constructed by working through these tensions; it cannot be assumed that such a solidarity is always already meaningful.

Some features may be present across most of the sexist, racist, capitalist and homophobic structures that we study, but those features should not be treated as if they were essences. Other characteristics may emerge in only a few cases, but they should not be dismissed as irrelevant accidents or anomalies. We can trace the birth, extension and decline of specific apparatuses, but we will never find teleological and predictable patterns according to which history is supposed to unfold. From non-teleological, genealogical historical research (Foucault 1977) and "family resemblances" comparative research, we can suggest probable outcomes, but we cannot produce a perfectly accurate map of future social structures. As soon as we discover a "rule" that seems to govern the operation of a given institution in one context, we will find that that rule has to be more or less reformulated as we apply it to a different context. It is nevertheless crucially important that radical democratic theory traces systematic and yet incomplete patterns of repetitions, normalizations, and institutionalizations, for effective counter-hegemonic strategies must always take the prevailing configuration of power relations into account.

It should also be recognized that Laclau adds a political supplement to Wittgenstein's theory. Having displaced essence with "family resemblances," Wittgenstein contends that the boundaries that shape meaning are built up over time as the members of the social group who share the language game in question engage in imperfectly repetitive usages. Laclau would add that the arbitrariness of the boundaries of meaning implies that the boundaries that do appear to operate as hard and fast rules – rules that seem to be absolutely necessary – only have that appearance thanks to the concealed effects of power relations. If it appears that only one form of "femininity," "masculinity," "marriage" or "the family" is "natural," then what we are dealing with is concealed power. For this reason, apparently "neutral" terms can at times become the object of tremendous controversy. For example, conservatives from many countries criticized the United Nations' documents relating to the 1995 International Conference On Women in Beijing because these texts used the term "gender" rather than "male" and "female." It was alleged that "gender" signaled the promotion of homosexuality – since lesbianism, male homosexuality and transsexuality are understood by some conservatives as third, fourth and fifth genders – and the rejection of biologically-determined sex roles (Flanders 1997: 7). Again, sexist, homophobic and other authoritarian forces are heavily invested in the maintenance of certain boundaries of meaning; they will always resist any analysis that challenges their attempts to govern the meaning of key terms. The very tools that we use to study power configurations may at times become the objects of political struggle.

Critics of post-structuralist feminist theory have often argued that the claim that "woman" and "women" are nothing but strategic fictions ultimately undermines political solidarity. The response to such a charge is best stated in an almost self-contradictory manner. As Spivak argues, we inevitably speak in fictitious universalizing terms whenever we think strategically. The simple repudiation of all universalizing formulations in the name of theoretical correctness is not only a self-defeating gesture, but is often motivated by an unacknowledged claim to intellectual superiority. Spivak contends instead that we should engage in the impossible and yet tactically crucial attempt to master universalizing rhetoric where it may serve our purposes, and remain all the while vigilant about its totalizing effects. Universal claims, for all their fictitious character, can have tremendous pragmatic value as provisional starting points for activism; the task for radical democratic activists is to examine the ways in which they conceal antagonisms and foreclose alternative practices (1988a, 1988b; Spivak and Grosz 1990: 11–12; Spivak et al. 1990: 117–18).

Haraway points out that the female biological category is itself highly contested in scientific discourse, and that the mere fact that some persons share the common experience of being categorized as "female" does not automatically give rise to solidarity between them. Where some type of "gender consciousness" does become meaningful and effective, it does so in response to political contingencies. "Gender, race or class consciousness is an achievement forced on us by the terrible historical experience of the contradictory social realities of patriarchy, colonialism, and capitalism" (Haraway 1991: 155).

Although post-structuralist feminist theory shares many constructivist assumptions with Kuhn's paradigm theory, it also suggests that there can only be a partial resolution to the process of discursive contestation in any given historical moment. Wherever sex and gender have become the sites of intense social contestation, many different gendering interpretative frameworks will compete with one another in their bid to hegemonize the social. Feminist interpretations of gender solidarity must struggle against the interest-driven "experts" who are deeply invested in the perpetuation of disciplinary constructions of the "woman" identity. Medical, psychoanalytic and aesthetic experts "do the work of limiting and regulating what it means to be a woman in line with the exigencies of their own discursive fields and legitimating truths" (Martin 1988: 14). Regulatory discourses with tremendous authority are able not only to set the agenda on gender issues; they also establish the rules that shape the boundaries of acceptable discourse and set out in advance a table of the subjects who qualify for recognition as legitimate social agents. This is but one of the many double binds that feminism confronts: where feminists work to unify women, they must ensure that they are not doing so according to the terms established by the patriarchal "experts" and thereby unintentionally promoting reactionary gender frameworks and exclusions. Where the patriarchal "experts" build misogynist, racist and heterosexist elements into their apparently "natural" definition of "woman," feminists must strive to ensure that their models of gender solidarity do not perpetuate these exclusions. The risk is that where the boundaries of the very categories that define the limits of feminist solidarity are rigidly determined in advance, some interests, issues and minority women subjects may be excluded. Butler contends that it is only a feminist movement that keeps the boundaries of feminist solidarity open to renegotiation that can avoid such exclusionary practices (Butler 1990a: 15). Martin concludes that "the question for those of us engaged in the development of new forms of discourse is how to enter struggles over the meaning(s) of woman in ways that do not repress pluralities, without losing sight of the political necessity for fiction and unity" (Martin 1988: 14).

The fully constructivist conception of identity adopted by Butler and Laclau and Mouffe is therefore not incompatible with political strategizing. In some situations, their approach can be indispensable for theorizing radical democratic political practices. A rigorous application of constructivist theory would not contradict the discourses that call for feminist action against sexist forces; it would only contradict those arguments that take women's unity as always already given.

The hegemony debate: a defense of Stuart Hall

The term, "hegemony," is often read as a synonym for "domination." Theorists working in the Gramscian tradition, however, take Gramsci's "centaur" metaphor (1971: 169–70) as their starting point. According to Gramsci, political authority in contemporary societies has two dimensions, force and the organization of consent. The organization of consent refers to the cultural dimension that is present in every political project, namely its promotion of popular identifications in terms of its corresponding imaginary. Again, Althusser holds that in a social formation that is structured by domination, a functional relationship will ultimately be established between the "repressive State apparatus" and the "Ideological State Apparatuses"

(1971: 150). Laclau and Mouffe would argue, by contrast, that social formations are never perfectly sutured together such that this sort of functional fit is obtained.[6] We will never find, for example, a perfect fit between governmental policies in the public education system and the goals of the global multi-media corporations. Private corporations can gain a marketing foothold in the classroom by sponsoring internet instruction. But, at the same time, students using the internet may get access to information about homosexuality, feminism, safer sex education and anti-corporate environmental activism that would have been otherwise difficult for them to obtain. Further, the disciplinary and cultural aspects of power are never neatly segregated in distinct institutions. There is, for example, a cultural moment in policing and a violent exclusionary moment in popular culture.

While Foucault developed a highly sophisticated theory of disciplinary bio-power relations – which is in some ways remarkably similar to Gramsci's conception of the organization of consent – he failed to give adequate attention to the presence of subtractive strategies within contemporary disciplinary regimes. Although Foucault asserts that bio-power fully displaced sovereign power during the early modern period, we are now witnessing the deployment of new forms of brutal subtractive power in key points within complex Western societies. When police and immigration officials brutally beat blacks, Latinos and Latinas only a few miles away from Los Angeles' financial district, when it is revealed that that violence has become a systemic aspect of inner-city post-colonial policing, and when capitalist greed promises to produce increasingly large "surplus populations," we can expect more and more complex articulations of brutal violence with disciplinary modes of social control. Instead of seeing power in terms of an either/or model – either brute subtractive domination or sophisticated productive bio-power normalization – we should think instead in terms of hybrid formations in which subtractive modes – domination, exclusion, genocide and so on – are combined with productive modes – the organization of consent.

Hall's interpretation of Thatcherism as a hegemonic formation (1988a) has been the subject of numerous debates. His critics claim that he portrayed Thatcherism as a dominant regime that had successfully incited the normalization and acceptance of its basic values (Jessop *et al.* 1988; Hirst 1989; Crewe 1988). However, when they point to opinion polls that apparently show that many of the people who voted for Thatcher actually disliked her policies, they miss the most innovative aspect of Hall's argument. Hall did not actually claim that the Conservative Party had turned a majority of British voters into a camp of enthusiastic Thatcherites. He held that Thatcherism engaged in a hegemonic struggle in the following sense: it disorganized the prevailing political formation, namely the post-war bi-partisan consensus; it waged a cultural war to redefine key values in different spheres of the social: the economy, civil society, intellectual and moral life; it deployed a large and highly differentiated set of strategies; and it neutralized the opposition while creating a small group of fervent supporters who could synecdochically stand in for the whole electorate (1988a: 7).

It is of course true that the "pocket-book" strategy was one of the factors that

contributed to Thatcher's electoral success. Some key sectors of the voting population gained substantially from Thatcherite policies such as the deregulation of
the private sector, tax-cutting schemes and the sale of council housing. But
"pocket-book" politics cannot explain why the numbers of Thatcherite voters
vastly exceeded the numbers of economic gainers, or why Thatcherism enjoyed
substantial success in its bid to transform the entire political agenda and political
culture. Hall usefully insists that "elections are not won or lost on so-called 'real'
majorities, but on (equally real) 'symbolic majorities'" (1988a: 262). There is in
fact substantial evidence that many voters supported Thatcher in spite of their
dislike for her actual policies because she seemed to be a "strong leader," and she
made them feel "good to be British again." Her success is also due in part to the
fact that the Conservatives stigmatized the Labour Party by effectively associating
it with unpopular groups such as militant trade unions, radical blacks and lesbians
and gays (Smith 1994b: 28–69). Only an analysis that combines the measurement
of "pocket-book" politics with the study of political symbols and their material
effects can adequately explain the paradoxical success of formations such as
Thatcherism.

From organic crisis to the institutionalization of a new imaginary

Laclau and Mouffe's theory of hegemony provides many valuable theoretical
formulations that allow us to extend Butler's and Hall's analyses. Following
Gramsci, Laclau insists in his early work that every analysis of a strategic discursive
intervention must begin with historical contextualization. In what Gramsci calls
an "organic crisis," there is a dramatic collapse in popular identifications with
institutionalized subject positions and political imaginaries. At this point, the
prevailing discursive formations are peculiarly vulnerable to critique from any
number of perspectives. The meaning of key signifiers, such as "democracy,"
"freedom" and "equality," are unusually available for multiple alternative articulations (Laclau 1977: 103). Although identification with subject positions never
fully meets the subject's goal of making herself "at home" in her given structural
positionings, she tends to experience the gap between the explanations provided
by her subject positions and the material effects of her structural positionings in a
particularly acute manner during an organic crisis. The 1960s in the United States
is a case in point. Traditional patriotism failed to incite mass support for the
Vietnam War, while traditional patriarchal, racial and political discourses were
denounced as morally bankrupt by growing numbers of activists. In these and other
similar conditions, we could say that more and more subjects become caught up in
an "identity crisis"; their sense of alienation can become especially unbearable at
this moment, such that their drive to seek out alternative explanatory frameworks
is intensified. We should also note that in a fully-fledged breakdown of the social
order, the experience of an identity crisis is shared not only by many of the disempowered but also by a significant proportion of the dominant groups as well.

Hegemonic strategies are particularly effective during an organic crisis. More and more subjects become unusually open to innovative political discourses; they therefore begin to experience the network of social structures into which they have been thrown as antagonistically blocking them from becoming what they believe to be their true selves – a phantasmatic construction that is itself always shifting. As this experience of lack becomes more and more acute, competing political forces will attempt to "hegemonize" the social: they will attempt to offer their specific "systems of narration" as a compensatory framework, and they will represent that framework as the only one that can resolve the identity crisis (Laclau 1977: 103; 1996h: 44). The emerging hegemonic discourse works simultaneously to deepen the identity crisis by further undermining the crumbling traditional regime, to construct a new framework for identification, and to represent that framework as if it exhausted the terrain of legitimate discourse.

Gramsci makes an important distinction between different strategic situations. In moments in which power is heavily concentrated in a singular state apparatus, as was the case in Tsarist Russia at the turn of the century, then resistance should be deployed according to a "war of maneuver" strategy: a single front that is mobilized directly against the single power center. In contemporary complex societies, however, we are rarely confronted with a situation in which power is heavily concentrated in a single center and wielded like a subtractive instrument according to a uniform logic. With Foucault, Gramsci contends that we are now generally confronted with situations in which power is concentrated in diverse institutional centers and deployed in complex and productive relations throughout the social according to multiple and hybrid logics. In these conditions, resistance should take the form of a "war of position": a complex ensemble of struggles that take place at multiple strategic sites in state apparatuses, civil society and the family (Gramsci 1971: 236–9).

The multiple struggles that take place in a "war of position" deployment must be unified to gain maximum effectiveness, but in a site-specific manner such that their difference is not canceled out. In Gramsci's terms, an increasingly sophisticated and strategically effective unifying strategy should move through three stages. In the first and crudest stage, a social movement is organized according to what Gramsci, invoking Hegel's *Philosophy of Right*, calls its "economic-corporate" interests. At this stage, the social group's solidarity is defined in the most particularistic terms. As the movement begins to act more and more as a hegemonic agent, redefining its demands in the light of other demands, and offering its discourse as a nodal point that symbolically sums up the interests of the other movements, it becomes first a "social class" and then a "party" (Gramsci 1971: 181). The hegemonic discourse functions as the political "glue" that holds the historic bloc together as it stands in opposition against its enemy bloc. The process of this transition is enormously complicated, and involves complex reconstructions of identities and values. Further, each movement's influence in these multilateral negotiations varies according to its institutionalized authority; I will return to this difficult problem in the Conclusion.

Against Gramsci, Laclau and Mouffe argue that we cannot predict which movement will become the hegemonic agent, for this depends upon the specific conditions that obtain in a given historical formation. In his more recent work, Laclau also apparently differs with Gramsci in his emphasis on the formal character of hegemonic discourse. As we have seen, Laclau argues in these texts that the compelling aspect of a hegemonic discourse consists primarily in the orderly and coherent nature of its social imaginary, and not in its actual content.

The difference between Laclau and Gramsci on this point is not as great as it may appear at first glance. Gramsci contends that although every party is in one sense "the expression of a social group," a party can, in hegemonic conditions, "exercise a balancing and arbitrating function between the interests of their group and those of other groups, and succeed in securing the development of the group which they represent with the consent and assistance of the allied groups." In an especially provocative phrase, he claims that the arbitration function of the party is analogous to that of the constitutional monarch who "reigns but does not govern," and that the party must always strive "by various means to give the impression that it is working actively and effectively as an 'impartial force' " (1971: 148). In these passages, Gramsci refines his conception of hegemony: hegemony consists not merely in the unification of diverse social groups through articulation, but also in the construction of a political leadership that offers itself as an apparently "neutral space" for the inscription of a broad range of political demands – as nothing less than the horizon that makes all political discourse possible.

This formal aspect of hegemonic discourse is also emphasized in Lefort's analysis of what he calls the "invisible ideology" that prevails in contemporary Western societies. The discourse of consumption, for example, constructs an apparently closed universe in which multiple demands can be satisfied, but its framing function remains invisible insofar as totalization becomes latent. Following Baudrillard, Lefort suggests that our desire for a consumer product is not driven by any specific interest for that commodity in its particularity; on the contrary, we desire the particular product because it synecdochically symbolizes the entire "system of objects" (1986: 234–5). Further, in the fake intimacy that characterizes much of popular discourse, the distance between political leaders and the led appears to have shrunk to zero such that "everything is in principle sayable, visible [and] intelligible" (1986: 229). Ideology brings about the closure that structures discourse and desire itself, but it simultaneously makes that closure imperceptible (1986: 235). Similarly, Barthes contends that "myth" constructs a "universal order" that de-politicizes contingent and historical discourse such that they appear to be legitimate, eternal, normal and natural (1973: 143, 155). And Marx himself analyzed the various ways in which bourgeois ideology naturalizes commodity fetishism and structurally excludes revolutionary discourse from the realm of coherent thought. For Marx, liberal democratic discourse suppresses its bourgeois particularity in order to offer itself as an apparently class-neutral framework in which all demands for human rights could be resolved (Marx 1977; Barrett 1991: 14–15; Mepham 1979: 152).

166

Working in this tradition, Laclau contends that the emerging hegemonic discourse must aim to position itself not just as one alternative among many, but as the only possible framework for the resolution of the crisis. A political discourse that aims to become hegemonic initially offers itself as a "myth." Its individual concrete demands must be transformed such that they symbolize much more than its particular content (Norval 1996: 9). A narrowly-defined single issue campaign, for example, could offer itself as the defining framework within which every legitimate demand ought to be expressed. In this sense, the emerging hegemonic discourse in its mythical form operates as a "surface of inscription" or a "space of representation." By operating in this manner, it promises to explain, to compensate for, and to suture over, the dislocation in the social structure. And yet, at the same time, there is nothing in the dislocation itself that guarantees that any specific discourse could take on this mythical function (Laclau 1990a: 61). With these developments, each demand in the emerging hegemonic discourse is constructed so that it appears to be organically linked to a chain of other demands; ultimately, each position evokes an entire series of positions (Laclau 1977: 102–3). The hegemonic bloc or Hall's synecdochical "symbolic majority" "now emerges not with isolated demands, nor as an organized alternative *within the system*, but as a political alternative to the system itself" (Laclau 1977: 116). A truly hegemonic discourse will suppress its literal content – its specific demands, its specific origins as a single issue movement – in favor of its metaphorical dimension – its self-representation as the principle of order itself. In this later stage, a hegemonic discourse becomes an imaginary, for it claims to embody the whole "principle of reconstruction of the entire ideological domain" (Laclau 1977: 103).

We could, then, propose the following political cycle. First, we have the development of an organic crisis and the weakening of the traditional hegemonic discourse. Alternative discourses compete to offer myths to account for the crisis, and horizons that organize identifications with their respective versions of popular subject positions. One discourse begins to prevail over the others, thanks not only to its linkages with residual, enduring and emerging institutions, but also to its form. Where other alternatives tend to retain a "single issue" focus, the concrete demands contained in the hegemonic discourse are "metaphorized." It offers itself as an interpretation of the crisis, and then as a "surface of inscription," that is, as a powerful explanatory and legitimizing framework for a wider and wider set of political demands (Norval 1996: 96). Ultimately, it begins to signify not just a single literal political position, but an entire new social order (Laclau 1990a: 64). As the emerging hegemonic discourse begins to construct a normalized horizon of intelligibility, it begins to reconstruct the prevailing networks of subject positions, for its own table of authorized subject positions will be at least somewhat unique. The cycle of the hegemonic regime's reproduction is set into motion as the newly transformed subject positions tend to incite practices along the lines of "regulated improvisations." At the same time, consciousness of the fact that the emerging hegemonic discourse obtains its coherence and unity

167

only because of its negativity – its antagonistic relation with its enemy figures – increasingly recedes. This is, of course, an ideal version of this process; once again, the complex and contradictory character of identification will ensure the proliferation of unpredictable and dysfunctional incitements.

During the first days of a new hegemonic order, identifications with the newly transformed subject positions may be somewhat unstable, as their novelty remains readily apparent. Over time, however, these identifications may become increasingly routinized. Routinization of course introduces a whole new set of challenges for the hegemonic formation within its own power centers such as unpredictable careerism, alienation, unintended acts of subversion as rules are applied in new contexts, the exhaustion of popular demonizations, and so on. In the more effective moments of a hegemonic formation, however, identifications with the subject positions that have been reshaped under the influence of the new horizon of intelligibility will be experienced as a recovery of a "nature" that has been there all along (Norval 1996: 13). Awareness of the paradox at the center of this experience, namely that "nature" has to be constantly produced through intensive intervention, will tend to be foreclosed. In some cases, identifications will become so normalized and so heavily supported by an almost seamless web of institutional props that the whole process of identification will disappear from view altogether. In some moments, "nature" will be experienced not so much as something that has to be "recovered" but as something that has always reigned supreme through time. At other moments, even as normalization has reached this intensity, alienation will reassert itself, necessitating an endless and mobile set of tactics on the part of hegemonic forces to manage the social.

The ability of one hegemonic strategy to prevail over the others in these conditions is primarily based on its linkages with institutions that retain some degree of authority throughout the organic crisis, its embodiment in emerging institutions that quickly obtain authority, and its iterations of already normalized traditions. As McClintock argues, the deployment of archaic signifiers can paradoxically play a key role in this process insofar as they effectively symbolize what is new in the emerging hegemonic formation, while simultaneously creating the sense that that formation is nothing more than a return to an imaginary golden age (1995: 376). The formal characteristics of a political discourse are of course also important. As Laclau, following Gramsci, points out, a discourse can only become hegemonic if its "system of narration" operates as a surface of inscription for a wide variety of demands. However, as we have already seen in Chapter 2, Laclau's almost exclusive emphasis on the formal aspect of hegemony in his later work is such that the Gramscian principle of historical contextualization is suppressed. Like Žižek, Laclau sometimes gives the impression that a hegemonic discourse becomes compelling simply because of its abstract formal operation, namely its provision of an orderly space for the inscription of political demands.

Laclau and Zac, for example, cite a passage in Mann's *Lotte in Weimar* in which the citizens of the city shift their support from the Napoleonic occupying force to the Prussians. The Prussians were initially regarded as "barbarians," but as their victory over the French became more certain, they were hailed as noble "liberators." Mann's narrator explains that the Weimar residents identified with the Prussians because " 'we human beings are by nature submissive. We need to live in harmony with outward events and situations' " (1994: 16). Laclau and Zac remark that the Weimar citizens were not being merely opportunistic; they were searching for a political force that could secure order in their community. They emphasize the formal aspects of the Prussian discourse in their commentary.

> The possibility of identification with a certain political order depended not only on its political virtues or attractiveness abstractly considered, but on its ability to guarantee the continuity of the community. But this continuity, precisely because it did not coincide with any of the political forms that would make it possible at particular moments in time – precisely because it would have no content of its own – would be nothing other than the name of an absent plenitude that could not be exhausted by any of the concrete forms that would attempt to realize it.
>
> (1994: 16)

Laclau does qualify his emphasis on the formal characteristics of an effective hegemonic discourse. Laclau and Zac state, for example, that the "filling function" of a hegemonic discourse as it offers compensation for ruptures in the social "requires an empty place," that is, a subject that is the subject of the lack, who is, therefore, condemned to the endless search for compensation through identification. This "empty place," the subject, "is, to some extent, indifferent to the content of the filling, though this filling function has to be incarnated in *some* concrete contents, whatever those contents might be" (1994: 15). Indifference to content, then, is only partial, never total. Further, Laclau does recognize that there must be some organic link between an effective hegemonic discourse and the traces of traditional identities among "the people" (1990a: 66). Laclau nevertheless claims that elements such as "[the] 'collective will,' 'organic ideology,' 'hegemonic group' and so forth become empty forms that can be filled by any imaginable political and social content" (1996f: 81).

In my approach, by contrast, I am attempting to give greater emphasis to Gramscian contextualization without losing the psychoanalytic insights in Laclau's recent work. Again, where one discourse prevails over the others and begins to assert itself effectively as hegemonic, its achievement is due not only to its abstract form, but also to its linkages with residual, enduring and emerging institutions. The moment in which virtually every institution would crumble to the ground, every traditional discourse would collapse and every individual would fall into a total identity crisis is infinitely postponed. The social is always "partially structured and partially unstructured" (Laclau 1996h: 46). Some traditions and institutions retain authority even as others disintegrate. The emerging hegemonic discourse must quickly gain strategic advantage by developing its appropriations from residual traditions, and by becoming embodied not only in the emerging institutions, but in the institutions that retain authority throughout the organic crisis as well. Hegemonic articulations also tend to work more effectively to the extent that previous traditions and institutions have been weakened, such that key political practices and values become more vulnerable to reinterpretation. Traditions that have remained more or less intact will resist redefinition more effectively. As Laclau himself admits, popular traditions cannot be manipulated in a voluntaristic manner, for they are "a residue of a unique and irreducible historical experience" (Laclau 1977: 167).

My position, then, is closer to that of Butler's post-structuralist theory of performativity than to Laclau's formalism. Although Butler often constructs her argument as an explicit critique of voluntarism, her remarks remain suggestive for the construction of a non-formalistic approach to hegemony.

> If a performative succeeds (and I will suggest that "success" is always and only provisional), then it is not because an intention successfully governs the action of speech, but only because that action echoes prior actions, and *accumulates the force of authority through the repetition or citation of a prior and authoritative set of practices*. It is not simply that the speech act takes place *within* a practice, but that the act is itself a ritualized practice. What this means, then, is that a performative "works" to the extent that *it draws on and covers over* the constitutive conventions by which it is mobilized. In this sense, no term or statement can function performatively without the accumulating and dissimulating historicity of force.
>
> (1997a: 51)

To follow Butler's example, a racial slur can have a tremendous material effect: it can link the speaker with a racist community, and it can disempower the listener (assuming here that she is a person of color) by reminding her that the present moment is in part structured, officially and unofficially, by a powerful racist tradition. If the listener attempts to reverse the tactic – if she in turn mobilizes her identification with other people of color and cites a collective response from the anti-racist tradition – then the dissimulation dimension goes to work. American law tells her that the speaking situation is not one in which the traces of past traditions have been cited and collective identifications mobilized, that it is merely a singular moment involving two utterly isolated individuals, and that unprotected speech ("fighting words") cannot be defined with respect to their content (Butler 1997a; Matsuda *et al.*1993; Williams 1991: 112–15). Ironically enough, if there is an "empty signifier" in this story, it is the racial slur – not in the moment of its operation as a credible threat, since that depends upon its citationality, but after its historicity has been strategically suppressed by the neo-conservative judiciary. Signifiers such as the Confederate flag only appear to be totally "empty" and therefore perfectly open to a new articulation – in this case, articulation as a harmless emblem of "Southern culture" – insofar as the

170

political forces that are interested in the erasure of its historicity have prevailed (Williams 1995: 29–30).[7]

As a hegemonic discourse gains authority, it becomes the framework through which more and more identifications become possible, as more and more subject positions are reconstructed with reference to its logic. At its highest moment of authority, the hegemonic discourse becomes an imaginary.

> The imaginary is a horizon: it is not one among other objects but an absolute limit which structures a field of intelligibility and is thus the condition of possibility for the emergence of any object.
>
> (Laclau 1990a: 64)

In the terms used by the Thatcherites, a hegemonic discourse strives to represent itself not just as a list of political positions or a bloc of concrete social agents, and not just as one alternative among many, but as the only possible alternative to total chaos.

This is the key element in Hall's analysis of Thatcherism, for Hall asserts that the hegemonic advance of Thatcherism depended in large part on its ability to operate as a social imaginary. Many of the political demands in the Thatcherite program were constructed such that they signified much more than their literal content. The Thatcherites did not, for example, merely depict their attack on local government autonomy as a sound constitutional reform; they consistently linked local governments with wasteful spending on programs that primarily benefited blacks, Asians, unions and homosexuals. In this and many other cases, the Thatcherites' demands signified an authoritarian populist common sense that responded effectively to everyday concerns about the economy, the family, race, gender and sexuality. Thatcherism became a defining framework for British politics, and a framework for identification on the part of just enough British voters – including many voters who rejected Thatcher's literal positions. This is not to say that given the popularity of racism and homophobia, any political demand whatsoever would have been accepted as long as it had been promoted in specifically racist and homophobic terms. The equation of local government autonomy with homosexual elements had to be "plausible" in order for this to work, and the boundaries of the "plausible" are always somewhat rigid in a given historical moment. New articulations, such as the equation of local government autonomy with the promotion of homosexuality, can gain plausibility insofar as they model themselves after already normalized traditions. In the Thatcherite case, for example, homophobic articulations gained plausibility because they borrowed extensively from racist traditions (Smith 1994b).

As it becomes an imaginary, the hegemonic discourse becomes embodied in a number of different key institutions, thereby ensuring the incitement of identifications within its framework in as many different sites in the social as possible. This is a crucial aspect of its operation: "The constitution of a social identity is an act of power [and] identity as such *is* power" (Laclau 1990a: 31). To the extent that a hegemonic discourse becomes an institutionalized horizon, it rules out alternative frameworks for identification as increasingly illegitimate, immoral, irrational and, finally, incoherent. Institutionalization therefore always entails an exercise of power: the brutal exclusion – concealed or explicit – of alternative frameworks. Further, institutionalization itself involves all sorts of complex strategic maneuvers to support this exclusion. In this sense, the condition of possibility of every identification is the effective operation of power mechanisms – either the institutionalization of a hegemonic discourse, or the advance of a counter-hegemonic discourse. Without power, there would be no "objectivity," in the sense that there would be no identities, and, without identities, nothing would incite the political practices that build up social structures (Laclau 1990a: 32). "Even in the most radical and democratic projects, social transformation thus means building a new power, not radically eliminating it" (Laclau 1990a: 33). Although identities and social structures always remain incomplete, they can become highly stabilized through normalization and institutionalization in favorable historical conditions.

The objectivity that we are confronted with, then, is like the accumulation of the traces that are left behind by power relations, and the institutionalization of these traces through regulated acts of iteration. Laclau, borrowing from Husserl, calls this accumulation of the traces that are built up by social apparatuses "sedimentation." Through sedimentation, practices that were at one time strange and unusual tend to become routinized, novel exclusions are increasingly taken for granted, and the political character of identity formation is more or less suppressed. In a metaphorical sense, sedimentation "spatializes" temporality: every series of iterated institutionalizations seeks to master the dislocations that remain fundamental to every social structure (Laclau 1990a: 41–5). In this condition, for example, one political slogan or metaphor seems to naturally evoke several others (Laclau 1977: 102).

The social never actually becomes fully colonized by hegemonic institutions; it always to some extent "overflows the institutionalized frameworks of 'society'" (Laclau 1994: 3). While images of perfect closure are necessary for the extension and intensification of hegemony, these images are wholly illusory (Laclau 1996i). If "sedimentation" consists of institutionalization and the forgetting of an institution's political origins, "reactivation" takes the form of re-politicization. A truly subversive counter-discourse will construct an alternative framework through which the forgotten political and contingent character of normalized identities and institutionalized social structures can be grasped (Laclau 1990a: 34). However, once a specific articulation is institutionalized, it will be increasingly difficult to promote a radically different articulation in an effective manner (Laclau 1996i). This is not because of anything inherent in the signifiers themselves; in logical terms, the possibilities for alternative articulations are infinite in number. In actual historical conditions, however, a given articulation only becomes effective, in the sense that it becomes a popular interpretative framework through which structural positionings are lived, insofar as it is embodied in authoritative institutions. The relative balance of power between institutions is always a contextually specific matter. We could say, therefore, that while alterna-tive articulations are always logically possible, a given alternative may or may not be strategically effective, depending on the given historical conditions.

The political meaning of reactivation, considered in and of itself, is politically undecidable. The mere demonstration of the contingency of the social formations that appear to be necessary does not, on its own, lead to any particular sort of ethical position. New racist discourse, for example, demonstrates the contingency of Western whiteness by portraying the latter as profoundly vulnerable to contami-nation and corruption, but then proceeds from this demonstration to promote the cleansing of racial and ethnic otherness from Western culture. A critique that only demonstrates the impossibility of closure does not necessarily lead to an "ethical imperative to 'cultivate' that openness" or to a commitment to democratic values (Laclau 1996f: 77).

The work of a hegemonic discourse is never finished; it remains endlessly trou-bled by alienation – a condition that can become acute even among its most fervent supporters – dysfunctional incitements, and resistances inspired by "outsider" discourse. Even with, for example, the massive shift towards the forma-tion of multi-media conglomerates that operate on a global scale, Hollywood films still make up only a fraction of world cinematic production (Shohat and Stam 1994: 30–1). Although Disney's foreign policy is now more influential than that of many countries, American mass culture has not fully succeeded in unilat-erally imposing its products on the "Third World." Using a rich conception of hegemony, Shohat and Stam conclude that even the most powerful media conglomerates cannot extinguish the possibility of resistant cultural work. They do nevertheless insist that this potential will only become effectively activated to the extent that it is politically organized (1994: 354).

One weakness of a hegemonic discourse is paradoxically exacerbated insofar as it becomes institutionalized as the very horizon of the social itself. Laclau considers, for example, a society in which the resistance tradition of an indige-nous people expresses the principle of popular opposition. Other communities and movements, such as radical peasants, urban squatters and militant trade union workers, will tend to appropriate indigenous symbols as they position themselves in opposition against dominant institutions (Laclau 1977: 180). At some point in this borrowing process, the previous connotation of the indigenous symbols will be weakened and their new connotations will become more vague, allowing more and more diverse groups to position themselves under their banner. This representational strategy of condensation (Laclau 1977: 177) will eventually make the unifying symbols so vague that the specificity of their opposi-tional meaning will be lost (Laclau 1996h: 45). Radical democratic pluralist traditions are equally vulnerable to the value dilution process. Although feminist discourse has not exactly achieved hegemonic status, it has nevertheless been subjected to complex processes of appropriation by right-wing political forces and corporate marketing discourses. Key feminist principles have been made into increasingly vague and empty symbols and then re-articulated with de-politicized discourse and even right-wing values (Eisenstein 1996; Smith 1997a). A defense of a radical democratic pluralist feminist politics in the face of these hostile appropriations would have to include what Laclau calls "reactivation," namely radicalizing counter-appropriations.

Hegemony, equivalence and difference

When a hegemonic project attempts to articulate more and more symbols and demands, it quickly comes up against the following problem: many of these elements stand in antagonistic relations against each other. Right-wing hegemonic forces in the United States, for example, are constantly faced with the challenge of redefining neo-conservatism and religious fundamentalism such that they can be integrated into a common worldview. A hegemonic discourse must strive to neutralize these antagonisms – with or without the conscious consent of the social agents in question – by effectively representing them as a bloc that stands opposed to a common enemy. It achieves this unification-effect by representing its articulated elements as equivalent signifiers in a chain that stands antagonistically opposed to another chain of signifiers, such as the opposition between "the people" and "the establishment." Each of the articulated elements retains some degree of specificity, but in this moment, the sense that all of them stand together in solidarity against the enemy bloc comes to the fore.

As we have seen, this type of constitutive representation is called the logic of equivalence. The effects of the logic of equivalence are limited, however, by the contrary effects produced by representations that are structured according to the logic of difference. The two logics limit each other such that neither one completely defines the social; the effects of a differential representation is suppressed insofar as it is displaced by an equivalential representation, and vice versa (Laclau and Mouffe 1985: 127–34). Much of hegemonic political strategizing consists in the management of political representation – the deployment of the logic of difference and the logic of equivalence – according to the prevailing tactical conditions. Each of the articulated elements takes on a fundamental ambiguity: it simultaneously connotes both its position as a differential element and the general principle of the opposition between its hegemonic bloc and the enemy bloc (Laclau 1996h: 41).

The hegemonic bloc must appear to provide a surface of inscription for the satisfaction of every legitimate demand. Of course, part of this appearance is achieved through concealed acts of exclusion. A center-right democratic discourse, for example, might construct itself as a universal surface of inscription by articulating multicultural symbols. Given its actual political orientation, however, it will probably embrace a conservative type of multiculturalism. The center-right movement will wage a concealed war against radical anti-racist, anti-sexist and anti-heterosexist forces, and, when it presents its multicultural face to the public, it will showcase only its carefully hand-picked conservative minority allies. In short, the appearance won by a hegemonic discourse as a space in which all the demands of all the people can be heard is supported by aggressive "behind-the-scenes" exclusionary campaigns to manage the boundaries between legitimate and illegitimate demands; and between "genuine citizens" and "surplus populations."

The tension between the logics of difference and equivalence is not necessarily fatal for political discourses. Norval contends, for example, that this tension constituted an undecidability that became central to the effectiveness of the apartheid regime (1996: 139, 169–73). As we saw in Chapter 3, Dole's 1996 Republican Presidential campaign was also marked by a fundamental undecidability with respect to representational management. In one moment, Dole emphasized a logic of equivalence strategy: he depicted himself as the leader of an all-out fight against liberal extremists to return the United States to its former "glory." He attempted to appeal to both the religious right and the neo-conservatives, embracing anti-Hollywood, homophobic, school prayer and anti-choice demands while suddenly converting to supply-side economic policies. At the same time, however, Dole took note of the declining popularity of House Speaker Gingrich's extremist Contract with America and the damage that had been done to the Republicans by its religious fundamentalist leaders during their 1992 Convention. Consequently, he deployed a logic of difference strategy as well: he attempted to create an imaginary national space in which the Republicans presided over a moderate, inclusionary and multiculturally diverse social order. Dole launched various symbolic efforts to construct the Republicans as a broad-based coalition. He made secret deals with the Christian Coalition to stop Buchanan's demagogic campaign. He worked for months, with limited success, to include language in the party's extremist platform that recognized the legitimacy of pro-choice Republicans. Republican officials ran a tightly scripted Convention that featured numerous women and people of color as speakers. Having achieved a voting record that won the approval of the Christian Coalition, Dole mostly avoided controversial issues such as welfare, abortion and homosexuality during his campaign. His campaign solicited, returned and then welcomed contributions from Republican homosexuals. He only emphasized his opposition to affirmative action and his demands for stricter immigration controls at the very end of his campaign, when it had become clear that he was not going to win, and his leadership was needed to encourage the "party faithful" to turn out to vote for the other Republican candidates.

Dole attempted to manage these contradictory representations by deploying them in different theaters of operation: the logic of equivalence "total war" images were concentrated in those sites in which Dole was speaking to the "party faithful," while the logic of difference images were emphasized wherever the nominee was speaking to the electorate as a whole. In any event, Dole and his supporters never succeeded in their bid to master the terrain of hegemonic politics. They did not bring the neo-conservatives and religious right into a thoroughly articulated relation, and they failed to construct Dole as a compelling leader with credible solutions.

Finally, it was Clinton, not Dole, who seemed to set the political agenda for the election campaign. The symbolic meaning of Clinton's leadership was produced by a modified hegemonic representational strategy. On the one hand, his leadership seemed to operate as a surface of inscription for popular identifications thanks to his largely symbolic policy proposals on juvenile smoking, gun control, youth curfews and school uniforms. The structure of Clinton's public discourse – his frequent therapeutic claims that he "feels the pain" of Americans, his use of phrases such as "I hear you," or "I identify with your suffering" – enhances this aspect of his discourse.[8] On the other hand, however, the electorate's expectations with respect to what his leadership can accomplish were sharply reduced. On welfare reform, for example, Clinton has masterfully portrayed himself as a weak President who was forced by a Republican-led Congress to do something that he would not have otherwise done. Clinton had actually embraced a neo-conservative position on welfare well before the 1992 election. Because he emerged from the pre-election session with the image of an embattled President and a reluctant compromiser, it was the Republican Congress rather than Clinton himself who had to bear the political costs of "Contract with America," when he himself supported an only slightly more moderate version of their agenda (Smith 1997a). In this case, a single political discourse, namely neo-conservatism, effectively operates as the hegemonic horizon of intelligibility for both the Clinton Democrats and the mainstream Republicans. Hegemonic struggles do not always correspond neatly to partisan boundaries; in some situations, political leaders such as Clinton merely deploy small-scale tactical maneuvers within an already hegemonized space.

CONCLUSION
Multicultural difference and the political

As we have noted at various points, Laclau tends to embrace an increasingly formal conception of hegemony in his recent work. This tendency is problematic because it suppresses a historically specific analysis of the success and failure of rival political discourses. In this final chapter, I will offer some concluding remarks on Laclau and Mouffe's hegemony theory and the implications of their work for understanding historical contextualization and multicultural difference.

Authoritarian versus radical democratic pluralist hegemonic practices

As we have already seen in Chapter 1, radical democratic pluralism stands utterly opposed to all forms of domination, for it seeks to create the conditions for free individual self-development, and this requires in turn the elimination of oppression and exploitation. Radical democratic pluralism is also opposed to domination insofar as it fully accepts the legitimacy of democratic differences. Authoritarian hegemonic discourses perpetuate domination and yet may become "organic" to the extent that they resonate with already mobilized popular anxieties and incorporate fragments of some popular traditions. Given the fact that the democratic revolution remains one of the defining discourses of contemporary politics, authoritarian hegemonic projects often construct themselves as a pseudo-"democratic" mobilization of "the people" against "the establishment." They might, for example, represent multicultural forces, trade union strategies, feminist movements and even an imaginary gay voting bloc as if they constituted an omnipotent apparatus that threatened to violate the rights of the "general population." Further, authoritarian projects do at times recognize the plural character of the social, but they aim to manage difference through the deployment of assimilatory, disciplinary and exclusionary strategies. Authoritarian discourses may make impressive attempts to construct apparently diverse social imaginaries, but ultimately they seek to reduce difference, to turn difference against itself, to incite self-surveillance and demonization, and to separate difference from what it can do (Smith 1994b).

Contemporary authoritarian hegemonic strategies often attempt to appropriate key elements from the democratic tradition, and to redefine democratic forces precisely as the anti-democratic "establishment," thereby allowing them to represent profoundly reactionary causes as nothing less than popular liberation struggles. Various right-wing interest groups in the United States have borrowed substantially from the civil rights movement in the construction of their demands, including the National Rifle Association ("freedom to defend one's family"); the tobacco industry ("freedom of choice"); the corporate lobby ("freedom from oppressive regulation"); the corporate medical insurance lobby ("freedom from socialized medicine"); mining, timber and real estate interests ("freedom from unjust 'takings'") and opponents of civil rights laws ("freedom from quotas") (Pertschuk 1995). Homophobic forces often conceal their total rejection of liberal democratic pluralism by replacing their blatant genocidal language with pseudo-democratic denunciations of lesbian and gay "special rights." Leaders of the Christian Coalition have attempted to construct their extremist movement as a democratic struggle by denouncing the Ku Klux Klan, George Wallace and anti-Semitism, and by calling for new coalitions between the religious right, African-Americans and Jews.

In actuality, the religious right, neo-conservatives and new racists only pretend to champion liberal democratic rights and freedoms in order to defend traditional class, race, gender and sexual inequalities. We can explore the fundamentally contradictory structure of authoritarian hegemonic strategies with reference to the Gramscian distinction between "passive" and "popular" revolutions. A "passive revolution," or "transformism," portrays itself as a popular and democratic movement, but it actually engages in profoundly anti-democratic strategies. It neutralizes social movements by satisfying some of their demands in a symbolic and reformist manner, and co-opts some of the symbols and representatives of popular movements or popular political parties and includes them – albeit in disempowered roles – within the hegemonic bloc, while it shifts authority towards disciplinary apparatuses. Where a radicalized form of resistance would construct its opposition to the hegemonic bloc as an antagonistic relation, a co-opted form of resistance would abandon this antagonistic interpretation, and express its relation with hegemonic elements as simple, power-free difference (Laclau 1977: 173). A co-opted form of multiculturalism, for example, would construct the social as a peaceful system of competing interest groups, while a more radical form would emphasize the oppressive and exploitative relations that obtain between dominant and subordinate groups.

Strictly speaking, Gramsci makes a clear distinction between "passive" revolution and hegemony, for a "passive" traditional moment is largely statist and bureaucratic; the "masses" do not take an active part, and brute force, rather than the organization of consent, becomes predominant. Further, Gramsci insists that the "passive revolution" includes substantial economic intervention by the state, a dimension that is almost anachronistic in contemporary globalizing economies. Gramsci's conception of the "passive" revolution nevertheless contains the provocative image of a pseudo-popular movement that wins some small degree of consent by responding to some of the popular demands from the grass-roots, while it actually uses that appearance of popular consent only to gain strategic ground for its fundamentally anti-democratic project (Laclau 1977: 116; Buci-Glucksmann 1979: 216–17, 224).[1]

Contrary to received wisdom about the right, authoritarian political projects usually owe their effectiveness to their deployment of war of position strategies. Unlike a totalitarian state formation, the state apparatuses in an authoritarian formation never become the mere instruments of dominant social groups, and never completely dominate or displace liberal democratic institutions. An effective authoritarian hegemony can nevertheless achieve a substantial transformation of key institutions such that they increasingly express its principles. An effective authoritarian hegemony would be able to advance simultaneously in multiple institutional settings; to adapt to the unique conditions at different sites in the social; to develop a specific form of political intervention at each site that best facilitates its extension and intensification; and to unify these plural micro-projects in pseudo-popular and pseudo-democratic terms, thereby foreclosing the possibility of radical resistance in advance.

Authoritarian hegemonic projects seek to absorb and to assimilate democratic forces by appropriating key elements of alternative popular worldviews, neutralizing their critical potential by redefining them, and then articulating these colonized elements – that is, integrating them in a transformative matter – into its worldview (Mouffe 1979b: 182; Laclau 1977: 161; Smith 1997a, 1997b). At this point, the limits of Laclau and Mouffe's invocation of singular social movements ("the women's movement, the environmental movement, the gay movement" etc.) become clear. Many authoritarian forces subversively borrow identity politics strategies from the Left and either promote right-wing elements within existing social movements or invent their own sanitized versions of grass-roots activism and "diversity." In conformity with the American mainstream media's rules, role models are substituted for political analysis, such that political struggle is displaced by a privatized discourse on identity-specific experiences (Williams 1995: 128), with a right-wing twist. Anti-feminist women intellectuals, for example, are celebrated as the spokespersons for the attack on Women's Studies that is launched in the name of vague pseudo-feminist principles, while mothers are featured as National Rifle Association leaders. Some black men and non-Anglo immigrants have emerged as prominent figures in the anti-affirmative action and anti-multiculturalism movements. Speaking from what they call their special black and ethnic minority perspectives, they condemn affirmative action and multiculturalism for promoting racist divisions, thereby identifying the anti-racists as the worst racists. In addition to their legitimation of right-wing policies, these tactics also threaten to redefine feminist and anti-racist politics.

The deployment of these pseudo-popular strategies is of course a dangerous operation for authoritarianism, for expectations are raised and a limited degree of popular mobilization does actually take place. Even under the auspices of the tightly controlled religious fundamentalist organizations, for example, leaders' promises are made, rallies are organized, cross-class and multiracial male-only retreats are held, parents' groups are formed, petitions are gathered, conference motions are approved, fax, phone and internet networks are set into motion, local participants are trained to run for office and so on. Authoritarian hegemonic forces strive to manage their pseudo-popular mobilizations with great care, such that genuinely autonomous grass-roots movements do not emerge (Laclau 1977: 81–142). Demonized figures such as foreign leaders, invading immigrants, hedonistic single mothers, greedy minorities, the drug-ridden and disease-spreading urban underclasses, corrupt union "bosses," excessive queers and so on, must be constantly offered as popular enemies, such that the partially mobilized masses are united in a manner that forecloses genuinely democratic articulations. Authoritarian leaders engage in a complex attempt to inflame their followers' hatred while steering the movement's activism towards effective networking rather than the publicly visible expressions of vicious hatred that might damage the movement's reputation (Smith 1994b, 1997a, 1997b).

Authoritarian forms of hegemony remain fundamentally contradictory, for they attempt to represent themselves as popular democratic movements, even though they engage in all sorts of containment strategies and pursue initiatives that perpetuate the unequal distribution of power. Often hegemonic politics only requires the construction of a minority of enthusiastic followers who can be synecdochically positioned as an imaginary majority, instead of actual popular mobilizations. This synecdochical substitution and the populist façade depend in turn on the demobilization of key sectors of the populace through blatant disenfranchisement tactics. In some cases, hegemonic forces drag the political center so far to the right that more and more people have no reason to participate in the political system. We are now witnessing extensive efforts to lower political participation in the United States: popular expectations about what governments ought to achieve have been dramatically reduced, while popular paranoias about evil forces lurking within state apparatuses have been deliberately promoted. To the extent that more centrist political projects, such as Clinton's conservative Democratic movement, borrow key strategies from the authoritarian hegemony tradition, we should anticipate a greater tendency on their part towards the neutralization of democratic contestation (Smith 1997a).

There is nothing in the contradictions within authoritarianism, however, that will by themselves lead to its decline. Not only can contradictory political discourses remain brutally effective, they can also make their contradictions a source of strength. One of the virtues of Laclau and Mouffe's redefinition of hegemony – from Gramsci's vision of an articulated bloc of actual subjects to their conception of the institutionalization of a new horizon, the taken-for-granted background knowledge that supplies the hidden assumptions behind authorized political discourse – is that it allows us to grasp the subtle and complex aspect of hegemony politics. As Hall argued with respect to Thatcherism, an authoritarian hegemonic project only needs to achieve the disorganization of the potential opposition and a minimal degree of mobilization such that the regime can pass itself off as the expression of the popular will (Hall 1988a).

Gramsci contends that where authoritarian "passive revolutions" have become institutionalized, democratic forces will have to wage a protracted "war of position" and struggle to advance an "expansive hegemony." Multiple struggles that are plural and contextually sensitive in form will have to be deployed at each of the various sites throughout the social in which the "passive revolution" has become entrenched. Where a "passive revolution" seeks to neutralize the democratic opposition and to construct a simulacrum popular movement while perpetuating structural inequality, an "expansive hegemony" seeks to promote a genuinely democratic mobilization of progressive social movements (Buci-Glucksmann 1979: 228–9; Mouffe 1979b: 182–3).

The Gramscian distinction between "passive revolution" and "expansive hegemony" also allows us to clarify Laclau and Mouffe's conception of radical democratic pluralism. Authoritarian hegemony aims to achieve a maximum disciplining of difference; even as it pretends to endorse pluralism, it can only promote a pseudo-multiculturalism that is entirely compatible with institutional racism. Radical democratic pluralism, by contrast, attempts to construct the sorts of hegemonic discourses that enhance and promote democratic forms of plurality and difference. Confronted with a plurality of progressive struggles already in motion, it seeks to release each of their democratic potentials, while bringing them together in mutually constitutive articulatory relations. It values the autonomy of each struggle, not only as a good in itself, but also for its practical value. In many cases, autonomy facilitates the sort of contextually specific contestation of oppression and exploitation that is needed in today's complex and hybrid social formations. Further, it values the promotion of hybridized democratic identities, for "hybridization does not necessarily mean decline through the loss of identity: it can also mean empowering existing identities through the opening of new possibilities" (Laclau 1996e: 65). Where authoritarian hegemony strictly regulates the development of political contestation, radical democratic pluralist hegemony multiplies the points of contestation and seeks to broaden the terrain of politicization or reactivation (Laclau 1996d: 99). The universalistic effects of the radical democratic pluralist horizon tend to institutionalize deeper and deeper recognition of the plurality and autonomy of the public spaces created by democratic struggles. To the extent that the specific discourses of the relatively autonomous progressive struggles are successfully articulated with a radical civic sense, the multiplication of these public spaces becomes a source of strength for a democratizing society (Laclau 1996b: 120–1).

If authoritarian hegemony has a fundamentally contradictory structure, radical democratic pluralist hegemony has a paradoxical central principle: the more that we advance towards its realization, the more impossible its realization becomes. Radical democratic pluralism is a good that remains a good only insofar as it is not fully institutionalized (Mouffe 1993b: 4, 6). The challenge of radical democratic pluralism is that it must gain strategic ground not only by subverting dominant institutions, but by founding and defending new ones as well. At the same time, it must guard against the potential that is inherent in its own institutions simply because they are institutions, namely the bureaucratization and disciplining of the social according to exclusionary principles. In a radical democratic pluralist movement, the definition of the good life must always be kept open to contestation; "nothing is definitely acquired and there is always the possibility of challenge" (Laclau 1996d: 100). No blueprint for an ideal society could fully grasp all of the exclusions that are built into contemporary institutions and anticipate the unintentional anti-democratic effects of apparently democratic strategies. We can only begin to imagine subjects who have yet to be invented, let alone their rights and responsibilities in communities that will only faintly resemble our own. Democratic activists of all kinds from only a few centuries ago would be bewildered by contemporary democratic politics. We have no reason to assume that we are peculiarly endowed with an ability to make all contemporary and future antagonisms transparent. A space for permanent democratic dissent must therefore be built into the radical democratic pluralist imaginary, for it is through contestation and struggle that exclusions can be brought to light and new democratic institutions can be imagined and established.

This point can be illustrated with reference to the debate on multicultural curricula. Radical multicultural educators are not arguing that we ought to include works by women, gays, blacks, Latino/as, Asians, indigenous people and peoples of the Third World in the Western "canon" because they are the only texts that are meaningful for our minority students. Their argument is that traditions of resistance among oppressed and excluded peoples have built up tremendous resources of wisdom, and that that wisdom is embedded within minority discourses. As Gutmann contends, "There are books by and about women, African-Americans, Asian-Americans, and Native Americans that speak to neglected parts of our heritage and human condition, and speak more wisely than do some of the canonical works" (1992: 18). Shohat and Stam similarly assert that their "polycentric multiculturalism" "grants an 'epistemological advantage' to those prodded by historical circumstances into what W.B. DuBois has called 'double consciousness,' to those obliged to negotiate both 'margins' and 'center' (or even with many margins and many centers), and thus somewhat better placed to 'deconstruct' dominant or narrowly national discourses" (1994: 48–9). Alexander and Mohanty, citing Moya, also claim an "epistemological advantage" for the oppressed, but insist on the mediating role of interpretation.

> The experience of repression can be, but is not necessarily, a catalyst for organizing. It is, in fact, the *interpretation* of that experience from within a *collective* context that marks the moment of transformation from perceived contradictions and material disenfranchisement to participation in women's movements.
>
> (1997: xl)

Structural positioning in itself does not guarantee a political outcome; it is only when the experience of oppression is organized in terms of the interpretative framework that is provided by radical subject positions that subversive texts and practices are produced.

Further, a radical multicultural curriculum does not embrace any kind of separatism, for it aims to raise students' awareness about the constitutive relations between different cultures. For Shohat and Stam,

> polycentric multiculturalism is reciprocal, dialogical; it sees all acts of verbal or cultural exchange as taking place not between discrete bounded individuals or cultures but rather between permeable, changing individuals and communities. Within an ongoing struggle of hegemony and resistance, each act of cultural interlocution leaves both interlocutors changed.
>
> (1994: 49)

Shohat and Stam extend their radical approach into their critique of Eurocentrism. Such a critique would remain conservative if it depicted Europe as a naturally distinct entity unmarked by political struggle and internal and external exclusions; constructed Europeans as a singular people bound together by a homogeneous and timeless cultural tradition; and represented European power as an omnipotent evil capable of achieving total victory on a global scale. Within their approach, an anti-Eurocentric multiculturalism also has to attend to the hybrid differences and complicated histories that constitute Europe itself (1994: 4). In this sense, Shohat and Stam (1984) reproduce Bernal's radical intervention; the point is not merely to find hybridity and difference on the margins, but to interrupt the metropole's foundational myths as well.

Multiculturalism, according to then Modern Language Association President Stimpson, is the "necessary recognition that we cannot think of culture unless we think of many cultures at the same time" (Levine 1996: 143). As Levine indicates, radical multiculturalism studies women, immigrants, workers, lesbians and gays and racial minorities not just to bring ethnic and gender difference into our curricula, but to promote a better understanding of socio-economic power.

> It is crucial to study and understand as many of the contributing cultures and their interactions with one another as possible, not as a matter of "therapeutic" history, as the opponents of multiculturalism keep insisting, not to placate or flatter minority groups and make them feel good, as they also assert, but as a simple matter of *understanding* the nature and complexities of American culture and the process by which it came, and continues to come, into being.
>
> (Levine 1996: 160)

Even a society that approaches radical democratic pluralism will tend to institutionalize a specific way of thinking; the danger is that domination will become normalized and the democratic wisdom at the margins of the social will not be heard. It is only through permanent contestation that every "canon" – even the most apparently radical "canon" – will be constantly exposed to democratic challenges.

Against Habermas, who constructs power-free communication as a regulative ideal, Laclau and Mouffe affirm the permanence of power relations. Although Rorty wants to expand the community of "we liberals" through persuasion and the incitement of solidarity-oriented sentiment, rather than argumentation that seeks to ground itself exclusively on context-independent rationality, he also places far too much faith on the construction of consensus, and fails to grasp the practical value of perpetual contestation (Mouffe 1996a: 8). In the spirit of Gramsci's centaur metaphor, Laclau and Mouffe argue that every form of communication, including persuasion, negotiation, and dialogue, is necessarily intertwined with power relations, and that this would remain true in any possible society. Like all post-structuralists, they hold that we cannot ground our ethical decisions in a necessary foundation; every political position that we take is in this sense contingent. Again, this is not to endorse relativism: since our choices are always conditioned by normative traditions, we never inhabit a space in which all the choices before us have equal validity. The traditions that shape our normative decision-making are the residual effects of contingent political struggles. This means that every normative decision taken within historical traditions – traditions that are only partially of our choosing – could have been taken in a different way; none of them express absolute necessity. Where one alternative is chosen instead of others, this decision is ultimately based on force rather than rational necessity. The force in question may be quite minimal, such as the suppression of a given set of alternatives when a choice is made, or it may involve the most brutal forms of exclusion (Laclau 1996b: 112).

In other words, social change is achieved not because the arguments of some historical groups are morally better than others when measured according to a universal standard, and not because the triumphant group's discourse expresses a necessary moment in the unfolding of reason. For Laclau, the very notions of universal standards and historical necessity are strategic myths. In contemporary complex societies, social change is achieved because some political struggles and historical forces strategically prevail over the opposing groups and forces. We have seen that Laclau tends to argue that the success of a hegemonic strategy depends on its form – its provision of an orderly space for the inscription of political demands. Differing slightly with Laclau on this point, I would argue that a hegemonic force prevails to the extent that it deploys a combination of tactics – involving violence, exclusion, articulation and redefinition, persuasion, the general framing of the political terrain, institutionalization and so on – that allows it to exploit the unique opportunities that are available in a given historical configuration. It should also be noted that in both this formulation and Laclau's theory, the hegemonic agent is not a concrete subject; it is instead an historical force. As Nietzsche and Foucault argue, historical forces are always prior to the formation of subjects. Hegemony and power are not instruments that can be wielded by individuals or groups; they are the conditions of possibility of any subjectivity.

The permanence of power relations is not, however, a fatality for radical democratic pluralism. The political aim of radical democratic pluralism is not the elimination of power, but the transformation of the prevailing forms of power, such that they become more compatible with democratic principles (Mouffe 1995: 502). The space for contestation will have to be kept open against all sorts of closure strategies; new decisions must always be taken; and alternative possibilities will have to be suppressed (Laclau 1996b: 115). Perhaps an egalitarian policy will have unforeseen consequences with respect to the limitations of some individuals' freedom; perhaps a progressive conception of civil liberties and civil rights will have serious inegalitarian effects in a new context; or perhaps an apparently innocent identification with radical principles is actually influenced by an unspeakable demonization. While democracy tends to enhance an awareness of contingency and to create the space in which difference in identity can be affirmed, it also creates the potential for a reactive politics of dogmatic identitarianism (Connolly 1991: 193). By creating and defending the space for contestation, and by keeping the tension between the principles of equality and liberty alive, radical democratic pluralism seeks to sustain the conditions in which these sorts of problems could be brought to light and addressed (Mouffe 1992a: 13).

Further, there is no reason to assume that an awareness of the contingency of decision-making would necessarily lead to political paralysis. Laclau contends that to the extent that we become aware of contingency, we are much more likely to submit a given formation to democratic contestation and to grasp the vulnerability of the democratic revolution's historical gains. Awareness of historicity can enhance a sense of social responsibility for the "consciousness of the historicity [of values] . . . will make us more responsible citizens, more ready to engage in their defense" (Laclau 1996b: 123). Mouffe similarly writes, "When we realize that, far from being the necessary result of a moral evolution of mankind, liberal democracy is an ensemble of contingent practices, we can understand that it is a conquest that needs to be protected as well as deepened" (1993b: 145).[2] Fish would be somewhat more pessimistic. Criticizing what he calls the "anti-foundationalist theory hope," Fish asserts that every political discourse necessarily closes off some set of differences as legitimate, and necessarily fails to express a complete consciousness of contingency and historicity (1994: 172–9).

Universalism and particularism, multiculturalism and social control

The promotion of radical democratic pluralism fundamentally depends upon the maintenance of the tension between opposed and mutually limiting social logics. The principle of equality is ultimately incompatible with the principle of liberty.

Democracy, the participation of the many in decision-making, is ultimately opposed to diversity, the defense of unassimilated difference. For Mouffe, these irreducible tensions are not fatal; on the contrary, they keep the very possibility of radical democratic pluralism alive (Mouffe 1993b: 133; Coles 1996: 379).

The debates on multiculturalism turn precisely on this problem. The imperfect communitarian mechanisms that we use to organize democratic participation can threaten difference with assimilation, discipline, colonization and neutralization; the diversity principle in this sense productively limits the democratic principle. At the same time, the diversity principle can be mobilized to legitimate exclusionary and reactionary demands by those social groups who wish to defend the privileges that they have won thanks to the work of exploitative and oppressive structures. Some Afrikaner South Africans have sought special education programs for their children (Nkomo et al. 1995) while some white Americans from the South have defended the Confederate flag. Both groups have made these arguments on the grounds that the "special way of life" of their "minorities" ought to be defended. Commenting on the deployment of the principle of "minority rights" by white conservative South Africans in the post-apartheid era, Norval remarks that although this tactic is launched in the name of democracy, it ultimately aims "to foreclose [democracy's] radically egalitarian thrust" (1996: 279). Here the diversity principle must be limited by the democratic principle; diversity rights should be upheld only in the cases in which those rights do not contradict democratic values.

The evaluation of multiculturalism requires a differentiated approach to difference. A voluntary multicultural program that serves an ethnic, racial, cultural, gender or sexual minority that has been historically excluded from democratic participation may, depending upon its precise structure, be compatible with the democratic principle. It may, for example, promote civic values while enhancing the minority members' understanding of their rich traditions, thereby providing them with the tools that they need to make valuable contributions to robust public debates. A program that serves only to enshrine the anti-democratic symbols and values that have been passed down in exclusionary traditions, such as those of racist white Afrikaners and racist white Americans from the South, would not have the same beneficial effect. Multicultural projects that celebrate the identity of a disempowered group can also be problematic in those cases in which they perpetuate capitalist exploitation, sexism, homophobia and the denigration of other racial/ethnic differences. Some traditions are more homogeneous while others consist of complex hybrid articulations of democratic and anti-democratic elements. As such, no abstract rules can be drawn up in advance with respect to the evaluation of diversity claims; each claim must be carefully assessed within a specific historical context.

Laclau's innovative theory of universalism provides a useful framework for understanding these problems. Instead of constructing the universal and the particular as separate elements, or positing the universal as a moment in which differences are canceled out, Laclau contends that we should consider the universal as "the symbol of a missing fullness." Like Spivak (1988a, 1988b; Spivak and Grosz 1990: 11–12; Spivak *et al.* 1990: 117–18) Laclau argues that particular social groups inevitably invoke universalist discourse – that is, the principles of the broader community as a whole – whenever they advance their demands for access to education, employment, consumer goods and so on. Every demand is framed in some minimal way with reference to the larger community's shared horizon. A particularistic discourse in this sense employs universal principles to fill in the gaps in its own identity: that element of legitimacy which extends beyond the limits of its own self-referentiality. Laclau's argument paradoxically situates the universal as a necessary moment of compensation for incompletion within every particularism. Further, whenever a particular social group affirms its difference as it advances its demands for rights, it also tends to cancel out its difference – precisely because it tends to frame its demands in terms of the broader community's values (1996g: 28). The "universal" never becomes a dialectical category, for Laclau's "universal" space remains a contested terrain, and the moment in which the difference between particularism and universalism would be finally overcome through dialectical negation is infinitely postponed. With Mouffe, Laclau affirms that the community's shared norms remain incomplete and vulnerable to political reactivation and subversive recitation (1996g: 28, 33).

Laclau's provocative formulation deserves careful analysis. He contends that a specific group attempts to fill out its incomplete identity by invoking the common principles of the broader community. We should note, first, that this is a very complex operation that takes place in the context of multiple and antagonistically opposed political discourses that compete with one another to perform this compensatory function. Laclau contends, for example, that an ethnic minority might advance its own particularistic demands by invoking "some universal principles" that are shared in a broader social space (1996g: 28). While Laclau does recognize that those universal principles are always open to contestation, we should also consider the multiplicity of "universal" spaces. In the debates on Quebec separatism, for example, different groups invoke different "universalities": separatist francophones may refer to the Québecois nation, to their position within the Quebec–United States economic community, and to the ties between their Québecois nation and France; the anglophones, federalist francophones and the allophones (immigrants for whom both English and French are second languages) may refer to their rights as Canadian citizens; while the indigenous peoples may refer to their federal rights and their rights under the United Nations Charter as sovereign First Nations. The development of Laclau's theory requires a detailed investigation of the multiple and sometimes contradictory character of broader community affiliations.

Laclau's privileging of formalism in his more recent work has profound implications for his argument on universalism and particularism. A "universal" discourse is necessarily invoked within a particularistic discourse as an ultimately vain attempt to fill in the constitutive lack that penetrates every identity. However, as we have already seen in Chapters 2 and 5, Laclau's argument tends to emphasize the formal characteristics of hegemonic discourse. He asserts, for example, that in an organic crisis,

> people need *an* order, and the actual content of it becomes a secondary consideration. "Order" as such has no content, because it only exists in the various forms in which it is actually realized, but in a situation of radical disorder "order" is present as that which is absent; it becomes an empty signifier, as the signifier of that absence. In this sense, various political forces can compete in their efforts to present their particular objectives as those which carry out the filling of that lack. To hegemonize something is exactly to carry out this filling function. (We have spoken about "order," but obviously "unity," "liberation," "revolution," etcetera belong to the same order of things. Any term which, in a certain political context becomes the signifier of the lack, plays the same role. Politics is possible because the constitutive impossibility of society can only represent itself through the production of empty signifiers.)
>
> (1996h: 44)

In the case of a specific group's particularistic demand for rights, the universal performs this "filling function"; it is the universal that sutures the group's dislocated identity. If we combine Laclau's remarks on particularism and universalism with his formalistic analysis of hegemonic discourse's ordering effect, then we have the following argument: in an organic crisis, the actual content of the "universal" discourse that performs this compensatory suturing work in particularistic discourse is much less important than its form, that is, its promise to provide some sort of order.

Laclau does admit that the content of the hegemonic discourse has some importance; while its content becomes a "secondary consideration," it is never totally irrelevant. It should also be noted that Laclau is dealing with an almost impossible case, for indifference to the content of a hegemonic discourse increases to the extent that the social formation is disrupted by an organic crisis. On this account, complete indifference to historical traces and residual traditions would only make sense in the context of a total breakdown of the social. The occasions in which actual historical circumstances even begin to approach these conditions are indeed very rare. Perhaps the problem with these formulations, then, is simply that they focus exclusively on an extreme case. In more normal conditions, there are multiple factors that make it more or less likely that one discourse will prevail over others in a hegemonic manner. In most cases, a discourse becomes effectively hegemonic not only because of its abstract form, but also because of its non-essentialist continuities with residual, enduring and emerging institutions.

Laclau explicitly criticizes Eurocentrism for representing its exclusionary particularism as the universalism that can include all differences (1996g: 24–5). He contends that oppressed cultural and ethnic groups should both appropriate the common values of their broader communities and engage in the struggle to redefine those common values at the same time. He recognizes that emerging racial and ethnic minorities perform valuable work when they bring the exclusionary effects of our society's common ideals to light, for they can thereby make way for the construction of a more democratic, egalitarian, and pluralistic society (1996g: 34).[3]

In these passages, Laclau identifies a key resistance tactic, namely the attempt to undermine the hegemonic discourse's universalistic pretensions by drawing attention towards its particularistic dimensions. Where hegemonic discourse promises to deliver "all things to all people," or claims that it establishes neutral standards that apply equally to everyone, resistance discourse aims to expose its limits and to bring its exclusionary character to light. Marx, for example, insisted that although the liberal democratic system promised to deliver equal rights to every individual, it actually constructed the conditions in which the particularistic interests of the bourgeoisie in exploiting the proletariat could be perpetuated (1975a, 1975b, 1977). Where hegemonic discourse suppressed its literal character during its ascendance in order to symbolize the principle of order itself, counter-hegemonic discourse attempts to reverse that process by foregrounding its literality. The ultimate aim of counter-hegemonic discourse, then, is to provoke an organic crisis by attacking the hegemonic discourse's universalistic pretension and its metaphoristic operation (Norval 1996: 274, 301–2). Laclau concludes,

> The democratic process in present-day societies can be considerably deepened and expanded if it is made accountable to the demands of large sections of the population – minorities, ethnic groups and so on – who traditionally have been excluded from it. Liberal democratic theory and institutions have in this sense to be deconstructed.
>
> (1996g: 33)

Laclau therefore rightly differentiates his argument on universalism from Eurocentric discourse. He also distances himself from yet another political strategy.

> The construction of differential identities on the basis of total closure to what is outside them is not a viable or progressive political alternative. It would be a reactionary policy in Western Europe today, for instance, for immigrants from Northern Africa or Jamaica to abstain from all participation in Western European institutions, with the justification that theirs is a different cultural identity and that European institutions are not their concern. In this way, all forms of subordination and exclusion would be consolidated with the excuse of maintaining pure identities. The logic of apartheid is not only a discourse of the dominant groups; as we said before, it can also permeate the identities of the oppressed.
>
> (Laclau 1996g: 29)

We should note, in passing, that Laclau does not support his invocation of "Northern African-" and "Jamaican-"European discourse with any textual references, making an evaluation of his remarks rather difficult. Theorists who have conducted extensive concrete research in this area do not construct European racial minorities as embracing an exclusively isolationist strategy. Gilroy, Hall and Bhabha, for example, demonstrate that black and Asian European cultural formations are the complex products of multiple overdeterminations and hybrid appropriations (Gilroy 1987, 1993; Hall 1988b, 1990; Bhabha 1990). Even at the height of the Salman Rushdie affair, the British–South Asian community was deeply divided on the problem of upholding Rushdie's right to free speech while opposing, at the same time, racist depictions of the Muslim as inherently opposed to modern Western values (Appignanesi and Maitland 1989).

Laclau's use of examples in this passage, and his use of the term, "the logic of apartheid," to describe the identities of the oppressed, are problematic. The theoretical argument that he is advancing, however, is rather straightforward: the assertion of a "pure particularism" is self-defeating. Where two or more antagonistic groups demand their rights in the name of a pure particularism, they will have to invoke some sort of more general principle in order to resolve their conflict.

Laclau further states that particularism as a principle on its own leads to an agnosticism that becomes dangerous for disempowered groups.

> I can defend the right of sexual, racial and national minorities in the name of particularism; but if particularism is the only valid principle, I have to also accept the rights to self-determination of all kinds of reactionary groups involved in anti-social practices.
>
> (Laclau 1996g: 26)

It is at this point that Laclau introduces his apartheid analogy: the conception of "separate developments" strategically affirms "difference" while ignoring the terrain of hierarchical power relations upon which difference is constructed (Laclau 1996g: 27).

It could be noted once again that Laclau does not offer any historically specific reference to a particular movement's discourse. Actual anti-racist, black nationalist and multicultural strategies rarely take the form of extremist particularism. In any event, Laclau's concern is that the invocation of particularism may lay the basis for the legitimation for anti-democratic movements. If, for example, we are dealing with a group that has traditionally won privilege over other groups through exclusions, exploitation and oppression, then allowing that group to assert its right to particularism is to "sanction the *status quo* in the relation of power between the groups" (1996g: 27). Mouffe, for her part, fully concurs on this point. Referring to the work of Marcil-Lacoste (1992), Mouffe argues that the "extreme" pluralistic valorization of all differences is highly dangerous for democracy, because it fails to engage in a differentiated approach to difference, namely the distinction between "differences that exist but should not exist and differences that do not exist but should exist" (Mouffe 1996b: 247).

Laclau and Mouffe, then, agree that not all differences can be accepted; the principles of difference, diversity and autonomy must be limited by the principles of liberty, equality and democracy. Perhaps the only serious problem with this argument is that Laclau consistently refers throughout these passages to hypothetical cases in which racial and ethnic *minorities* deploy purely particularist demands for rights. In this sense, Laclau risks reproducing the discriminatory representation of ethnic and racial difference as inherently particularistic. As Christian points out, apparently progressive figures often perpetuate this viewpoint when they congratulate an "extraordinary" minority intellectual for transcending her naturally "narrow" frame of reference to produce a "universally" significant work (1994: 176–7).

Laclau continues,

> These remarks allow us to throw some light on the divergent courses of action that current struggles in defense of multiculturalism can follow. One possible way is to affirm, purely and simply, the right of the various cultural and ethnic groups to assert their differences and their separate development. This is the route to self-apartheid, and it is sometimes accompanied by the claim that Western cultural values and institutions are the preserve of white, male Europeans or Anglo-Americans and have nothing to do with the identity of other groups living in the same territory. What is advocated in this way is total segregationism, the mere opposition of one particularism to another.
>
> (1996g: 32)

For Laclau, such an argument would collapse into "perpetual incoherence": it would aim to win the legal reforms necessary for the official recognition of its legitimacy, but it would simultaneously claim that the legal system is inherently rooted in the "traditional dominant sectors of the West *and that [it has] nothing to do with that tradition*" (1996g: 33).

In the cases in which racial minorities do embrace what Gilroy calls "ethnic absolutism" (1993), their projects can become antithetical to radical democratic pluralist values. Thomas notes, for example, that the apparently progressive conception of black "authenticity" is often used to disavow or to demonize lesbians and gays of color (1997). Attention should also be paid to the contexts in which "ethnic absolutism" thrives. It could be the case that such a phenomenon takes hold more effectively wherever the space for more democratic forms of expression are closed off by corporate, political and educational institutions. Norval suggests, for example, that dogmatic forms of resistance may become more compelling in conditions of severe economic deprivation and political, educational and cultural exclusions (1996: 304). In an important intervention, Lubiano notes the parallels between the patriarchal and homophobic positions embraced by hegemonic factions within the black nationalist movement on the one hand and the moral authoritarianism of the prominent American new right/new racist/neo-conservative movements on the other. She contends that "even as [black nationalism] functions as resistance to the state . . . it reinscribes the state in particular places within its own narratives of resistance. That reinscription most often occurs within black nationalist narratives of the black family" (Lubiano 1997: 236).

Laclau does not adequately acknowledge, however, the radical democratic pluralist potential that is expressed in the vast majority of anti-racist and radical multicultural struggles. These struggles affirm Baldwin's principle: disempowered minorities ought to win recognition without being asked to pay the price of assimilation in return (Baldwin 1985: 375). Far from isolating themselves from the dominant community, these struggles often attempt to subject dominant groups and hegemonic authoritarian values to the democratic critique that can be found in the discourses of the disempowered. Minority rights claims do sometimes take the form of a demand for separation, but they can also be phrased as radical communitarian demands for the authorization of an anti-racist, anti-sexist, anti-homophobic and anti-capitalist definition of "our common tradition" or "our shared values" (Williams 1995: 82). Again, as Levine notes with respect to multicultural curricula, the aim is to value difference so that the operation of power – discrimination, exploitation and erasure – can be brought to light. A radical multiculturalism, for example, would not only celebrate democratic differences; it would also shed light on the power relations that structure cultural expression by studying, for example, trends in employment and the distribution of wealth, media ownership, affirmative action in universities, public arts grants and so on. Instead of thinking culture according to a simplistic pluralist logic, it would explore the complexities of transnational cultural appropriations, hybrid cultural articulations and intra-cultural antagonisms.[4]

Against the weight of Laclau's examples, I would argue that in contemporary American politics, the most dangerous forces of particularist politics actually favor dominant groups. The American wealthy are pursuing an increasingly segregationist agenda that is fundamentally eroding the concept of collective responsibility. Income taxes and capital gains taxes for the rich are cut, necessitating not only massive cuts in federal government programs, but also increases in the regional and local government taxes that are less fair for the lower-middle-class, workers and the poor. The geographical mobility of the poor is reduced through public transportation cuts while their already minuscule opportunity for socio-economic mobility is all but eliminated through education cuts. School zoning boundaries isolate the middle class from the rest of the population; school voucher programs and tax-free savings accounts transfer public funds from public school investment to subsidies for wealthy children's private education; and local government tax schemes cut the wealthy suburban communities off from the inner city. Urban planning and policing techniques systematically protect the wealthy by cordoning off urban unrest and targeted forms of criminality (Davis 1991, 1992).

Not-in-my-backyard-style lobbying by middle-class suburban communities has led to the concentration of environmental hazards in areas populated by the poor. The Republican Congress approved an experimental plan that sets up government subsidies for individuals who want to opt out of private group health insurance to obtain their own personal coverage. More and more corporations are eliminating the pension plans that used to cover their entire work force and replacing them with generous tax-subsidized plans for the highest-paid managers. For the American wealthy, neo-conservative individualism and privatization are not enough; they are now demanding segregationist forms of individualism and privatization.

Because race and class are so thoroughly intertwined in the United States (Takaki 1993; Omi and Winant 1994), much of these developments have an especially negative impact on the black and Latino communities, and on many Asian American communities as well. And yet, even as economic globalization and restructuration lock these peoples into perpetual poverty, and the backlashes against immigration, affirmative action, crime, teenage pregnancy, welfare, education spending and governmental excess are blatantly used to harness racist sentiment, dissimulation tactics are deployed such that the charge of racism becomes rebuttable. Bush puts Thomas on the Supreme Court, the media dwells on the O.J. Simpson case, the Republicans flirt with Colin Powell, Clinton launches a "national conversation" on race, and the Promise Keepers positions itself as a leader in the movement for multiracial harmony.[5]

While Laclau's critique of particularist politics is sound – and entirely compatible with Mouffe's democratic theory – his emphasis on inappropriate strategic choices by ethnic and racial minorities is problematic. It is not clear, however, that Mouffe would agree with Laclau as he develops another aspect of his argument.

> I cannot assert a differential identity without distinguishing it from a context, and, in the process of making the distinction, I am asserting the context at the same time. And the opposite is true: I cannot destroy a context without destroying at the same time the identity of the particular subject who carries out the destruction. It is a very well known historical fact that an oppositionist force whose identity is constructed within a certain system of power is ambiguous *vis-à-vis* that system, because the latter is what prevents the constitution of the identity and it is, at the same time, its condition of existence. And any victory against the system also destabilizes the identity of the victorious force.
>
> (Laclau 1996g: 27)

It is once again rather difficult to assess this passage, for Laclau does not direct us towards the historical sources that he has in mind. In theoretical terms, Laclau – with reference once again to a hypothetical "ethnic minority" – argues that demands for "access to education, to employment, to consumer goods and so on . . . cannot be made in terms of difference, but [in terms] of some universal principles that the ethnic minority shares with the rest of the community" (1996g: 28).

From Laclau's perspective, the danger is that progressive movements might stop short at aiming only to invert power relations, such that they neglect the importance of transforming the entire social structure. Assuming that a democratic struggle's opposition to a specific type of domination is integral to its identity, Laclau asserts that that struggle is always tempted to stop short at the mere inversion of the relation of domination, such that the logic of domination is largely preserved.

> If the oppressed is defined by its difference from the oppressor, such a difference is an essential component of the identity of the oppressed. But in that case, the latter cannot assert its identity without asserting that of the oppressor as well.
>
> (Laclau 1996g: 29)

We could note, in passing, that Žižek similarly contends that "each position is only its negative relation to the other" and that "man is a reflexive determination of woman's impossibility of achieving an identity with herself (which is why woman is a symptom of man)" (Žižek 1990: 253).[6]

Referring to Norval's research on apartheid and to the dimensions of South Africa's post-apartheid society, Laclau comments,

> If we simply *invert* the relation of oppression, the other (the former oppressor) is maintained as what is now oppressed and repressed, but this inversion of the *contents* leaves the form of oppression unchanged.
>
> (1996g: 31)

Although Laclau originally wrote these passages in 1991, and published them in 1995 and 1996, he does not actually examine South Africa's contemporary history to investigate whether or not this simple inversion took place. Based on the information that we have available about the transition process, the new South African Constitution, the policies of the African National Congress (ANC), and the bi-partisan pattern of cooperation with Bishop Tutu's Truth and Reconciliation Commission, we would estimate that the ANC itself never really needed Laclau's warning. Ash comments,

> Of course, history knows many examples of people who fought heroically against one dictatorship, only themselves to erect another one. But the fight against apartheid inside South Africa also nourished a feisty attachment to democracy, and the ANC movement is itself a rainbow coalition.
>
> (1997: 10–11)

Norval estimates that the ANC government has been particularly impressive in its deployment of affirmative action and equal opportunity programs, and in its interpretation of non-racist discourse such that the latter has become consistent with these programs. She notes, however, that the ANC's record with respect to the colored population and the labor movement is less than perfect (1996: 294–6). There are social agents in South Africa who actually do continue to threaten to perpetuate the "closed, organic identities" that were central to apartheid discourse, namely the far right, the new National Party and Buthelezi's Inkatha (1996: 302). This complex map of social agents does not, however, correspond to Laclau's model of a formerly oppressed agent who merely inverts the prevailing power relations. Even the racist Inkatha cannot be held up as an example in this regard, for with its historical record of cooperation with the apartheid regime and its embrace of free market principles, its positions within the prevailing configurations of power relations are multiple and complex in nature.

Laclau's emphasis on the danger of an oppressed group embracing a strategy of simple inversion also seems to be at odds with Mouffe's approach, for Mouffe consistently affirms the complex character of the social, and the plural, overlapping and even contradictory character of the social spheres and institutions in which antagonisms develop. Even in those conditions in which two chains of equivalence (racist/anti-racist; capitalist/anti-capitalist; etc.) stand antagonistically opposed to one another in what appears to be a total struggle at one site in the social, the ethical "universe" in which each element in those chains orients itself will always extend beyond the site of the antagonism. A student group, for example, might throw itself into a bitter struggle against a university administration, but, even in the most antagonistic circumstances, its discourse will be influenced by sources outside that site, such as the students' links with other struggles and their previous residential communities. Even in a total war situation, such as the anti-apartheid struggle in South Africa, the terms of the struggle always go far beyond the oppressor/oppressed dyad. Anti-apartheid organizations, for example, drew extensively upon traditions of anti-imperialist struggles throughout Africa and the developing world, the democratic struggles of racial minorities in Europe and the United States, and the socialist tradition. It is precisely this richness of overdetermination that infinitely postpones the moment in which an oppositional struggle would inhabit such an impoverished ethical universe that it would aim simply to "invert" the prevailing power relations without altering their content. Norval contends that the non-racist aspect of the discourse that was embraced by the majority of anti-apartheid activists was in fact strengthened by its opposition to the apartheid regime, for the regime placed before their eyes the utterly brutal consequences of an identitary political logic (1996: 304).

Laclau's overall emphasis remains firmly centered on a critique of Western Eurocentrism and on an investigation of the conditions necessary for opening communitarian universalistic principles to democratic contestation (1996g: 34–5). He recognizes that the "struggles of new social actors show that the concrete

195

practices of our society restrict the universalism of our political ideals to limited sectors of the population" (1996g: 34). It could be argued, however, that his assessment of the political context of these struggles is insufficient. Again, the weight of his examples tend to suggest that the dangers of particularistic discourse reside, for the most part, among racial and ethnic minorities. I have argued, by contrast, that in contemporary American politics, it is mainly the wealthy – an overwhelmingly white Anglo population – that is embracing the new segregationism. Further, Laclau comments that "the decline of the integrationist abilities of the Western states makes political conformism a rather unlikely outcome" (1996g: 34).

While it is certainly true that we are currently witnessing a dramatic shrinkage in the welfare state and massive cuts in public programs, the situation with respect to political conformism may be much more complicated than Laclau's diagnosis would suggest. First, we should note that the current transformations in the state structures are uneven in nature. As Fraser, citing Skocpol, notes, the state is not a singular entity; it is instead a "complex and polyvalent nexus of compromise formations in which are sedimented the outcomes of past struggles as well as the conditions for present and future ones" (1989: 157). In the United States, huge cuts are being made in education, welfare and health programs, but massive expansions in policing, high technology domestic surveillance, border patrols, immigration monitoring, penitentiary systems, and the tracking of welfare recipients are taking place. We are witnessing an acceleration in the differentiation of social control technologies as bio-power strategies are deployed with more and more productive finesse in the disciplining of the middle-class and professional strata, while the brute tactics of banishment and capital punishment – tactics that Foucault believed had been more or less replaced in the early modern era (Foucault 1979) – are routinely used against the dangerously unassimilable elements of the "underclass." Norval argues that the apartheid regime was supported by a dual strategy: the organization of consent among the "insiders" and the deployment of brute force against the "outsiders" (1996: 4). It is perhaps the case that this aspect of apartheid logic, namely its "combined and uneven development" – its articulation of multiple modes of power relations in complex overdetermined formations – is exemplary with respect to the emerging structure of American society rather than exceptional. The political center and the right have virtually declared a war on what they call the "underclass," the disproportionately non-white impoverished peoples of the inner cities. (We could note here that poor of the rural areas and indigenous peoples on remote reservations have all but disappeared from public discourse altogether.) These peoples are not only blamed for their own impoverishment; they are increasingly constructed as sub-humans who, because of their anti-social cultural traditions and biological tendencies towards addiction, excessive sexuality, criminality and inferior intelligence, simply cannot be helped through education and skill training. Popular texts such as The Bell Curve (Herrnstein and Murray 1994) and actual policies such as the elimination of welfare entitlement (Smith 1997a) and the militarization of inner city policing that aims at total containment of these peoples (Davis

1991, 1992) express the idea that the "underclass" has become a "disposable population."

Only a few years ago, American adult workers from working-class communities who held basic educational qualifications had a fairly good chance of obtaining a semi-skilled or skilled job that paid a livable wage. With the profound transformation of the American economy, workers with these same qualifications now find themselves cycling between non-unionized low-paid work – usually in unskilled service sector and manufacturing employment – and welfare. The "disposable population" discourse legitimates the sharp decline in their standard of living and the large-scale reduction in government expenditures on housing, education and health programs that might ameliorate their conditions. It is of course a myth that the state apparatuses evenly deployed large-scale education, housing and health programs that aimed to assimilate the entire population, white and non-white, wealthy and poor, citizen and immigrant alike. Many populations in the United States never experienced this "golden age" of disciplinary public investment on a massive scale in the first place. But, to the extent that these programs were indeed deployed, especially between the New Deal years and the 1970s, the public policy emphasis with respect to the "underclasses" has now shifted from assimilation to policies of deliberate neglect. To return to Laclau's remark, what we have in this case is not simply a "decline in the integrationist abilities" of this particular Western state; we have a shift towards banishment and quarantine with respect to the "underclass." Laclau's question about the incitement of conformist political participation is not really an issue with respect to the "underclass," because the poor, and poor minorities in particular, have already been structurally excluded from participation in the most important arenas of decision-making (Hero 1992; Guinier 1991).

Laclau's equation of the decline of the welfare state with the increasing inability for the state to incite conformism – along the functionalist lines, say, of Althusser's "ideological state apparatuses" (Althusser 1971) – nevertheless remains problematic. We may be entering into a terrain in which other hegemonic forces are producing basically the same effect. Consider, for example, the reduction in public support for cultural projects. As private capital displaces public investment in this sphere, we are certainly not entering into a new era of radical multicultural expression. The huge oligopolies in the media, entertainment and information technology sectors may embrace Disney-fied images of multiculturalism, such as *Pocahontas*, *The Lion King*, *Aladdin* and Puerto Rican "Barbie," and their "synergistic" niche marketing might give us sanitized images of rebellion, such as *To Wong Fu, Thanks for Everything! Julie Newman*, *First Wives Club* and *Waiting to Exhale*, but they are certainly not embracing radical multicultural projects. In fact, there is an expanding demand for these neutralized depictions of difference as transnational corporations and state apparatuses become increasingly interested in "diversity management": the domestication of racial and gender antagonisms and the marketing of simulated multiculturalism (Lubiano 1997: 239).

Education cuts, to take another example, are creating the conditions in which fewer minorities obtain the advanced training that they need to engage in effective political resistance, as fewer of them are able to attend the best schools, colleges and universities, and the quality of the rest of the education system rapidly declines. Education cuts also strike first at the most vulnerable institutions and programs, but their effects are transmitted throughout academia. The substitution of adjunct professors for tenure-track and tenured faculty has a much greater chilling effect on unconventional scholarship than the most vociferous anti-multiculturalism campaign. Where the Kuhnian principle – namely that innovation comes largely from the margins of a discipline (Kuhn 1962) – obtains, the loss of tenured positions at the lower and middle ranges of the highly stratified academic market will have an impact on the entire system: professors at elite institutions will practice their craft in an increasingly isolated, rarefied, nepotistic, routinized and backward context. Within a single institution, cuts or even their mere threat heighten interdepartmental and intradepartmental antagonisms; all too often, multicultural programs become a synecdochical signifier of excessive proliferation of specializations that urgently requires administrative rationalization. This in turn not only escalates criticism of the multicultural programs that have barely gained a foothold in the education system, but also promotes the sort of self-disciplining within these programs that endangers the careers of the more creative multicultural educators. Gifted students witnessing these conditions choose either to leave academia altogether, or to gain credentials in the most mainstream aspects of their profession, contributing further to the ossification of the multicultural programs that survive the cuts. None of these developments can even remotely be interpreted as a gain for radical multiculturalism. As Readings argues, the university's role in producing and protecting national culture has indeed been sharply reduced, but this transition has only made way for the intensive corporatization and transnational bureaucratization of the academy (1996).[7]

From the primitivization of difference to oppositional consciousness

Laclau's critique of what he regards as excessive particularism may be rooted in part in Gramsci's problematic conception of the relation between the intellectuals and the masses. As we have seen in Chapter 2, Gramsci rejects Lenin's vanguard party theory, and argues that the organic intellectual must engage in an extensive democratic dialogue with the "common sense" philosophy of "the people" (1971: 330, 365, 377). Even with these radical departures from the vanguard party tradition, some strains of elitism continue to shape Gramsci's theory of the organic intellectual. Gramsci contends that a particular political movement becomes hegemonic insofar as it expresses universal rather than particular interests. He assumes that the organic intellectuals who lead this hegemonic movement have obtained a worldview that is superior in its coherence and systematic organization to that of the masses (1971: 335). Gramsci's vision of a dialogue between the leaders and the led has a precise structure: the led bring historical specificity and concrete experience, while the leaders supply sophisticated intellectual frameworks. The masses are therefore portrayed as fundamentally dependent upon the organic intellectuals, for without them, they would remain trapped within a pre-modern, incoherent, episodic, provincial and anachronistic perspective (1971: 152, 153, 324, 325).

Gilroy demonstrates, by contrast, that when the African slaves submitted the modern institution of slavery to critique, they drew effectively upon pre-modern images, symbols, aesthetic expressions, rituals and practices. Their construction of a hybrid – or what Haraway (1991) would call "cyborg" – pre-modern/modern/post-modern discourse may have been the most effective form of anti-slavery resistance, for the "racial terror" of slavery was both fully compatible and "cheerfully complicit" with modern Western rationality. As such, an immanent critique that turned the tools of modernity against modernity itself to rescue its liberatory promise would have been insufficient (Gilroy 1993: 56, 71, 221). Insofar as it is premised upon the hierarchical distinctions between modernity and pre-modernity, or coherent universal rationality and incoherent particularisms, Gramsci's theory cannot be reconciled with the way in which Gilroy and Haraway value syncretistic and cyborg discourses of resistance.

A discourse that represents itself as democratic on the grounds that it promotes a dialogue between theorists and "the people" and yet decides in advance that the theorists have exclusive access to a superior rationality while "the people" can only bring particularistic experience to that dialogue is also highly problematic. We need to pay close attention in this respect to the strategic exclusions that are constitutive of the universality/particularity distinction. Scott notes that "man," the mythical universal subject of history, becomes a plausible figure only insofar as his development is constructed as a unified story. That unified story in turn depends upon the exclusion of the so-called particularisms – that is, the stories about "man"'s "others," the exploited and the oppressed (1988: 197). The problem is not resolved, however, merely by adding these excluded stories into a historical account. Even with these additions, their exclusion could be perpetuated, for they could be treated as expressions of an inferior rationality. Hooks, for example, criticizes feminist discourse that invokes the experience of women of color only to illustrate a theoretical formulation, without considering the possibility that the works by women of color could be theoretical discourses themselves (1984: 30–1). In this case, an apparently egalitarian exchange is actually operating like an Orientalizing primitivism, thereby normalizing the strategic assertion that the discourse of otherness would remain utterly fragmented and incoherent without the superior rationality provided from the outside by a Western intellectual elite (Said 1978).

Both Gramsci and Laclau imply that a movement's political practice corresponds to its worldview. Laclau states, for example, "If . . . feminist demands enter into chains of equivalence with those of black groups, ethnic minorities, civil rights activists, etcetera, they acquire a more global perspective than is the case where they remain restricted to their own particularism" (Laclau 1996e: 57). Similarly, Laclau and Mouffe contend that the "equivalential articulation between anti-racism, anti-sexism and anti-capitalism... requires a hegemonic construction which, in certain circumstances, may be the condition of consolidation of each one of these struggles" (1985: 182).

While Laclau and Mouffe signal the importance of contextualization in this passage, they do not actually investigate the complex combinations of worldviews and strategies that characterize concrete social movement politics. They tend instead to suggest that shifts in theoretical perspectives on the part of a given social movement will give rise to shifts in its actual strategies. Some minority groups, however, develop highly sophisticated and non-foundationalist analyses of the social, and deploy subversive appropriations of "universalistic" discourse in Laclau's sense, and yet – because of the ways in which they are historically positioned in contexts that are not wholly of their choosing – decide to mobilize their struggle in a highly autonomous manner. If a democratic movement finds itself thrown into a political terrain in which the only emerging democratic hegemonic forces are deploying "passive revolution" strategies that promote absorption, neutralization and colonization, then that movement has very little room to maneuver. It may be obliged to engage in the short-term maximization of its autonomy to strengthen its constituency, even if it would prefer, on the basis of its political values, to engage in hegemonic politics. The maximization of a movement's autonomy in these difficult conditions may nevertheless become beneficial for radical democratic pluralism in the long term. Neutralizing articulations may reduce the democratic potential in every movement's discourse in order to safeguard the status quo. The rejection of neutralizing articulations may allow the movement to deepen its anti-assimilatory identity and to develop further its specific democratic critique, and that may in turn give its democratic critique more force in future articulations with other political movements.

Sandoval and Anzaldúa make precisely this point in their theoretical analyses of women of color feminist discourse (Sandoval 1990; Anzaldúa 1990; Mohanty 1991: 36–7). If a hegemonic democratic movement is dominated by white heterosexual men who have not even begun to engage in anti-racist, anti-sexist and anti-homophobic politics, and if that hegemonic movement offers only an assimilatory form of articulation, then the minority leaders' decision to maximize their movements' autonomy would be entirely justified. Gitlin insists that demands for the recognition of multicultural diversity be kept "in proportion," and asks, "What is a Left if it is not, plausibly at least, the voice of the whole people?... If there is no people, but only peoples, there is no Left" (1995: 165). Sandoval and Anzaldúa might reply, "What is the value of a pretend leftist unity that fails to address the contestations that have justifiably emerged within and between democratic social movements?" Because democratic demands are often unjustly suppressed within apparently progressive blocs, Sandoval and Anzaldúa strongly endorse a theory of "oppositional consciousness" that embraces a mobile strategy for women of color feminist movements. They maintain that the latter are right when they engage in the constant tactical re-evaluation of hegemonic conditions. They defend women of color feminists' decisions to shift their primary allegiances back and forth between many different bloc-oriented positions and autonomous positions, depending on the prevailing conditions.

Sandoval and Anzaldúa want to see the development of robust leftist political activism in which multiple democratic movements would learn from each other and work productively together. Unless minority movements possess some authority when they engage in these leftist articulations, however, they will be reduced to assimilated tokens. Short-term autonomy strategies involving, for example, voluntary multicultural programs, affirmative action, and minority caucusing, may allow minority movements to gain the authority that would add more force to their demands. Speaking from an already empowered position at the bargaining table where articulation and identity reconstruction take place is something the traditionally dominant forces in democratic struggles take for granted. This is rarely, if ever, the case with traditionally excluded minorities.

Sandoval and Anzaldúa have not entirely resolved these problems. Their arguments tend to rest on the implicit assumption that the minorities in question can become completely aware of their strategic position and then freely choose an appropriate course of action. We are never fully conscious of the ways in which we are always being deployed and positioned, and we must make decisions – or, more precisely, we find that we have already been positioned as having decided – in conditions that are not wholly of our choosing. In any event, their theories open the way towards a contextually-sensitive analysis of hegemonic strategies.

Radical democratic pluralism does face some criticism from liberal democratic and leftist sources: from individual social democrats who do not accept that bureaucratization can have tremendously anti-democratic and anti-pluralist effects; from the traditional Marxists who see virtually every aspect of liberal democracy as irretrievable for socialism given its historical emergence within capitalist societies (Cunningham 1987: 151, 156–60); from the liberal multiculturalists who opportunistically deploy identity politics rhetoric but fail to grasp the effects of class differences (Ahmad 1992); from the traditional leftists who either contend that radical democratic pluralism's post-structuralist approach to difference is inherently incompatible with socialist principles[8] or who fail to value radical multicultural, anti-racist, anti-sexist and anti-homophobic politics altogether;[9] from those who believe that the transition to socialism must be won by any means necessary, including the "temporary" suspension of democratic rights and freedoms (Harrington 1993: 67); and from those "pragmatists" who believe that the electoral victories of a center-right figure such as Clinton justifies the abandonment of civil rights and leftist principles. Notwithstanding these liberal democratic and leftist critics, however, the strongest opposition against radical democratic pluralism comes from the right. In these conditions, as democratic movements are engaged in a life or death struggle against almost omnipotent reactionary forces, we need to balance our critique of these movements' struggles with a careful study of the ways in which common sense continues to reside in every moment of popular resistance.

What is needed in this respect is an historical investigation of the popular that underlines its organic character without collapsing into uncritical celebration. If oppressed and exploited peoples are responding to Le Pen, Buchanan, reactionary men's religious movements and right-wing militias, then we need to investigate the ways in which right-wing discourses resonate effectively with their everyday concerns. If they support anti-corruption and grassroots activist slates in American trade union elections and put leftist parties like Blair's "New Labour," Jospin's Socialists and Prodi's Olive Tree alliance into office, then we ought to engage with these historical opportunities in a constructive manner. If "the people" are withdrawing from political participation altogether, and if they are finding more meaning in media-packaged celebrity trauma, such as Princess Diana's death or Clinton's consensual sex life, rather than in key political debates, then we must examine the ways in which social, cultural and political institutions will have to be radically transformed to make way for genuine democratization. The solutions to these problems require a close analysis of the genealogical continuities and contextual specificities of hegemonic formations. Laclau and Mouffe's discourse has been central to the work of a whole generation of researchers who are studying right-wing politics and the "new social movements" in concrete historical conditions (Escobar 1992; Adam 1993; Epstein 1990; Norval 1996; Smith 1994b). Our conversations with their work have been indispensable, for they have outlined a political theory that allows us to grasp the fragile possibilities for the extension of the radical democratic revolution in our complex contemporary conditions.

NOTES

Introduction

1 Laclau and Mouffe's critics include Burawoy (1990), Callinicos (1989), Dickens (1990), Eagleton (1991), Geras (1987, 1988), Hunter (1988), Massey (1992), Mouzelis (1988), Osborne (1991), Rustin (1988) and Wood (1986).

2 I would like to acknowledge my debt to my University of Toronto and York University teachers, especially Dušan Pokorný, Gad Horowitz, Alkis Kontos, Frank Cunningham, Harvey Dyck, Donna Andrew, Mel Watkins, David Wolfe, Bob Gallagher, Sue Golding and Juan Maiguashca.

1 Retrieving democracy: the radical democratic imaginary

1 On the concept of institutions, I am following Balibar's definition: "As for 'institution', it is generally a name signifying that any human practice involves a certain *distribution of statuses* (or obligations) *and functions* (utility, efficiency, communication), susceptible of being expressed and legitimated in discourses – whether they be codes, stories or programs" (1995: 183; original emphases).

2 Laclau and Mouffe's interpretation of Arendt's term, "the social," is quite similar to that of Fraser. Like Fraser and Arendt, they understand the social as a space that has emerged within modernity, and that tends to embrace both the private and the public spheres. With Fraser, however, they would oppose Arendt's understanding of the private/public distinction as an appropriate expression of the human condition. They would also support Fraser insofar as she values the politicization of heretofore "private" needs as a positive development, and contends that that process does not necessarily lead to the triumph of bureaucratization and instrumental rationality (1989: 160).

3 For a critique of Tocqueville's pluralism, which was developed in part out of his extremely hostile and distorted representation of the American native people as nomadic savages, see Connolly (1995: 163–73).

4 Many would argue that the upward mobility of white ethnic groups such as the Irish immigrant population proves that the United States is a basically meritocratic society, with the implication that impoverished minorities have only themselves to blame for their condition. For a refutation of this "ethnicity theory" argument, see Takaki's *A Different Mirror* (1993).

5 In the Soviet workforce in the late 1980s, women were heavily concentrated in low-paid, low-status occupations. Although the Soviet Union did enact "protective" provisions for child care and maternity leave, abortion was the only widely available form of family planning, women's unequal burdens in terms of domestic labor and

consumer labor were not addressed, and women's rights were inextricably linked to motherhood. The continuities in gender discrimination in the Soviet and Western economies are remarkable: in both workforces, women were enormously over-represented in precisely the sorts of unskilled manual labor that would prove so vulnerable to displacement with the acceleration of restructuration and globalization, and the gap between the average wages of men and women was approximately 30 percent (Eisenstein 1994: 19–35).

6 I thank Martin Bernal for sharing his thoughts on this point with me.

7 The work of demonstrating the plural character of Marx's text, and the continuing force of its heterogeneous traces in contemporary global capitalist conditions, has also been performed by Derrida in his *Specters of Marx* (1994).

8 Individuals were categorized as "poor" in 1995 if their total family income was less than $15,569. It was assumed that there were four members in their family.

9 It should be noted that there may be some tensions between the theoretical framework that is being developed here and this survey of American inequality data. Class in the Marxist tradition is a relational position that is constituted in exploitative conditions; it can never be reduced to an individual's socio-economic status. Wherever the smallest possibility for mobility exists, an individual's class may not necessarily coincide with the socio-economic status into which they were born (Barrett 1988: xv). A more class-oriented analysis of inequality in the United States would have to trace the production and appropriation of surplus value. Such an analysis would become enormously complicated insofar as we took the global character of American capital into consideration. On race and inequality in the United States, see also Quadagno (1994) and Oliver and Shapiro (1997).

10 Although Connolly's outline for an egalitarian political economy is useful, it is not entirely clear how his general emphasis on the transnationalization of the political might be integrated into this program. The costs and benefits relating to different types of consumption do not necessarily obey nation-state boundaries. A country might actually transfer some of its public subsidies to favor inclusionary consumption, but it could do so without addressing the environmental costs that it imposes on other countries in the form of air- and water-borne pollution, exported nuclear waste, ozone-depleting consumption and production practices, massive deforestation and hydro-electric projects, and a high per capita consumption of non-renewable resources.

11 My thanks to Susan Buck-Morss and Nancy Hirschmann for helping me to clarify this summary of Lefort's argument.

12 "La liberté pour les seuls partisans du gouvernement, pour les seuls membres d'un parti – aussi nombreux soient-ils – ce n'est pas la liberté. La liberté est toujours au moins la liberté de celui qui pense autrement" (Löwy 1981: 74).

13 Leftist theorists have rarely addressed homophobia and heterosexism. Notable exceptions include Weeks (1977, 1981, 1985), Rubin (1975), the Gay Left Collective (1980), D'Emilio (1993), Chauncey (1990), Davis and Kennedy (1990), Newton (1993) and Bérubé (1990).

14 For example, the best answer to the demand for "gay marriage" would be the construction of an alternative family values bloc, in which the rights of sexual minorities, single parents, unmarried heterosexuals, divorced women, children born out of wedlock and welfare recipients would be promoted. The aim here would be to stop the state from pursuing the moral management of the population through the public subsidization of patriarchal heterosexual marriage. Such a campaign would demand, for example, the dismantling of marriage as a legal category and its replacement with domestic partner status, and universal access to public goods such as health care and education on an individual basis. Where the public subsidization of personal relationships – relationships involving, for example, impoverished families, or individuals

caring for the disabled and the elderly – is entirely appropriate, it should be imple-
mented in a truly secular manner without the imposition of official moral standards. In
this manner, lesbian and gay rights could be aligned with the rights of poor women to
make free decisions about childbearing and the rights of heterosexuals to construct
their consensual adult relationships according to their own personal values. The state
should only intervene in cases of exploitation and abuse, and these terms should be
given feminist definitions to preclude their covert usage as legitimations for right-wing
social engineering. This is not to say that we should not celebrate every kind of
romantic commitment that is freely chosen by consenting adults, but that we should
do so without the involvement of state apparatuses. For a more detailed discussion of
the gay marriage issue, see Hunter (1995).

15 Plotke contends that the post-Marxist concern about the preservation of a social
movement's autonomy only makes sense in the context of a political terrain that is
dominated by a powerful Communist Party on one side and a highly centralized state
and homogeneous culture on the other. From this perspective, he concludes that
because these conditions do not exist in the United States, and power is "relatively
dispersed" in the American setting, the autonomy principle does not have the same
value here (Plotke 1990: 93). Plotke's critique has some merit; it could be argued that
Laclau and Mouffe do not pay enough attention to historical specificities in advancing
their argument about autonomy. However, the problems of assimilationism and
tokenism remain serious obstacles for radical political activism in the United States,
even if the assimilating agents are neither a strong Leftist party nor a centralized
welfare state, but the Democratic and Republican parties, powerful transnational
corporations and media conglomerates.

16 Slavenka Drakulic, for example, criticized Clinton for declaring in December 1997
that peace in Bosnia depended on the will of the Bosnians alone. She pointed out that
there could be no peace in Bosnia when extremist nationalists remained in power in
Croatia and Serbia. From her perspective, Milsovic, Tudjman, and, to a lesser extent,
Izetbegovic are merely using the illusion of free elections to legitimate their authoritarian "demokratura" regimes (Drakulic 1997).

17 The whole issue of "population control" has been the site of numerous complex articulations whose political meaning cannot be determined according to a simple typology
or content analysis. The Clinton administration, for example, has taken an apparently
"feminist" "pro-choice" position in international contexts, such as the 1994 United
Nations' International Conference on Population and Development in Cairo. While
it should be recognized that with the Republican grip on the Congress, Clinton pays a
price for preserving any degree of official support for abortion rights, feminists have
charged that the administration is interested in population control for the sake of
international security first and foremost, and has only adopted feminist language in
order to disguise its policies (Flanders 1997: 89–91, 92–4).

18 For a critical analysis of the Rock Against Racism and the Anti-Nazi League movements, see Gilroy (1987: 117–35).

19 Gramscian intellectuals also influenced the British Communist Party (CP) during this
period. They argued in Party policy documents published in the late 1970s that the CP
should recognize the importance of cultural struggles, attack narrow economistic
strategies in the labor movement, and pursue alliances with popular movements, but
without imposing a vanguardist leadership upon them (Forgacs 1989: 80–2).

20 A right-wing anti-gay rights campaign, for example, might argue that although heterosexuality is "natural," sexuality remains socially constructed, for homosexuality can be
promoted. Or right-wing anti-immigration and anti-multiculturalism campaigns might
charge that racial otherness can have a corrupting effect on white Anglo culture
(Smith 1994b).

2 Essentialism, non-essentialism and democratic leadership: from Lenin to Gramsci

1 The Second International was an international workers' organization that flourished between 1889 and the First World War. Established by Marxists and dominated by the European labor movement, the Second International aimed to promote socialist struggles.
2 "Structures" include not only economic relations, but all sedimented and institutionalized practices. Structures therefore include "modes of identification, social institutions and legal and economic practices [,] all of which, in principle, are open to dislocation and resedimentation" (Norval 1996: 26).
3 Here I am paraphrasing Hall, who contends that in contemporary Britain, "race is ... the modality in which class is 'lived', the medium through which class relations are experienced, the form in which it is appropriated and 'fought through'" (Hall 1980: 341).
4 We cannot have a perfectly solipsistic subject position in the same sense that we cannot have an utterly private "language game" (Wittgenstein 1958).
5 Based on my own experience as an activist in the United Auto Workers' Livable Wage campaign at Cornell University, I would acknowledge that even the most apparently neutral "fact" can, in the context of a labor dispute, become quite controversial.
6 For a critique of functionalism, see Barrett (1988: 22–3).
7 It could be noted here, following Dallmayr (1987: 284), that where Laclau and Mouffe affirm that every social formation remains an incomplete totality, the authors not only distance themselves from Lukács, but also from the sociologistic claim that we can fully comprehend the logic of the social. For Laclau and Mouffe, we can – and indeed we must – deploy theoretical concepts to interpret social forces, but there will always be some untheorizable remainder that exceeds our grasp.
8 Mercer points out that there are strong continuities between the Gramscian argument that subjectivity is constituted through political discourse, and the Foucauldian principle that within the bio-power regime, power brings its objects into subjectivity (1980: 126).
9 Maquiladoras are, generally speaking, labor-intensive light-manufacturing factories that are owned by transnational corporations and are located in northern Mexico near the US border. Under the NAFTA accord, they are able to benefit from the lower Mexican wage rate while simultaneously enjoying low tariff access to the US market. Women often make up the majority of the maquiladora's workforce. Although NAFTA side agreements are supposed to ensure environmentally sound production processes and workers' rights, there has been extensive evidence that pollution, dangerous work conditions and anti-independent union practices prevail in the maquiladora sector. The US labor movement is paying increasing attention to the maquiladoras. The relocation of factories to this sector has caused profound dislocations in the American low-skilled manual labor market. Further, US unions are experimenting with new forms of transnational solidarity involving both Mexican and US workers.
10 LaCapra further argues that Žižek's theory is problematic in that it does not adequately conceptualize the possibilities for organizing political resistance.

It is difficult to find in this ... theoretical formulation a place for critical, responsible agency within a noninvidious normative framework, even if one carefully distinguishes the desirability of such agency from its self-serving, indiscriminate use that is justifiably criticized by Lacan: the nonexplanatory, moralizing tendency to blame the victim by seeing ethical failure as the "cause" of "pathology."

(1994: 207)

11 Salecl (1994), for her part, has begun the very important work of bridging Lacanian formalism and Foucauldian genealogy. See also McClintock (1995), who attempts to integrate psychoanalytic insights into her post-structuralist paradigm. From this perspective, she takes Bhabha and Irigaray to task for perpetuating a "fetishism of form" that precludes a historically specific analysis of social antagonisms and concrete practices (1995: 62–5, 67–8).

12 Although this analogy with Lacan's mirror stage argument is suggestive, we must set aside its developmental aspect. (Mis)identification is of course a permanent condition rather than a single "stage" in human life, and societies in "organic crisis" are certainly not more "infantile" than relatively stable societies.

13 It could be suggested that Žižek's attempt to quarantine the historical in this manner is itself the product of historically specific anxieties that structure that text. A full exploration of this possibility would necessitate reading Žižek's theory against the background of contemporary East European politics. These remarks are inspired by Rose's contention that Freud's writing retreated towards modernist closures in the face of the unbearable character of mourning, and that that unbearability came to the fore for him when he was faced with specific historical events. Rose argues that because the work of mourning can never be brought to an end, our lost attachments will continue to haunt and to threaten with pulverization our identifications in the present. With this formulation, Rose underlines the complex and ultimately unmasterable character of identification (1997). As I will note in Chapter 4, this approach has implications for understanding identifications with both right-wing and radical democratic discourses.

14 Butler nevertheless points out the repetitions that can be found in Žižek's various attempts to describe the operation of the real. Insofar as the real is understood as the unsymbolizable threat of castration, Žižek's text tends to proceed as if Oedipally induced sexual difference were always already established in the prediscursive. As a result, Žižek's theory

> evacuates the "contingency" of its contingency. Indeed, his theory valorizes a "law" prior to all ideological formations, one with consequential social and political implications for the placing of the masculine within discourse and the symbolic, and the feminine as a "stain", "outside the circuit of discourse."

(1993: 196)

3 Subject positions, articulation and the subversion of essentialism

1 If democratic demands are "undecidable" in abstraction – if their political value can only be determined in specific contexts – the same is certainly not true for anti-democratic demands. All racisms are wrong; obviously, we do not need to do a contextually-specific analysis to arrive at this conclusion. Of course, it is always strategically important that we ask which sorts of reactionary discourses we are dealing with in a particular situation, but we can say unequivocally in advance that radical democratic pluralism opposes all anti-democratic positions.

2 See, for example, Miles (1984).

3 Hall refers to a different edition and translation of *Capital*, Vol. III (London: Lawrence & Wishart, 1974: 791–2), but the differences between the translations are minimal.
4 We could note in passing that Cohen's argument rests on an essentialist conception of human nature, for he refers to humans' natural interest in resolving the problem of scarcity through rational action in his account of the productive forces' development (Cohen 1978: 150–60).

4 Self-determination, community and citizenship

1 Rorty's dependence upon the incitement of solidarity-oriented sentiments for the construction of a liberal consensus could be challenged precisely on these grounds. From a psychoanalytic perspective, the promotion of specific identifications will always remain complex and notoriously vulnerable to dysfunctional effects.
2 We could also note that Schmitt is not the only thinker who has issued a warning about the dangers that are inherent in the construction of an illusory agnosticism towards political differences on the part of the liberal democratic state. Marx's own critique of liberal democracy (Marx 1975b, 1977) might have been suggestive in this regard.

5 Power and hegemony

1 Chodorow has also been criticized for suggesting that gender difference and feminist social change are primarily concerned with the family and household experience, thereby making it impossible to link the familial institution with economic, political and broad-based socio-cultural relations (Scott 1988: 37–8). See also Brown (1995: 83), who argues that MacKinnon exaggerates the totalizing and ontologically reductionist dimension of Marx's theory while failing to adopt its historical and dialectical elements. Hartsock's theory is similarly limited insofar as it is structured by an analogy with the most reductionist moments in Marx's theory of ideology (Hartsock 1983: 283–5; Marx 1976: 42, 67; Barrett 1991: 3–17). Hartsock revises her standpoint theory in a later text; she acknowledges, for example, that women are indeed differentiated in terms of class, racial and colonial status (1990: 161). Hartsock nevertheless continues to theorize power as a purely negative and external force, and does not address Alarcón's challenge concerning intragender antagonisms (1990). Hartsock does refer to the existence of multiple marginalized groups, but she constructs the social as a simple antagonism between two unified blocs – the marginalized and the dominant – without recognizing the persistence of antagonisms among the marginalized and across the marginalized/dominant divide (1990: 171). Finally, she reiterates her basic argument that the social is divided into the rulers and the ruled and that the rulers only have access to a "partial" and "reversed" view of material reality; feminism is again positioned as a superior rational, objective and universal discourse that can unmask false consciousness and recover women's authentic identities (1990: 172). With respect to the general issue of feminist essentialism, it should be noted that many women activists have in fact organized their projects according to a complex understanding of gender that is highly sensitive to class, race and sexual differences throughout the current post-1960s period of feminist mobilization. Part of the problem consists in the fact that insofar as feminists have won mass media attention, the "sound-bite" and "niche-oriented" logic of that coverage is such that only the more binaristic feminist struggles have been featured, while the intersectional and transnational aspects of women's activism have been ignored (Flanders 1997: 4–5).

2 Zerilli makes a similar point with respect to feminist interpretative strategies. She contends that feminist readings of canonical political theory are inadequate where they merely trace the ways in which the texts in question assign political significance to gendered signifiers, as if the meaning of gendered signifiers were already established elsewhere. Political theorists do not, of course, invent the category of "woman" out of nothing, but they do intervene in gendered discourse in a performative manner. Zerilli aims to bring this constitutive dimension to light:

> Rather than treat woman either as an embodied social referent or as a term whose meaning preexists its figuration, narrative invocation, and circulation in the political text, I examine woman as she is produced symbolically and deployed rhetorically in theoretical interventions in historical debates about the crisis in political meaning.
>
> (1994: 4)

On the racialized performativity of gender and sexuality discourse in the imperial context, see McClintock (1995) and Stoler (1995).

3 Appiah's Kantian rationalism, however, yields very little in the way of anti-racist strategies. Where racists resist anti-racist rational dialogue and scientific evidence, Appiah bleakly concludes that they suffer from a "deformation of rationality in judgement," that may in turn "threaten an agent's autonomy, making it appropriate to treat or train rather than to reason with them" (1990: 9).

4 See, for example, Herrnstein and Murray (1994) and the texts on *The Bell Curve*, including Devlin *et al.* (1997), Fischer *et al.* (1996), Fraser (1995) and Kinchloe *et al.* (1996).

5 For a critique of *The Bell Curve* and race-based conclusions from "intelligence testing," see S. Gould (1981), Johnson (1994), Gardner (1994), Holmes (1994), Holt (1994), Lewin (1994), Herbert (1994), Passell (1994), Hirsch (1994), Ryan (1994) and Lane (1994).

6 This critique of Althusser does not, however, amount to an endorsement of Scott's rejection of hegemony theory. From a Gramscian–Foucauldian perspective, Scott's argument becomes problematic insofar as he constructs significant formal continuities between radically different formations, such as slavery and late capitalism, and treats the identities of the disempowered as if they were prior to power relations (Scott 1990).

7 Butler notes that although the American judiciary has allowed for an expansion of the category of obscenity, it has consistently rejected the claim that a person of color who has been subjected to racist speech – including cross-burnings – has suffered an injury that would legitimate the abrogation of the First Amendment. Under the First Amendment, speech can be regulated only if it violates the obscenity "community standards," or if it fails the "clear and present danger" test. By ruling in *R.A.V. v. St. Paul* (1992) that a burning cross on a black family's lawn remained protected speech, even though there is a well-documented historical relationship between burning crosses and racist acts of arson and murder in the United States, the Supreme Court effectively drained that deadly historicity out of the burning cross signifier. Butler also demonstrates that some officials regard blacks as the primary source of racially incendiary speech (1997a: 62–5). Her critique can be compared in this respect to that of the British leftists who took aim against the British Race Relations Act (1965). Citing the fact that black activists have been charged under this law with the incitement of racial hatred against whites, they have argued that it was designed solely to promote the state's social control agenda in the name of safeguarding the "public order" (Sivanandan 1982: 17–18).

8 There are, of course, several risks involved in the use of this compassionate discourse. To the extent that Clinton transforms himself into an empathetic figure and uses phrases that are usually found in the context of a discourse between equal members of a therapeutic support group, he decreases the symbolic distance between his office and his constituents, thereby endangering his Presidential stature. In contemporary American society, a successful populist would probably have to move back and forth between the compassionate position and the dignified elder statesman position, thereby symbolically inciting both egalitarian sibling/sibling-style identifications and hierarchical parent/child-style identifications. His critics would point out, in any event, that Clinton has also lost Presidential stature because of his own wrongdoings with respect to campaign finance scandals and Jones' sexual harassment charge, and that his "downsizing" of the dignity in his office synecdochically represents the general "downsizing" of public institutions and the decline in popular trust in the government.

Conclusion: multicultural difference and the political

1 As Mercer points out, Gramsci develops this distinction between "passive revolution" and hegemony through a comparison of the relatively conservative Italian *Risorgimento* and the popular French Revolution (1980: 129–30).
2 Laclau and Mouffe's conception of permanent contestation can be usefully compared with Nancy's "la communauté désoeuvrée" (1991: 40) and Readings' "community of dissensus" (1996: 185, 187–93).
3 Laclau's remarks can be usefully compared with Balibar's argument, namely that "racism reveals the non-universalistic component of nationalism," insofar as it operates as a "symptom of the contradiction between particularism and universalism which primordially affects nationalism, a symptom of the double-bind to which any claim of *identity* as *national* identity, both individual and collective, is unavoidably subject" (1994: 194, 195). From Balibar's perspective, racism does not simply use universalistic discourse to conceal its exclusionary program; nor is it only the case that racist particularism can be made compatible with universalism. He contends that racism and universalism are like Hegelian contraries; each concept is "inside" the other and affects the other from the "inside." Universalism has no essence; it can in principle be thought without being affected from the inside by racism. But because the weight of tradition bears so heavily on the present – there has never been a single definition of the human that did not contain within itself the principle of human hierarchy; there has never been a nationalism that has not attempted to resolve the tension between its promised egalitarianism and the persistence of inequality by referring to natural differences – the ground for such radically new universalistic thought would have to be prepared, and that would require, in turn, extensive collective struggle and profound social change (1994: 191–204).
4 See, for example, the work of Fusco (1995), Shohat and Stam (1994), the Chicago Cultural Studies Group (1994), Gutierrez (1994), Christian (1994), Spivak (1997) and Minh-ha (1997). Although Walzer's remarks about "footloose" individuals, "postmodern vagabonds," the divorce rate, and the political strategies of radical social movements are problematic, he nevertheless rightly argues that genuine multicultural tolerance must entail a defense of group differences and an attack on economic inequality (1997: 98–112).
5 It could be objected that excluded minorities see through this sort of displacement and tokenism, but given the contemporary political structure, that is often beside the point. Actual minorities usually lack organized access to our imperfect democratic institutions; in some cases, their votes do not matter at all (Guinier 1991; Hero 1992).

From the perspective of a hegemonic force, political strategies must aim first and fore-most to constantly remobilize popular identifications among the imagined "majority." As I have argued with respect to homophobia, when an official insults a minority and then apologizes, it does not really matter whether or not the apology's ostensible audi-ence believes that the apology is sincere. What matters is that the "soft-core" bigots who support the official because he or she is a bigot, and yet enjoy fantasizing that they are "mainstream" and "tolerant," are thereby reassured and taught yet again how to identify with bigotry in a rebuttable manner (1997b). Balibar, referring to fake scien-tific racist discourses, institutional racism, Eurocentric cultural policies and colonization, states, "Such political and ideological processes work effectively *only* if those who carry them out actually *believe* in their legitimacy and, indeed, in their truth, or in their being grounded in true doctrines" (1994: 195). The task for a hege-monic formation is not just to make sure that it builds a supporters' bloc by appealing to individuals' socio-economic interests, for subjects never make decisions based on instrumentalist analysis alone. It also has to offer compelling frameworks for popular identifications – even among, and sometimes especially among, the individuals who stand to make socio-economic gains from its policies – and it has to constantly adjust those frameworks as the mobile strategic terrain presents new challenges.

6 Ironically enough, D'Souza makes the same point about anti-racism: "By a curious somersault of history, the *anti-racist* has become the mirror image of his enemy." He claims that liberal anti-racists are mainly responsible for the perpetuation of racism since they promote a cultural relativism that conceals blacks' cultural deficiencies, perpetuates dependency among blacks, and censors whites' "natural" and "rational" antagonistic feelings towards their cultural inferiors (1995: 243).

7 While Readings' study of corporatization in the contemporary university (1996) is insightful and suggestive, there are many weaknesses in his text. He gives a problem-atic historical account of the university's development (see, for example, Levine 1996 for an alternative account of the debates on the American academy's mission in the nineteenth and twentieth centuries), he equates "ideology" with the needs of the nation-state, he constructs the social as a totalistic functionalist system that is driven solely by capital, and he oversimplifies the effects of capital's globalization. Because the restructuration that Readings identifies is accompanied by the accelerated stratifi-cation of the academic job market, increased differentiation between well-endowed private institutions and their more vulnerable private and public counterparts, and intensified competition between academic departments – and even between the sub-fields within a single department – for institutional legitimation and access to resources, it becomes all the more urgent that we grasp the complex and sometimes contradictory relationship between the rise of transnational capital and the contem-porary transformation of the academy. Readings is also not sufficiently critical on the question of the corporatized academy's standards; rather than taking its discourse at its word and treating its standard of "excellence" like an empty signifier, we should analyze the ways in which the corporatized academy deploys intensive paradigm management techniques as it "rationalizes" its structure. Where Readings claims that women's studies and ethnic studies programs, for example, are perfectly assimilable within the corporatized academy as long as they achieve a proper degree of "excel-lence," it should be noted that that achievement is often reserved in advance solely for the most neutralized forms of these programs, namely the ones that successfully mimic the mainstream discourses within their parent disciplines. Finally, Readings does not pay enough attention to the insidious character of market rationality. A single elite institution could adopt his alternative standards; it could transform itself into a "dissensual community" and provide for permanent contestation on the meaning of academic standards. But if it acted in isolation, if it did not simultaneously work in

solidarity with less elite institutions, it might find that its special "anti-corporatization" approach will ultimately become transformed into a highly marketable commodity. Anti-capitalist cultural criticism does not necessarily resist commodification (Adorno 1990); "anti-corporatization" academic discourse could merely create favorable conditions for the construction of elite intellectual theme parks.

8 See, for example, Gitlin's *Twilight of Common Dreams* (1995).

9 For all his valuable historical scholarship, Hobsbawm's discourse becomes problematic when he embraces this position in his "Identity Politics and the Left" (1996).

BIBLIOGRAPHY

Adam, B. (1993) "Post-Marxism and the New Social Movements," *Canadian Review of Sociology and Anthropology*, 30, 3: 316–36.

Adams, P. (1979) "A Note on the Distinction between Sexual Division and Sexual Differences," *m/f*, 3: 51–7; repr. in P. Adams and E. Cowie (eds) (1990) *The Woman in Question: M/f*, Boston, MA: MIT Press.

—— (1990) "Introduction: The Nature of Feminist Argument," in P. Adams and E. Cowie (eds) *The Woman in Question: M/f*, Boston, MA: MIT Press.

Adams, P. and Cowie, E. (1986) "*m/f*: Interview 1984," in *m/f*, 11–12: 5–16; repr. in P. Adams and E. Cowie (eds) (1990) *The Woman in Question: M/f*, Boston, MA: MIT Press.

Adorno, T. (1990) "Cultural Criticism and Society," in T. Adorno, *Prisms*, Cambridge, MA: MIT Press.

Ahmad, A. (1992) *In Theory: Classes, Nations, Literatures*, London: Verso.

Alarcón, N. (1990) "The Theoretical Subject(s) of *This Bridge Called My Back* and Anglo-American Feminism," in G. Anzaldúa (ed.) *Making Face, Making Soul = Haciendo Caras: Creative and Critical Perspectives By Women of Color*, San Francisco, CA: Aunt Lute Foundation Books.

Alexander, J. and Mohanty, C. (1997) "Introduction: Genealogies, Legacies, Movements," in J. Alexander and C. Talpade Mohanty (eds) *Feminist Genealogies, Colonial Legacies, Democratic Futures*, New York: Routledge.

Almaguer, T. (1993) "Chicano Men: A Cartography of Homosexual Identity and Behaviour," in H. Abelove *et al.* (eds) *The Lesbian and Gay Studies Reader*, New York: Routledge.

Althusser, L. (1971) "Ideology and Ideological State Apparatuses (Notes towards an Investigation)," in L. Althusser, *Lenin and Philosophy and other Essays*, New York: Monthly Review Press.

Amos, V. and Parmar, P. (1984) "Challenging Imperial Feminism," *Feminist Review*, 17 (July): 3–19.

Anderson, P. (1976–7) "The Antinomies of Antonio Gramsci," *New Left Review*, November/January, 100: 5–78.

Angier, N. (1997) "New Debate Over Surgery on Genitals," *New York Times*, 13 May.

Anzaldúa, G. (1990) "Bridge, Drawbridge, Sandbar or Island," in L. Albrecht and R. Brewer (eds) *Bridges of Power: Women's Multicultural Alliances*, Santa Cruz: New Society Publishers.

Appiah, A. (1985) "The Uncompleted Argument: Du Bois and the Illusion of 'Race'," in H.L. Gates, Jr. (ed.) *"Race," Writing and Difference*, Chicago, IL: University of Chicago Press.

—— (1990) "Racisms," in D. Goldberg (ed.) *Anatomy of Racism*, Minneapolis, MN: University of Minnesota Press.

Appignanesi, L. and Maitland, S. (1989) *The Rushdie File*, London: ICA/Fourth Estate.

Aristotle (1958) *The Politics of Aristotle*, trans. E. Barker, Oxford: Oxford University Press.

Aronson, R. (1995) *After Marxism*, New York: Guilford Press.

Ash, T. (1997) "The Curse and Blessing of South Africa," *New York Review of Books*, 14 August: 10–11.

Avineri, S. (1970) *The Social and Political Thought of Karl Marx*, Cambridge: Cambridge University Press.

Bacon, D. (1995) "Labouring to Cross the NAFTA Divide," *The Nation*, 13 November: 572–4.

Badgett, M. (1997) "Beyond Biased Samples: Challenging the Myths on the Economic Status of Lesbians and Gay Men," in A. Gluckman and B. Reed (eds.) *Homoeconomics: Capitalism, Community and Lesbian and Gay Life*, New York: Routledge.

Baldwin, J. (1985) *The Price of a Ticket*, New York: St Martin's Press.

Balibar, E. (1991a) "Class Racism," in E. Balibar and I. Wallerstein, *Race, Nation, Class: Ambiguous Identities*, London: Verso.

—— (1991b) "Is There a 'Neo-Racism'?," in E. Balibar and I. Wallerstein, *Race, Nation, Class: Ambiguous Identities*, London: Verso.

—— (1991c) "Preface," in E. Balibar and I. Wallerstein, *Race, Nation, Class: Ambiguous Identities*, London: Verso.

—— (1991d) "Racism and Crisis," in E. Balibar and I. Wallerstein, *Race, Nation, Class: Ambiguous Identities*, London: Verso.

—— (1994) *Masses, Classes, Ideas: Studies on Politics and Philosophy Before and After Marx*, London: Routledge.

—— (1995) "Culture and Identity (Working Notes)," in J. Rajchman (ed.) *The Identity in Question*, New York: Routledge.

Barker, M. (1981) *The New Racism: Conservatives and the Ideology of the Tribe*, London: Junction Books.

Barnet, R. and Cavanaugh, J. (1994) *Global Dreams: Imperial Corporations and the New World Order*, New York: Simon & Schuster.

Barnett, A. (1986) "The Twots," unpublished paper.

Barrett, M. (1985) "Ideology and the Cultural Production of Gender," in J. Newton and D. Rosenfelt (eds) *Feminist Criticism and Social Change: Sex, Class and Race in Literature and Culture*, New York: Methuen.

—— (1988) *Women's Oppression Today: Problems in Marxist Feminist Analysis*, London: New Left Books.

—— (1991) *The Politics of Truth: From Marx to Foucault*, Cambridge: Polity Press.

Barrett, M. and Coward, R. (1982) "Letter to the Editorial Collective," *m/f*, 7: 88.

Barthes, R. (1973) *Mythologies*, London: Paladin.

Baudrillard, J. (1983) *In the Shadow of the Silent Majorities . . . Or the End of the Social*, New York: Semiotexte.

Bay, C. (1993) "The Structure of Freedom," in P. Green (ed.) *Democracy*, Atlantic Highlands, NJ: Humanities Press.

Bellamy, E. (1993) "Discourses of Impossibility: Can Psychoanalysis be Political?," *Diacritics*, 23, 1: 24–38.

Bem, S. (1993) *The Lenses of Gender: Transforming the Debate on Sexual Inequality*, New Haven, CT: Yale University Press.

Bennis, P. and Moushabeck, M. (1993) *Altered States: A Reader in the New World Order*, New York: Olive Branch Press.

Bergesen, A. (1993) "The Rise of Semiotic Marxism," *Sociological Perspectives*, 36, 1: 1–22.

Berlin, I. (1984) "Two Concepts of Liberty," in M. Sandel (ed.) *Liberalism and Its Critics*, New York: New York University Press.

Bernal, M. (1987) *Black Athena: The Afroasiatic Roots of Classical Civilization*, vol. I, *The Fabrication of Ancient Greece, 1785–1985*, London: Free Association Books.

Bérubé, A. (1990) "Marching To A Different Drummer: Lesbian and Gay GIs in World War II," in M. Duberman, M. Vicinus and G. Chauncey, Jr. (eds.) *Hidden From History: Reclaiming the Gay and Lesbian Past*, New York: Penguin.

Bhabha, H. (1990) "The Third Space," in J. Rutherford (ed.) *Identity: Community, Culture, Difference*, London: Lawrence & Wishart.

Bhabha, J., Klug, F. and Shutter, S. (eds) (1985) *Worlds Apart: Women Under Immigration and Nationality Law*, London: Pluto.

Big Flame (1979) *Sexuality and Fascism*, Liverpool: Big Flame.

—— (1981a) *Organizing to Win: A Political Manual About How to Stop Losing Struggles at Work*, Liverpool: Big Flame.

—— (1981b) *Walking a Tightrope: Big Flame's Women's Pamphlet*, Liverpool: Big Flame.

Blackburn, R. (1991) "Fin de Siècle: Socialism after the Crash," in R. Blackburn (ed.) *After the Fall: The Failure of Communism and the Future of Socialism*, London: Verso.

Bobbio, N. (1979) "Gramsci and the Conception of Civil Society," in C. Mouffe (ed.) *Gramsci and Marxist Theory*, London: Routledge & Kegan Paul.

Bourdieu, P. (1977) *Outline of a Theory of Practice*, Cambridge: Cambridge University Press.

Bowles, S. and Gintis, H. (1986) *Democracy and Capitalism: Property, Community and the Contradictions of Modern Social Thought*, New York: Basic Books.

Bradsher, K. (1995a) "Gap in Wealth in U.S. Called Widest in West," *New York Times*, 17 April.

—— (1995b) "America's Opportunity Gap," *New York Times*, 4 June.

Braidotti, R., Charkiewicz, E., Hausler, S. and Wieringa, S. (1994) *Women, the Environment and Sustainable Development*, London: Zed Books.

Brennan, T. (1990) "History After Lacan," *Economy and Society*, 19, 3 (August): 277–313.

Brown, B. and Adams, P. (1979) "The Feminine Body and Feminist Politics," *m/f*, 3: 35–50.

Brown, E. (1992) *A Taste of Power: A Black Woman's Story*, New York: Doubleday.

Brown, J. (1990) "Lesbian Sexuality in Medieval and Early Modern Europe," in M. Duberman, M. Vicinus and G. Chauncey, Jr. (eds.) *Hidden From History: Reclaiming the Gay and Lesbian Past*, New York: Penguin.

Brown, W. (1995) *States of Injury: Power and Freedom in Late Modernity*, Princeton, NJ: Princeton University Press.

Bryan, B., Dadzie, S. and Scafe, S. (1985) *The Heart of the Race: Black Women's Lives in Britain*, London: Virago.

Buchanan, A. (1982) *Marx and Justice: The Radical Critique of Liberalism*, Totowa, NJ: Rowman & Littlefield.

Buci-Glucksmann, C. (1979) "State, Transition and Passive Revolution," in C. Mouffe (ed.) *Gramsci and Marxist Theory*, London: Routledge & Kegan Paul.

Burawoy, M. (1990) "Marxism as Science: Historical Challenges and Theoretical Growth," *American Sociological Review*, 55: 775–93.

Burke, E. (1955) *Reflections on the Revolution in France*, ed. T. Mahoney, Indianapolis, IN: Bobbs-Merrill.

Butler, J. (1990a) *Gender Trouble: Feminism and the Subversion of Identity*, New York: Routledge.

—— (1990b) "Gender Trouble, Feminist Theory, and Psychoanalytic Discourse," in L. Nicholson (ed.) *Feminism/Postmodernism*, New York: Routledge.

—— (1992) "Sexual Inversions," in D. Stanton (ed.) *Discourses of Sexuality*, Ann Arbor, MI: University of Michigan Press.

—— (1993) *Bodies That Matter: On the Discursive Limits of "Sex,"* New York: Routledge.

—— (1997a) *Excitable Speech: A Politics of the Performative*, New York: Routledge.

—— (1997b) "Further Reflections on Conversations of Our Time," *Diacritics*, 27, 1 (spring): 13–15.

Butler, J. and Laclau, E., with R. Laddaga (1997) "The Uses of Equality," *Diacritics*, 27, 1 (spring): 3–12.

Callinicos, A. (1985) "Postmodernism, Poststructuralism, Post-Marxism?" *Theory, Culture and Society*, 2: 85–101.

—— (1989) *Against Postmodernism: A Marxist Critique*, London: Lawrence & Wishart.

Carter, S. (1991) *Reflections of an Affirmative Action Baby*, New York: Basic Books.

Chauncey, Jr., G. (1990) "Christian Brotherhood or Sexual Perversion? Homosexual Identities and the Construction of Sexual Boundaries in the World War I Era," in M. Duberman, M. Vicinus and G. Chauncey, Jr. (eds) *Hidden From History: Reclaiming the Gay and Lesbian Past*, New York: Penguin.

Chen, K. (1991) "Post-Marxism: Between/Beyond Critical Postmodernism and Cultural Studies," *Media, Culture and Society*, 13: 35–51.

Chicago Cultural Studies Group (The) (1994) "Critical Multiculturalism," in D. Goldberg (ed.) *Multiculturalism: A Critical Reader*, Oxford: Blackwell.

Chodorow, N. (1978) *The Reproduction of Mothering: Psychoanalysis and the Sociology of Gender*, Berkeley, CA: University of California Press.

Chomsky, N. (1988) *Manufacturing Consent: The Political Economy of the Mass Media*, New York: Pantheon Books.

Christian, B. (1994) "Diminishing Returns: Can Black Feminism(s) Survive the Academy?" in D. Goldberg (ed.) *Multiculturalism: A Critical Reader*, Oxford: Blackwell.

Clegg, S. (1989) *Frameworks of Power*, London: Sage.

Cockburn, A. (1991) "Radical as Reality," in R. Blackburn (ed.) *After the Fall: The Failure of Communism and the Future of Socialism*, London: Verso.

—— (1996) "The Kevorkian in the White House," *The Nation*, 14 October.

Cohen, G. (1978) *Karl Marx's Theory of History: A Defence*, Princeton, NJ: Princeton University Press.

Coles, R. (1996) "Liberty, Equality, Receptive Generosity: Neo-Nietzschean Reflections on the Ethics and Politics of Coalition," *American Political Science Review*, 90, 2 (June): 375–88.

Collins, P. (1991) *Black Feminist Thought: Knowledge, Consciousness, and the Politics of Empowerment*, New York: Routledge.

Connolly, W. (1991) *Identity/Difference: Democratic Negotiations of Political Paradox*, Ithaca, NY: Cornell University Press.

—— (1995) *The Ethos of Pluralization*, Minneapolis, MN: University of Minnesota Press, 1995.

Corn, D. (1995) "Retiring Newt," *The Nation*, 30 January: 117–18.

Cose, E. (1993) *The Rage of a Privileged Class: Why are Middle-Class Blacks Angry? Why Should America Care?* New York: HarperCollins.

Creet, J. (1991) "Lesbian Sex/Gay Sex: What's the Difference?" *Outlook*, 11 (winter).

Crenshaw, K. (1992) "Whose Story Is It Anyway? Feminist and Antiracist Appropriations of Anita Hill," in T. Morrison (ed.) *Race-ing Justice, En-gendering Power: Essays on Anita Hill, Clarence Thomas and the Construction of Social Reality*, New York: Pantheon.

Crewe, I. (1988) "Has the Electorate Become Thatcherite?" in R. Skidelsky (ed.) *Thatcherism*, London: Chatto & Windus.

Critchley, S. (1996) "Deconstruction and Pragmatism: Is Derrida a Private Ironist or a Public Liberal?" in C. Mouffe (ed.) *Deconstruction and Pragmatism*, London: Routledge.

Culler, J. (1986) *Ferdinand de Saussure*, Ithaca, NY: Cornell University Press.

—— (1988) *Framing the Sign: Criticism and Its Institutions*, Norman, OK: University of Oklahoma Press.

Cunningham, F. (1987) *Democratic Theory and Socialism*, Cambridge: Cambridge University Press.

Dahl, R. (1956) *A Preface to Democratic Theory*, Chicago, IL: University of Chicago Press.

—— (1961) *Who Governs? Democracy and Power in an American City*, New Haven, CT: Yale University Press.

—— (1982) *Dilemmas of Pluralist Democracy: Autonomy vs. Control*, New Haven, CT: Yale University Press.

—— (1989) *Democracy and Its Critics*, New Haven, CT: Yale University Press.

Dallmayr, F. (1987) "Hegemony and Democracy: A Review of Laclau and Mouffe," *Philosophy and Social Criticism*, 13, 3: 283–96.

—— (1993) "Postmetaphysics and Democracy," *Political Theory*, 21, 1 (February): 101–27.

Daly, G. (1994) "Post-metaphysical Culture and Politics: Richard Rorty and Laclau and Mouffe," *Economy and Society*, 2, 2 (May): 173–200.

Davis, A. (1981) *Women, Race and Class*, New York: Random House.

Davis, M. (1991) *City of Quartz: Excavating the Future in Los Angeles*, New York: Verso.

—— (1992) *Urban Control: The Ecology of Fear*, Westfield, NJ: Open Magazine Pamphlet Series.

Davis, M. and Kennedy, E. (1990) "Oral History and the Study of Sexuality in the Lesbian Community: Buffalo, New York, 1940–60," in M. Duberman, M. Vicinus and G. Chauncey, Jr. (eds) *Hidden From History: Reclaiming the Gay and Lesbian Past*, New York: Penguin.

217

Dean, C. (1992) *The Self and Its Pleasures: Bataille, Lacan and the History of the Decentred Subject*, Ithaca, NY: Cornell University Press.

Debonis, R. (1995) "The Normal Body and the Sex Error: A Foucauldian Analysis," Department of Government, Cornell University, unpublished undergraduate honours thesis.

De Giovanni, B. (1979) "Lenin and Gramsci: State, Politics and Party," in C. Mouffe (ed.) *Gramsci and Marxist Theory*, London: Routledge & Kegan Paul.

De Lauretis, T. (1987) *Technologies of Gender*, Bloomington, IN: Indiana University Press.

D'Emilio, J. (1993) "Capitalism and Gay Identity," in H. Abelove *et al.* (eds) *The Lesbian and Gay Studies Reader*, New York: Routledge.

Derrida, J. (1973) *Speech and Phenomena*, Evanston, IL: Northwestern University Press.

—— (1976) *Of Grammatology*, Baltimore, MD: Johns Hopkins University Press.

—— (1988) *Limited Inc*, Evanston, IL: Northwestern University Press.

—— (1994) *Specters of Marx: The State of the Debt, The Work of Mourning, and the New International*, New York: Routledge.

—— (1996) "Remarks on Deconstruction and Pragmatism," in C. Mouffe (ed.) *Deconstruction and Pragmatism*, London: Routledge.

Devlin, B. *et al.* (eds.) (1997) *Intelligence, Genes and Success: Scientists Respond to The Bell Curve*, New York: Springer.

Dickens, D. (1990) "Deconstruction and Marxist Inquiry," *Sociological Perspectives*, 33, 1: 147–58.

Dillon, S. (1997) "Union Vote in Mexico Illustrates Abuses," *New York Times*, 13 October.

Drakulic, S. (1997) "Misguided Words in the Balkans," *New York Times*, 24 December.

D'Souza, D. (1995) *The End of Racism*, New York: Free Press.

Dworkin, A. (1974) *Women-Hating*, New York: Dutton.

Eagleton, T. (1991) *Ideology: An Introduction*, London: Verso.

Eisenstein, Z. (ed.) (1979) *Capitalist Patriarchy and the Case for Socialist Feminism*, New York: Monthly Review Press.

—— (1981) *The Radical Future of Liberal Feminism*, New York: Longman.

—— (1994) *The Color of Gender*, Berkeley, CA: University of California Press.

—— (1996) *Hatreds*, New York: Routledge.

Elson, D. (1991) "The Economics of a Socialized Market," in R. Blackburn (ed.) *After the Fall: The Failure of Communism and the Future of Socialism*, London: Verso.

Elster, J. (1989) "Self-realization in Work and Politics: the Marxist Conception of the Good Life," in J. Elster and K. Moene (eds) *Alternatives to Capitalism*, Cambridge: Cambridge University Press.

Epstein, B. (1990) "Rethinking Social Movement Theory," *Socialist Review*, 20: 1, 35–65.

Escobar, A. (1992) "Culture, Economics, and Politics in Latin American Social Movements Theory and Research," in A. Escobar and S. Alvarez (eds) *The Making of Social Movements in Latin America: Identity, Strategy and Democracy*, Boulder, CO: Westview Press.

Fanon, F. (1968) *The Wretched of the Earth*, New York: Grove Press.

—— (1986) *Black Skin, White Masks*, London: Pluto.

Fausto-Sterling, A. (1992) *Myths of Gender: Biological Theories About Women and Men*, New York: Basic Books. ·

—— (1993) "The Five Sexes: Why Male and Female Are Not Enough," *The Sciences*, March/April: 20–4.

Feinberg, L. (1993) *Stone Butch Blues*, Ithaca, NY: Firebrand Press.

Femia, J. (1993) *Marxism and Democracy*, Oxford: Clarendon Press.

Feyerabend, P. (1993) *Against Method*, London: Verso.

Fischer, C. *et al.* (eds.) (1996) *Inequality By Design: Cracking the Bell Curve Myth*, Princeton, NJ: Princeton University Press.

Fish, S. (1994) *There's No Such Thing As Free Speech and It's a Good Thing Too*, New York: Oxford University Press.

Flanders, L. (1997) *Real Majorities, Media Minorities: The Costs of Sidelining Women in Reporting*, Monroe: Common Courage Press.

Forgacs, D. (1989) "Gramsci and Marxism in Britain," *New Left Review*, 176: 70–88.

Foucault, M. (1970) *The Order of Things*, London: Tavistock.

—— (1972) *The Archaeology of Knowledge*, New York: Pantheon.

—— (1977) "Nietzsche, Genealogy, History," in D. F. Bouchard (ed.) *Language, Counter-memory, Practice*, New York: Cornell University Press.

—— (1979) *Discipline and Punish: The Birth of the Prison*, New York: Random House.

—— (1980a) "Body/Power," in C. Gordon (ed.) *Power/Knowledge: Selected Interviews and Other Writings, 1972–1977*, New York: Pantheon Books.

—— (1980b) *The History of Sexuality*, vol. I, New York: Vintage.

—— (1980c) "Truth and Power," in C. Gordon (ed.) *Power/Knowledge: Selected Interviews and Other Writings, 1972–1977*, New York: Pantheon Books.

Frank, T. and Mulcahey, D. (1995) "Hunger Striking in the Corn Belt," *The Nation*, 6 November: 540–2.

Fraser, N. (1989) *Unruly Practices: Power, Discourse, and Gender in Contemporary Social Theory*, Minneapolis, MN: University of Minnesota.

Fraser, N. and Gordon, L. (1994) "A Genealogy of *Dependency*: Tracing a Keyword of the U.S. Welfare State," *Signs*, 19, 2: 309–34.

Fraser, N. and Nicholson, L. (1990) "Social Criticism Without Philosophy: An Encounter between Feminism and Postmodernism," in L. Nicholson (ed.) *Feminism/Postmodernism*, New York: Routledge.

Fraser, S. (ed.) (1995) *The Bell Curve Wars: Race, Intelligence and the Future of America*, New York: Basic Books.

Friedman, M. (1993) "Capitalism and Freedom," in P. Green (ed.) *Democracy*, Atlantic Highlands, NJ: Humanities Press.

Fusco, C. (1995) *English Is Broken Here: Notes on Cultural Fusion in the Americas*, New York: The New Press.

Fuss, D. (1989) *Essentially Speaking: Feminism, Nature and Difference*, New York: Routledge.

Gale, M. (1995) "Supreme Reactionaries," *The Nation*, 11 September: 242–5.

Gardner, H. (1994) "Cracking Open the I.Q. Box," *The American Prospect*, winter: 71–80.

Garrow, D. (1995) "On Race, It's Thomas v. an Old Ideal," *New York Times*, 2 July.

Gasché, R. (1986) *The Tain of the Mirror: Derrida and the Philosophy of Reflection*, London: Harvard University Press.

Gates, Jr., H.L. (1985a) "Talkin' That Talk," in H.L. Gates, Jr. (ed.) *"Race," Writing and Difference*, Chicago, IL: University of Chicago Press.

—— (1985b) "Writing 'Race' and the Difference It Makes," in H.L. Gates, Jr. (ed.) *"Race," Writing and Difference*, Chicago, IL: University of Chicago Press.

Gay Left Collective (1975–80) *Gay Left: A Gay Socialist Journal*, London: 1–10.

—— (1980) *Homosexuality: Power and Politics*, London: Allison & Busby.

Geras, N. (1987) "Post-Marxism?," *New Left Review*, 163: 40–82.

—— (1988) "Ex-Marxism Without Substance: Being a Real Reply to Laclau and Mouffe," *New Left Review*, 169: 34–61.

Gilroy, P. (1982) "Steppin' Out of Babylon: Race, Class and Autonomy," in *The Empire Strikes Back: Race and Racism in 70s Britain*, London: Hutchinson, 276–314.

—— (1987) *"There Ain't No Black in the Union Jack": The Cultural Politics of Race and Nation*, London: Hutchinson.

—— (1993) *The Black Atlantic: Modernity and Double Consciousness*, Cambridge, MA: Harvard University Press.

Giroux, H. (1993) "Living Dangerously: Identity Politics and the New Cultural Racism: Towards A Critical Pedagogy of Representation," *Cultural Studies*, 7, 1: 1–27.

Gitlin, T. (1995) *The Twilight of Common Dreams: Why America is Wracked by Culture Wars*, New York: Henry Holt & Co.

Glaberson, W. (1995) "Striking Newspaper Workers Out in Cold in a Union Town," *New York Times*, 11 November.

Gluckman, A. and Reed, B. (1997) "Introduction," in A. Gluckman and B. Reed (eds) *Homoeconomics: Capitalism, Community and Lesbian and Gay Life*, New York: Routledge.

Goldberg, C. (1997) "Hispanic Households Struggle As Poorest of the Poor in U.S.," *New York Times*, 30 January.

Golding, S. (1992) *Gramsci's Democratic Theory: Contributions to a Post-Liberal Democracy*, Toronto, Ont.: University of Toronto Press.

Gooding-Williams, R. (1993) *Reading Rodney King, Reading Urban Uprising*, New York: Routledge.

Goodwin, J. (1990) "The Limits of 'Radical Democracy'," *Socialist Review*, 20, 2: 131–44.

Gould, C. (1981) "Socialism and Democracy," *Praxis International*, 1, 1 (April): 49–63.

Gould, S. (1981) *The Mismeasure of Man*, New York: Norton.

Graham, J. (1988) "Post-modernism and Marxism," *Antipode*, 20, 1: 60–6.

Gramsci, A. (1971) *Selections From the Prison Notebooks*, trans. and eds Q. Hoare and G. Nowell Smith, London: Lawrence & Wishart.

Green, P. (1985) *Retrieving Democracy: In Search of Civic Equality*, Totowa, NJ: Rowman & Allanheld.

—— (ed.) (1993a) *Democracy*, Atlantic Highlands, NJ: Humanities Press.

—— (1993b) " 'Democracy' as a Contested Idea," in P. Green (ed.) *Democracy*, Atlantic Highlands, NJ: Humanities Press.

Guinier, L. (1991) "The Triumph of Tokenism: The Voting Rights Act and the Theory of Black Electoral Success," *Michigan Law Review*, 89: 1077–154.

Gutierrez, R. (1994) "Ethnic Studies: Its Evolution in American Colleges and Universities," in D. Goldberg (ed.) *Multiculturalism: A Critical Reader*, Oxford: Blackwell.

Gutmann, A. (1992) "Introduction," in C. Taylor, *Multiculturalism and "The Politics of Recognition*," Princeton, NJ: Princeton University Press.

Habermas, J. (1970) "Technology and Science as 'Ideology,' " in J. Habermas, *Toward a Rational Society*, trans. J. Shapiro, Boston, MA: Beacon Press.

—— (1975) *Legitimation Crisis*, trans. T. McCarthy, Boston, MA: Beacon Press.

—— (1984) *The Theory of Communicative Action, vol. 1, Reason and the Rationalization of Society*, trans. T. McCarthy, Boston, MA: Beacon Press.

—— (1987) *The Theory of Communicative Action, vol. 2, Lifeworld and System: A Critique of Functionalist Reason*, trans. T. McCarthy, Boston, MA: Beacon Press.

Hall, S. (1980) "Race, Articulation and Societies Structured in Dominance," in UNESCO (ed.) *Sociological Theories: Race and Colonialism*, Paris: UNESCO.

—— (1988a) *The Hard Road to Renewal: Thatcherism and the Crisis of the Left*, London: Verso.

—— (1988b) "New Ethnicities," in K. Mercer (ed.) *Black Film, British Cinema*, London: Institute of Contemporary Arts.

—— (1990) "Cultural Identity and Diaspora," in J. Rutherford (ed.) *Identity: Community, Culture, Difference*, London: Lawrence & Wishart.

—— (1993) "Deviance, Politics, and the Media," in H. Abelove *et al.* (eds) *The Lesbian and Gay Studies Reader*, New York: Routledge.

—— (1997) "Subjects in History: Making Diasporic Identities," in W. Lubiano (ed.) *The House That Race Built*, New York: Pantheon.

Hall, S., Critcher, C., Jefferson, T., Clarke, J. and Roberts, B. (1978) *Policing the Crisis: Mugging, the State and Law and Order*, London: Macmillan.

Hall, S. and Jacques, M. (eds) (1983) *The Politics of Thatcherism*, London: Lawrence & Wishart.

Hall, S., Lumley, B. and McLennan, G. (1977) "Politics and Ideology: Gramsci," *Cultural Studies*, 10: 45–76.

Halley, J. (1989) "The Politics of the Closet," *UCLA Law Review*, 36: 915–76.

—— (1993) "The Construction of Homosexuality," in M. Warner (ed.) *Fear of a Queer Planet: Queer Politics and Social Theory*, Minneapolis, MN: University of Minnesota Press.

Halperin, D. (1990) "Sex Before Sexuality: Pederasty, Politics, and Power in Classical Athens," in M. Duberman, M. Vicinus and G. Chauncey, Jr. (eds) *Hidden From History: Reclaiming the Gay and Lesbian Past*, New York: Penguin.

Hammonds, E. (1994) "Black (W)holes and the Geometry of Black Female Sexuality," *differences*, 6, 2/3: 126–45.

Haraway, D. (1991) *Simians, Cyborgs and Women: The Reinvention of Nature*, New York: Routledge.

Harding, S. (1986) *The Science Question in Feminism*, Ithaca, NY: Cornell University Press.

Harrington, M. (1981) "Marxism and Democracy," *Praxis International*, 1, 1 (April): 6–22.

—— (1993) *Socialism: Past and Future*, London: Pluto Press.

Harris, L. (1983) "Forces and Relations of Production," in T. Bottomore (ed.) *A Dictionary of Marxist Thought*, Cambridge, MA: Harvard University Press, 178–80.

Hartsock, N. (1983) "The Feminist Standpoint: Developing the Ground for a Specifically Feminist Historical Materialism," in S. Harding and M.B. Hintikka (ed.) *Discovering Reality: Feminist Perspectives on Epistemology, Metaphysics, Methodology, and Philosophy of Science*, Dordrecht: D. Reidel Publishing Company, 283–310.

—— (1985) *Money, Sex and Power: Toward a Feminist Historical Materialism*, Boston, MA: Northeastern University Press.

—— (1990) "Foucault on Power: A Theory for Women?" in L. Nicholson (ed.) *Feminism/Postmodernism*, New York: Routledge.

Hegel, G. (1953) *Reason in History: A General Introduction to the Philosophy of History*, New York: Liberal Arts Press.

Herbert, B. (1994) "Throwing a Curve," *New York Times*, 26 October.

—— (1995) "The Issue is Jobs," *New York Times*, 6 May.

Hero, R. (1992) *Latinos and the U.S. Political System: Two-tiered Pluralism*, Philadelphia, PA: Temple University Press.

Herrnstein, R. and Murray, C. (1994) *The Bell Curve: Intelligence and Class Structure in American Life*, New York: The Free Press.

Higginbotham, E.B. (1992) "African-American Women's History and the Metalanguage of Race," *Signs*, 17, 2: 251–74.

Hiro, D. (1971) *Black British, White British*, London: Eyre & Spottiswoode.

Hirsch, E. (1994) "Good Genes, Bad Schools," *New York Times*, 29 October.

Hirschmann, N. (1992) *Rethinking Obligation: A Feminist Method for Political Theory*, Ithaca, NY: Cornell University Press.

Hirst, P. (1989) *After Thatcher*, London: Collins.

Hobsbawm, E. (1991) "Goodbye to All That," in R. Blackburn (ed.) *After the Fall: The Failure of Communism and the Future of Socialism*, London: Verso.

—— (1996) "Identity Politics and the Left," *New Left Review*, May/June, 217: 38–47.

Holmes, S. (1994) "You're Smart If You Know What Race You Are," *New York Times*, 23 October.

—— (1995a) "Income Gap Persists for Blacks and Whites," *New York Times*, 23 February.

—— (1995b) "Low-wage Fathers and the Welfare Debate," *New York Times*, 25 April.

Holt, J. (1994) "Anti-Social Science?" *New York Times*, 19 October.

Honneth, A. (1994) "The Social Dynamics of Disrespect: On the Location of Critical Theory Today," *Constellations*, 1, 2: 255–69.

Hooks, B. (1984) *Feminist Theory: From Margin to Center*, Boston, MA: South End Press.

Howell, S. and Warren, S. (1992) "Public Opinion and David Duke," in D. Rose (ed.) *The Emergence of David Duke and the Politics of Race*, Chapel Hill: University of North Carolina Press.

Hull, G.T., Scott, P.B. and Smith, B. (eds) (1982) *All the Women Are White, All the Blacks Are Men, But Some of Us Are Brave*, Old Westbury, NY: The Feminist Press.

Hunt, A. (1980) "Introduction: Taking Democracy Seriously," in A. Hunt (ed.) *Marxism and Democracy*, London: Lawrence & Wishart.

Hunter, A. (1988) "Post-Marxism and the New Social Movements," *Theory and Society*, 17: 885–900.

Hunter, N. (1995) "Marriage, Law and Gender: A Feminist Inquiry," in L. Duggan and N. Hunter, *Sex Wars: Sexual Dissent and Political Culture*, New York: Routledge.

Hurston, Z. (1978) *Mules and Men*, Bloomington, IN: Indiana University Press.

Jenkins, R. (1992) *Pierre Bourdieu*, London, Routledge.

Jessop, B. *et al.* (1988) *Thatcherism*, Cambridge: Polity Press.

Johnson, B. (1987) *A World of Difference*, Baltimore, MD: The Johns Hopkins Press.

Johnson, G. (1994) "Learning Just How Little is Known About the Brain," *New York Times*, 23 October.

Justice For All (1996) "Straight Talk About the Real Issues" pamphlet, Ithaca, NY: Justice For All.

Keane, J. (1984) *Public Life and Late Capitalism: Toward a Socialist Theory of Democracy*, Cambridge: Cambridge University Press.

Kinchloe, J. *et al.* (eds) (1996) *Measured Lies: The Bell Curve Examined*, New York: St Martin's Press.

King, M.L., Jr. (1968) *Where Do We Go From Here? Chaos or Community*, Boston, MA: Beacon Press.

—— (1991) "Letter from Birmingham City Jail," in C. Carson *et al.* (eds) *The Eyes on the Prize Civil Rights Reader*, New York: Penguin Books.

Kitching, G. (1994) *Marxism and Science: Analysis of an Obsession*, University Park, PA: The Pennsylvania State University Press.

Kolakowski, L. (1978) *Main Currents of Marxism: Its Origins, Growth and Dissolution*, vol. 2, *The Golden Age*, Oxford: Oxford University Press.

Kuhn, T. (1962) *The Structure of Scientific Revolutions*, Chicago, IL: University of Chicago Press.

Kymlicka, W. (1990) *Contemporary Political Philosophy: An Introduction*, Oxford: Clarendon Press.

—— (1995) *Multicultural Citizenship: A Liberal Theory of Minority Rights*, Oxford: Oxford University Press.

Lacan, J. (1977) "The Mirror Stage as Formative of the Function of the I as Revealed in Psychoanalytic Experience," in *Écrits*, London: Tavistock.

LaCapra, D. (1994) *History, Theory, Trauma: Representing the Holocaust*, Ithaca, NY: Cornell University Press.

Laclau, E. (1977) *Politics and Ideology in Marxist Theory: Capitalism, Fascism, Populism*, London: Verso.

—— (1985) "New Social Movements and the Plurality of the Social," in D. Slater (ed.) *The New Social Movements in Latin America*, Amsterdam: Centre for Latin American Research and Documentation.

—— (1987) "Class War and After," *Marxism Today*, April: 30–3.

—— (1988) "Politics and the Limits of Modernity," in A. Ross (ed.) *Universal Abandon? The Politics of Postmodernism*, Minneapolis, MN: University of Minnesota Press.

—— (1990a) *New Reflections of the Revolution of Our Time*, London: Verso.

—— (1990b) "Totalitarianism and Moral Indignation," *Diacritics*, 20, 3 (spring): 88–95.

—— (1994) "Introduction," in E. Laclau (ed.) *The Making of Political Identities*, London: Verso.

—— (1996a) "Beyond Emancipation," in E. Laclau, *Emancipation(s)*, London: Verso.

—— (1996b) "Community and Its Paradoxes," in E. Laclau, *Emancipation(s)*, London: Verso.

—— (1996c) "Deconstruction, Pragmatism, Hegemony," in C. Mouffe (ed.) *Deconstruction and Pragmatism*, London: Routledge.

—— (1996d) "Power and Representation," in E. Laclau, *Emancipation(s)*, London: Verso.

—— (1996e) "Subject of Politics, Politics of the Subject," in E. Laclau, *Emancipation(s)*, London: Verso.

—— (1996f) " 'The Time is Out of Joint'," in E. Laclau, *Emancipation(s)*, London: Verso.

—— (1996g) "Universalism, Particularism and the Question of Identity," in E. Laclau, *Emancipation(s)*, London: Verso.

—— (1996h) "Why do Empty Signifiers Matter to Politics?" in E. Laclau, *Emancipation(s)*, London: Verso.

—— (1996i) "The Death and Resurrection of the Theory of Ideology," unpublished paper.

—— (1996j) "On the Names of God," unpublished paper.

—— (1997) "Converging on an Open Quest," *Diacritics*, 27, 1 (spring): 17–19.

Laclau, E. and Mouffe, C. (1985) *Hegemony and Socialist Strategy: Towards a Radical Democratic Politics*, London: Verso.

—— (1990) "Post-Marxism without Apologies," in E. Laclau, *New Reflections of the Revolution of Our Time*, London: Verso.

Laclau, E. and Zac, L. (1994) "Minding the Gap: The Subject of Politics," in E. Laclau (ed.) *The Making of Political Identities*, London: Verso.

Lane, C. (1994) "The Tainted Sources of *The Bell Curve*," *New York Review of Books*, 1 December.

Laplanche, J. and Pontalis, J.-B. (1973) *The Language of Psycho-analysis*, New York: W.W. Norton & Co.

Larrain, J. (1981) "On the Character of Ideology: Marx and the Present Debate in Britain," *Theory, Culture and Society*, 1:2, 5–22.

Lefort, C. (1986) *The Political Forms of Modern Society: Bureaucracy, Democracy, Totalitarianism*, J. Thompson (ed.), Cambridge, MA: Polity Press.

Lenin, V. (1989) *What is to be Done?* London: Penguin Books.

LeVay, S. (1993) *The Sexual Brain*, Cambridge, MA: The MIT Press.

Levine, L. (1996) *The Opening of the American Mind: Canon, Culture and History*, Boston, MA: Beacon Press.

Lewin, T. (1994) "Births to Young Teen-Agers Decline, Agency Says," *New York Times*, 26 October.

Lilla, M. (1997) "The Enemy of Liberalism," *New York Review of Books*, 15 May, 38–44.

Locke, J. (1963) *Two Treatises of Government*, P. Laslett (ed.), Cambridge: Cambridge University Press.

Löwy, M. (1981) "Rosa Luxemburg et la Democratie Socialiste," *Praxis International*, 1, 1 (April): 72–8.

Lubiano, W. (1997) "Black Nationalism and Black Common Sense: Policing Ourselves," in W. Lubiano (ed.) *The House That Race Built*, New York: Pantheon.

Lukes, S. (1974) *Power: A Radical View*, London: Macmillan.

Lyotard, J. (1984) *The Postmodern Condition: A Report on Knowledge*, Minneapolis: University of Minnesota Press.

Macdonald, B. (1988) "Towards a Redemption of Politics: An Introduction to the Political Theory of Ernesto Laclau," *Strategies* (Fall), 5–9.

MacIntyre, A. (1981) *After Virtue*, Notre Dame, IN: University of Notre Dame Press.

—— (1983) "Moral Arguments and Social Contexts," *The Journal of Philosophy*, 70, 12 (1983): 590–1.

MacKinnon, C. A. (1989) *Toward a Feminist Theory of the State*, Cambridge, MA: Harvard University Press.

Macpherson, C.B. (1962) *The Political Theory of Possessive Individualism: Hobbes to Locke*, Oxford: Oxford University Press.

—— (1965) *The Real World of Democracy*, Toronto, Ont.: CBC.

—— (1973) *Democratic Theory: Essays in Retrieval*, Oxford: Clarendon Press.

—— (1977) *The Life and Times of Liberal Democracy*, Oxford: Oxford University Press.

Malcolm X (1965) *The Autobiography of Malcolm X*, New York: Ballantine Books.

Malik, M.A. (1968) *From Michael de Freitas to Michael X*, London: André Deutsch.

Marable, M. (1983) *How Capitalism Underdeveloped Black America: Problems in Race, Political Economy and Society*, Boston, MA: South End Press.

—— (1991) *Race, Reform and Rebellion: The Second Reconstruction in Black America, 1945–1990*, Jackson, MS: University Press of Mississippi.

Marcil-Lacoste, L. (1992) "The Paradoxes of Pluralism," in C. Mouffe (ed.) *Dimensions of Radical Democracy: Pluralism, Citizenship, Community*, London: Verso.

Marshall, T. (1964) *Class, Citizenship and Social Development: Essays by T.H. Marshall*, Garden City, NY: Doubleday & Co.

Martin, B. (1988) "Feminism, Criticism and Foucault," in I. Diamond and L. Quinby (eds) *Feminism and Foucault: Reflections on Resistance*, Boston, MA: Northeastern University Press.

—— (1993) "Lesbian Identity and Autobiographical Difference[s]," in H. Abelove *et al.* (eds) *The Lesbian and Gay Studies Reader*, New York: Routledge.

Marx, K. (1952) *Theories of Surplus Value: Selections*, New York: International Publishers.

—— (1969a) "Preface to A Contribution to the Critique of Political Economy," *Selected Works*, vol. I, Moscow: Progress Publishers, 502–6.

—— (1969b) "Theses on Feuerbach," *Selected Works*, vol. I, Moscow: Progress Publishers, 13–15.

—— (1975a) "Economic and Philosophical Manuscripts," *Early Writings*, trans. R. Livingston and G. Benton, New York: Vintage Books.

—— (1975b) "On the Jewish Question," *Early Writings*, trans. R. Livingston and G. Benton, New York: Vintage Books.

—— (1977) *Capital: A Critique of Political Economy*, vol. I, New York: Vintage Books.

—— (1978) "The Eighteenth Brumaire of Louis Bonaparte," in R. Tucker (ed.) *The Marx–Engels Reader*, New York: W.W. Norton & Co.

—— (1981) *Capital: A Critique of Political Economy*, vol. III, New York: Vintage Books.

Marx, K. and Engels, F. (1969) "Manifesto of the Communist Party," *Selected Works*, vol. I, Moscow: Progress Publishers, 98–136.

—— (1976) *The German Ideology*, Moscow: Progress Publishers.

Massey, D. (1992) "Politics and Space/Time," *New Left Review*, 196: 65–84.

Massey, D., Segal, L. and Wainwright, H. (1984) "And Now for the Good News," in J. Curran (ed.) *The Future of the Left*, Cambridge: Polity Press & New Socialist.

Matsuda, M., Lawrence, C., Delgado, R. and Crenshaw, K. (1993) *Words That Wound: Critical Race Theory, Assaultive Speech and the First Amendment*, Boulder, CO: Westview Press.

McClintock, A. (1995) *Imperial Leather: Race, Gender and Sexuality in the Colonial Contest*, New York: Routledge.

McClure, K. (1990) "Difference, Diversity and the Limits of Toleration," *Political Theory*, 18:3 (August): 361–91.

—— (1992) "On the Subject of Rights: Pluralism, Plurality and Political Identity," in C. Mouffe (ed.) *Dimensions of Radical Democracy: Pluralism, Citizenship, Community*, London: Verso.

Mepham, J. (1979) "The Theory of Ideology in Capital," in J. Mepham and D. Ruben (eds) *Issues in Marxist Philosophy*, Atlantic Highlands, NJ: Humanities Press.

Mercer, C. (1980) "Revolutions, Reforms or Reformulations? Marxist Discourse on Democracy," in A. Hunt (ed.) *Marxism and Democracy*, London: Lawrence & Wishart.

Midgett, D. (1975) "West Indian Ethnicity in Great Britain," in H. Safa and B. du Toit (eds) *Migration and Development*, The Hague: Mouton.

Miles, R. (1984) "Marxism Versus the Sociology of 'Race Relations'," *Ethnic and Racial Studies* 7, 2: 217–37.

Miliband, R. (1991) "Reflections on the Crisis of Communist Regimes," in R. Blackburn (ed.) *After the Fall: The Failure of Communism and the Future of Socialism*, London: Verso.

—— (1994) "The Plausibility of Socialism," *New Left Review*, 206 (July/August): 3–14.

Mill, J.S. (1972) "On Liberty," in *Utilitarianism, Liberty, Representative Government*, New York: Dutton.

Minh-ha, T. (1997) "Not You/Like You: Postcolonial Women and the Interlocking Questions of Identity and Difference," in A. McClintock, A. Mufti and E. Shohat (eds) *Dangerous Liaisons: Gender, Nation and Postcolonial Perspectives*, Minneapolis, MN: University of Minnesota Press.

Mitchell, J. (1982) "Introduction – I," in J. Mitchell and J. Rose (eds) *Feminine Sexuality: Jacques Lacan and the école freudienne*, New York: Pantheon Books.

Mitchell, J. and Rose, J. (1983) "Feminine Sexuality: Interview – 1982," *m/f*, 8: 3–16.

Mohanty, C.T. (1991) "Introduction: Cartographies of Struggle," in C. Talpade Mohanty, A. Russo and L. Torres (eds) *Third World Women and the Politics of Feminism*, Bloomington, IN: Indiana University Press.

—— (1997) "Women Workers and Capitalist Scripts: Ideologies of Domination, Common Interests, and the Politics of Solidarity," in J. Alexander and C. Talpade Mohanty (eds) *Feminist Genealogies, Colonial Legacies, Democratic Futures*, New York: Routledge.

Moraga, C. and Anzaldúa, G. (eds) (1983) *This Bridge Called My Back: Writings by Radical Women of Color*, New York: Kitchen Table Press.

Morera, E. (1990) "Gramsci and Democracy," *Canadian Journal of Political Science*, 23, 1 (March): 23–37.

Morrison, T. (ed.) (1992) *Race-ing Justice, En-gendering Power: Essays on Anita Hill, Clarence Thomas and the Construction of Social Reality*, New York: Pantheon.

Mostov, J. (1989) "Karl Marx as Democratic Theorist," *Polity*, 22, 2 (winter): 195–212.

Mouffe, C. (1979a) "Introduction: Gramsci Today," in C. Mouffe (ed.) *Gramsci and Marxist Theory*, London: Routledge & Kegan Paul.

—— (1979b) "Hegemony and Ideology in Gramsci," in C. Mouffe (ed.) *Gramsci and Marxist Theory*, London: Routledge & Kegan Paul.

—— (1981) "Hegemony and the Integral State in Gramsci: Towards a New Concept of Politics," in G. Bridges and R. Brunt (eds) *Silver Linings*, London: Lawrence & Wishart.

—— (1983) "Working-Class Hegemony and the Struggle for Socialism," *Studies in Political Economy*, 12, fall: 7–26.

—— (1987a) "Le libéralisme américain et ses critiques: Rawls, Taylor, Sandel et Walzer," *Esprit*, 3: 100–14.

—— (1987b) "Rawls: Political Philosophy Without Politics," *Philosophy and Social Criticism*, 13, 2: 105–23.

—— (1990) "The Legacy of *m/f*," in P. Adams and E. Cowie (eds) *The Woman in Question: M/f*, Boston, MA: MIT Press.

—— (1992a) "Preface: Democratic Politics Today," in C. Mouffe (ed.) *Dimensions of Radical Democracy: Pluralism, Citizenship, Community*, London: Verso.

—— (1992b) "Democratic Citizenship and the Political Community," in C. Mouffe (ed.) *Dimensions of Radical Democracy: Pluralism, Citizenship, Community*, London: Verso.

—— (1993a) "Carl Schmitt, une politique du droit," *Esprit*, 12: 182–9.

—— (1993b) *The Return of the Political*, London: Verso.

—— (1993c) "Toward a Liberal Socialism?" *Dissent*, 40, 1: 81–7.

—— (1994) "For a Politics of Nomadic Identity," in G. Robertson *et al.* (eds.) *Travellers' Tales: Narratives of Home and Displacement*, London: Routledge.

—— (1995) "The End of Politics and the Rise of the Radical Right," *Dissent*, Fall.

—— (1996a) "Deconstruction, Pragmatism and the Politics of Democracy," in C. Mouffe (ed.) *Deconstruction and Pragmatism*, London: Routledge.

—— (1996b) "Democracy, Power and the 'Political,'" in S. Benhabib (ed.) *Democracy and Difference: Contesting the Boundaries of the Political*, Princeton, NJ: Princeton University Press.

—— (1996c) "Radical Democracy or Liberal Democracy?," in D. Trend (ed.) *Radical Democracy: Identity, Citizenship and the State*, New York: Routledge.

Mouzelis, N. (1988) "Marxism or Post-Marxism?" *New Left Review*, 167: 107–23.

Muller, J. and Richardson, W. (1982) *Lacan and Language*, New York: International Universities Press Inc.

The Nation (1996) "Grapes of Wrath," editorial, *The Nation*, 26 August/2 September.

Nancy, J. (1991) *The Inoperative Community*, Minneapolis, MN: University of Minnesota Press.

New York Times (1995) "The Rich Get Richer Faster," editorial, *New York Times*, 18 April.

Newton, E. (1993) "Just One of the Boys: Lesbians in Cherry Grove, 1960–88," in H. Abelove *et al.* (eds) *The Lesbian and Gay Studies Reader*, New York: Routledge.

Nicholson, L. (1994) "Interpreting Gender," *Signs*, 20:1 (Autumn): 79–105.

Nietzsche, F. (1969) *On the Genealogy of Morals*, New York: Vintage Books.

Nkomo, M., Mkwanazi-Twala, Z. and Carrim, N. (1995) "The Long Shadow of Apartheid Ideology: The Case of Open Schools in South Africa," in B. Bowser (ed.) *Racism and Anti-Racism in World Perspective*, Thousand Oaks, CA: Sage.

Norval, A. (1996) *Deconstructing Apartheid Discourse*, London, Verso.

Nove, A. (1983) *The Economics of Feasible Socialism*, London: George Allen & Unwin.

O'Connor, S., Scalia, A. and Thomas, C. (1995) "Adarand Constructors v. Pena," decision and concurring opinions, US Supreme Court, *New York Times*, 13 June.

Oliver, M. and Shapiro, T. (1997) *Black Wealth/White Wealth: A New Perspective on Racial Inequality*, New York: Routledge.

Omi, M. and Winant, H. (1994) *Racial Formation in the United States*, New York: Routledge.

Osborne, P. (1991) "Radicalism Without Limit? Discourse, Democracy and the Politics of Identity," in P. Osborne (ed.) *Socialism and the Limits of Liberalism*, London: Verso.

Paggi, L. (1979) "Gramsci's General Theory of Marxism," in C. Mouffe (ed.) *Gramsci and Marxist Theory*, London: Routledge & Kegan Paul.

Parenti, M. (1993) *Inventing Reality: The Politics of the News Media*, New York: St. Martin's Press.

—— (1995) *Democracy for the Few*, New York: St. Martin's Press.

Parmar, P. (1990) "Black Feminism: The Politics of Articulation," in J. Rutherford (ed.) *Identity: Community, Culture, Difference*, London: Lawrence & Wishart.

Passell, P. (1994) "Bell Curve Critics Say Early I.Q. Isn't Destiny," *New York Times*, 9 November.

Payne, C. (1989) "Ella Baker and Models of Social Change," *Signs*, 14, 4: 885–99.

Pertschuk, M. (1995) "How to Out-Talk the Right," *The Nation*, 26 June.

Pfaff, W. (1997) "Eugenics, Anyone?" *New York Review of Books*, 23 October.

Phelan, S. (1990) "Foucault and Feminism," *American Journal of Political Science*, 34, 2: 421–40.

Phillips, A. (1993) *Democracy and Difference*, University Park, PA: The Pennsylvania State University Press.

Plotke, D. (1990) "What's So New About New Social Movements?" *Socialist Review*, 20, 1: 81–102.

Pollard, P. (1972) "Jamaicans and Trinidadians in North London," *New Community*, 1, 5: 370–7

Pratt, M. B. (1984) "Identity: Skin Blood Heart," in E. Bulkin, M.B. Pratt and B. Smith, *Yours In Struggle: Three Feminist Perspectives on Anti-Semitism and Racism*, Ithaca, NY: Firebrand Books.

Przeworski, A. (1985) *Capitalism and Social Democracy*, Cambridge: Cambridge University Press.

Purvis, T. and Hunt, A. (1993) "Discourse, Ideology, Discourse, Ideology, Discourse, Ideology . . . ," *British Journal of Sociology*, 40:3, 473–99.

Quadagno, J. (1994) *The Color of Welfare: How Racism Undermined the War on Poverty*, New York: Oxford University Press.

Quine, W. (1960) *Word and Object*, Cambridge, MA: MIT Press.

Rawls, J. (1971) *A Theory of Justice*, Cambridge, MA: Harvard University Press.

Readings, B. (1996) *The University in Ruins*, Cambridge, MA: Harvard University Press.

Red Rag Collective (1973) *Red Rag: A Magazine of Women's Liberation*, London.

Reed, A. (1990) "The Underclass as Myth and Symbol," *Radical America*, 24, 1: 21–40.

Rich, A. (1993) "Compulsory Heterosexuality and Lesbian Existence," in H. Abelove *et al.* (eds) *The Lesbian and Gay Studies Reader*, New York: Routledge.

Riley, D. (1988) *Am I That Name? Feminism and the Category of "Women" in History*, New York: Macmillan.

Ritzer, G. and Schubert, D. (1991) "The Changing Nature of Neo-Marxist Theory: A Metatheoretical Analysis," *Sociological Perspectives*, 34, 3: 359–75.

Rorty, R. (1996a) "Remarks on Deconstruction and Pragmatism," in C. Mouffe (ed.) *Deconstruction and Pragmatism*, London: Routledge.

—— (1996b) "Response to Simon Critchley," in C. Mouffe (ed.) *Deconstruction and Pragmatism*, London: Routledge.

—— (1996c) "Response to Ernesto Laclau," in C. Mouffe (ed.) *Deconstruction and Pragmatism*, London: Routledge.

Rosaldo, M. (ed.) (1974) *Women, Culture and Society*, Stanford, CA: Stanford University Press.

Rose, J. (1982) "Introduction – II," in J. Mitchell and J. Rose (eds) *Feminine Sexuality: Jacques Lacan and the école freudienne*, New York: Pantheon Books.

—— (1997) "Virginia Woolf and the Death of Modernism," unpublished talk, Cornell University, 7 July.

Ross, A. (1986) review of E. Laclau and C. Mouffe, *Hegemony and Socialist Strategy: Towards a Radical Democratic Politics*, *m/f*, 11–12, 99–106.

Rousseau, J.-J. (1973) *The Social Contract and Discourses*, trans. G.D.H. Cole, New York: Dutton.

Rowbotham, S. (1981) "The Women's Movement and Organizing for Socialism," in S. Rowbotham, L. Segal and H. Wainwright, *Beyond the Fragments: Feminism and the Making of Socialism*, Boston, MA: Alyson Publications.

Rowbotham, S., Segal, L. and Wainwright, H. (1981) *Beyond the Fragments: Feminism and the Making of Socialism*, Boston, MA: Alyson Publications.

Rubin, G. (1975) "The Traffic in Women: Notes on the 'Political Economy' of Sex," in R. Reiter (ed.) *Toward an Anthropology of Women*, New York: Monthly Review Press.

—— (1984) "Thinking Sex," in C. Vance (ed.) *Pleasure and Danger: Exploring Female Sexuality*, New York: Routledge & Kegan Paul.

Rumble, P. (1984) review of A.S. Sassoon (ed.) *Approaches to Gramsci*, and E. Laclau and C. Mouffe, *Hegemony and Socialist Strategy: Towards a Radical Democratic Politics*, *Italian Quarterly*, 25: 97–8, 210–13.

Rustin, M. (1988) "Absolute Voluntarism: Critique of a Post-Marxist Concept of Hegemony," *New German Critique*, 43: 146–73.

Ryan, A. (1994) "Apocalypse Now?" *New York Review of Books*, 17 November.

Said, E. (1978) *Orientalism*, London: Penguin Books.

Salecl, R. (1994) *The Spoils of Freedom: Psychoanalysis and Feminism After the Fall of Socialism*, London: Routledge.

Sandel, M. (1982) *Liberalism and the Limits of Justice*, Cambridge: Cambridge University Press.

– (1996) *Democracy's Discontent: America in Search of a Public Philosophy*, Cambridge, MA: Harvard University Press.

Sandel, M. (ed.) (1984) *Liberalism and Its Critics*, New York: New York University Press.

Sandoval, C. (1990) "Feminism and Racism: A Report on the 1981 National Women's Studies Association Conference," in G. Anzaldúa (ed.) *Making Face, Making Soul = Haciendo Caras: Creative and Critical Perspectives By Women of Color*, San Francisco, CA: Aunt Lute Foundation Books.

Sargent, L. (ed.) (1981) *Women and Revolution: A Discussion of the Unhappy Marriage of Marxism and Feminism*, London: Pluto Press.

Sassoon, A.S. (1980) "Gramsci: A New Concept of Politics and the Expansion of Democracy," in A. Hunt (ed.) *Marxism and Democracy*, London: Lawrence & Wishart.

Saussure, F. de (1966) *Course in General Linguistics*, trans. W. Baskin, New York: McGraw-Hill.

Schmitt, C. (1976) *The Concept of the Political*, New Brunswick: Rutgers University Press.

Schulman, S. (1994) *My American History: Lesbian and Gay Life During the Reagan/Bush Years*, New York: Routledge.

Schwab, G. (1976) "Introduction," in C. Schmitt, *The Concept of the Political*, New Brunswick: Rutgers University Press.

Schwartz, J. (1995) *The Permanence of the Political: A Democratic Critique of the Radical Impulse to Transcend Politics*, Princeton, NJ: Princeton University Press.

Scott, J.C. (1990) *Domination of the Arts of Resistance*, New Haven, CT: Yale University Press.

Scott, J.W. (1988) *Gender and the Politics of History*, New York: Columbia University Press.

—— (1993) "The Evidence of Experience," in H. Abelove *et al.* (eds) *The Lesbian and Gay Studies Reader*, New York: Routledge.

Sedgwick, E. (1990) *Epistemology of the Closet*, Berkeley, CA: University of California Press.

Segal, L. (1989) "Still Seeking a Union," *Interlink* (February/March), 26–7.

—— (1991) "Whose Left? Socialism, Feminism and the Future," in R. Blackburn (ed.) *After the Fall: The Failure of Communism and the Future of Socialism*, London: Verso.

Shohat, E. and Stam, R. (1994) *Unthinking Eurocentrism: Multiculturalism and the Media*, New York: Routledge.

Sivanandan, A. (1982) *A Different Hunger: Writings on Black Resistance*, London: Pluto.

Skinner, Q. (1992) "On Justice, the Common Good and the Priority of Liberty," in C. Mouffe (ed.) *Dimensions of Radical Democracy: Pluralism, Citizenship, Community*, London: Verso.

Smith, A.M. (1993) " 'What is Pornography?' The Rhetoric of a Campaign," *Feminist Review*, 43: 71–87.

—— (1994a) "The Imaginary Inclusion of the 'Good Homosexual': The British New Right's Representation of Sexuality and Race," *Diacritics*, 24, 2–3: 58–70.

—— (1994b) *New Right Discourse on Race and Sexuality: Britain, 1968–1990*, Cambridge: Cambridge University Press.

—— (1995a) " 'By Women, For Women and About Women' Rules O.K.?: The Impossibility of Visual Soliloquy," in P. Burston and C. Richardson (eds) *A Queer Romance*, London: Routledge.

—— (1995b) "The Regulation of Lesbian Sexuality Through Erasure: The Case of Jennifer Saunders," in K. Jay (ed.) *Lesbian Erotics*, New York: New York University Press.

—— (1997a) "Feminist Activism and Presidential Politics: Theorizing the Costs of the 'Insider Strategy,' " *Radical Philosophy*, 83 (May/June).

—— (1997b) "Why Did Armey Apologize? Hegemony, Homophobia and the Religious Right," in A. Ansell (ed.) *Unraveling the Right: The New Conservatism in American Thought and Politics*, New York: Westview Press.

Smith, J., DeMoss, H. and Wiener, J. (1996) "Hopwood v. Texas," decision, US Court of Appeals for the Fifth Circuit, *Chronicle of Higher Education*, 29 March.

Smith, M. (1990) "Pluralism, Reformed Pluralism and Neopluralism: the Role of Pressure Groups in Policy-Making," *Political Studies*, 38, 2: 302–22.

Smith-Rosenberg, C. (1990) "Discourses of Sexuality and Subjectivity: The New Woman, 1870–1936," in M. Duberman, M. Vicinus and G. Chauncey, Jr. (eds) *Hidden From History: Reclaiming the Gay and Lesbian Past*, New York: Penguin.

Spillers, H. (1987) "Mama's Baby, Papa's Maybe: An American Grammar Book," *Diacritics*, summer: 65–81.

Spivak, G. (1988a) "Can the Subaltern Speak?" in L. Grossberg and C. Nelson (eds) *Marxist Interpretations of Literature and Culture: Limits, Frontiers, Boundaries*, Urbana, IL: University of Illinois Press.

—— (1988b) "French Feminism in an International Frame," in G. Spivak, *In Other Worlds: Essays in Cultural Politics*, New York: Routledge.

—— (1997) "Teaching for the Times," in A. McClintock, A. Mufti and E. Shohat (eds.) *Dangerous Liaisons: Gender, Nation and Postcolonial Perspectives*, Minneapolis, MN: University of Minnesota Press.

Spivak, G. and Grosz, E. (1990) "Criticism, Feminism and the Institution," in G. Spivak and S. Harasym (eds) *The Post-Colonial Critic: Interviews, Strategies, Dialogues*, New York: Routledge.

Spivak, G., Threadgold, T. and Bartkowski, F. (1990) "The *Intervention* Interview," in G. Spivak and S. Harasym (eds) *The Post-Colonial Critic: Interviews, Strategies, Dialogues*, New York: Routledge.

Staten, H. (1984) *Wittgenstein and Derrida*, Oxford: Basil Blackwell.

Steinmetz, G. (1994) "Regulation Theory, Post-Marxism and the New Social Movements," *Comparative Studies in Society and History*, 36, 1: 176–212.

Stoler, A. (1995) *Race and the Education of Desire: Foucault's History of Sexuality and the Colonial Order of Things*, Durham: Duke University.

Sypnowich, C. (1990) *The Concept of Socialist Law*, Oxford: Clarendon Press.

—— (1993) "Justice, Community and the Antinomies of Feminist Theory," *Political Theory*, 21:3 (August): 484–506.

Takaki, R. (1993) *A Different Mirror: A History of Multicultural America*, Boston, MA: Little, Brown & Co.

Taylor, C. (1975) *Hegel* Cambridge: Cambridge University Press.

—— (1992) *Multiculturalism and "The Politics of Recognition,"* Princeton, NJ: Princeton University Press.

Texier, J. (1979) "Gramsci, Theoretician of the Superstructures," in C. Mouffe (ed.) *Gramsci and Marxist Theory*, London: Routledge & Kegan Paul.

Thomas, C. (1988) "Civil Rights as a Principle Versus Civil Rights as an Interest," in D. Boaz (ed.) *Assessing the Reagan Years*, Washington, DC: Cato Institute.

Thomas, K. (1997) " 'Ain't Nothing Like the Real Thing': Black Masculinity, Gay Sexuality, and the Jargon of Authenticity," in W. Lubiano (ed.) *The House That Race Built*, New York: Pantheon.

Vicinus, M. (1993) " 'They Wonder to Which Sex I Belong': The Historical Roots of Modern Lesbian Identity," in H. Abelove, M. A. Barale and D. Halperin (eds) *The Lesbian and Gay Studies Reader*, New York: Routledge.

Walzer, M. (1983) *Spheres of Justice: A Defence of Pluralism and Equality*, Oxford: Oxford University Press.

—— (1990) "The Communitarian Critique of Liberalism," *Political Theory*, 18, 1: 6–23.

—— (1992) "The Civil Society Argument," in C. Mouffe (ed.) *Dimensions of Radical Democracy: Pluralism, Citizenship, Community*, London: Verso.

—— (1993) "A Credo for This Moment," in P. Green (ed.) *Democracy*, Atlantic Highlands, NJ: Humanities Press.

—— (1997) *On Toleration*, New Haven, CT: Yale University Press.

Watkins, F. and Kramnick, I. (1979) *The Age of Ideology: Political Thought, 1750 to the Present*, Englewood Cliffs, NJ: Prentice-Hall.

Weeks, J. (1977) *Coming Out: Homosexual Politics in Britain from the Nineteenth Century to the Present*, London: Quartet.

—— (1981) *Sex, Politics and Society: The Regulation of Sexuality Since 1800*, New York: Longman.

—— (1985) *Sexuality and Its Discontents: Meanings, Myths and Modern Sexualities*, London: Routledge & Kegan Paul.

—— (1990) "Inverts, Perverts and Mary-Annes: Male Prostitution and the Regulation of Homosexuality in the Nineteenth and Early Twentieth Centuries," in M. Duberman, M. Vicinus and G. Chauncey, Jr. (eds) *Hidden From History: Reclaiming the Gay and Lesbian Past*, New York: Penguin.

—— (1995) *Invented Moralities: Sexual Values in an Age of Uncertainty*, New York: Columbia University Press

Weir, A. and Wilson, E. (1984) "The British Women's Movement," *New Left Review*, Nov./Dec., no. 148, 74–103.

Williams, P. (1991) *The Alchemy of Race and Rights*, Cambridge, MA: Harvard University Press.

—— (1995) *The Rooster's Egg*, Cambridge, MA: Harvard University Press.

Williams, R. (1993) "Democracy," in P. Green (ed.) *Democracy*, Atlantic Highlands, NJ: Humanities Press.

Williams, R. M. (1993) "Accumulation as Evisceration: Urban Rebellion and the New Growth Dynamics," in R. Gooding-Williams (ed.) *Reading Rodney King, Reading Urban Uprising*, New York: Routledge.

Wilson, W. (1978) *The Declining Significance of Race*, Chicago, IL: University of Chicago Press.

Wittgenstein, L. (1958) *Philosophical Investigations*, Oxford: Basil Blackwell.

Wood, A. (1981) *Karl Marx*, London: Routledge & Kegan Paul.

Wood, E. (1986) *The Retreat From Class: A New "True" Socialism*, London: Verso.

Wright, A. (1986) *Socialisms: Theories and Practices*, Oxford: Oxford University Press.

Yamato, G. (1990) "Something About the Subject Makes It Hard to Name," in G. Anzaldúa (ed.) *Making Face, Making Soul = Haciendo Caras*, San Francisco: Aunt Lute Foundation Books.

Young, I. (1990) *Justice and the Politics of Difference*, Princeton, NJ: Princeton University Press.

Zerilli, L. (1994) *Signifying Woman: Culture and Chaos in Rousseau, Burke, and Mill*, Ithaca, NY: Cornell University Press.

Žižek, S. (1989) *The Sublime Object of Ideology*, London: Verso.

—— (1990) "Beyond Discourse Analysis," in E. Laclau, *New Reflections of the Revolution of Our Time*, London: Verso.

—— (1994) "Identity and Its Vicissitudes: Hegel's 'Logic of Essence' as a Theory of Ideology," in E. Laclau (ed.) *The Making of Political Identities*, London: Verso.

INDEX

INDEX

Lukács, G. 66
Luxemburg, R. 20, 24–5
Lyotard, J.-F. 144–5, 146

McClintock, A. 82, 168, 207n
McClure, K. 99
MacIntyre, A. 124
MacKinnon, C. 42, 152
Macpherson, C. B. 10, 11
Malcolm X 35, 122
maquiladoras 206n
Marcil-Lacoste, L. 144, 190
market socialism 21–2
Marshall, T. 127–8
Martin, B. 162
Marx, K. 20, 40, 43, 54–5, 60, 62, 66,
    101–2, 112–13, 114, 166, 189, 204n,
    208n
Marx, K. and Engels, F. 20, 44–5, 62–3
Marxist theory: critique of economic
    reductionism in 102–3, 103, 109–15,
    151; critique of essentialism in 2–3,
    25–6, 30, 36, 39–41, 42–3, 58, 63, 74,
    84, 98, 102; critique of 'scientific'
    claims in 24–5, 40, 49, 51, 53, 61; and
    cultural studies 4; and democracy
    19–25, 87, 90–1, 201; false
    consciousness 59, 91; and human rights
    31, 40; and power 151; Second
    International 206n; and socialist
    revolutions 13–15; see also class,
    Gramsci, Kautsky, Lenin, Luxemburg,
    Marx, Marx and Engels, Stalinism
Mercer, C. 206n, 210n
Miliband, R. 22, 23
Mill, J. S. 11, 35, 148, 149
multiculturalism 33–4, 46, 54, 89, 140–3,
    147, 157, 174–5, 178, 179, 182–4, 186,
    187, 190, 191, 192, 197, 198, 201,
    205n

Nancy, J. 210n
nation-state theory: critique of 137–8
nationalism 98, 145, 210n
neo-conservatism 10, 57, 59, 66–7, 69,
    70–1, 75, 107, 147, 150, 174, 175–6,
    178, 192–3, 196, 197; socialist critique
    of 12–13, 16
Nicholson, L. 153
Nietzsche, F. 77, 185
nodal point 32, 89, 98, 104, 105–6, 115
Norval, A. 78, 82, 175, 191, 194, 196

Nove, A. 21

Omi, M. and Winant, H. 27
overdetermination 88, 97, 101, 103, 110,
    115, 150, 160, 195

Paggi, L. 111
Parenti, M. 148
Phillips, A. 136
Plotke, D. 205n
positivism, critique of 60, 159–60

Québecois nationalism 4, 187
Quine, W. 60

race 72–3, 156–7, 158, 159, 189, 190, 191,
    192, 193–4, 195, 200, 210–11n; and
    class 27–8, 93–4, 95, 98, 110, 193,
    203n; and gender 94–5, 100, 105
racism 12, 70, 72–3, 75, 87–8, 93–4, 96,
    105, 106, 121, 122–3, 134, 143, 150,
    156–7, 158, 163, 171, 173, 178, 179,
    186, 196, 199, 207n; and economic
    inequality 17–18; hate speech 170–1,
    209n; and labour segmentation 27;
    South African apartheid 150, 175, 194,
    195, 196; South Africa post-apartheid
    186, 194–5
radical democratic pluralism 33, 34, 54,
    59, 66–7, 123–4, 125–6, 130, 132–3,
    135, 138–9, 139–40, 143–4, 146, 147,
    149–50, 173, 177, 181–2, 185, 186,
    192, 201–2; and anti-essentialism 40,
    42–3; and authenticity claims 91–2,
    100; autonomy principle 32;
    democratic limits of 34, 119–20,
    143–4, 146–7, 186, 191; and hegemony
    32; and liberal democracy 31–2, 39;
    and Marxism 31–2, 39–40, 50, 52,
    114–15; and political economy 30–1;
    and power 40, 41; see also
    multiculturalism
Rawls, J. 116–17, 119–20, 149
Readings, B. 198, 210n, 211–12n
relations of oppression 8
relations of subordination 8
relativism 77, 103–4, 107–9, 184
religious fundamentalism 49, 57, 59, 66–7,
    69, 90, 131, 141, 142, 145, 146, 174,
    175, 178, 179–80, 193, 202
reproductive rights 15, 31

235